Essays in Education
and Judaism in Honor
of Joseph S. Lukinsky

Essays in Education and Judaism in Honor of Joseph S. Lukinsky

Edited by
Burton I. Cohen and Adina A. Ofek

The Jewish Theological Seminary of America

The editors wish to thank Mr. Michael Terry of the
Dorot Jewish Division, New York Public Library,
for his kind assistance in securing the images for
Adina A. Ofek's article.

Contents

Contributors

Walter I. Ackerman
Ben Gurion University
and The Schechter Institute
of Jewish Studies, Israel

Brenda Bacon
The Schechter Institute
of Jewish Studies, Israel

Yehuda Bar-Shalom
David Yellin College
of Education, Israel

Zvi Bekerman
Melton Centre for Jewish
Education
The Hebrew University, Israel

Stephen I. Brown
State University of New York,
Buffalo

Burton I. Cohen
The Jewish Theological
Seminary, New York

Jonathan Cohen
Melton Centre for Jewish
Education
The Hebrew University,
Israel

Gail Zaiman Dorph
Mandel Foundation, New York

Elan Ezrachi
Charles Bronfman Mifgashim
Centre, Israel

Seymour Fox
Mandel Foundation, Israel

Neil Gillman
The Jewish Theological
Seminary, New York

Marc Hirshman
Melton Centre for Jewish
Education
The Hebrew University, Israel

Barry W. Holtz
The Jewish Theological
Seminary, New York

Alvan H. Kaunfer
Temple Emanu-El, Rhode Island

William Bean Kennedy
Union Theological Seminary,
New York

Chaim Licht
Haifa University, Israel

David Marcus
The Jewish Theological
  Seminary, New York

Adina Ofek
The Jewish Theological
  Seminary, New York

David E. Purpel
University of North Carolina

Eduardo Rauch
The Jewish Theological
  Seminary, New York

David Resnick
Bar Ilan University, Israel

Michael Rosenak
The Hebrew University, Israel

Lifsa Schachter
Cleveland College of Jewish
  Studies

Israel Scheffler
Harvard Graduate School
  of Education

Frances Schoonmaker
Teachers College,
  Columbia University

Asher Shkedi
Melton Centre for Jewish
  Education
The Hebrew University,
  Israel

Douglas Sloan
Teachers College,
  Columbia University

Chaim Zins
Haifa University, Israel

Preface

So many of us have been enriched by Joseph Lukinsky, the scholar, the rabbi, and the teacher. In all these roles, Joe moves comfortably from theory to practice and from practice to theory. He is particularly attracted to problems and ideas that are related to practice. He locates these ideas, analyzes them, and in his publications, he enriches the conversation in both Jewish and general education.

Joe applies many of these theoretical concepts to practice in the classroom, in informal educational settings, and in the life of the synagogue. The list of his publications is a powerful demonstration of his contributions to theory and to practice, as is the table of contents listing the articles written in his honor in this significant Festschrift.

Let us briefly consider some examples from his own publications. In "Morality and the Teaching of Mathematics," written with Professor Stephen I. Brown, he describes the potential moral thrust entailed in the teaching of mathematics. In "Scholarship and Curriculum: What Jewish Scholarship Means for Jewish Education," he explicates his commitment to the role that scholarship must play if content and subject matter are to be rendered authentically and are to make a significant impact on Jewish education.

His influence in the field of informal education is best illustrated by his work in the Ramah camps. Joe is a legendary figure in the Ramah movement, where he began as a counselor and sports specialist. In his essay "Sports and Jewish Education: A Personal and Curricular Note," he explains how he used sports at Camp Ramah to enrich and deepen Jewish education. In later years, at Camp Ramah in Nyack, New York, Joe was encouraged to build on his ideas and specify how a summer camp could become an institution where character education is the central goal. Many of us believe that in the process, he developed an "existence proof"—in this case, a camp that demonstrated that it is possible to transform the thinking, feeling, and behavior of young people and the staff who work with them. He shares these ideas with us in "Teaching Responsibility: A Case Study in Curriculum Development."

As rabbi, Joe Lukinsky had a lasting influence on member families of Congregation Kehillath Israel of Brookline Massachusetts, where he served as both assistant rabbi and educational director. I often meet former congregants and students from his religious school who continue to see him as their role model. He helps us understand why this is so in "Starting with Yourself: A Model for Understanding the Jewish Holidays and Teaching Them." To this day, he is still rabbi to many, who turn to him for guidance in dealing with the myriad complicated issues they face.

As a teacher and a professor of Jewish education, Joe inspired students, many of whom subsequently assumed leading positions in Jewish education in North America and in general education in the State of Israel. Many wrote their doctoral dissertations in Jewish education under his guidance. As their mentor, he insisted that they could not write about Jewish education without a deep understanding of the world of general education. Furthermore, it is Joe's belief that the Jewish educator can and should contribute to the analysis and understanding of key issues in general education. His two-part essay "Structure in Educational Theory" helps us understand why philosophical analysis should precede and accompany experimentation and implementation in the field of curriculum. For many years, these articles have been required reading in the courses that I teach in universities in both Israel and the United States.

But above all, Joe is to be treasured as a friend. We learn from him by example. We turn to him for advice. We know that he will respond with wisdom and sensitivity. May he continue to teach and inspire us for many years to come.

SEYMOUR FOX
President
Mandel Foundation, Israel

Introduction

Jewish communities, from ancient times through the present day, have given lifelong education the highest priority on the communal and personal agenda of each Jew; however, it was only in the first decades of the twentieth century that an academic field of Jewish education began to develop. Since the mid-twentieth century, Professor Joseph S. Lukinsky, the Baumritter Professor of Jewish Education at the Jewish Theological Seminary, has taken a key role in the development of the field: first, as a practitioner in Conservative synagogues and in the Ramah summer camps; and later, concomitant with and subsequent to his studies at the Harvard Graduate School of Education, as an academician and theorist. His doctoral dissertation, "Teaching Responsibility: A Case Study in Curriculum Development," documents how the program at Camp Ramah in Nyack, New York, functioned and the educational theory that undergirds it.

This volume comprises articles and scholarly studies written in honor of Professor Lukinsky on the occasion of his seventieth birthday by his teachers, colleagues, and students. As for the last, there is no doubt that he has nurtured and guided the writing of more dissertations in the field of Jewish education than any other senior scholar, producing a gifted group of young educational practitioners and scholars who are noted for making profound contributions to the field in both North America and Israel.

He has excelled in the application of social scientific methodologies and in fostering the application of liberal religious thought to the teaching of Jewish texts and religious practices. From the beginning of his scholarly work, he emancipated himself from the constraints of quantitative research—the then regnant methodology in educational research, both general and Jewish—and embraced the newly developing qualitative approaches. He passed along this affinity for the qualitative approach to many of his students, and it is reflected in their dissertation research as well as in some of the articles that appear in this volume.

In his own work, he has been deeply committed to applying and promoting the application of the religious theory of Conservative Judaism to the practice of Jewish education, whether at the elementary or at the graduate school level. He has sought out the significant educational ramifications of the writings and lives of major Jewish thinkers and theologians, especially Abraham Joshua Heschel and Mordecai M. Kaplan.

When the editors proposed the creation of this book, there was a broad and immediate positive response from individuals in all the categories mentioned above. All the papers presented reflect both the high esteem in which his teachers, colleagues, and students hold Professor Lukinsky and the personal warmth with which he related to them, sharing freely of his knowledge and insights, as together they tackled the many complex problems that characterize the field of Jewish education.

Jewish education is a very broad field, and the various types of scholarship and topics that appear in the papers in this book reflect both the nature of the field and Professor Lukinsky's broad range of interests. Often, scholars limit the students whose dissertations they accept to supervise to those whose interests correspond to their own. Joe Lukinsky never turned down a student or discouraged a student whose area of interests did not correspond to the areas that he had previously investigated. He looked forward to the opportunities that each new dissertation gave him to learn about new branches of Jewish education and Jewish knowledge, or to master new methodologies of educational research.

It is no accident that a large portion of these studies were written by scholars residing and working in the State of Israel. In large measure, they are a reflection of Joe's deep commitment to Eretz Yisrael and the warmth of the hospitality that he and his wife, Betty, extended to the many Israeli students who came to New York to study education at the Jewish Theological Seminary. In this sense, Joe has been a true builder of bridges between diaspora Jewry and Eretz Yisrael Jewry. He has invested untold hours in striving to understand the unique dynamic of education in the Jewish state, and in providing Israeli scholars with the tools that they need to have an impact upon the course of Israeli education.

•   •   •

In the first section of the book, "Philosophy of Education," the authors attack some of the thorniest, if frequently avoided, problems inherent in the field of education. Barry Holtz opens our volume by addressing what is perhaps the fundamental question of all Jewish education in the liberal branches of Judaism, namely, how to bridge the gulf between the two sources of our knowledge: classical Jewish texts; and general educational philosophy, theory, and practice. He asks how we can remain loyal to the contributions of the academic fields while at the same time advancing the agenda of Jewish education.

The other three papers in this section, by Israel Scheffler, Frances Schoonmaker, and Douglas Sloan, all deal with philosophic problems in the field of general education, all of which indirectly have great relevance for the Jewish educator. Scheffler's paper addresses the basic question of what use philosophy is to education, and suggests several ways in which educators are hampered in their tasks to the extent that they neglect subjecting them to philosophical analysis. Schoonmaker's essay on the place of theory in education, a practical profession, discusses the perceived tension between the academician theorist in the university and the practitioner in schools, and offers a model for visualizing how teachers tend to deal with those tensions. Sloan analyzes the modern way of knowing, assesses the historical responses to these modern assumptions and their inadequacies, and finally suggests what might be involved in transforming the modern approach so as to foster a way of knowing that stresses the primacy of meaning in all experience.

The second section of this volume presents ten studies that deal directly with the field of Jewish education. They are reflective of the breadth of the field of Jewish education and offer an opportunity to observe how a number of scholars in the field have responded to the challenge presented by Holtz of how to remain loyal to the contributions of the academic fields while advancing the agenda of Jewish education.

The first essay, by Brenda Bacon, is mainly a narrative in which she describes her work in creating an elementary Hebrew school curricular unit on the Rambam, and she offers her retrospective analysis of how she met the challenge of utilizing Joseph Schwab's model for construction of the curriculum. Burton Cohen offers the reader an action-research study in which, with the aid of insights from general and Jewish educational researchers, he describes his experience teaching an adult Talmud study group in a non-Orthodox synagogue. Gail Dorph responds to the question that is the title of her essay, "What Do Teachers Need to Know to Teach Torah?" by asserting that teachers need what education theorists have defined as subject-matter knowledge and pedagogic-content knowledge, concepts that she unpacks with the aid of the transcript of an actual Torah lesson.

Neil Gillman explains how Joe Lukinsky's invitation to him to attend a workshop on mythic reenactment, led by Samuel Laeuchli and focused on the story of the *akedah,* forever changed the manner in which he taught the Bible and other classic Jewish texts. From that time forward, he began to demand that his rabbinical students, in examining a biblical text, go beyond the confines of the words of the biblical text and try to project the living experience that generated the text in the first place. Alvan Kaunfer presents an innovative method for the teaching of biblical narrative, which would replace the regular synagogue sermon. His proposal, based upon the theory of reader-response literary criticism, invites the congregation in the sanctuary on Saturday morning to respond to midrashim that have been previously selected by the rabbi, based upon the weekly Sabbath Torah reading. Adina Ofek, in her historical survey of Hebrew language textbooks, traces their development over the course of a century, from their origins in Eastern Europe in the mid-nineteenth century under the influence of the Haskalah. She suggests a solution to the puzzle presented by the changes made over time in the pedagogic style of these textbooks.

Eduardo Rauch describes the mutually beneficial relationship between the settled mature German Jewish women and the newly arrived Eastern European young women in New York City at the beginning of the twentieth century. He relates how the German Jewish women set for themselves a goal of establishing programs and institutions aimed at preventing the young immigrant women from slipping into poverty and immorality. Readers may be taken by surprise at David Resnick's use of the military experience, largely drawn from classic Jewish sources, as a metaphor for gaining an understanding of the dilemmas facing Jewish education. He brings many useful analogies from one field to the other.

Michael Rosenak broadens and deepens for us the discussions contained in the earlier essays in a most unusual fashion: by challenging the reader to give serious consideration to the writings of one of the important modern ideologues of *haredi* education, Rabbi Eliyahu E. Dessler. He strives to convince us that were Dessler's disciples agreeable to discussing Judaism and Jewish education with us, we might have as much to learn as to say.

Chaim Zins, beginning with a phenomenological analysis, has done a study aimed at creating a knowledge outline for the field of Jewish education. He suggests that such a study can prepare the theoretical ground for future academic education curriculum design, determine prospective areas for future research, and facilitate quick access to relevant information if implemented in information systems and Web resources.

The third section of the book deals with the potential role of Judaism as a resource for general education. The three essays—by Stephen I. Brown, William Bean Kennedy, and David E. Purpel—are exciting examples of Joe Lukinsky's facility in establishing mutually beneficial relationships with scholars of education working outside the field of Jewish education. Stephen I. Brown not only aims to demonstrate that there is no inherent contradiction in utilizing talmudic method to prepare teachers of mathematics; to the contrary, talmudic experience can illuminate mathematical issues and enable the mathematics teacher trainees to see the subject matter and themselves in ways previously rarely attained.

William Kennedy expresses appreciation to Joe Lukinsky for the appreciation of Judaism that he achieved through their collegial relationship in the joint seminar in religion and education that these two professors of religious education conducted for over a decade, along with Douglas Sloan from Columbia University's Teachers College. David E. Purpel calls for intensive Jewish involvement in the discourse surrounding American public education. He suggests that the introduction by Jews of aspects of Jewish thought and tradition into that discourse would make a significant contribution toward thoughtful and textured public debate on the current state and future direction of public education in American society.

In the fourth section of the book, six education researchers—one a colleague of Joe Lukinsky and five of them his former doctoral students—write about issues relating to different educational settings in the State of Israel. In the first article in this section, Walter Ackerman, going back to the pre-State period, limns the history of the debate regarding the place of Jewish studies in the curriculum of the state teacher-training institutions in Israel, noting that the programs offered by national school systems generally reflect the ethos of the society.

The next study in this section, by Yehuda Bar-Shalom, is one of two in this section that address the topic of the *mifgash*, the programmed encounter between Israeli and Jewish youth from the diaspora. After explaining the nature of the *mifgash* experience and its theoretical underpinnings, Bar-Shalom presents the results of his study of fifteen *mifgashim* that took place in Israel over the course of a single summer. He presents tentative general conclusions reached about the usefulness of this technique with specific examples of the views that the Israeli and diaspora youth expressed about each other.

Zvi Bekerman, in his essay "Art in Cultural Education," suggests that if, as Bateson and others would assert, art encodes information about psychic integration, then art might well become a partial remedy for the perceived modern disintegration and fragmentation of our ailing community education.

Elan Ezrachi describes and analyzes one encounter between Israeli and American youth in a *mifgash* setting that took place on American soil. This encounter was focused on the possibility of a joint spiritual experience between some American Jewish and Israeli teenagers who had met five months earlier in Israel and had maintained contact through correspondence and by telephone in the interim.

Chaim Licht discusses an M.A. program in Jewish history and talmudic literature that he and other colleagues who teach in these fields at Haifa University created in response to the 1993 recommendations of the Shenhar committee (the origins, mission, and final report of this committee are presented in Ackerman's paper in this section). This particular program was based on the premise that the recommendation of the Shenhar committee to reinstate studies in Oral Law into the high school curriculum, from which they had been removed over time, could not be achieved without training a cadre of experienced high school teachers in these disciplines. Asher Shkedi's paper reports on research done with teachers of Bible as subjects, to ascertain how their pedagogical beliefs about students affect their roles in teaching Bible.

It should not surprise readers that this volume honoring Joseph Lukinsky, the noted scholar of Jewish education, should close with a number of contributions that address themselves directly, if not always strictly, to areas of Jewish knowledge. Throughout his career, Lukinsky has insisted that scholars and practitioners of Jewish education need to prepare themselves with a sophisticated and up-to-date background in the areas that provide the content of Jewish education. In the preceding section, Ackerman and Licht, among others, concerned themselves with the implementation of this principle. In the final section of the book, a number of scholars add to our knowledge of Jewish texts and ideas.

Jonathan Cohen, a philosopher of education, urges educators to examine Levinas's concept of "religious maturity" and consider it as an orienting notion for Jewish education. Presenting some of Levinas's core ideas before discussing their educational implications, he challenges Jewish "educationalists" to turn to the writings of modern Jewish thinkers as a resource for the enrichment of discourse on the goals of Jewish education.

With supporting texts from biblical and talmudic literature, Marc Hirshman demonstrates that from the biblical period onward, the seeds of the struggle within Judaism between a land-centered religion and a Torah-centered portable religion are in evidence. Talmudic sources record how the two ancient centers of rabbinic learning, Israel and Babylonia, continued the debate, each fiercely advocating its own unique calling.

David Marcus's essay gives recognition to Joe Lukinsky's long-standing interest in the external form of the Masoretic text of the Hebrew Bible by discussing an aspect of this topic. Using *parashat Va'era* as an example, he demonstrates that when the openings of the chapters do not correspond to the division into *parashiyyot*, the discrepancy seems to have its source in differing exegesis of the Bible text.

Lifsa Schachter comments in the final essay in our volume on the well-known Torah story of Abraham's hospitality and the significance given to it in Jewish tradition. She suggests that a deeper and broader meaning for the story emerges when it is read in the context of biblical stories about travelers and in connection with the verses that serve as "bookends" to the story.

•   •   •

We are deeply grateful to all the writers of the essays and studies included in this volume. Through their contributions, they have not only paid honor to their colleague and teacher, Joe Lukinsky; they have significantly enriched the literature of Jewish education. What they have written will serve as a foundation and an inspiration for scholars of Jewish education for many years to come.

In closing, we wish to thank the Jewish Theological Seminary Press Publications Committee, and especially its chairperson, Alan Cooper, for their thoughtful consideration of our manuscript. Also, we want to thank our magnificent copy editor, Janice Meyerson, for her sympathetic, meticulous, and swift response to all that we asked of her.

Finally, we are thankful to the Teacher-of-All, that he gave us the strength, enthusiasm, and wisdom to carry through this important endeavor to an elegant conclusion.

Burton I. Cohen and Adina Ofek
New York, New York
October 2001/Cheshvan 5762

PHILOSOPHY OF EDUCATION

Whose Discipline Is It, Anyway?

Barry W. Holtz

Joseph Lukinsky's career has been rooted in two sources of knowledge: his profound engagement with Jewish classical texts; and his deep understanding of general educational philosophy, theory, and practice. His work has often tried to bridge these two domains, whether it is reflecting on John Dewey and Rav Kook, on Judaism and sports, or on theater and modes of Jewish pedagogy. He has taught us ways to find subtle and complex linkages between these worlds, and he has also reminded us that the differences between these worlds need to be part of our exploration.

In essence, these two worlds live in a kind of tension. Ideally, this is a generative tension, and deep engagement with both worlds will be of benefit to both. Of course, that ideal is not always realized, and even when it is approached, considerable attention must be paid and work must be done. Michael Rosenak has written at some length about the problem of "translation"[1] between the two domains of the Jewish and the general and has argued for the viability of what he calls "partial translation."[2]

But are there times that translation, even partial translation, is not possible? In what way does Jewish education present categories ultimately unique or, at the very least, essentially particular to its own world, worldview, or context? In this article, I want to explore one case of such a divide and some of the educational problems that it engenders. What I wish to explore is disciplinary knowledge as it is commonly understood and the challenges that it presents to the practice of Jewish education.

Barry W. Holtz is associate professor of Jewish education at the Jewish Theological Seminary of America.

When Jerome Bruner declared that "the curriculum of a subject should be determined by the most fundamental understanding that can be achieved of the underlying principles that give structure to that subject,"[3] he launched an emphasis on disciplinary knowledge that became the hallmark of curricular thinking in American education in the 1960s and beyond. This perspective—the "structure of the disciplines" approach—had profound implications, not only for curriculum making, but also for teaching and learning in schools. Thus, in a book that appeared not long after Bruner's, King and Brownell argued that a course in school taken by students should be "a planned series of encounters with the structure of any single discipline. . . . A course will be based on the historic and current nature of the discipline."[4] Tanner and Tanner note:

> Some educationists went so far as to advocate that all subject matter in the curriculum be based on the structure-of-a-discipline principle. In the words of [Philip] Phenix, "all curriculum content should be drawn from the disciplines, or to put it another way, *only* knowledge contained in the disciplines is appropriate to the curriculum," because "the disciplines reveal knowledge in its teachable forms" and "non-disciplined knowledge is unsuitable for teaching and learning."[5]

The structure-of-the-disciplines orientation presented a number of difficulties for educators, both of a theoretical and practical sort. For example, Bruner's oft-quoted notion that "intellectual activity anywhere is the same, whether at the frontier of knowledge or in a third-grade classroom"[6] led inevitably to the idea that the model for a child's classes should be the activities of advanced practitioners of the specific discipline at hand. The "schoolboy learning physics *is* a physicist"[7] (emphasis his), as Bruner memorably put it. But such a formulation seems to ignore any insights that developmental psychology offers about the way children learn at different ages. Bruner's concept has been characterized as arguing that "the young learner [i]s a miniature scholar-specialist whose intellectual activity is not qualitatively different from that of the scholar on the frontier of knowledge."[8]

Dewey's warnings about the difference between subject matter as viewed by the teacher and subject matter as seen by the learner—particularly a child learner—are especially relevant here. From the educator's point of view, Dewey noted, the academic disciplines represent working resources, available capital. Their remoteness from the experience of the young is not, however, seeming; it is real. The subject matter of the learner is not, therefore, it cannot be, identical with the formulated, the crystallized, and systematized subject matter of the adult. . . . Failure to bear in mind the difference in subject matter from the respective standpoints of teacher and student is responsible for most of the mistakes made in the use of texts and other expressions of preexistent knowledge.[9]

The critique of Bruner from a Deweyan perspective, then, revolves around the experience of learning from the student's point of view, but Bruner's concept of the "structures" could be challenged even by the structuralists themselves. Joseph Schwab's approach represents a different way of thinking about the structures of the disciplines. For Bruner, as Lukinsky has put it,

[t]he structures are "there"; they are the best generalities that we can derive from the facts or the most inclusive ways of summarizing the facts that we can develop. . . . Schwab and others see the structures in a discipline differently. The structures precede the facts. Moreover, they determine what will be considered a fact.[10]

The structures, for Schwab, are (as Lukinsky notes) essentially "heuristic" devices, not end products of inquiry, but frameworks for the process of discovery. Thus, Schwab delineates "substantive" and "syntactic" structures of a discipline.[11] The substantive structures of a discipline are the large organizing interpretive frames that "are used for defining, bounding, and analyzing the subject matters they investigate."[12] They are the lenses through which the entire field is understood. The syntactic structures are the "different methods of verification and justification of conclusions"[13]—in other words, those tools that scholars use to introduce new knowledge to a field and the canons by which evidence is viewed as acceptable or not.

Schwab was concerned about the dangers of reifying the perceived structures, locking in the definition of the structure of any given discipline. Seymour Fox has argued that Schwab describes alternative conceptions of structure, and he indicates the dangers of distortions which inevitably occur when one adheres to a limited and rigid conception of a structure of a discipline, such as the one which guided the curriculum reforms of the fifties and sixties. . . . Schwab argues that it is not the role of curriculum to simplify or to parrot a favored or accepted conception of a discipline, but to reflect on what contribution the various conceptions within a discipline can make to the thinking, the feeling and the behavior of the student.[14]

In the long run, however, as Lukinsky points out, despite the various points of view about structure of the disciplines and "despite other internal distinctions, . . . the emphasis on having school subjects reflect the structure of the academic discipline"[15] is what characterizes all the proponents of this approach, Schwab included.

Although the structure-of-the-disciplines approach was challenged by a number of critics, in recent years it has emerged once again as a central element in educational thinking. But in its newer incarnation, the focus has shifted away from what students should learn and toward what teachers need to know. Teacher preparation and the professional development of teachers need to rediscover the "missing paradigm"[16] (in Lee Shulman's words) of subject-matter knowledge. But the kind of knowledge that Shulman envisions is of a particular sort. It includes elements of "structures of the disciplines" along with a new category, which Shulman terms "pedagogical content knowledge." Shulman, his colleagues, and his former students have spent a good deal of time advancing our understanding about the kinds of knowledge that teachers need to have. Substantive and syntactic structures play an important role in defining the parameters.[17] Equally important, however, is the way that the teacher needs to know his or her subject matter and how it differs from the way that scholars know their disciplines.[18]

What matters to the teacher (as opposed to the scholar)[19] is the subject matter from the learner's point of view. Note how the discourse has changed from Bruner and Schwab in the 1960s. Here we are looking at what the teacher needs to know, not how the student needs to grasp the structure of the discipline. Shulman and his colleagues have added other dimensions to the picture of knowledge, in an effort to take into account the emphasis now placed on the teacher. Teachers have knowledge, but they also have beliefs and attitudes about the subjects that they teach and the reasons that they teach them. The amalgam of knowledge and beliefs has been termed the teacher's "orientation," and this concept plays a significant role in contemporary educational literature.[20] But whether the issue be that of the student or that of the teacher, the ultimate anchor point for the knowledge of the discipline still remains the discourse of the university.

In Schwab's description of the importance of the structures of a discipline, he points out:

> [E]nquiry has its origin in a conceptual structure, often mathematical, but not necessarily so. It is this conceptual structure through which we are able to formulate a telling question. It is through the telling question that we know what data to seek and what experiments to perform to get those data. Once the data are in hand, the same conceptual structure tells us how to interpret them, what to make of them by way of knowledge. Finally, the knowledge itself is formulated in the terms provided by the same conception.[21]

As is obvious from this passage, Schwab was most comfortable expressing his ideas through the example of science, but the overarching concept in his view applies to the humanities and social sciences as well. As he says later in the same article, "While different substantive structures tend to succeed one another in physics, chemistry, and biology, other disciplines are characterized by the concurrent utilization of several sets of structures."[22] That is, what is typical of science is the successive development and replacement of specific substantive structures, in the manner of Thomas Kuhn's description of "revolutions" in scientific "paradigms."[23]

Schwab goes on to describe the simultaneous structures of different psychological theories of personality. Thus Freud, Jung, and Adler could hold different conceptions of the substantive structure of psychology all at more or less the same historical moment. One could, just as well, choose a different example—the various stances within contemporary historical studies such as feminist history, Marxist history, intellectual history, or social history—to make the same point.

But here we see a significant difference in regard to the situation of Jewish education. Despite the multiplicity of substantive structures possible for any discipline—existing either in chronological succession (as Schwab believes generally holds in science) or in temporal simultaneity (as he believes characterizes the humanities and social sciences)—

Schwab's perspective assumes an overarching criterion of authority: namely, the world of the university and its culture, rules, and modes of discourse. That is, there may be different substantive structures represented by, say, the approach of social historians versus the approach of intellectual historians; two Nobel Prize–winning economists may have widely diverging approaches to fundamental ideas in the field; and two university Bible scholars may differ greatly in approach, with one focused on literary approaches to the text while the other looks at ancient Near Eastern parallels. Nonetheless, in all these cases the rules of argument, inquiry, and acceptable analysis will be shared by all, even if the conclusions are different in the extreme. For a professor such as Schwab sitting at the University of Chicago, such an assumption would have seemed almost tautological—as it would to most educators working within the central educational institutions in the Western world.

But taking the example of Jewish education, let us look at Bible as our subject matter. In this case, the authority of the discipline may reside in multiple locations, not all of which are within the university. Certainly for those in the academy, the disciplinary authority resembles that of any other subject area. It is probably no accident that Schwab's work in Jewish education came in connection with the Jewish Theological Seminary and its faculty and institutions—the Melton Research Center and Camp Ramah. JTS is a religious institution that has always prided itself on its adherence to the rules of academic scholarship, and Schwab no doubt felt very comfortable in such a context.[24]

There are other possibilities as well. In the world of the ultraorthodox yeshiva, for example, the rules of discourse are completely different, as is the definition of acceptable "syntactic" structures, to use Schwab's term. If in the university, the tools of archaeology, comparative philology, anthropology, and historical documentation are all basic and acceptable means of exploring the biblical text, in the yeshiva these are completely irrelevant or forbidden.

The substantive structures are, in the same manner, completely different as well. For the yeshiva teacher, the meaning of the text is what the classical commentators reveal it to be. More significantly, the Bible is God's word, not a human document, and even the way that university scholars might talk about the genres and subgenres of the Bible—narrative, law, prophecy, and so on—is unimaginable. The Bible, for the yeshiva teacher, is not a collection of different types of literature; it is a seamless whole.

Thus, Schwab's description of substantive structures does not take into account the possibility that there may be modes of discourse that do not fit the basic rules of university life. Perhaps in the context of general education, these difficulties are less likely to appear. But in the realm of Jewish religious education, we find ourselves face-to-face with the reality of multiple approaches to the discipline, some of which are governed by the comfortable rules of university discourse, and others of which are quite different[25]—so different, in fact, that even the word "discipline" is outside of realm of discourse.

In many ways, my argument here resembles the notion of "interpretive communities" of textual interpretation, as it appears in the work of the literary critic Stanley Fish. That is, the way we read texts—and, in our case, the way we teach texts—is deeply connected to the community to which we belong. Fish claims that the "interpretive strategies" employed by individual readers "exist prior to the act of reading and therefore determine the shape of what is read rather than, as is usually assumed, the other way around."[26] I am hesitant to go quite as far as Fish does and claim that "since the thoughts an individual can think and the mental operations he can perform have their source in some or other interpretive community, he is as much the product of that community (acting as an extension of it) as the meanings it enables him to produce."[27] But I do believe that the idea of interpretive communities allows us to see how related, in Schwab's language, the "commonplace" of subject matter is to that of milieu. We live in communities that help us understand texts, what we want to accomplish when we teach them, where we see ourselves, and where we see our students and their futures.

The goals of an individual teacher, surely related to the community in which he or she is located (though not, I believe, entirely determined by it), will profoundly influence how he or she teaches, even down to the very definition of the discipline itself. What, for example, are the rules of textual interpretation that are "allowed" or encouraged? Is Rashi—representing here traditional exegesis—the source of "truth" for a teacher, or is it the academic "truth" of the modern academic Bible commentary? Note, in addition, that the word "located" in my words above does not necessarily mean the literal community in which the teacher works. Often, teachers work in one school but are, one might say, psychologically located in quite another place! The not uncommon phenomenon of a *haredi* (ultraorthodox) teacher working in a Conservative or modern Orthodox day school, for example, shows such a "dislocated" location.

Perhaps the best way to understand alternative, "nonuniversity," educational orientations is to look at the curriculum materials used by teachers as an indication of the way that they may actually approach their particular subjects in the classroom. Certainly, it is true that decisions about the books that a class uses are not entirely in the hands of teachers alone. But the popularity of certain books and the ways that those books attempt to reflect the real-life practices of teachers make looking at textbooks a valuable and instructive exercise.[28] As Ball and Cohen note:

> Unlike frameworks, objectives, assessments, and other mechanisms that seek to guide curriculum, instructional materials are concrete and daily. They are the stuff of lessons and units, of what teachers and students do. That centrality affords curricular materials a uniquely intimate connection to teaching.[29]

If we turn to one popular example, we can see an orientation to the teaching of Bible very different from that which would be based on Schwab's sense of the discipline's structures. *A Child's Bible* by Seymour Rossel aims to look at the narratives in the Bible as a means of instructing us today in the way that we should behave. "The people in the stories," we read in the introduction for the student, "are always a lot like us. So the stories help us learn how we should live, what we should do, and how we should behave."[30] The aim is to see "what [the stories] mean to us today" and in order to do so, students should ask themselves: "'What truth is this story teaching me?' 'What does this story say that I should do?' 'How does this story say that I should behave?'"[31] We see the method exemplified in the textbook's explanation of various biblical tales. Thus, in its discussion of the Tower of Babel story (under the headline "What Does It Mean?"), the student reads:

> The builders on the tower looked down and saw everything below getting smaller and smaller. It made them feel stronger and more important than the people below. They began to think that they were as mighty as God.

> You do not have to be on top of a tall tower to look down on other people. You can just say or think that a person is someone to "look down on," someone less important than you.

But really, God makes each of us special, so every person is important. Every person has something special to offer the world. "Looking down" on people is always a mistake. It's like "making war with God."[32]

In the curriculum's approach to teaching the Joseph story, we see a discussion that includes, under "What Does It Mean?": "Your dreams teach you things you need to know. Even a bad dream can help you grow stronger."[33] And under "What Does It Teach?" (the distinction between this and "What Does It Mean?" is not entirely clear to me):

Joseph heard Pharaoh say that there were two dreams. But he listened very carefully. And that is how he discovered that both were really one and the same dream. If you want to help people by listening to them, you must first listen to their words. But then you must also try to hear what their words mean. Joseph was a good listener.[34]

The biblical stories, according to this view, are important for the moral lessons that they communicate. Unlike the academic literary method—and the pedagogic approach that emanates from it—which aims at opening up the complexity, indeed, the ambiguity, of the biblical narrative, A Child's Bible is oriented toward simplifying the biblical tale into a specific "teaching," as Rossel puts it in his introduction. Contrast this with Robert Alter's comment that "an essential aim of the innovative technique of fiction worked out by the ancient Hebrew writers was to produce a certain indeterminacy of meaning, especially in regard to motive, moral character, and psychology."[35] Perhaps for this reason, A Child's Bible does not use the actual biblical text itself, but rather retells the stories, leaving out the inconvenient complexities of the original and adding clarifying points on its own.[36]

The underlying assumption of this approach is that the Bible communicates clear lessons, and the details of the narratives are to be understood as pointing us in the way of good moral behavior. Educationally, A Child's Bible has the advantage of being accessible to children and clear about its outcomes. The Bible, in these lessons, has something to tell us, and in each case we will be able to define what that something (to be fair, it is "some things," in the plural) is. Children can take home these messages and feel that the Bible speaks to them.

Alter and others would no doubt argue that such an educational approach sends a not-so-hidden message that the Bible is simple, perhaps even simplistic. The Bible becomes a kind of Jewish Aesop's Fables. That, those critics would assert, is an unfortunate message to communicate to children: not only is it an inaccurate portrayal of the Bible, but it also works to the detriment of Jewish education in the long run. The Bible will be understood as far less sophisticated than other literatures that children will encounter, and therefore they will always think of it as a childish thing.[37]

Though this may be true about the approach of A Child's Bible, at the same time we can see quite clearly its attempt to personalize the experience of learning Bible. The stories are meant to teach us lessons. Because of that, I would characterize this orientation as a "didactic" or "moralistic" approach to Bible. Thus, even though A Child's Bible is aimed at the liberal sector within the Jewish religious spectrum, ironically, it resembles more traditional approaches, such as the textbook called Gateway to Torah.[38] What is striking in light of the "structures of the disciplines," however, is that the orientation represented by this textbook is completely outside the purview of any academic discipline or university approaches to scholarship—and even to university models of teaching. Yet at the same time, it is clear that A Child's Bible, whether one agrees with its approach or not, works out of an orientation that legitimately asks how we can speak directly to the concerns of children who wish to find meaningful content in the words of the Bible.

We live in a time in which the whole notion of the "disciplines" is under some attack or reconsideration in the academic community. Beginning perhaps with Clifford Geertz's influential article "Blurred Genres: The Refiguration of Social Thought,"[39] we have witnessed a considerable debate about the question of what it means to do research in any "discipline." Anthropology is used to study history; literary theory to study law. Various perspectives such as cultural studies or "interdisciplinarity" have challenged the particular uniqueness and contribution of the classic university disciplines and have suggested that "disciplines are ephemeral, barely existing entities, transitory, shifting, permeable in their boundaries, riven by internal conflict, and in some sense unreal since they are but epiphenomena of larger structural movements."[40]

Challenges about the nature of a discipline—what constitutes the very core of the discipline itself—inevitably will affect teaching, at all levels of the educational landscape. But the issues that I have raised in this paper also raise a different set of questions. In particular, we can ask; What are the limitations of disciplinary knowledge—"disciplinary thinking," one might call it—for Jewish education? In what ways can we remain loyal to the contributions of the academic fields as they have been defined in university culture, while at the same time advancing the agenda of Jewish education, an agenda that goes beyond the academy's emphasis on the acquisition of knowledge? But once we open up that question, what are the limits of disciplinary "authority" in the world of Jewish education? For if authority does not lie in the familiar realms of university scholarship, where does it lie? How are decisions to be made, then, about what is "worthwhile"[41] for students to learn? These are not simple problems, but as Joseph Lukinsky has often reminded us, the excitement of Jewish education lies precisely in its dilemmas, its tensions, and in the power of the questions that we as educators are required to confront. As he once put it, though, "truth is one. . . . [T]he paths to that ultimate are multiple, leading through diversity, tension, overlap and challenge."[42]

Notes

1. See, for example, Michael Rosenak, *Roads to the Palace: Jewish Texts and Teaching* (Providence: Berghahn, 1995), 98ff.
2. Ibid., xiv.
3. Jerome S. Bruner, *The Process of Education* (New York: Vintage, 1960), 31.
4. Arthur R. King, Jr., and John A. Brownell, *The Curriculum and the Disciplines of Knowledge* (New York: John Wiley, 1966), 122.
5. Daniel Tanner and Laurel N. Tanner, *Curriculum Development*, 2d ed. (New York: Macmillan, 1980), 527. The quotation from Phenix is found in *Curriculum Crossroads*, ed. A. Harry Passow (New York: Teachers College Press, 1962).
6. Bruner, *The Process of Education*, 14.
7. Ibid.
8. Tanner and Tanner, *Curriculum Development*, 535.
9. John Dewey, *Democracy and Education* (1916; New York: Macmillan, 1944), 182–83.
10. Joseph Lukinsky, "Structure in Educational Theory," pt. 1, *Educational Philosophy and Theory* 2 (1970): 20.

11. See my discussion of substantive and syntactic structures in "Reading and Teaching: Goals, Aspirations and the Teaching of Jewish Texts," in *Abiding Challenges: Research Perspectives on Jewish Education,* ed. Yisrael Rich and Michael Rosenak (London: Freund, 1999).

12. Joseph J. Schwab, "Education and the Structure of the Disciplines" (1961), in his collected essays, *Science, Curriculum, and Liberal Education,* ed. Ian Westbury and Neil J. Wilkof (Chicago: University of Chicago Press, 1978), 246.

13. Ibid.

14. Seymour Fox, "The Vitality of Theory in Schwab's Conception of the Practical," *Curriculum Inquiry* 15, no. 1 (1985): 69. See also Israel Scheffler, "The Practical as a Focus for Curriculum: Reflections on Schwab's View," in *Reason and Teaching* (Indianapolis: Bobbs-Merrill, 1973), 181–97.

15. Lukinsky, "Structure in Educational Theory," 17.

16. Lee S. Shulman, "Those Who Understand: Knowledge Growth in Teaching," *Educational Researcher* 15, no. 2 (1986): 7.

17. See, for example, Pamela L. Grossman, Suzanne M. Wilson, and Lee S. Shulman, "Teachers of Substance: Subject Matter Knowledge for Teaching," in *Knowledge Base for the Beginning Teacher,* ed. M. Reynolds (New York: Pergamon, 1989), 23–36.

18. See, for example, Samuel Wineberg and Suzanne M. Wilson, "Subject Matter Knowledge in the Teaching of History," in *Advances in Research on Teaching,* ed. Jere Brophy (Greenwich, Conn.: JAI, 1991), 2:335.

19. Note that we are talking about "pure" categories here—in most cases, historians are also teachers of history, at universities or colleges. But when they are sitting in the library wearing their scholar hats (and not thinking about the courses that they offer across the campus), their goals and tasks and focus differ greatly from those of teachers, some of whom may also be scholars—in their spare time, so to speak.

20. The term is most associated with Pamela Grossman's work; see her *The Making of a Teacher: Teacher Knowledge and Teacher Education* (New York: Teachers College Press, 1990). Elsewhere, I have described orientation as a "description not of a teacher's 'method' in some technical meaning of the word, but in a deeper sense, of a teacher's most powerful conceptions and beliefs about the field he or she is teaching" (Holtz, "Reading and Teaching," 414).

21. Joseph J. Schwab, "Structure of the Disciplines: Meanings and Significances," in *The Structure of Knowledge and the Curriculum,* ed. G. W. Ford and Lawrence Pugno (Chicago: Rand McNally, 1964), 12.

22. Ibid., 28.

23. Thomas S. Kuhn, *The Structure of Scientific Revolutions,* 2d ed. (Chicago: University of Chicago Press, 1970).

24. See the discussion of Schwab's role at JTS in the following articles in Jack Wertheimer, *Tradition Renewed: A History of the Jewish Theological Seminary of America,* 2 vols. (New York: Jewish Theological Seminary, 1997): David

Kaufman, "Jewish Education as a Civilization: A History of the Teachers Institute," esp. 1:617; Michael Brown, "It's Off to Camp We Go," esp. 1:839–41; Virginia Leson Brereton, "Religious Educators at JTS and the Wider Educational World," esp. 2:755.

25. For a related issue, see Jonathan Cohen's discussion of the problem of defining Jewish philosophy as a discipline in his "Enacting the Eclectic: The Case of Jewish Philosophy," *Journal of Curriculum Studies* 30, no. 2 (1998): 207–31.

26. Stanley Fish, *Is There a Text in This Class?* (Cambridge: Harvard University Press, 1980), 171.

27. Ibid., 14.

28. See Miriam Ben-Peretz, *The Teacher-Curriculum Encounter: Freeing Teachers from the Tyranny of Texts* (Albany: State University of New York Press, 1990), on the potential of curriculum and its limitations; and for some of the difficulties, Sharon Feiman-Nemser and Deborah Loewenberg Ball, "Using Textbooks and Teachers' Guides: A Dilemma for Beginning Teachers and Teacher Educators," *Curriculum Inquiry* 18 (1988): 401–23.

29. Deborah Loewenberg Ball and David K. Cohen, "Reform by the Book: What Is—or Might Be—the Role of Curriculum Materials in Teacher Learning and Instructional Reform," *Educational Researcher* 25, no. 9 (1996): 6.

30. Seymour Rossel, *A Child's Bible* (West Orange, N.J.: Behrman, 1988), 7.

31. Ibid.

32. Ibid., 43.

33. Ibid., 118.

34. Ibid.

35. Robert Alter, *The Art of Biblical Narrative* (New York: Basic Books, 1981), 12.

36. Thus, in the Tower of Babel story, we read: "God saw the bricks becoming a city and a tower. God watched as the hearts of the people became as hard as bricks. The people of the earth stopped loving one another. They forgot how to love God," etc. (Rossel, 41). See the original version in Gen. 11:5–7, by contrast, where none of these motivational details is given. In answer to those who would argue that *A Child's Bible* adds these details because it is meant for children, see the retelling in Shirley Newman, *A Child's Introduction to Torah* (New York: Behrman and Melton Research Center, 1972) for an approach much more faithful to the original.

37. See, by contrast, Sarna's views on the importance of the "intellectual challenge" involved in studying the Bible, *Understanding Genesis* (New York: Melton Research Center and Schocken, 1966), xxii–xxiii.

38. Miriam Lorber and Judith Shamir, *Gateway to Torah* (New York: Ktav, 1991).

39. The article originally appeared in 1980. It was collected in Geertz's volume *Local Knowledge: Further Essays in Interpretive Anthropology* (New York: Basic, 1983), 19–35.

40. Stanley Fish, *Professional Correctness* (Cambridge: Harvard University Press, 1995), 73–74. Fish rejects this attack on the disciplines, stating that, in his view:

"The vocabularies of disciplines are not external to their objects, but constitutive of them. Discard them in favor of the vocabulary of another discipline, and you will lose the object that only they call into being" (85).

41. R. S. Peters, *Ethics and Education* (London: Allen and Unwin, 1966).

42. Joseph Lukinsky, "Integrating Jewish and General Studies in the Day School: Philosophy and Scope," in *Integrative Learning: The Search for Unity in Jewish Day School Programs,* ed. Max Nadel (New York: American Association for Jewish Education, 1980), 14.

Some Contributions of Philosophy to Education*

Israel Scheffler

O f what use is philosophy to education? What do philosophical pur-poses, skills, and attitudes bring to educational practice? What might they accomplish? My concern in what follows is not with any particular set of philosophical doctrines, nor am I inquiring after the ed-ucational implications of this or that philosophical viewpoint. Rather, my questions pertain to philosophical activity itself. The questions are thus quite general and are certainly not new. But they take on special ur-gency when viewed in the perspective of current trends that are likely increasingly to affect our future circumstances of life and our operative conceptions of education.

Current Trends

What are these trends? We have been living through a period that has seen a remarkable burst of technological energy that has already trans-formed, and will continue to transform, a wide variety of human activi-ties, including education, in ways that can hardly be foreseen. Advances in the underlying special sciences have, concomitantly, proceeded apace, spawning a welter of new technical conceptualizations in the physical, biological, social, and professional fields and challenging our prior as-

Israel Scheffler is the Victor S. Thomas Professor of Education and Philosophy Emeritus in the Graduate School of Education at Harvard University.

*This paper was presented at a plenary session of the 20th World Congress of Philosophy in Boston (August 1998); it appears in David M. Steiner, ed., *Philosophy of Education* (*Proceedings of the 20th World Congress of Philosophy*) (Philosophy Documentation Center, 1999), 193–200.

25

sumptions concerning life and death, morality, and society. Modes of transportation, communication, and interaction in every sphere have been radically accelerated, with the result that our globe has shrunk in physical size while cultural distances have, ironically, often widened and become more opaque to mutual understanding. And while the sciences and the global technical culture that they have made possible base themselves on appeal to stringent empirical tests, open theoretical debate, and objective criteria of evidence, large segments of our public have increasingly rejected the very notions of objective inquiry and the pursuit of truth, replacing them with the idea that subjectivism rules and (almost) anything goes.[1] Clearly, there is work for philosophy to do in responding to our new intellectual and cultural situation. I shall here outline some types of philosophical work that seem to me pressing under present circumstances and of particular importance in and for education.

The Rationale of Scientific Inquiry

First, I consider the task of developing a broad intellectual approach to the advancing scientific specializations that surround us on all sides. These specializations pose difficult challenges to the understanding when they are seen either as self-enclosed authorities embodying indubitable truths or else as arbitrary forms of social self-expression. What is urgently needed, by students and public alike, is an insight into the rationale of scientific inquiry—a grasp of the basic logic animating the provisional conclusions of the special sciences. These conclusions need to be understood, explicated, and related to the methods of inquiry by which they are developed and evaluated. The more such specializations impinge on public policy, the more urgent it is to make the rationale of their deliverances as well as their limitations understandable to a broad public, beginning, first of all, with the students in our schools. The desired aim in this context is to present science not as primarily an engine of technology, but rather, and above all, as a dynamic form of self-critical thought powered by the imagination yet answerable to the demands of logic and credible evidence.

This requires not only that the special idioms of scientific specialties be interpreted in terms accessible to the layman, to whatever extent this is possible, but also that the structures of their reasoning be grasped—that their assertions be viewed not as isolated and inert facts but as provisional judgments arising out of a creative search for explanatory theories, tempered by an empirical assessment of their adequacy. In turn, this requires that basic curricula in the schools be designed accordingly, so as to interpret their specialized materials to the novice rather than presenting them as fixed and final. Understood in the context of scientific reasoning, such materials are to be seen as bounded by the methodology supplying whatever authority they can claim.

In this curricular task, thinkers concerned with the history and philosophy of science have the capability to contribute significantly, both in explicating technical concepts and in setting forth the inferential patterns motivating the data of specialized investigations. Such thinkers may thus assist in overcoming the narrow treatment of subject matter and help in exhibiting such matter as neither dogmatic nor arbitrary but rather as exemplifying principles of critical thought.

Practice and Disciplinary Variety

When we turn from understanding the data of particular specializations to the question of understanding their applications to practice or policy, we confront additional problems. For such applications do not flow directly from given scientific disciplines taken one at a time. When the findings of a special discipline are to be brought to bear on practice, they need to be conjoined with other special findings, since practical problems are never exhaustively solvable by the single discipline. Thus, it is not only the internal rationale of any given scientific specialization that needs to be grasped but also its conjoint bearing, along with other relevant specializations, on practical problems of interest. Each specialization to be acquired by our students is to be presented not only in terms of its internal disciplinary context, but also with reference to its foreign relations, that is, the points of potential contact between it and other special studies.

The disciplines are, in effect, to be taught to our students not only linearly but also as ranged around the common practical problems to which they may be applied as relevant groups. Since the members of these groups are typically organized by different concepts and interests, the learner must, if he is to apply his learning to practice, acquire the ability to step outside the bounds of the discipline that may be most familiar to him. He cannot retire into the core of this discipline and stay there; he needs to hear the voices of those without who speak in foreign tongues and needs also to make himself understood to those who dwell beyond. A sensitivity to the languages and procedures of diverse inquiries is required, along with the willingness to hear others who have been differently trained. Further, the learner needs an ability to use disparate disciplines jointly in attacking practical problems, linking them, where possible, through translation or partial translation and—beyond the reach of translation altogether—an ability to assign the items of varying specializations to different segments of the practical problems in question.[2]

In fostering the requisite sensitivity to linguistic and procedural variation, philosophy has another important contribution to make. For philosophers are professionally disposed to deal with a plurality of subject matters and a variety of languages, seeing the commonalities as well as the differences between them, translating back and forth where possible and putting relevant varieties together in application to problems. Trained in the history of thought, philosophers are committed to making sense of diverse abstruse systems and committed also to seeing how such systems relate to one another, how they may be intertranslatable, and how they may, on the contrary, repel one another in content, style, or procedure. Such predispositions are of inestimable value in curricular formation and in teaching, not just for disciplinary understanding but also for disciplinary application to practice and policy.

Appreciation and Human Understanding

We have so far spoken of enhancing the understanding of specialized data by placing them within a context of logical structure and relevant methodological constraint. In dealing with applications to practice and policy, we have, further, emphasized the need for avoiding tunnel vision in order to profit from the various specializations bearing on practical solutions. In both these respects, philosophy has much to offer. But this is not all.

The application of special scientific studies to practical problems goes beyond disciplinary specializations altogether. For "the awareness of such problems is not the monopoly of any special discipline nor is it the exclusive province of any set of disciplines. Pooling the specialized perspectives of the several forms of inquiry does not yet guarantee human understanding,"[3] that is, comprehension of the human problems on which such perspectives are brought to bear.

Applications affect the activities, values, thoughts, and feelings of various people, and these require to be taken into account in evaluating the applications in question. Taking them into account means that we understand what people say when they describe their circumstances and express their opinions, fears, and hopes. It means that we have access to the way affected persons understand themselves and define their situations, that "we hear what they say when they speak in their own voice."[4] Here what is required is not just the sensitivity to language that we have described as a philosophical virtue, but also the willingness to listen genuinely, to enter sympathetically into the thought worlds of others, as expressed not in the locutions of any specialized inquiry, but the informal, and often idiosyncratic, expressions of everyday life, colored by personal habit and predilection. The philosopher, trained to enter into the systematic worlds of radically diverse thinkers, to attempt to gauge their circumstances, motivations, and expressions—in short, to reconstruct their thought sympathetically—has a vital contribution to make to the formation of pupils, who will be applying, as well as absorbing, the data of specialized studies in the whole of their future lives.

Application and Value

Application to practice involves choice. It is not enough to have the requisite knowledge to realize a variety of alternatives for dealing with a practical problem. Nor is it enough to know how each alternative will impinge on the lives of those it affects. To choose an alternative for realization is an expression of preference, a conferring of value upon such alternative, which creates a precedent, thus, in effect, creating a presumptive principle of action. R. M. Hare has emphasized the fact that decisions are the germs of principles that reverberate into other cases without limit.[5] Awareness of the incipient principles that one is thus expressing in application is awareness of one's actual values and facilitates their critical review.

A critical self-consciousness respecting one's values is a primary aim of education. It is one that is particularly urgent in a time of rapid technological change, when its momentum threatens to sweep all before it, overwhelming both moral scruple and human feeling. To attain this educational aim, it is essential to be able to discourse about values, to navigate fearlessly in the conceptual areas where factual and value considerations intermingle. To avoid blindness in action, it is essential to grapple with the task of formulating a code of moral principles by which one may act reflectively. Here, philosophy is of inestimable assistance, for unlike modern dispositions to avoid value discussions altogether or to consider values beyond rational treatment, philosophy embodies a tradition of over two millennia in which value considerations are treated seriously, subtly, and comprehensively. To build elements of this tradition into educational curricula is an important contribution of philosophy to an educational future of ethical substance.

The Past and the Present

The mention of the long tradition of philosophical discussion raises for consideration another important benefit that philosophy renders to education. This benefit lies in the very fact that philosophical discussion inevitably recalls its past. Unlike scientific and mathematical training, which move ever onward, leaving past developments behind, philosophical study never outgrows its past, recalling earlier thinkers and arguments even as it forges ahead. Placing the intellectual, literary, and moral contents of school curricula in the context of a long history of relevant treatments, philosophy thus breaks the tenacious hold of the present upon the consciousness of modern youth.

The present is, of course, the scene of all activity to be undertaken by our pupils and must therefore retain its centrality for their deliberations. Yet, untempered by memory, a focus on the present is a source of blindness, eliminating the funded experience of our predecessors from consideration as a resource for current understanding and perception. Strengthened by the momentum of technological advance that looks ever toward the potential transformation of prevailing arrangements by new devices and never looks back, the present-centeredness of much contemporary schooling runs the risk of distorting educational values by its cultural amnesia.

A current example is the impact of the computer on educational thinking. The computer is, of course, the agent of vast changes in social arrangements in recent years, and technical concepts of information and algorithm are its intellectual underpinnings. Opportunities for increased efficiency in teaching and enhanced individualization of learning are but two promises of computer applications that prudent educators need to explore. But the basic hazard that educators need to confront is a narrowing of their educational vision—a reduction of their fundamental concepts to presumed technological correlates. It is in helping to overcome this hazard that philosophy may now serve education as an important resource.[6]

Traditional epistemology, to take one central instance, views knowledge—even in its purely propositional form, as distinct from know-how or skill—in the broad contexts of truth, evidence, and belief. Knowledge, it insists, cannot be reduced to information alone, in the technical sense, i.e., to bits of bare propositional content. An item of knowledge, to qualify as such, must also be true. Education, insofar as it concerns knowledge, must therefore rest on an appeal to truth, assessing the truth value of available content and referring implicitly to operative standards of truth.

Nor, as epistemology shows, can knowledge be presumed to depend solely on algorithm. A claim to knowledge bears reference to evidence, but such evidence in general comprises good reasons in support of a conclusion rather than only algorithms or decision procedures, or even proofs. Even where proof is indeed available, it is important to note that, whereas it is subject to check by routine process, it cannot be discovered by routine process. The generation of proofs is a creative rather than an algorithmic outcome of inquiry, a matter of heuristics, ingenuity, and luck rather than mechanical routine.

Finally, knowledge is, for epistemology, no merely impersonal unit of propositional content, even if true and, moreover, grounded in adequate evidence. For such content is always formulated in the concepts of a historical language, and it is embodied in belief, evidenced not only in assertions but also in actions and purposes. To assess a claim to knowledge thus involves inquiry into concepts channeling relevant beliefs as well as the purposes expressed in related conduct. To view knowledge not as an inert corpus of informational items to be manipulated by algorithm, but rather as a domain of human belief aspiring to truth, advancing through creative discovery and evidenced in statement, action, and purpose is thus the perspective that the heritage of philosophy lends to educational practice.[7]

Information and Educational Aims

When we move beyond the educational aim of enhancing knowledge to consider educational aims in general, we find the popular computer concept of information to be clearly inadequate.

The everyday notion of information refers to material we can understand and interpret in context. Grasping what it expresses, we can paraphrase it and evaluate its contextual relevance, criticize and reject it or back it up appropriately, respond to it with feeling, sense its metaphorical echoes, appraise its bearing on our purposes, and apply it in our activity. The computer itself cannot be properly described as doing any of these things, in the everyday senses of the terms involved. To characterize the electronic state of computer circuitry in terms of information is to employ the word under a different interpretation. Further to construe the mind in terms of "computer information" empties the human notion of virtually all its content.[8]

Even the full-blooded human sense of information is incapable of expressing all our educational aims with respect to knowledge. As Ryle has put it, knowing a fact requires "having taken it in, i.e., being able and ready to operate with it, from it, around it and upon it. To possess a piece of information is to be able to mobilize it apart from its rote-neighbors and out of its rote-formulation in unhackneyed and *ad hoc* tasks."[9] And learning, even in the context of problem solving, goes well beyond information, in any sense. For it does not simply acquire information but

> entertains suppositions, rejects the accepted, conceives the possible, elaborates the doubtful or false, questions the familiar, guesses at the imaginable, improvises the unheard of. An intelligence capable only of storing and applying bits of information would be profoundly incapacitated for the solving of problems.[10]

Beyond the language of information altogether are those traditional educational formulations that speak of insight, skill, and norm. The first of these, i.e., insight, describes educational aims in terms of perception, vision, and illumination, intuition of nuance and pattern, imaginative grasp of overtone and undertone. The second, i.e., skill, discusses aims in terms of the forming or strengthening of abilities, the know-how commanded by a person rather than the know-that, the capability to deal with the tasks and challenges in every domain of life. The last of the three formulations focuses on norms rather than either information or capacities, on the tendencies and dispositions of a person, on what he does do rather than what he can do. Here again, we have left the notion of information behind. For we are dealing here not with what people believe or with what they are equipped to do, but with their character, what they can reliably be expected to do—with their predictable patterns of conduct, taste, and emotion.

These various realms of educational aims all need to be kept steadfastly in view as we make progress on any educational front. The whole array of ends embodied in the traditional locutions we have described must serve as the context within which we gauge our educational situation. Rather than cutting this array down to the size of our technology, we should strive to look beyond our technology, to determine the future purposes and directions of our further efforts. And in this task, philosophy serves a vital function by keeping the broadest conceptions of human learning in view as we move into a new and uncharted technological future.

Notes

1. For my defense of the ideal of objectivity in science, see I. Scheffler, *Science and Subjectivity*, 2ᵈ ed. (Indianapolis: Hackett, 1982).
2. For the application of scientific disciplines to practice, see "The Education of Policy Makers," chap. 4 in my *Of Human Potential* (London: Routledge and Kegan Paul, 1985), esp. 100ff.
3. Ibid.
4. Ibid.
5. R. M. Hare, *The Language of Morals* (Oxford: Clarendon, 1952), 56–78.
6. See my "Computers at School?" chap. 8 in I. Scheffler, *In Praise of the Cognitive Emotions* (New York: Routledge, Chapman and Hall, 1991), 80–96.
7. See my *Conditions of Knowledge* (Chicago: University of Chicago Press, 1965).
8. Scheffler, *In Praise of the Cognitive Emotions*, 91.
9. Gilbert Ryle, "Teaching and Training," in *The Concept of Education*, ed. R. S. Peters (London: Routledge and Kegan Paul, 1967), 111.
10. Scheffler, *In Praise of the Cognitive Emotions*, 93.

The Place of Theory
in a Practical Profession*

Frances Schoonmaker

There is probably no more intriguing or elusive question in education than the relationship between theory and practice. Understanding the connection between theory and practice is as compelling a challenge now as it was in 1904, when Dewey wrote his essay "The Relation of Theory to Practice in Education."[1]

In the mind of the public, theory is something done by scholars and researchers who probably know very little about actual practice. In education, practice is thought of as the day-to-day work of teaching children and youth in classrooms. Learning to teach is often seen as having very little to do with what goes on at universities, including colleges of education, because teaching is a practice-based profession. This public understanding of teaching is reinforced by the fact that many successful teachers have not been through formal teacher-preparation programs. As Dewey pointed out, success in teaching "is often not in any direct ratio to knowledge of educational principles," reinforcing the notion that teaching seems to be something that is learned by doing.[2] So compelling is this view of teaching that in many countries, there is a strong movement to place teacher preparation in the hands of schools, with universities serving a consultative role. Two examples that come immediately to mind are England, where local educational authorities have an initial teacher-training function, and the United States, where "alternative routes" into teaching allow aspiring college graduates with no background in teaching to participate in a few weeks of preparation before

Frances Schoonmaker is professor in the Department of Curriculum and Teaching at Teachers College, Columbia University.

*This paper was delivered at the Hong Kong Institute of Education, Department of Curriculum and Instruction, January 1999.

being apprenticed to schools. So while the question about the place of theory in a practical profession is not a new one, it is still a pertinent one.

The connection between theory and practice seems direct and obvious: theories are generated by scholars, tested by researchers, and implemented by practitioners. This perceived link is not only firmly entrenched in a public mindset about education, but has also shaped expectations of the college of education within universities and is tied to a university work culture of knowledge production. Given this social expectation, it is not surprising that university professors who are interested in schools (including those in colleges of education) are primarily interested in schools as laboratory sites for production of new knowledge through research. Sometimes, the purpose of knowledge production becomes obscure to those outside the university, and the result appears to be that scholars do research and theorizing in order to submit papers for publication—to be read by other scholars and researchers while life at the local school goes on unaffected by research on the school and its inhabitants. Theory and practice remain in their separate domains, the one belonging to the university and the other to the school.

Neither universities nor schools have been well served by this entrenched pattern of thinking about theory and practice as separate domains. It feeds two destructive fallacies. One is the fallacy that teaching does not require special knowledge and skills, but is learned by doing and the university has no special role to play in teacher education except to provide a grounding in the content that is to be taught. This is associated with a second fallacy, that great teachers are "born and not made." While it is true that many gifted teachers are "relatively ignorant of educational history, psychology, approved methods" and the like, "the successes of such individuals tend to be born and to die with them."[3] As for the remainder, those teachers who are not born with great gifts, the trial and error of day-to-day practice is a dubious teacher.

These fallacious notions have contributed to the demeaning of practice and to a diminishing of the intellectual role of the teacher in shaping classroom curriculum. When theory and practice belong to separate domains, the teacher tends to be separated from the intellectual life of teaching, and the process of curriculum development is seen as something separate from that of instruction. This, in effect, limits the teacher's role to making decisions about which of an array of prescribed teaching strategies to use, discipline of students, and preparation of the teaching environment—all technical aspects of teaching that do not require a great deal of original thought on the teacher's part. Teachers who need to experience intellectual stimulation in their work are left to seek it elsewhere, often in additional courses that enable them to develop their content knowledge, with little attention to pedagogy. But the teacher who becomes more knowledgeable in an academic discipline may find that choices about content are already made by the curriculum that is required.

Curriculum development involves the intellectual work of theorizing about content, human growth and development, and pedagogy. This is the quintessence of what Dewey described as the "soul action" of the classroom.[4] But this work is too often left to "off-site" experts while teachers are expected to put the ideas of curriculum developers into practice. Their task is not a curricular task, but one of implementation. This reduces teaching to the techniques of delivery and management, diminishing the appeal of teaching to the academically able candidates we most need to attract into the profession. As Zumwalt observed:

> By assigning curricular decisions elsewhere and relegating teachers to instructional and managerial decisions, one limits the discretionary freedom expected of most professionals and restricts teachers' ability to create effective educational experiences for their students. The current technological orientation with its mandated methods and curriculum strips teachers of their professionalism and undermines the attainment of excellence in the long run.[5]

The technological view of teaching that guided the major curriculum-change projects of the seventies and eighties found its way into programs of staff development and supervision of teaching. It continues to be one of the strongest strands in research on teaching. This is the view held by Berliner and Gage, who argue that "the teacher's job is to find ways, within the framework of classroom teaching, in which the different teaching methods, each with its own advantages for different purposes and different students, can be used."[6] Along similar lines, Gagne says that the teacher's essential task is "to arrange the conditions of the learner's environment so that the processes of learning will be activated, supported, enhanced, and maintained."[7] The training task, then, is to get teachers to integrate these various facets into a smooth performance.[8]

While these are all unarguably important facets of the teacher's work, they are essentially curriculum-neutral. They do not require the teacher to evaluate the appropriateness of curriculum goals, content, and recommended strategies except within the narrow boundaries of prescribed choices. The teacher is not one who is expected to raise questions of the worth of what is being delivered. Nor does the narrowed perspective on teaching expect or require the teacher to re-create the curriculum in order to meet the specific learning needs and interests of a particular group of students.

When the teacher's role is to implement curriculum designed off-site, staff development and supervision focus on instructional behaviors. The installation task is that of training teachers in the skills necessary for implementation of a particular curriculum. This has undoubtedly contributed to the fact that academically able students tend to leave the teaching profession within the first five years of teaching. A profession that focuses on "how to" and ignores, or refers, questions of "what if" and "how come" to authorities outside the classroom has little to offer the highly intelligent graduate who is capable of advancing our understanding of the complex life of schools from the inside.

The separation of theory from practice has also taken a toll on the university-based teacher educator. Research that is practice-based—not in observing practice from the corner of the classroom, but through involvement with teachers in their struggles about practice—is time-consuming. Until recently, university scholars seemed to get as far from practice as possible.[9] Even within research-intensive schools of education where research on schools has come to be in vogue, researchers are more eager to do research *on* than *with* school people. Furthermore, universities have not sorted out how to reward practice-based work, which yields less of what the university seems to value most: published research.

Historically, theory and research have been seen as offering practical things for teachers to do. Many teachers are eager for such tips, as evidenced by the popularity of *What Works* in the 1980s.[10] Teacher educators often hear cooperating teachers say that they are looking forward to "fresh new ideas" from student teachers who, presumably, are learning the latest in techniques generated by theory and research. This underscores the persistence of the commonplace belief that the real place of theory is in furnishing teachers with things to do. Despite the eagerness of many teachers to receive new ideas, the perception of the university as the place where ideas are produced is a source of tension between school and university. Teachers often resent the fact that their own ideas about practice seem to have less cachet than those disseminated by the university.

Knowledge production also becomes a problem to teachers when it generates educational solutions that become mandates for practice. Joseph Schwab suggested that the characteristic of theory is "the possibility of successful neatness, dispatch, and sweeping generality," which ambitiously set out to solve "by one mighty coup the problem of what to teach, when, and how."[11] It is this characteristic of theory that school people find most unsettling because the history of school reform suggests that today's "mighty coup" is tomorrow's outdated curriculum.

The Symbiotic Relationship between Theory and Practice

The separation of theory from practice is not only dysfunctional; in reality, it is a false separation. Theory always leads practice in education, whether by conscious design of people who call themselves "theorists" or in the form of tacit beliefs that guide the complex choices and actions of those who call themselves "practitioners." This is apparent in the following anecdotal recollection, drawn from field notes kept in my work in a Professional Development School: "When we interviewed Tina for the position of clinical faculty, she had one major reservation. 'I'm not at all theoretical,' she announced, leaning back in her chair and putting both hands up as if in protest. 'If you want practical ideas, I'm okay. But I don't know anything about theory!'"[12] Tina was initially unaware that the acts of teaching are always grounded in theoretical conceptions of teaching and learning that form teacher constructs, or naturalistic theories in use. Later, after about five weeks of team-teaching with university faculty, Tina said during a planning meeting, "So that's what you mean by theory! I guess I really am theoretical. I thought theory had to be what other people—you know, big university scholars—said. I do have things I believe about how kids learn. But I didn't think that was theory." Tina was beginning to identify her own constructs about teaching. Teacher constructs have theoretical underpinnings that are linked to commitments. These commitments are related to beliefs about what is worth knowing, how knowledge should be made available, to whom and by what authority. Hence, the question "What is the place of theory in a practical profession?" is not a relevant question. The more relevant questions are "What are the theories that are in use in a given context, and how are they related to one another?"

In recent years, there has been considerable interest in teacher reflection and the "contents" of teacher theories in use, or constructs. It is apparent from the robust body of literature on this subject that while there is considerable agreement that teacher reflection is a good thing, there is less agreement on what teacher reflection is.[13] When I use the term, I am thinking about what is often referred to as praxis, or reflective or thoughtful action.[14] Paulo Freire saw praxis as standing between intellectualism, or reflection without action, and activism, or action without reflection. James MacDonald argued that curriculum development should be seen as praxis, but he did not connect curriculum development with implementation, falling short of real praxis, in my view.[15] It is at this point, the juncture between the intended curriculum and the curriculum in use, that the teacher stands. When the teacher focuses on teaching practice as the skillful delivery and management of a curriculum (the instructional task), she or he is engaged in activism.[16] When the researcher or university-based teacher educator focuses on theory and research as creation of knowledge, apart from their practical context, the result is intellectualism.

The real place for theory in a practical profession is in bridging the intellectual work of theorizing about learning and what is to be learned and the people in the classroom—teachers and students—with their own theories in use, usually expressed as interests, wishes, preferences, and needs. Instruction, then, is not a manipulative process in which the teacher uses motivational psychology to get students to behave themselves and to learn things that may not be worth learning. Instead, it is a dynamic process in which the teacher's own theoretical constructs play a part along with the theoretical constructs of educational psychology, curriculum theorists, and the like. Teachers, teacher educators, and curriculum thinkers all have a role to play that is both theoretical and practical, though their roles are not redundant. The classroom is a laboratory for learning in which teachers draw on multiple resources—human and material—to create, try out, and assess curriculum and learning. The university offers another perspective, one that is not caught up in the day-to-day life of the classroom but that values this life and nurtures it through multiple levels and arenas of involvement that encompass university, classroom, and school community.

Teachers often have difficulty in accepting university involvement in their work, just as they have difficulty accepting theory and educational theories. This resistance is in part due to the fact that they usually encounter the university when they are required to take courses, when a researcher wants to study some classroom phenomenon, or when reformers and policy makers have staged another "mighty coup." University "involvement" usually means university intrusion. The most common form of intrusion is in the form of curriculum reform. Teachers are constantly faced with the task of implementing curricula that have been adopted, whether at the national, state, or local level, and that are based on someone else's notion of teaching and learning. Whether these curricular solutions come in the form of textbooks and accompanying materials, or comprehensive curricular packages, their shelf life is usually so short that teachers are just becoming expert in dealing with one before the next "mighty coup" comes along.

Curriculum prescriptions are based on some theoretical formulation that usually consists of a series of logically related statements that explain past events and predict future outcomes. In simplest terms, a theory is the articulation of an idea of how something works and will work under certain conditions. Top-down theories prescribe actions that are to be implemented or actualized in practice. These have been embodied in a curriculum model. Any new model usually requires changes in curriculum goals, organization, content, instructional strategies and materials, evaluation, and classroom management. Decisions regarding what is to be taught and how are made by experts and built into the curriculum, minimizing the power that teachers have in making decisions about the curriculum. Yet the degree to which any theoretical principles are to be implemented in practice is dependent on teachers and their expertise. This has meant that every major reform effort has required its own support network of supervision and staff development.

This is another reason that teaching can be so uninteresting to intellectually engaged teachers. There is a point at which learning new techniques and strategies becomes unsatisfying, no matter how novel they may be. After a certain number of experiences with new and innovative curricular solutions mandated by the central office, teachers become skeptical of staff-development days and resentful of in-class supervision. As a veteran teacher explained to me early in my own career as a classroom teacher, "I've seen them all. The things they were 'selling' me as a new teacher have already come back around." The demeaning of the professional role of teacher, teacher resistance to change, and flight from the profession are among the consequences of top-down curriculum that does not acknowledge and honor the teacher's own theoretical constructs about teaching and learning. Apple has identified another, the "de-skilling" of the teacher.[17] That is, the teacher's own skills and knowledge become stale because they are not exercised when curriculum decisions are made for them.

Teachers do not cope with mandated curricula in the same way, in part because not all mandates require the same kind of implementation. Curriculum theories seem to have hard and soft versions.[18] In a hard version of top-down theory, decisions about means and ends are made for teachers and for students as a curriculum is being designed. Even when teachers are part of a design team, the design is formulated outside of the classroom, and the expectation is that it will be installed as designed with a maximum degree of fidelity. Usually, such programs come with textbooks, supplementary materials, and training packages so that teacher decision making is kept to a minimum. In this case, power resides with the outside experts and the head of the organization, who agree to the adoption of a curriculum.

Not all top-down models require the same degree of specificity in implementation. Some top-down theories have soft prescriptions for practice. These are focused on a particular process—for example, cooperative learning. Or they may focus on a set of beliefs about how people learn—for example, Developmentally Appropriate Practice, in early-childhood education. Such models are less concerned with highly specific subject content and activities and leave many curriculum decisions to teachers, requiring their judgment and adaptation. Rather than specifying conceptual content, classroom management, and materials, soft theory delineates strategies, processes, or principles to be followed and criteria by which programs are to be evaluated. Soft versions of top-down theory are no less rigid and imposing in insistence on adherence to particular principles or processes than hard top-down models and maintain the theory-practice dichotomy. The difference between the two is on focus and latitude. A soft theory leaves the teacher with latitude in curriculum design as long as particular practices or processes are consistent with the theory. A hard theory is more specific along all dimensions of curricular choice.

Despite the persistent illusion held by many theorists that teachers will serve as the vehicle for transmission of their ideas into the classroom, teachers' own constructs about teaching and learning come into play when they teach a curriculum. Studies of curriculum implementation suggest that, broadly speaking, there are three approaches that teachers may be expected to take to implementation.[19] The first is to attempt to implement a curriculum with as high a degree of fidelity to a design as is possible. The harder the version of top-down theory, the greater the need for congruence between the curriculum model and classroom practice. Soft versions of top-down theory support a process of mutual adaptation, the second way in which teachers tend to implement curriculum. Adjustments are made in project goals and methods as well as in the needs, interests, and skills of various participants and organizations.[20] The third approach to implementation occurs when teachers involve themselves in curriculum theorizing, whether they do this consciously or unconsciously. Such teachers are likely to implement a curriculum through enactment, a process by which the curriculum is shaped in practice by teachers and students and may be entirely transformed.

In a process of enactment, teachers will utilize curriculum based on hard and soft theories, but may not follow the theorist's intentions. These teachers see the university-based theorist, the curriculum designer, teacher educator, and other off-site or out-of-classroom education workers as potential partners in uncovering the meaning of classroom events. They recognize that partners will bring in new perspectives and information. Partners may pursue different facets of a problem but will be working toward similar goals. This may be the greatest promise of Professional Development Schools, which attempt to bring together school and university collaboration around problems of teaching and learning.

It is not clear how teachers who seem to be consciously engaged in theorizing actually make use of formal theory. Those who have hope that teachers would clearly identify well-recognized formal psychological or educational theories in talking about their classroom practice have been disappointed.[21] It appears that teachers are more likely to draw on their own implicit theories of practice rather than technical theories.[22] Furthermore, teachers tend to be eclectic, integrating some aspects of formal theoretical knowledge into their own implicit constructs. Personal experience and the social context of teaching seem to be stronger influences on practice than formal theory.[23] In attempting to understand teacher use of theory, Sharon Ryan and I have developed a framework for thinking about teacher constructs as these are illustrated in their use of top-down curriculum theories and mandates for practice.[24]

Teachers' Constructs about Top-Down Theory: A Framework

Teachers' constructions of ideas around teaching and learning may be conceived of as points along a continuum of practice in which they will: focus the techniques of instruction; or engage in constant refining of ideas about knowledge and pedagogy.

The first of the extremes, getting the techniques right, may be labeled as a "practical construct"; the emphasis is on best methods and their efficient and effective mastery. This is an example of what I referred to earlier as "teacher activism." When teachers who are practically oriented engage in the everyday work of teaching, their choices of what to do and how are derived from the belief that particular activities work. By this, they usually mean that students like the activities and that they produce desired outcomes. Beyond this, they are not involved in thinking about the theoretical assumptions, philosophical commitments, and goals of the curriculum.

Other teachers have an experimental construct. The experimental teacher is involved in a continuous process of invention based on understanding of subject matter (content), social context (including the immediate classroom and community), and pedagogy (including learning, development, and organizational theory). Experimentally oriented teachers engage in a great deal of conscious deliberation. These are teachers whose actions I have described as "praxis." When deciding what to do, such teachers select particular activities based on children's interests not simply because they work, but because they are seen as essential instruments of experimentation in their evolving constructs about teaching and learning. They are concerned about theoretical assumptions, philosophical commitments, and goals of a curriculum, though they may not express these concerns in educational jargon.

The continuum suggests how teachers relate to top-down theory, how they use top-down curricula, and their own reaction to theory. This is represented in the figure below, which shows the relationship of constructs and approaches to implementation. Both practical and experimental constructs inform the way that teachers relate to top-down theory. Research on implementation suggests that there are at least three approaches teachers take to top-down theory, which are parallel to the ways in which they implement curriculum:

Teacher Constructs

Practical   Experimental

▪ ─────────────────────── ▪ ─────────────────── ▪

conservative   eclectic   creative

conservative	eclectic	creative
Mandated curriculum is implemented with a maximum degree of fidelity to the model.	Mandated curriculum is implemented with adaptations that are in keeping with the model but meet unique classroom needs	Mandated curriculum is utilized along with other resources in creation of unique classroom experiences.

1. Teachers with practical constructs grounded in beliefs about knowledge as something belonging to experts consider theory the domain of outside experts. At one extreme will be teachers holding a more conservative practical construct. Such teachers look for prescriptions for practice. Initially, they are likely to be responsive to hard versions of top-down theory when they are looking for "good things to do." They will expect a curriculum to include detailed teaching plans with accompanying materials. They may persist in using a curriculum long after it has been replaced and be resistant to changing from "one best way" to another.

2. Other teachers will examine a curriculum that has been adopted (perhaps with their input) and make adaptations as these are consistent with their own sense of how things ought to be in the classroom. They are not necessarily looking for fixed prescriptions. An eclectic practical construct holds that "if it works, do it." An array of materials, activities, and techniques are used by this teacher, regardless of the particular theoretical perspective from which they were generated. The eclectic practical teacher is more likely to respond to a soft version of top-down theory but may go along with a hard top-down theory long enough to try out the techniques it prescribes. Such teachers are not likely to stay with any particular curriculum, because of contextual factors such as school goals that are not consistent with a model or because they are focused on doing what seems to work. "What works" does not always seem congruent with the expectations of a given model.

3. Still other teachers assume responsibility for articulating and defending strongly held beliefs about how students learn what they need to know, and appropriate pedagogy and materials. These are teachers who hold an experimental construct. Such teachers are likely to rationalize their actions in language that suggests a commitment to the struggle between educational ideals, demands of a discipline of knowledge, psychological theories, and the social realities of the classroom. They are constantly weighing practice. Teachers with an experimental construct are likely to favor emergent models of practice, but may try a top-down model and attempt to implement it as precisely as possible in order to test its applicability to their own situation. However, if the goals of the model are too far from the teacher's own goals, adaptations will be seen, and over time the curriculum may be abandoned unless it has been completely transformed. Such teachers see their classrooms as learning laboratories where they are constantly learning along with their students.

The continuum illustrates the complexity and diversity of teacher constructs and their relationship to theory and practice. A teacher may typically act in ways that appear to be practical or experimental, but a teacher will not necessarily remain in one position along the continuum over a career. In fact, it is likely that a teacher who is given the freedom to do so may move from one position to another at different times, engaging in enactment for some classes or periods of the day and relying on a mandated curriculum for others. One of the interesting challenges that faces us is to figure out what prompts teachers to become experimental in their practice.

What Is the Place of Theory in a Practical Profession?

I have suggested that while the question "What is the place of theory in a practical profession?" is often asked, more useful questions are "What are the theories that are in use in a given context, and how are they related to one another?" What teacher educators really need to know is, "How can we make sense of the theories that are present in practice?"—those generated off-site and the teacher's own, often unconscious, constructs. The literature on curriculum change and implementation over the past several decades suggests that we can seriously question whether top-down theory has guided practice. And, judging from the literature, we can question whether educational and psychological theory has had more than a cursory impact on teaching practice. It appears that teachers do not utilize the theories that they learn in their teacher-preparation programs and that they drag their feet about implementing new curricula because, at least in part, they find them impractical and irrelevant to realities of classroom life. This presents a problem for teacher educators who believe that formal theory and curricula have a place in teaching.

One way of addressing this problem is through making problematic how theory is conceptualized and taught. A theory needs to be understood as an ambiguous and complex human construct inviting interpretation and critique rather than being delivered as great truth. This requires teacher educators and teachers becoming articulate about their own theoretical perspectives and the experiences that have led to their formation. When teachers make explicit some of their tacit theories, these theories become available for analysis, critique, and reconstruction. Teachers can then consciously select from top-down theory and theoretical models those principles or ideas that illuminate aspects of their own experience and make sense for their own practical work context. In such a context, top-down theory becomes relevant and meaningful.

The same is true when teacher educators make explicit their own struggles to deconstruct particular theories as well as their own constructs. When teacher educators are self-reflective and critical, they provide a safe environment for teachers and student teachers to engage in deliberation. They also model or provide intellectual scaffolding for understanding the nature of knowledge as dynamic, and the complex, symbiotic relationship between theory and practice. Teacher preparation that accounts for teacher constructs challenges student teachers to examine their prior experiences, beliefs, and commitments. It provides student-teaching environments that are *uncomfortable* enough to stimulate growth without discouraging it.

When curriculum development and change programs are undertaken with an understanding of teacher constructs, the process of implementation will be altered. There is much more emphasis on change as a process rather than as a static event. Implementation efforts, even those with fidelity to a model as the goal, account for the fact that teachers bring a range of commitments and interests to their work. Not all teachers are content to take on the role of technician. These teachers need to know why a particular curriculum requires adherence to strict guide-lines and see its implementation as an experimental process. Other teachers are interested in the technical aspects of teaching and are un-concerned about the broader picture. In their enthusiasm for teacher empowerment, some researchers make the assumption that all teachers are waiting to be liberated in order to do research on their own class-room practice, engage in curriculum enactment, and restructure the pro-fession. It is as unreasonable to suppose that all teachers desire to engage in curriculum enactment as it has been to assume that all teach-ers are content with the role of curriculum "implementer." There ought to be a place within the profession for both. Those who treat teachers as a homogeneous group who have the same interests and needs or who have the same interests and needs all the time are doomed to failure in their efforts to change the schools. Curricular options need to be avail-able to reflect societal needs, needs of a community, and individual needs of teachers and students.[25]

I have argued that the separation of theory from practice is unrealis-tic and has been a dysfunctional way of thinking about both. Such thinking has contributed to a separation of curriculum and teaching, which has had a negative effect on teacher morale and has limited our understanding of teaching. The relationship between theory and prac-tice is symbiotic; all teaching issues from some theoretical perspective, however unconscious. As Sharon Ryan and I conclude in our initial dis-cussion of the framework for thinking about teacher constructs:

> There is no such thing as practice without theory. Teachers have their own constructs about teaching, which influence their reac-tion to theories of learning and models of practice. How teach-ers respond to formal theory and the extent to which it leads practice in large part depend on these constructs. The challenge facing us all is how to bridge top-down theory with teachers' personal and theoretical constructs in a way that recognizes the power of both and honors the critical contribution of each.[26]

Notes

1. John Dewey, "The Relation of Theory to Practice in Education," in *The Rela-tion of Theory to Practice in the Education of Teachers*, ed. C. A. McMurry, Third Yearbook of the National Society for the Study of Education, pt. 1 (Chicago: University of Chicago Press, 1904), 10.

2. John Dewey, *The Sources of a Science of Education*, Kappa Delta Pi Lecture Series (New York: Horace Liveright, 1929).

3. Dewey, *The Sources of a Science of Education*, 10.

4. Dewey, "The Relation of Theory to Practice in Education."

5. Karen K. Zumwalt, "Are We Improving or Undermining Teaching?" in *Critical Issues in Curriculum*, ed. L. N. Tanner, Eighty-Seventh Yearbook of the National Society for the Study of Education, pt. 1 (Chicago: University of Chicago Press, 1988), 169.

6. David C. Berliner and Nathaniel L. Gage, "The Psychology of Teaching Methods," in *The Psychology of Teaching Methods*, ed. N. L. Gage, Seventy-Fifth Yearbook of the National Society for the Study of Education, pt. 1 (Chicago: University of Chicago Press, 1976), 19.

7. Robert M. Gagne, "The Learning Basis of Teaching Methods," in *The Psychology of Teaching Methods*, 42.

8. Richard J. Shavelson, "Teachers' Decision Making," in *The Psychology of Teaching Methods*.

9. Harry Judge, *American Graduate Schools of Education: A View from Abroad* (New York: Ford Foundation, 1982).

10. U.S. Department of Education, *What Works: About Teaching and Learning* (Washington, D.C.: U.S. Dept. of Education, 1986).

11. Joseph Schwab, "The Practical: A Language for Curriculum," in *School Review* 78 (1969): 1–23.

12. PDS log, 1991, personal research notes.

13. See Frances S. Bolin, "Helping Student Teachers Think about Teaching: Another Look at Lou," in *Journal of Teacher Education* 39, no. 2 (1988): 48–55; Frances Schoonmaker, "Promise and Possibility: Learning to Teach," in *Teachers College Record* 99, no. 3 (1998): 559–91; John Smyth, "Developing and Sustaining Critical Reflection in Teacher Education," in *Journal of Teacher Education* 40, no. 2 (1989): 2–9; Georgea M. Sparks-Langer and Amy B. Colton, "Synthesis of Research on Teachers' Reflective Thinking," in *Educational Leadership* 48, no. 6 (1991): 37–44; Alan Tom, *Inquiry into Teacher Education*, paper presented at the meeting of the American Educational Research Association, Chicago, April 1985; Kenneth Zeichner, "Preparing Reflective Teachers: An Overview of Instructional Strategies in Preservice Teacher Education," in *International Journal of Educational Research* 11 (1987): 565–75.

14. Paulo Freire, *Pedagogy of the Oppressed*, trans. Myra Bergman Ramus (New York: Herder and Herder, 1970).

15. James B. MacDonald, "Curriculum and Human Interests," in *Curriculum Theorizing: The Reconceptualists*, ed. W. Pinar (Berkeley: McCutchan, 1975).

16. Frances S. Bolin, "The Teacher as Curriculum Decision Maker," in *Teacher Renewal: Professional Issues, Personal Choices*, ed. F. Bolin and J. McConnel Falk (New York: Teachers College Press, 1987).

17. Michael Apple, *Teachers & Texts: A Political Economy of Class and Gender Relations in Education,* (Boston: Routledge and Kegan Paul, 1987).
18. Frances Schoonmaker and Sharon Ryan, "Does Theory Lead Practice? Teachers' Constructs about Teaching: Top-Down Perspectives," in *Advances in Early Education and Day Care* 8 (1996): 117–51.
19. Jon Snyder, Frances Bolin, and Karen Zumwalt, "Curriculum Implementation," in *Handbook of Research on Curriculum,* ed. P. W. Jackson (New York: Macmillan, 1992), 402–35.
20. Paul Berman and E. Pauley, "Federal Programs Supporting Educational Change," in *Factors Affecting Change Agent Projects,* vol. 2 (Santa Monica, Calif.: Rand, 1975); Milbrey W. McLaughlin and David D. Marsh, "Staff Development and School Change," in *Teachers College Record* 80, no. 1 (1976): 69–94.
21. Magdalene Lampert, "Teaching about Thinking and Thinking about Teaching," in *Journal of Curriculum Studies* 16, no. 1 (1984): 1–18.
22. N. Bell, "Early Childhood Teachers' Theories in Practice: What Do Teachers Believe?" paper presented at the fifth early-childhood convention, Dunedin, New Zealand, 1991.
23. Ibid.; K. L. Siefert, "What Develops in Informal Theories of Development," ERIC Document Reproduction Service no. ED 34289, 1991; Bernard Spodek, "Thought Processes Underlying Preschool Teachers' Classroom Decisions," in *Early Child Development and Care* 29 (1987): 197–208.
24. See Schoonmaker and Ryan, "Does Theory Lead Practice?"
25. See Snyder et al., "Curriculum Implementation."
26. Schoonmaker and Ryan, "Does Theory Lead Practice?

Opening the Gates of Knowledge

Douglas Sloan

For nearly fifteen years, Professor Joseph Lukinsky and I have participated, first with Professor William Bean Kennedy of Union Theological Seminary, and, more recently, with Professor Mary Boys, also of UTS, in a unique program in religion and education offered cooperatively by Teachers College, Union Theological Seminary, and the Jewish Theological Seminary. Joe has been a wonderful colleague and friend and a source of inspiration to me in our work together. It is a great pleasure to be able to join in this tribute to him.

This paper will explore the necessity and possibility of a transformation of our dominant ways of knowing. Let us consider, first, the necessity for such a transformation.

Assumptions of the Modern Mindset

During the nineteenth and twentieth centuries, three assumptions about knowing and knowable reality came increasingly to dominate thinking and consciousness. All three are coming under question today. Nevertheless, they are peculiarly modern, and their influence remains strong, often determinative, for modern knowledge and experience. So deeply ingrained are these assumptions that, even when we become seemingly sophisticated and aware of them, they repeatedly reassert themselves in our thinking in unexpected, often undetected, ways.[1]

Douglas Sloan is Professor of History and Education Emeritus, Teachers College, Columbia University, and is director of the Center for the Study of Spiritual Foundations of Education at Teachers College.

The first has been described as the objectivistic assumption, which derives from the now notorious Cartesian split between subject and object. It has also been called the assumption of the "onlooker consciousness." This view supposes that the knower is a detached onlooker standing over against, and describing, a world of mind-independent objects, as though neither knower nor known were fundamentally interrelated and mutually affected in the process. On this assumption, if we truly want to know something, we must detach ourselves from it as much as possible and describe it as mere onlookers.

The second is the further epistemological assumption that we can know only that which is given through our ordinary physical senses and through abstractions from sense experience. On this view, invisible realities are sometimes regarded as sensory in principle, but too small or too large to be perceived by our ordinary sensory apparatus; nevertheless, they could be perceived, had we the requisite instruments (a powerful-enough microscope or telescope, for instance). Or, they are regarded simply as unknowable; they may, indeed, exist, but they cannot be known.

The third is the related metaphysical assumption that reality is ultimately quantitative—without qualities, without consciousness or life—and is to be understood in terms of physical cause and effect, of external relationships, that is, mechanistically. In the nineteenth century, this quantitative-mechanistic view of knowable reality was expanded into an all-encompassing picture of a dead, meaningless, mechanical universe: the so-called scientific and technological worldview. While this view has had its critics from the beginning, it also has had, and continues to have, a powerful influence over modern consciousness.

What have been some of the major consequences of these assumptions for human understanding and modern culture? The picture is both positive and negative, and it is important that both sides be acknowledged. In criticizing the modern mindset, as I shall, I will not be urging (contrary to some contemporary critics) that we jettison each and everything about it. Indeed, sight must not be lost of the positive potentials contained in modern consciousness, whatever criticisms may otherwise be brought against modernity.

First, what are these positive potentials? Some years ago, the French sociologist Jacques Ellul described three great positive elements of modern Western culture: technical reason, an emerging sense of individuality and of individual worth, and the possibility of genuine freedom.[2] A strange thing, which we can only note without exploring in detail in this paper, is that these positive potentials are mysteriously entwined with the subject-object dichotomy and with the quantitative-mechanistic assumptions of the modern world. With the objectivity of controlling (or technical) reason and the sense of an objective world over against the feeling, human subject, there is interwoven a sense of separation from that world, and therewith also a growing sense of individual identity. Given clear, powerful thinking and the sense of individuality, there is also the possibility of free, self-determined action; in H. Richard Niebuhr's terms, there is the possibility of the responsible self.[3] Nor should it be overlooked that individual worth and freedom are the prerequisites for genuine love and community among persons.

Whatever criticisms are directed against the modern mindset, no response to these criticisms can be deemed adequate that does not preserve and strengthen the positive potentials of that mindset. These positive potentials, however, seem rapidly to be disappearing. And the reason for their evanescence is to be found, paradoxically, in that same modern mindset. The negative consequences of modernity's assumptions are now threatening the positive.

In the first place, a purely quantitative, mechanistic, and sense-bound way of knowing cannot deal with the most important dimensions of human experience. By definition, it cannot deal with the entire realm of quality. Under quality may be included such things as color, sound, scent, and so on, which are entwined with sense experience, but whose full reality—as I shall maintain—transcends the sensibly given. But also included under quality are those larger realities that we experience as meaning, value, purpose, truth, beauty, goodness, and so on. Neither can a purely quantitative way of knowing deal with life and growth in nature, nor with personal beings of any kind, except in their physical-mechanical aspects. Under this way of knowing, the human being—no less than beings of the animal and plant kingdoms—is reduced to bare, material elements; hence, the moral and spiritual can be dealt with not at all.

Because our dominant ways of knowing cannot deal with the qualitative and non-sensory, everything having to do with these is increasingly regarded not only as unknowable, but as actually unreal. Religion, ethics, the arts, and personal-communal meanings and values have been put on the defensive and are constantly forced to justify their places in our lives. We see this within the university curriculum: subjects having to do with the qualitative—religion, metaphysics, literature, poetry, the fine arts—are constantly forced to justify their place in the higher learning on an equal standing with all those subjects having to do with quantity. It is often remarked that the arts are always the "first to go" in times of financial exigency—not biochemistry, not computer science.

A second, related consequence of this narrow way of knowing is that truncated models and images of the human being and of nature abound and predominate in our thinking, guiding our research and practice and our education at every level. Some of the models are reductionist in the extreme. But even those scientists who, in their own thinking, would not subscribe to full-scale reductionism—on the order, e.g., of that expressed recently by Francis Crick: all human joys and sorrows, memories, ambitions, and personal identity itself are, as he puts it, "no more than the behavior of a vast assembly of nerve cells and their associated molecules"[4]—are almost all bound in their actual research entirely to mechanistic and reductionist models of reality.

In medicine, agriculture, biology, cognitive science, brain research—in nearly every field—mechanistic models of inquiry and application prevail. In our laboratories and classrooms, mechanistic images and models of the human almost exclusively guide research, teaching, and technological development. The results are wrenching ethical, medical, ecological, and cultural dilemmas, as the fullness of the human being is reduced to conformity with the less than human realities that are generated in the laboratory and are then released upon a hapless public. And all the while, qualitative nature—the nature around us and in us, the nature of beauty and life—continues, relentlessly, to be taken apart. Our science and technology reserve almost no place for this beauteous nature in their prevailing models of knowing.

This points to a third consequence of our modern ways of knowing, the creation and perpetuation of the central dualism of the modern world—namely, the split that exists between knowledge on the one hand, and faith, values, and meaning, on the other. An exclusively quantitative, sense-bound way of knowing has no place for intrinsic values and ethical ends. These can only be seen as arbitrary and irrational. But values that cannot be dealt with in connection with genuine knowledge can only be irrationally and dogmatically asserted, whether by the individual or by the community. As selfhood, community, and nature are eroded by our modern ways of knowing, the values that they support also disintegrate. As people cling to endangered values but can find no grounding for them in what is taken to be knowable reality, they are increasingly moved simply to assert them dogmatically, and if the threat increases, either to give them up or to kill for them. So we witness the rise of two major phenomena of our modern world, reinforcing and feeding off each other: the evaporation of all sense of truth and morality; and burgeoning, nationalistic, ethnocentric, and religious-political-scientific fundamentalisms of every description.

Finally, perhaps the most serious consequence of the modern mind-set is that it undercuts its own best, positive potentials. Thinking loses its creative foundation and becomes increasingly fragmenting and destructive, or dogmatic. Individuality loses its connection to a larger meaning and to other human beings, becoming rugged and rapacious, or disappears into the collective. And freedom without qualitative direction simply evaporates.

Toward a Transformation of Knowing

Today, many indications suggest that such a qualitative transformation of our knowing is becoming ever more conceivable. We can see this in the three main assumptions of modernity with which we began. The on-looker stance in knowing has been seriously challenged by participatory conceptions of knowing coming from many directions: from ecological studies, from hermeneutics, and, above all, from quantum physics. The mechanistic worldview has been challenged by organic metaphors deriving from sources as diverse as Whiteheadian process thought, ecological studies (again), and philosophical phenomenology. Even the assumption that all genuine knowledge is sense-bound is being questioned in some quarters—by those, for example, who have discovered ancient paths of consciousness-science, and by health-mind-body research.

All these challenges to the central assumptions of modernity encourage us to contemplate the possibility of a fundamental transformation in our ways of knowing. However, as they now stand, these challenges are severely limited, incomplete, and often inconsistent and confused. And it is crucial that these limitations and confusions be recognized if the real transformation that is needed is to take place. For example, while the ideal of the objective, detached knower-as-onlooker is increasingly rejected, other mechanistic and naïvely empirical assumptions remain intact. Thus, modern physics has taken the lead in criticizing older objectivistic, nonparticipatory ways of knowing, and, in such phenomena as nonlocality, it seems to have reached the boundaries of mechanistic explanations. But modern physics remains quantitative through and through and, to that extent, reductionist. Of course, the quantities in point are no longer measures of the old hard, palpable objects; these have evaporated into the purely formal quantities of number, force, and motion, but the latter motivate purely quantitative thinking, nonetheless. As the biologist Richard Lewontin has remarked, "matter ain't what it used to be"—good old-fashioned, hard matter has dissolved into mathematical relations and force fields—"but then neither is materialism."[5] Not quite, but materialism—and reductionism—it remains, because the only ultimate realities it recognizes are those of quantity. Moreover, in certain areas of science—genetic research, for example—mechanistic and reductionistic approaches to the whole of living nature, including human nature, could hardly be stronger.

To prevent misunderstanding, however, a caution may be in order. To call for an ongoing critique of what have been the dominant assumptions concerning knowing and knowable reality that now guide the practice and determine the ends of our current science and education is not to reject science, including quantitative science. The assumptions that we have looked at are historically associated with modern science, and, as we have seen, they have had an enormous influence on the directions, and limitations, of scientific research and technological practice. But they are not intrinsic to science as such. They have been imported into science from the larger social-historical context in which science developed and actually constitute scientifically foreign and scientifically corrupting elements within science. To criticize these assumptions is not, therefore, to abandon science; it is, rather, to begin to liberate science from obstructions to the realization of its own possibilities—the possibility of knowledge, for example, of the qualitative, of life, and of growth and development, which can only be denied, severely truncated, or reduced to something else by an exclusively mechanistic and quantitative way of knowing.

What, then, might a fundamental transformation of our knowing entail in its essentials? Certainly a rigorous and sustained probing and testing of the assumptions that guide and shape our thinking constitute a *sine qua non.* And there are abundant resources available in the work of many people in a variety of fields for this. A genuine transformation, however, will also require as essential not merely new theories and categories (important as these are), but new capacities—new capacities for insight and understanding, new capacities for perception and experience.

There are two points within modern science and religion alike where the germs of these capacities already exist. The starting points, therefore, are already at hand. But they seem so commonplace, so "ho-hum," as my students might say, that their radical potential goes largely unnoticed. These are the areas of thinking and of seeing, of conception and of perception. I will close by simply pointing to the potential for a radical transformation of knowing (and of ourselves) contained in these two capacities of the human being, a transformation that would embrace both sides of the faith-knowledge relationship.

Some people today have recognized and called our attention to the power of thinking. Stanislauf Ulam, the noted mathematician involved in the development of the atomic bomb, once expressed his own amazement at the power of thought. "It is still an unending source of surprise for me," he said, "to see how a few scribbles on a blackboard or on a sheet of paper could change the course of human affairs."[6] Erwin Chargaff, the great biochemist, has observed the power of thinking in penetrating and splitting the two nuclei of matter, the nucleus of the atom and the nucleus of the cell—and, in both instances, Chargaff expressed his uneasiness with what thinking has wrought.[7] To take one last example, the historian John Lukacs has described as the most important fact of our time what he calls "the mental intrusion into the structure of events." In our century, this mental intrusion has attained new powers of penetration, capable of what Lukacs calls, on the one hand, the destructive "insubstantialization of matter," and, on the other, the creative "spiritualization of matter."[8] What he and others are pointing to is the power of thinking both to create and to destroy—right down to the foundational level of the material world itself. If thinking has this power, then we are well advised to pay attention to it, for the quality of our world is going to depend directly on the quality of our thinking.

One of modern science's attendant myths—now called into question by most philosophers of science, but still flourishing in textbooks and popular accounts—is that science, and experience generally, involve thinking about the world by means of ideas, theories, and hypotheses, then checking these out *against* our perceptions of the world, which are given to us *independently* of our thinking and of our ideas. The so-called facts, it is assumed, are given in pure perception apart from our concepts, which are then added on. Philosophers sometimes call this account "naïve realism," or, better, "naïve empiricism," or "sensationism."

It is an account that cannot be sustained. There are no facts apart from ideas that make them facts. We have a world of experience because our concepts conspire with our perceptions to give us this world. The world of our experience, its possibility, depends upon our ideas, our concepts, and our theories shaping and giving us a world. Without thinking, without concepts, we would have no world. At most, we would have an unintelligible, chaotic "experience" of colors, sounds, and motions. If we could successfully separate our thinking from our perception, we would be left not with a world of "pure" facts and objects, but with no world at all. Pure perception would be, as William James recognized long ago, "buzzing, blooming confusion."

We perceive an object as object because we have a concept of that object that we bring to our perception. Seeing, as Henri Bortoft expresses it, is "a cognitive perception," not just a "sense perception."[9] As the philosopher of science Norwood Hanson has put it, "There is more to seeing than meets the eye."[10] And as David Best has written, "Someone who suffers a total loss of memory does not, as a consequence, understand reality directly. On the contrary he understands nothing. For example, he could no longer directly see a tree, since he no longer knows what a tree is."[11] To eliminate concepts would not bring us a purer experience of the world; it would eliminate the world with the concepts.

In science, there are no unalterable facts, because the facts themselves are shaped and determined by our theories and concepts. The kind of world that we find ourselves living in depends, then, on the quality of the concepts by means of which we perceive and experience it *as* a world. As Owen Barfield has observed, "If enough people go on long enough perceiving and thinking about the world as mechanism only, the macroscopic world [*scil,* the world of our lived experience] will eventually *become* mechanism only."[12]

A critical part of our work in any transformation of knowledge would be to develop, and bring to bear in our knowing, heightened powers of concentration and attention that can enable us to break the hold of conventional, habitual ways of thinking and seeing and attain to new insight. We can speak, in this regard, of bringing volitions into our thinking—volitions that can be variously developed through cognitive and artistic exercises, and through patient, diligent observation itself, exercises that are integral to the education of our thinking.[13] The physicist David Bohm has pointed out that all genuinely new knowing, of whatever provenance, comes not primarily through calculation or discursive reason, but through prior acts of insight. Bohm describes insight as a highly concentrated, attentive awareness capable of piercing the habitual and the given in a grasp of meaning in its immediacy and wholeness.[14] Similarly, Own Barfield has called imagination—in the sense of

Bohm's "insight"—thinking with will in it. The development of inner forces of will, of directed concentration and attention, is necessary to move us out of the ruts of our habitual assumptions and dead concepts into the radically new and vital.

A transformation of knowing will also require a new understanding and new capacities of perception. Here one can even speak of a new empiricism, in William James's words, "a radical empiricism," quite different from the naïve empiricism that separates fact from meaning, percept from concept. Insight and understanding require new concepts; they also require a concentrated attending to the phenomena, an attitude of enhanced attention and of radical openness to what the phenomena have to reveal in and of themselves, and a developed willingness and ability not to force the phenomena prematurely and inappropriately to fit our theories, explanations, thought models, and other reigning ideas. Insight and understanding demand an attitude of enhanced attention and of radical openness to the qualitative depths of the phenomena themselves. The phenomena attended to can, then, educate our thinking.

This realization was one of the main contributions of the scientific work of Goethe, who—in addition to his literary work—spent years developing a scientific approach in the fields of color theory, plant metamorphosis, morphology, and meteorology. Only now are his method's radical implications for the development of a truly qualitative science of nature gaining attention and appreciation.[15]

This is not the place to attempt a presentation of Goethe's method in any detail whatever. Suffice it for our purposes, at the risk of oversimplification and distortion, to point out one of the mainstays: the phenomena themselves carry their own meaning within them. To grasp this meaning, we have to attend to the phenomena ever more attentively, ever more openly, ever more assiduously and, at the same time, hold at the highest pitch our powers of thinking and conception. We must not project into the phenomena too quickly our antecedent conceptions, our explanations. These may enable us to control the phenomena for purposes actually alien to them, but controlling concepts—in nature as in personal relationships—seldom lead to deeper understanding. If, instead, we attend to the phenomena without prematurely forcing them under our own thought-models and assumptions, the ideas, the concepts, and the meanings in nature will begin to nurture and call forth within us sensitivities, the requisite organs of cognitive perception. Qualities carefully attended will serve to build up within us corresponding capacities for qualitative awareness. As Goethe himself puts it, "Each new object, well contemplated, opens up a new organ within us."[16] Attention to the qualities of the phenomena can build capacities, new organs of cognition, for discerning qualitative reality and meaning.

Religious feelings themselves, for example, can become more than subjective attitudes; they can also become organs of cognition. Owen Barfield provides an example: "Reverence is not simply a virtue for which we may expect full marks in heaven, or a device for bolstering up the social establishment. It is an organ of perception for a whole range of qualities that are as imperceptible without it as another whole range is imperceptible without an ear for music."[17] Methodologically, qualitative ways of knowing in the religious realm are not different in their essence from qualitative ways of knowing in the scientific realm.

In both realms, however, a radical transformation of knowing that can enable us to begin to grasp the qualities of existence will require a radical transformation of ourselves. Knowledge of qualities must by definition be both subjective and objective—in current jargon, participatory. I can only come to know qualities in the world—the world of nature, the world of others, the world of the spiritual—to the extent that I can bring to birth those qualities in myself. The fruits of the spirit—love, joy, peace, patience, goodness, and so forth—are non-sensory realities, but they are perceived and become realities for me only to the extent that I am able to identify with them and bring them to birth in myself. Such an inner transformation requires the participation of the whole human being—thinking, feeling, and willing. Acquaintance with living nature, involvement in meaningful social relationships, a deepening experience of the richness of language, active engagement with arts of every kind, inner discipline and concentration: these emerge as primary modes of education, for these are primary carriers of qualities in our experience. This suggests that a critical task in the transformation is to find ways to counter all those cultural influences that work to coarsen the feelings, to impoverish and deaden our senses, and to harden and rigidify our pictorial, imaging, and conceptual capacities, and that foster diminished and debased images of the human being itself—all the forces that impoverish and dampen our capacities for knowledge of the qualitative fullness of life.

What we require are ways of knowing that can open, in all their creative newness and life, the realms of the qualitative in both nature and spirit, and, if genuine knowledge is involved, knowledge in one realm will have consequences for the other.

Notes

1. As Owen Barfield has pointed out, these assumptions lie deep within us as unconscious habits, constituting our real, modern collective unconscious. They are the foundations of what Huston Smith has called the "modern mind-set." Neither he, in coining this term, nor I, in borrowing it, mean to suggest that there exists a monolithic mindset that unambiguously characterizes every modern thinker. Rather, the term suggests that certain assumptions about knowledge and the world have become so deeply embedded in modern consciousness that they influence everything we moderns do—our expectations, our actions, our perceptions—even at those moments when we may also be consciously incorporating premodern and antimodern assumptions. Cf. Owen Barfield, *Habit, Guilt, and History* (Middletown, Conn.: Wesleyan University Press, 1979), 79. Huston Smith, "Excluded Knowledge: A Critique of the Modern Western Mind-Set," *Teachers College Record* 80 (February 1979).

2. Jacques Ellul, *The Betrayal of the West* (New York: Seabury, 1978).

3. H. Richard Niebuhr, *The Responsible Self: An Essay in Christian Moral Philosophy* (New York: Harper and Row, 1978, c. 1963).

4. Francis Crick, *That Astonishing Hypothesis: The Scientific Search for the Soul* (New York: Scribners, 1994). It always seems to escape those who make this kind of claim that this is self-canceling. If true, Crick's claim is meaningless, because it is no less the product of his pack of neurons, totally determined and without meaning, so we would have no reason to want to read it. Of course, as is often the case with those who write this way, Crick may be making an exception for himself and, presumably, for at least one reader.

5. Richard Lewontin, "Science and 'The Demon-Haunted World': An Exchange," *The New York Review of Books,* 6 March 1997, 52.

6. Quoted in Richard Rhodes, *The Making of the Atomic Bomb* (New York: Simon and Schuster, 1986), 11.

7. Erwin Chargaff, *Heracletian Fire: Sketches from a Life before Nature* (New York: Rockefeller University Press, 1978).

8. John Lukacs, *Outgrowing Democracy* (Lanham, Md.: University of America, 1986).

9. Henri Bortoft, *The Wholeness of Nature: Goethe's Way toward a Science of Conscious Participation in Nature* (Hudson, N.Y.: Lindisfarne, 1996). Also see Owen Barfield, *Saving the Appearances: A Study in Idolatry* (New York: Harcourt, Brace and World, n.d.), passim. For a groundbreaking account of the primacy of thinking and its far-reaching implications, see Rudolf Steiner, *Philosophy of Freedom,* often translated in English as *Philosophy of Spiritual Activity* (1922; repr., Kila, Mont.: Kessinger, 1999). Also, Rudolf Steiner, *Truth and Knowledge* (Blauvelt, N.Y.: Multimedia, 1981).

10. Norwood Hanson, *Perception and Discovery: An Introduction to Scientific Inquiry* (San Francisco: W. H. Freeman, 1969), 61.

11. Quoted in Bortoft, *The Wholeness of Nature*, 131.

12. Owen Barfield, "Science and Quality," in Barfield, *The Rediscovery of Meaning and Other Essays* (Middletown, Conn.: Wesleyan University Press, 1977), 185.

13. While it is beyond the scope of this paper, to begin to explore the nature of such exercises, an example of what is necessary is presented in Georg Kühlewind, *From Normal to Health* (Hudson, N.Y.: Lindisfarne, 1993).

14. Cf. David Bohm, "Imagination, Fancy, Insight and Reason in the Process of Thought," in *Evolution of Consciousness*, ed. Shirley Sugerman (Middletown, Conn.: Wesleyan University Press, 1976); "Insight, Knowledge, Science, and Human Values," *Teachers College Record* 82 (spring 1981); and "On Insight and Its Significance for Science, Education and Values," in *Education and Human Values*, ed. Douglas Sloan (New York: Teachers College Press, 1980).

15. For examples of the growing interest in Goethe's scientific method and its implications for the transformation of science, cf. Bortoft, *The Wholeness of Nature*; Frederick Amrine, ed., *Goethe and the Sciences: A Reappraisal*, Boston Studies in Philosophy of Science, vol. 97 (Boston: D. Reidel, 1987); Arthur Zajonc, *Catching the Light: The Entwined History of Light and Mind* (New York: Bantam, 1993); Douglas Miller, ed., *Goethe: Scientific Studies* (New York: Suhrkamp, 1988); David Seamon and Arthur Zajonc, eds., *Goethe's Way of Science: A Phenomenology of Nature* (Albany: State University of New York Press, 1998). For examples of the radical results of Goethe's method when applied to contemporary scientific research, see Craig Holdrege, *Genetics and the Manipulation of Life: The Forgotten Factor of Context* (Hudson, N.Y.: Lindisfarne, 1995); Wolfgang Schad, *Man and Mammals* (New York: Waldorf, 1977); Jochen Boekemühl and Andreas Suchantke, *The Metamorphosis of Plants* (Cape Town, South Africa: Novalis, 1995); E. M. Kranich, *Thinking beyond Darwin* (Hudson, N.Y.: Lindisfarne, 1999).

16. Quoted in Arthur Zajonc, "Facts as Theory," in Amrine, *Goethe and the Sciences*, 241.

17. Owen Barfield, *What Coleridge Thought* (Middletown, Conn.: Wesleyan University Press, 1971), 10–11.

JEWISH EDUCATION

Developing a Curriculum:
Between the Personal and the Professional

Brenda Bacon

> Decisions that confront educators are notoriously varied, complex and far-reaching in importance, but none outweighs in difficulty or significance those decisions governing selection of content.[1]

The question of what knowledge is worth teaching to students at a specific age in the supplementary Jewish school has challenged the staff of the Melton Research Center from its inception. The guiding principle in selecting content for the Melton curriculum was to give the students in the afternoon school the "intellectual power"[2] so crucial for making and carrying out the students' personal and moral decisions, especially as relating to their Jewish identity and commitment to Jewish tradition.

In this article, I will trace how decisions were made as to the contents of one curriculum of the Melton Research Center. Reflection on the process of developing *Teaching Rambam: His Thought and His Times,* written for twelve- and thirteen-year-old students, raises questions about the extent to which decision making in curriculum writing is a rational process.

Ralph Tyler, in his classic *Basic Principles of Curriculum and Instruction,*[3] presents the process of curriculum development as rational and linear. After deciding upon the aims of a curriculum, the staff selects and organizes those learning experiences that can maximize the possibility of reaching the aims. Evaluation of the students' learning de-

Brenda Bacon is a senior lecturer in Jewish education at the Schechter Institute of Jewish Studies in Jerusalem, where she heads the M.A. track in teaching Jewish studies and in informal/values education. She was a doctoral student of Professor Joseph Lukinsky at the Jewish Theological Seminary of America.

termines whether the aims were indeed reached. However, Goodlad and Richter doubt that curricular decisions can ever be completely rational. "No matter how carefully any rationale is set forth, human frailty will prevail to some degree in constructing the rationale itself as well as in following it in curriculum planning."[4]

The process of deliberation, as elucidated by Schwab,[5] can help limit the effects of human frailty, for the members of a group deliberating on a curriculum have different concerns and different backgrounds and can serve as "checks and balances" on the biases of their colleagues, as well as on their natural tendency to emphasize their specialties. Representatives of the four commonplaces—the academic discipline, the teachers, the students, and society—when guided by a well-prepared curriculum-deliberation leader, can reach the best possible decisions as to the contents of a curriculum. To what extent did this process take place in the development of *Teaching Rambam?*

The Melton Curriculum: An Idea-Centered Curriculum

Teaching Rambam: His Thought and His Times is but one component of a comprehensive curriculum for the six-hour-a-week afternoon Jewish school, for ages eight to twelve or thirteen. Various curricula include units of study on history, Bible,[6] prayer, holidays and mitzvot (commandments), Hebrew language, and contemporary Jewish life.

In 1963, Seymour Fox, then dean of the Teachers' Institute of the Jewish Theological Seminary, convened the faculty seminar of the Melton Research Center. The seminar participants, faculty members of the Jewish Theological Seminary, were assigned to select the "motifs or values inherent in the Jewish tradition that should be given special emphasis in the educational program for Jewish children,"[7] basing their selection of material on the "logic intrinsic to the subject matter."[8] These motifs were to serve as a frame of reference for the development of materials for Jewish schools. The participants agreed that Jewish thought should serve as the focal point for all subjects in the curriculum of the afternoon school. An understanding of the worldview of Judaism, as compared with the worldview of the surrounding culture, would enable the student "to respond to his society as a Jew."[9] The participants in the seminar shared the belief that the results of the critical scholarly study of Judaism, when turned into curriculum, could promote Jewish commitment.[10] This commitment would ensue as a result of the understanding that the ideas of the Jewish tradition deal with existential issues of eternal concern. The Melton Research Center plan envisioned a faculty member in each discipline writing a book to clarify the subject matter for teachers and supervisors. In addition, in the beginning stages of discussion, character education received heavy emphasis.[11]

After the selection of motifs and materials, developmental psychologists were to act as consultants and

> alert the faculty to the suitability or unsuitability of the materials and the means of presentation to the child in order to achieve the desired goals. They will guide the determination of the order (with respect to the age or maturity of the child) in which the various motifs should be presented in the curriculum.[12]

Professors Joseph Schwab and Ralph Tyler of the University of Chicago served as consultants in this process of curriculum development. They both warned against repeating the mistakes of the curriculum projects in general education, which had put great emphasis on subject matter, without being balanced by the needs of students, teachers, and the community. They also emphasized the requirement of careful testing in the classroom before a unit could be sent out to the public. Their view was accepted, and it was decided that the final step would be that "the materials so developed will be submitted to test and criticism by teachers and principals in the Jewish schools."[13]

Seymour Fox recognized from the outset that the six-hour-a-week supplementary Jewish school could not alone foster Jewish commitment. He viewed the junior congregation, the youth group, and summer camp as necessary adjuncts. However, because of the pressing needs of the congregational school as well as budgetary constraints, the Melton Research Center decided to focus on the supplementary school alone.

In 1971, before the publication of the Melton Research Center idea-centered curriculum proposal, Fox met with educators in the field to hear their reactions. While the educators generally concurred with the need for a new curriculum, several raised objections to the proposal, since they considered such a curriculum appropriate for upper grades rather than for the elementary school. Alvin Mars and Philip Arian, for example, stressed the need for experiences to help the child attain a feeling of Jewish identity even within the formal framework of the six-hour-a-week school. In their opinion, ideas alone could not serve as a vehicle for building the Jewish identity of the American Jewish child.[14]

Responding to the educators' criticisms, Fox argued that the introduction of an idea-centered curriculum based on traditional sources was a practical enterprise for the six-hour-a-week supplementary school. Other means of instilling Jewish identity could be fostered by the informal frameworks of the youth group and junior congregation. Fox also thought it necessary to teach traditional Jewish concepts before the age of thirteen, since only 20 percent of the graduates of the Jewish supplementary school continue their Jewish education beyond that age.[15]

The Melton curriculum maintained its idea-centered orientation. In doing so, the Melton Research Center decided, in effect, that the school can do best what it has done in the past: foster Jewish literacy, but now with an emphasis on key ideas of the Jewish tradition. The Melton curriculum, different from other curricula in Jewish education, would base itself on the most current scholarship, thus engaging the students' intellectual curiosity. The children's commitment to Judaism was to grow out of their knowledge of Jewish tradition.

The "Outline for the Afternoon School," published in the *Melton Research Center Newsletter* in 1977, set out the contents of the history curricula. It suggested that ten-year-old students study the beginning of the postbiblical period, with emphasis on the nature of rabbinic exegesis; that eleven-year-olds study the medieval period, with emphasis on the medieval Jewish commentator Rashi and the worldview of Ashkenazic Jewry; and that twelve-year-old students study selections from Maimonides' works as a way of understanding the worldview of medieval Sephardic Jewry. This plan differed considerably from the standard Jewish history curriculum for the supplementary school, which concentrated on "heroes" in the early grades and presented a chronological survey of history in the upper grades. The curriculum was partially a response to what Ackerman termed in 1970 the "deplorable state of instruction in history."[16] In most schools, history was taught as a description of the past that the child had to memorize, without any effort to relate those events to the present and with no time devoted to projects or meaningful discussion.

In their approach to the history component of the Melton curriculum, the faculty seminar found a solution to what Scheffler called "the basic problem" of curriculum decision making: "how to avoid both ignorance and superficiality." He had suggested that "the solution lies not in rapid survey courses but in the intensive cultivation of a small but significant variety of areas."[17]

The Melton Colloquium:
An Exemplar of Deliberation

How to present one of these areas was exemplified by the historian Gerson Cohen. Speaking at a Melton Center conference in Columbus, Ohio, in 1973, Cohen used the example of medieval Spanish Jewry to demonstrate how the study of history, "frequently presented as a series of disjointed facts," can take on meaning for students.

> What is required above all is a clear formulation of the changing syntheses that the Jewish leadership developed at any particular time and place as these became expressed in a new conception of *paideia*, or of the ideal Jew, and to relate these syntheses to the "external forces" shaping the Jewish community and its ideals.[18]

Cohen described the emergence of a Jewish aristocracy in Muslim Spain. This aristocracy prospered and even enjoyed political power bestowed by rulers who viewed Jews as a trustworthy group above partisan interest. These Jews developed a Hebrew culture meant to be the equal of the surrounding Arabic culture. In Sephardic Jewish society, the ideal Jew knew poetry, grammar, philosophy, and science, in addition to Torah.

For Cohen, the effort to define the *paideia* of each age and community should constitute the "connective thread" in the teaching of Jewish history. He thought that this approach was especially important for Jewish education in America, since the American Jew has yet to forge his own unique cultural response to the external influences of American society.

Cohen's presentation of Spanish Jewry became the subject of deliberations during a Melton Center colloquium in the spring of 1974. Chaired by Seymour Fox, the colloquium's participants included Gerson Cohen, the sociologist Seymour Martin Lipset, the social psychologist Shalom Schwartz, and Harold Gorvine, a teacher of Jewish history at Akiba Academy in Philadelphia. The choice of participants ensured that the subject matter, the child, the community, and the teacher would all have a voice in determining the content of the curriculum, as Schwab had enjoined.

During the discussion of Cohen's presentation, Schwartz and Lipset raised issues dealing with the child and the community. Both wondered whether children raised in a democratic society could relate to an elitist society such as the one that Cohen described.[19] There is no evidence in the protocols that consensus was reached on this issue. As will be shown below, the curriculum writer was the person who made the decision on this and similar matters.

Teaching Rambam: Decisions as to Content

The Melton project necessitated the training of curriculum writers. As a graduate student in Jewish history at the Jewish Theological Seminary, and a social studies teacher, I was approached by Sylvia Ettenberg, then assistant dean of the Teachers' Institute, to participate in a writing seminar led by Seymour Fox. The seminar met in 1975 and 1976. Tyler's *Basic Principles of Curriculum and Instruction* and Schwab's articles[20] on curriculum as an eclectic and practical endeavor, as opposed to a theoretical one, served as the basis for discussions in the seminar. The experience of the Melton Research Center in developing its Bible curriculum in the 1960s provided examples from the field.

The seminar participants were asked to choose one topic of the many in the curriculum plan and to submit a sample chapter. My interest in Jewish history and thought made it natural for me to choose to develop a curriculum on Rambam. And beyond my intellectual interest, I felt emotionally connected to Rambam, having studied in Yeshiva Rambam elementary school in Brooklyn, New York, during which time a picture of Rambam was printed on the cover of all notebooks used in Hebrew studies. In addition, I have a strong memory of Mr. Lefkowitz, the principal, asking my eighth-grade graduating class, "Who was Rambam?" To his great chagrin, no one could give a complete answer! I was determined that graduates of the supplementary school would know who Rambam was.

The original plan of the Melton curriculum was that the writing staff would follow the outline set out by the faculty seminar. This curriculum outline, written by academic specialists, would be the subject of a deliberation by representatives of the community, students, and teachers. In reality, the process recommended by Schwab proved almost impossible to carry out. It was too difficult to arrange meetings of sociologists, psychologists, teachers, and scholars, and the pressing needs of the field precluded such a lengthy deliberation process. Very often, a deliberation took place only at the outset of formulating the contents of the curriculum. As a result, the curriculum writers were central to the decision-making process.[21]

In the preparation of *Teaching Rambam: His Thought and His Times,* the concerns of Lipset and Schwartz did not pose a problem, for I had decided that the major focus was not to be on the nature of Spanish Jewish society. I chose to follow the model presented by George Boas in *The History of Ideas,*[22] thinking that it would pose a more appropriate intellectual challenge for students. Boas wrote that the historian of ideas wants to find out how a logical principle became a guide for behavior. In *Teaching Rambam,* I chose several key ideas in Judaism and examined the varied expressions that these ideas took in a specific period in Jewish history and how these ideas influenced Jewish behavior. Although this approach overlapped Cohen's in that it, too, dealt with the *paideia* of Spanish Jewry, including a chapter on the ideal of study, emphasis was not placed on the elites themselves but rather on their ideas.

I decided that the first chapter I would write would be on Rambam's concept of the Messiah. This decision was justified by the fact that messianism is a central idea in Judaism and that Maimonides dealt with the idea both theoretically, in his law code, and practically, when he responded to an incident of a false messiah in Yemen. However, other ideas central to the thought of Maimonides could easily have been justified. Upon reflection, the overriding factor in this decision is that the messianic idea has always fascinated me, as evidenced by my having written as an eighth-grade student an essay entitled "What Will Happen When the Messiah Comes." In addition, as a daughter of Holocaust survivors, I had always been especially moved by the story of victims going to their death, singing the *Ani Ma'amin* formulation of the twelfth principle of Maimonides' thirteen principles of Jewish faith, "I believe with perfect faith in the coming of the Messiah, and even though he tarries, I will wait daily for his coming."

The contents of this chapter underwent few changes from the initial draft until the final version of the curriculum, because teachers' reactions to the material during classroom testing were very positive. Having learned in the seminar with Professor Fox of the dangers of relying on the inquiry method alone, and basing myself on my experience as a social studies teacher, I included a large variety of learning activities, such as creative writing and simulations, in addition to the reading and analysis of texts.

The chapter on the concept of the Messiah includes a section from the *Mishneh Torah*, Maimonides' legal code, on the messianic era. This selection, which reflects a rationalistic view of messianism, is contrasted with a selection from *The Book of Beliefs and Opinions* of Saadia Gaon, the ninth-century Jewish leader in Babylonia. Saadia Gaon presents an apocalyptic view in which the order of the universe would undergo drastic change after the Messiah's arrival. The purpose of the comparison is to demonstrate the pluralism in Jewish thought, one of the aims of the curriculum as a whole. After the discussion of the contents of the messianic idea, the curriculum deals with concrete expressions of this idea, such as the phenomenon of false messiahs. The influence of messianism on contemporary life is examined in movements such as Zionism and Reform Judaism. For the closing activity of this chapter, I suggest that students participate in a project that would help less fortunate people have a glimpse of the messianic era.

For the second chapter, I chose the problem of evil, a theological issue discussed in a section of Rambam's philosophical work *The Guide for the Perplexed*. In retrospect, it is difficult to explain this choice, other than perhaps on a personal level. Working on this issue in the framework of developing a curriculum may have offered me an excellent opportunity to grapple with it. The chapter on the problem of evil proved to be problematic, as was pointed out by some teachers who tested the material in Camp Ramah in 1977. The difficult material from *The Guide for the Perplexed* demanded a level of sophistication that many students did not possess and worked well only in classes with exceptionally bright students. Also, the solution proposed by Maimonides was not satisfactory to the students. If one goal of the curriculum was to help students to identify with Maimonides and his worldview, then this chapter would not further that goal. My own experience in teaching that chapter, as well as the reactions of other teachers, contributed to my decision to discard it.

The experience of that summer also determined that a chapter on the biography of Maimonides should be written. The teachers thought that an introductory chapter was necessary to serve as a framework for Maimonides' ideas. A biography would enable students to gain a sense of the times in which Rambam lived, the problems he faced, his major achievements, and possibly to find points of identification with his life.

After discarding the chapter on evil, two chapters remained: one on Rambam's biography and the other on the Messiah. I was in a quandary as to how to continue. Which other key ideas should be presented to these students? An article written by Michael Rosenak of the Hebrew University, which was opportunely published in 1978, provided direction. In the article, "Education for Jewish Identification," Rosenak proposes that students in the supplementary school should study:

> (a) the ideational facts, the basic conceptual data that invite ideological or theological interpretation (such as God, Torah, and so on); (b) the historical facts, such as King David, Hebrew, and the State of Israel; and (c) sociological facts, those pertaining to community, anti-Semitism, "belonging," and "being different."[23]

Knowledge of these facts can help students make realistic and meaningful choices about their Jewishness, and if such an education succeeds, a student will "gain an understanding of diverse ways of Jewish belonging."[24] The ideational facts must be understood in relation to one another, as well as in their distinct interpretations as they took diverse forms in different periods of Jewish history. For Rosenak, the five key ideas are God, Torah, the Land of Israel, the people of Israel, and the Messiah.[25]

Rosenak's article dovetailed with the approach set out by Boas in *The History of Ideas* and helped complete the process of locating crucial ideas to include in the curriculum. In addition, it reinforced my decision to retain the chapter on the Messiah, one of Rosenak's five key ideas, and to eliminate the chapter on the problem of evil.

Thus, the ideas of God and Torah became the subjects of the following chapters. They seemed more central to Maimonides' thought than the concepts of the Land of Israel and the people of Israel. Also, the latter two concepts could be dealt with in a separate curriculum on the Land of Israel, which was part of the Melton plan for the *hey* class.

I divided the chapter on Torah into two parts: the study of Torah; and the rationale for the commandments of the Torah. The first topic poses basic questions for both the medieval and the modern Jew: What should an educated person know? Is there a difference between the kind of learning that students do and the learning undertaken when fulfilling the commandment of studying Torah?

In this chapter, students read selections from Rambam's code of Jewish law, the *Mishneh Torah,* on the regulations pertaining to Torah study. They then read an adaptation of the ethical will of Judah ibn Tibbon, the translator of many of Rambam's writings, to his son Samuel. The first source presents the ideal of Torah study, while the second shows its actualization in the everyday life of a Jew in Rambam's era. This chapter includes activities comparing the place of study in the lives of medieval and modern Jews. A project on illuminated manuscripts concludes this chapter, thus giving the students a sense of the aesthetic elements of medieval Jewish culture.

The second topic, the rationale for the commandments, could be important in helping students make personal choices. The genre of writings about *ta'amei hamitzvot,* explanations of the commandments, flourished in societies in which Jews faced intellectual challenges from the surrounding culture, such as those that Jews in America face. Usually not from ritually observant families, most of these students would not continue their Jewish education after the *hey* class, so this would be the last formal opportunity for them to learn about this idea. In addition, since the topic of mitzvot was central during the previous four years of the Melton curriculum,[26] a chapter on the rationale for the commandments would reinforce what the students had already learned.

This chapter opens with a selection describing the daily routine of a medieval Jew in Toledo, for whom observance of mitzvot was a natural part of life, thus presenting a model with which the students might be unfamiliar. Selections from two philosophical works, *The Guide for the Perplexed* by Maimonides and *The Kuzari* by Judah Halevi, offer explanations for kashrut and Sabbath observance. The concluding project involves researching the explanations given in past generations for various commandments and encourages students to suggest their own explanations.

The chapter on God seeks to remedy the omission of this concept from curricula and classroom discussions.[27] A person who believes in God views the world differently from one for whom the scientific way of looking at the world presents the whole truth. Therefore, the chapter opens with a lesson on different ways of looking at an object, in this case a dog, demonstrating that the scientific way of looking at the world is limited.[28] Rational indicators of God's existence by Rambam and experiential ones by Judah Halevi are presented. For Rambam, belief in God implies *imitatio dei,* imitating His compassionate acts. The curriculum concretizes this concept through study of the section from the

Mishneh Torah on *tzedakah* (charity), and concludes with suggestions for a *tzedakah* project.

In sum, the various chapters deal with questions that many students ask in other contexts—for example, whether God exists, or the purpose of the commandments—showing how thinking Jews in previous eras dealt with those same issues and gave answers that might have contemporary significance. They learn that just as Rambam had to face the challenge of an outside culture (Islam), so students today must contend with the influences of secularism and Christianity.

The fifteen sessions originally planned for the curriculum on *Teaching Rambam* seemed inadequate for a serious discussion of all these concepts. Since this conceptual framework necessitated the inclusion of a large amount of material, the Melton Research Center agreed to expand the original fifteen lessons to thirty. In preparation for the writing of each chapter, I read the major scholarly works on each idea and then considered how to translate the scholarship into curriculum appropriate to the *hey* class. David Silverman, of the philosophy department of the Jewish Theological Seminary, read each completed chapter for scholarly accuracy.[29] I thought that I could draw sufficient conclusions from the testing done at various Camps Ramah and supplementary schools as to the suitability of the material for teachers and students, except for the chapter on God. Elaine Morris, then director of the Melton Research Center, invited supplementary-school teachers and principals to offer their views on the chapter, after which I inserted minor changes. A deliberation among representatives of all the commonplaces was too difficult to arrange.

I felt a heavy responsibility in developing this curriculum, especially in the writing of the teacher's guide. Because not all teachers in supplementary schools had a good Jewish-studies background, the teacher's guide was to transmit content as well as pedagogy. As Fox wrote, "The curriculum writer will be communicating conceptions of Jewish thought and Jewish history, as well as suggesting ways of teaching this material."[30] What this meant, in effect, is that I would be determining how students and teachers would understand the worldview of Maimonides; I would be determining in part the canon of the graduate of the Jewish supplementary school.

Weiss and Cutter point out that canonical literature acts as "a support to memory—the collective memory that makes people feel part of a history. . . [They] have a tendency to tie the reader or the learner back to a community." We also need to recognize that many build their models of Judaism . . . largely from what we make available in synagogue, schools and bookstores. This is where the idiosyncratic and the normative connect. Consider the even more eccentric or particularistic aspects of canon formation such as the personal friendships of authors and editors or the size of print or quantity of illustrations. These observations draw attention to some of the unconscious or inadvertent factors that shape what we consider the canon of a community. A speaker may appeal to our public, or several volumes of a certain work suddenly become available, and we are in the process of adding to the canon. Idiosyncrasy and utility are inevitable, but we can prevent them from becoming the overriding determinants of canon by ongoing discourse and evaluation. A little self-awareness helps as well. . . . we want to measure what we value, and we want to have a reason for choosing *this* theory to teach.[31]

To what extent were the factors that determined the contents of the curriculum on Rambam inadvertent or unconscious? It is clear that my choice of the first two chapters, on messianism and on the problem of evil, were a result of my autobiography and my interests. However, the final content was determined by my study of the disciplines of Jewish thought and Jewish history and by a consideration of the needs of the community, students, and teachers. In the case of the first chapter written, on the Messiah, the choice was successful. In the case of the second chapter, on the problem of evil, "ongoing discourse" may have prevented my time being spent in writing the chapter, but fortunately, "ongoing evaluation" determined that efforts would not be expended in having it become part of the canon of the students of the supplementary school.

One inadvertent factor in the formation of the curriculum on Rambam was the appearance of the article by Rosenak just as I was groping for direction. If that article had not appeared, the curriculum might have had a different content. Indeed, if a different Melton staff member had chosen to work on this curriculum, its contents might also have been very different, with other concepts of Maimonides receiving attention.

To what extent is my experience as described in this paper true of the experience of other writers in developing new curricula? Educational research in the past two decades has pointed to the overwhelming influence of biography and values on teachers' curriculum decisions in the classroom.[32] This paper raises the question of their influence on the decisions involved in curriculum development as well, specifically in Jewish education.

Conclusions

To what extent was Schwab's curriculum-development model actually implemented, to what extent was it modified, and to what extent was it ignored during the past thirty years of curriculum development? Schwab presented a model of curriculum deliberation that was impossible to implement in the case of *Teaching Rambam*. His call for the active involvement of representatives of the commonplaces proved to be too expensive and too time-consuming. A more appropriate model for the field might be a modification of his ambitious proposal, one in which the representatives of the commonplaces would be involved in the early stages of development and would be consulted as individuals by the writer when needed. This places the burden of responsibility on the curriculum writer, who must balance the needs of the discipline, the students, the teachers, and society. Thus, it is all the more important for curriculum writers to become aware of the influence of their life experience on their curriculum decisions. In my case, this retrospective awareness confirmed Goodlad and Richter's view that human frailty prevails to some degree in curriculum planning.

This paper on the process of developing the curriculum *Teaching Rambam* follows Schwab's view that "the recovery and report of deliberations and of tactical judgments constitute a labor of great importance. Only a large and growing body of them will provide us with a ground for testing our views of what constitutes better and worse in these critically important arts."[33] It is my hope that reports of the development of other curricula in Jewish education will be forthcoming so that more opportunities for testing our views will become available.

Notes

1. I. Scheffler, "Justifying Curriculum Decisions," in *Curriculum and Evaluation*, ed. A. A. Bellack and H. Kliebard (Berkeley, Calif.: McCutchan, 1977), 497.
2. Ibid., 505.

3. R. W. Tyler, *Basic Principles of Curriculum and Instruction* (Chicago: University of Chicago Press, 1949).

4. I. J. Goodlad and M. N. R. Richter, Jr., "Decisions and Levels of Decision Making: Processes and Data Sources," in *Curriculum and Evaluation*, 507.

5. See J. J. Schwab, "The Practical 3: Translation into Curriculum," *School Review* 81, no. 4 (1973): 501–22.

6. For a history of the Bible curriculum, see R. Zielenziger, "A History of the Bible Program of the Melton Research Center" (Ph.D. diss., Jewish Theological Seminary, 1989).

7. "Developing the Melton Curriculum," *Melton Research Center Newsletter* 7 (fall 1977): 4. This followed the trend in general education in which first-rate scholars, such as Jerome Bruner in psychology and Jerrold R. Zacharias in physics, played a leading role in curriculum development. See E. Clinchy, "The New Curricula," in *The New Social Studies,* ed. E. Fenton (New York: Holt, Rinehart and Winston, 1966), 498–514.

8. Melton Research Center, *A Program for Jewish Education* (unpublished, 1963), 1. A more common term for the "logic intrinsic to the subject matter" is the "structure of the discipline." For the various uses of this term, see J. Lukinsky, "Structure in Educational Theory," *Educational Philosophy and Theory* 2, no. 2 (1970): 15–31.

9. "Developing the Melton Curriculum," 2.

10. See E. Schweid, "The Critique of the 'Science of Judaism,'" *Jerusalem Quarterly* 45 (winter 1988): 85–109, for a perceptive critique of this stance in Israeli education, particularly higher education. Schweid states, "It was not at all clear that the academic study of Judaism was equipped to fulfill a social and popular function in the realm of education, as traditional Torah study did." He notes that "the science of Judaism has indeed supplied material for the national Jewish educational system in Israel, but the cumulative result has been one of failure" (103). As will be shown later in this paper, in the early stages of the development of the curriculum, some educators expressed opposition to the idea-centered approach of the Melton curriculum.

11. See the exercises in ethical reasoning developed by B. Cohen and J. Schwab in *Genesis: The Teacher's Guide* (New York: Melton Research Center, 1966), 493–97, which reflect this emphasis.

12. "Developing the Melton Curriculum," 8.

13. Ibid.

14. This debate still continues. The difficulty of integrating knowledge and experiential activities can be seen in the recommendation of Shimon Frost, formerly executive vice president of Jewish Educational Services of North America. He suggested that two types of supplementary schools are needed: the present congregational school, which will focus on identity development, emphasize the experiential, and involve the entire family; and a regional supplementary school that would emphasize the transmission of knowledge. See S. Frost, "Any

Change Will Be for the Better: On the Future of Supplementary Schooling," *Jewish Education* 56, no. 2 (1988): 32–34. The 1987 report of the Board of Jewish Education of New York, entitled *Jewish Supplementary Schooling: An Educational System in Need of Change*, recommends that a weekend fellowship program should be instituted as a replacement for some classroom sessions of the supplementary school, because in the upper grades the need for Jewish experiences far outweighs that of academic learning. The 1990 Jewish Population Survey, which showed that half of all American Jews marry outside their faith, encouraged the trend of educators who focused on instilling a positive attachment to Judaism and the Jewish people rather than on the transmission of information. See J. Wertheimer, "Jewish Education in the United States: Recent Trends and Issues," *American Jewish Year Book* (1999), 3–115.

15. E. Morris, "Notes" (Melton Research seminar with educators, unpublished, 1971).

16. W. Ackerman, "An Analysis of Selected Courses of Study of Conservative Congregational Schools," *Jewish Education* 40, no. 2 (1970/71): 39. See also W. Ackerman, "Let Us Now Praise Famous Men and Our Fathers in Their Generations: History Books for Jewish Schools in America," *Dor Le'dor: Studies in the History of Jewish Education in Israel and the Diaspora* 2 (1984): 1–35.

17. Scheffler, 505.

18. G. D. Cohen, "Translating Jewish History into Curriculum," in *From the Scholar to the Classroom*, ed. S. Fox and G. Rosenfield (New York: Melton Center for Jewish Education, 1977), 36. The presentations of Cohen and other speakers at the conference were published in this volume.

19. E. Morris, "Notes" (Melton Center colloquium, unpublished, 1974). No record exists of Gorvine's comments, but an article by him published in 1975 indicates that he had similar objections, but for different reasons. He wrote that teaching Jewish history as the history of elites does not teach the whole truth about a historical period because it emphasizes the ideal rather than the reality. He would teach social history about the lives of ordinary Jews and would focus on conflicts in Jewish society. See H. Gorvine, "Jewish History and the Raising of Jewish Consciousness," *Reconstructionist* 41, no. 5 (1975): 7–13.

20. J. J. Schwab, "The Practical: Arts of the Eclectic," *School Review* 79, no. 4 (1971): 493–542; "The Practical: A Language for Curriculum," *School Review* 78, no. 1 (1969): 1–23; "The Practical 3: Translation into Curriculum" (see n. 5 above).

21. See B. Holtz, "Making the Practical Real: The Experience of the Melton Research Center in Curriculum Design," *Studies in Jewish Education* 6 (1992): 196–97 (English abstract); 33–45 (Hebrew).

22. George Boas, *The History of Ideas* (New York: Charles Scribner and Sons, 1967).

23. M. Rosenak, "Education for Jewish Identification," *Forum* 28 (1978): 122.

24. Ibid., 118.

25. Ibid., 123.

26. See, for example, G. Z. Dorph and V. Kelman, *Holidays/Mitzvot/ Prayer* (New York: Melton Research Center, 1979–80).

27. See F. S. Rothschild, "The Concept of God in Jewish Education," *Conservative Judaism* 24, no. 2 (1970): 2–20.

28. Eduardo Rauch, editor of the curriculum, wrote this introductory lesson on God because I had difficulty deciding how to introduce the chapter in a way that would be meaningful to twelve- and thirteen-year-old students.

29. This process may reflect an academic bias of the Melton Research Center, an arm of the Jewish Theological Seminary. While the curriculum material underwent infrequent supervision by developmental psychologists and the curriculum writers enjoyed almost complete freedom on this score, no curriculum was published without a scholar's checking for subject-matter accuracy. It should be noted that all writers were experienced teachers and thus had had much contact with children.

30. S. Fox, "The Scholar, the Educator and the Curriculum of the Jewish School," in *From the Scholar to the Classroom,* 109.

31. A. Weiss and W. Cutter, "Canon and Curriculum: How We Choose What We Teach," *Religious Education* 93, no. 1 (1998): 86.

32. See B. Bacon, "The Impact of the Life Experience of the Teacher in Curriculum Implementation: Implications for Jewish Education," in *New Trends in Jewish Educational Research,* ed. B. Bacon, D. Scherz, and D. Zissenwine (Tel Aviv: Tel Aviv University Press, 2000), 9–38; K. Carter, "The Place of Story in the Study of Teaching and Teacher Education," *Educational Researcher* 22, no. 1 (1993): 5–12; F. M. Connelly and D. J. Clandinin, *Teachers as Curriculum Planners* (New York: Teachers College Press, 1988); A. Hargreaves, "Revisiting Voice," *Educational Researcher* 25, no. 1 (1996): 12–19; W. Louden, *Understanding Teaching* (New York: Teachers College Press, 1991); P. S. G. Millies, "The Relationship between a Teacher's Life and Teaching," in *Teacher Lore: Learning from Our Own Experience,* ed. W. H. Shubert and W. C. Ayers (London: Longman, 1992); C. L. Paris, *Teacher Agency and Curriculum Making in the Classroom* (New York: Teachers College Press, 1993).

33. J. J. Schwab, foreword to *Case Studies in Curriculum Change,* ed. W. A. Reid and D. F. Walker (London: Routledge and Kegan Paul, 1975), viii.

An Accidental Teacher Researcher Looks at a Synagogue Talmud Study Circle

Burton I. Cohen

Much has been written about the role of teacher as researcher, usually within the framework that has been identified as "action research." As a rule, in this form of educational research, the teacher adopts the role of researcher or the researcher adopts the role of teacher, in both cases so as to examine some particular aspect of teaching that has drawn their attention. In the case study discussed in this paper, this writer "fell into" the role of teacher of a synagogue-based Talmud study group for adults. A neighbor invited me to join a Shabbat afternoon Talmud study circle that met in the Conservative synagogue with which we were both affiliated on the South Shore of Long Island, and when the leader took ill, I assumed the group's leadership at the request of its members. Only after some time had passed after having assumed that role did I recognize that this particular teaching responsibility raised interesting research questions, especially as regards the relationship (1) between my observations of the learning process in this group that I was teaching and resultant changes that I would make in my style of teaching; and (2) between the preceding and some of the published research in areas such as action research, adult education, and informal Talmud study.

An exploration of action research literature[1] convinced me that as unintended as my course of research may have been, it did lie within the parameters of this style of educational research.

Action research divides into two main strands: experimental and practitioner-researcher. . . . Experimental action research refers

Burton I. Cohen is associate professor and chair of the Department of Jewish Education at the Jewish Theological Seminary. He has specialized in informal Jewish education, having spent many years as director of Camp Ramah in Wisconsin and national director of the Ramah Camps and Israel Programs.

to that which begins with a hypothesis, is tested in an experimental action project, and is then evaluated for its effects. . . . In
the practitioner-researcher strand, however, research and action
are not carefully segregated. Although intentional and systematic, the process is more emergent than prescribed, and the researchers are practitioners inquiring into their own practice. . . .
The research grows out of practitioners' questions of their own
practice. They gather, record, and make meaning of data which
they, themselves, may have had a part in generating.[2]

The observations and findings that appear in this paper reflect this latter
type of action research.

The Current Interest in Talmud Study

My personal observations have led me to conclude that more than any
other single area of Jewish study, the Talmud has maintained and even
increased in its attractiveness to adults in the American Jewish community. I see evidence of its popularity on all sides. Perhaps this is best epit-
omized by the presence, a few years ago, of more than thirty thousand
Orthodox men at Madison Square Garden in Manhattan and at the
Nassau Coliseum on Long Island to celebrate their having studied the
three thousand pages of the Babylonian Talmud, a page per day, over a
seven-year period. Similar gatherings took place in other cities around
the country and around the world.[3]

There is strong evidence, however, that interest in Talmud study extends far beyond the Orthodox community. Over the past few years, Random House publishing company has been bringing out, a volume at a
time, an English/Hebrew edition of the Talmud, prepared by Adin Steinsaltz and his staff in Jerusalem and surely intended for a much broader
constituency than the aforementioned Orthodox community.[4] As the
number of adults studying Talmud has increased, so have the types of
venues for Talmud study increased and begun to extend far beyond the
traditional face-to-face study group, usually composed of Orthodox Jews,
of whom contemporary examples are described by Samuel Heilman in his
important book dealing with the topic.[5] The traditional venues have been
augmented by the innovation of Talmud *shi'urim* on tape and offered
over the Internet (mainly from *yeshivot* in Israel). This was carried a step

further by the Jewish Theological Seminary in autumn 1997, when it in-
augurated a program of interactive distance Talmud learning on the
World Wide Web with its "Introduction to Talmud" course.

For centuries, groups of Jewish men have spontaneously organized
themselves into leisure-time study circles focused on texts drawn from
the Babylonian Talmud. The religious, historical, sociological, and anthropological significance of the old and the contemporary versions of
such study circles in the Orthodox community are perceptively described by Heilman in his *The People of the Book*. Heilman utilizes the
Yiddish term *lernen* (the word that the students he observed use to refer
to their study activity) to distinguish such Talmud study from the organized didactic Talmud study that goes on in day schools, *yeshivot, kole-
lim*, seminaries, and universities; he uses the Yiddish word *khavruse* to
denote the fellowship of such *lerners* or students.[6] In this paper, those
terms will be used only to refer to the groups that Heilman studied.

My Talmud Group

It has been my good fortune to have the opportunity to lead a group of
enthusiastic laypeople in the study of Talmud every Saturday afternoon
for the past five years in the context of a Conservative synagogue. As
was mentioned earlier, the founder of the study group, a layman, urged
me to participate, and when he fell ill, the leadership devolved upon me.
The consistent membership and attendance of the group from week to
week throughout the year testify to the attractiveness of Talmud study
to a group of Jews who do not pursue Talmud study to fulfill a religious
obligation (a mitzvah)—which is how Heilman characterizes the motivation of the Orthodox Jews who constituted the membership of most
of the *khavruses* that he studied.[7]

I do not know if I can identify exactly what common factors draw
the members of my group to pursue this study so diligently. While they
do seem to have a genuine desire to increase their knowledge of the contents of the Talmud, they seem not much concerned to find authoritative
religious guidance in it or even to try to retain the specifics of what they
have learned.[8] None of them tries to take home copies of the Talmud
text to review the material studied over the course of the intervening
week; and when, after a week or two, I review what we have studied,
most do not recall the specifics without my coaching.

So why do they come to study regularly, on Saturday afternoon, week after week and year after year, when they could be napping or enjoying some recreational activity? My observations suggest that it is because they enjoy participating in the pleasurable experience of Talmud study, within a traditional-like framework, with a congenial group of men and women, within the walls of the synagogue, and at a time contiguous to the Shabbat afternoon services. It is not so as to absorb a background of authoritative Jewish teachings that will guide their behavior, or to fulfill the mitzvah of study, as do the *khavruse* members studied by Heilman. While not binding themselves by the authority of the Talmud text and its classical interpreters, they seem to understand intuitively that the study of Talmud, as arcane as it may be at times, will enable them to better understand the Jewish religion to which each of them is deeply committed (though in non-Orthodox fashion). It is clear that our Talmud circle lies well within the general understanding of what makes any adult-learning setting attractive to its participants.

> Support for adult learners is provided through a learning environment that meets both their physical and psychological needs. . . . An ideal adult learning climate has a non-threatening, non-judgmental atmosphere in which adults have permission for and are expected to share in the responsibility for their learning.[9]

Like many long-established Talmud study circles with a stable membership, ours was not initiated by a synagogue rabbi or an administrator, but by the study-group members themselves. As Heilman suggests in his description of the failure of the "Jerusalem Social Club Talmud Group," there is probably something intrinsically beneficial in a program (exemplified by the other five Talmud study groups that he observed) that flows from the psychic energy of its participants rather than from a programmatic framework such as a synagogue or Jewish community center seeking to round out its program or respond to the assumed interests of its members. Heilman emphasizes that you cannot arbitrarily schedule a Talmud *khavruse* as you would an activity in a JCC or a course at a university and then wait to see who registers for it.

> One should not be surprised to learn . . . that [in the case of] the people meeting in the class . . . scheduled. . . . by the administration of the club [that] felt an obligation to offer something in the way of "sacred study," the course never really managed to

become anything like a genuine study circle. . . . Lacking a sense of fellowship, the people simply could not sustain the experience of *lernen*. . . . That left only the interest in Talmud, apparently an insufficient basis for *lernen*.[10]

What Heilman says reminds one of Joseph Schwab's assertions regarding the role of Eros in education:

Appetite, emotion, and reason, then, can be abstracted from one another for purposes of thought but not in action. If we are to act upon and with another human person, as in his education, these factors must be understood and employed in their interaction and interpenetration. . . . Eros, the energy of wanting, is as much the energy source in the pursuit of truth as it is in the motion toward pleasure, friendship, fame or power. Any means or method of education taps this energy source to the extent that the method is at all effective.[11]

While the synagogue did make available to us a space for study and see to it that tables and chairs were provided and lights turned on for our group, for the first two years, the *shi'ur* was not included in the standard Saturday morning pulpit announcements, because we were a self-generated activity and not an official activity of the synagogue or its various auxiliaries. During this period, word of our weekly Shabbat afternoon meetings was disseminated solely by word of mouth. Possibly, the low profile of the group led to the intensification of commitment to the group among those who were later to become its core participants. Also, it meant that during the first years in which the class met, there would be few drop-by participants, something that became quite regular once the Talmud group was added to the public announcements each week and counted among the synagogue's official adult-education activities.

Beginning But Not Starting

At first, like a professor who feels obligated to give students the full value for their tuition (though, in this case, my students were not paying tuition, nor was I being compensated for teaching), I felt compelled to start the *shi'ur* as soon after the designated time as possible. Among the first things that I learned from my action-research observations was that although the *shi'ur* had a set sixty-minute time frame (from one hour before the time designated for *Minchah* services until *Minchah* time), it need not, nor should not, begin on time!

After a few weeks, I grasped the fact that the class had a rhythm of its own, which was well suited to the informal manner in which we studied and to the expectations of the adult learners who constituted the group. A successful session did not require our exploiting every moment of the hour in study narrowly focused on the Talmud text. Consequently, our "hour" always began with informal conversation among the participants, which began when they arrived and extended into the hour. My being present at the time that the students arrived, even at the announced meeting time, did not inhibit this initial conversation.

These initial moments after the arrival of the group members always turned out to be a time for discussion of such matters as "synagogue politics," talking about news items from the Jewish or general press, or sharing personal news—all totally unrelated to the subject matter of our studies. As far as the mechanics of the lesson, this delayed start of our studies created an opportunity for late-arriving students (there were always some) to be present for the actual start of our learning and may have been an unconscious tactic on the part of the students to allow for this. After a while, I reached the conclusion that this initial interchange among the students not only was not a deterrent to learning, but served as a sort of a revving-up period for the study session to follow. Often the topics discussed in this initial period would be recalled by the students during the *shi'ur* and even related by them to our studies. I came to see that there was no reason for me to feel guilty that we did not begin the study of the Talmud text promptly at the appointed time. The importance of this pre-study social activity is confirmed by Heilman:

> During these liminal periods, the beginnings and endings of class, there always seemed some business that members of the circle had to transact with one another. That is, they found additional ties to one another and used the occasion of their meeting to reaffirm and strengthen those ties.[12]

I was to see this same pattern of initial conversation, unrelated to the topic of study, and a delayed beginning to the session when I visited a weekly Bible group for adults that met in the home of participants in Berkeley, California.

Selecting Texts and Resources

The system for selecting study texts that I ultimately adopted was one that had long been used by the West Side (Manhattan) Talmud group: study a chapter in one tractate or an entire short tractate (to give students the stylistic and topical flavor of that particular talmudic text) and then switch to another tractate.[13] In this way, after a number of years, the continuing students (in our group, the same students did tend to come back from week to week and from year to year) would gradually be exposed to most of the areas of Jewish law and literary styles reflected in the Talmud. (The talmudic orders *Kodoshim* and *Toharot* were not studied.) The manner in which I borrowed this system from the West Side group was a reminder of the way in which schools often borrow promising innovations from one another.

Before proceeding to a new Talmud text, I always gave students a choice of materials. To my surprise, and contrary to what I had been led to expect of adult learners, they usually said, "Rabbi, you decide!" But an examination of research on this topic in adult-education literature showed that the adult educators see this seeming inconsistency as normal for adult learners. On the one hand,

> [adult learners] see themselves as being able to make their own decisions and face the consequences, to manage their own lives. In fact, the psychological definition of adulthood is the point at which individuals perceive themselves to be essentially self-directing. At this point people also develop a deep psychological need to be seen by others as being self-directing.[14]

On the other hand,

> [a]dults have been so deeply conditioned by their previous schooling (under the pedagogical model) to perceive the appropriate role of learner to be that of a dependent, more or less passive recipient of transmitted content, that even though they

may be completely self-directing in all other aspects of their lives, the minute they enter into any activity labeled "education," they sit back, fold their arms, and say, "Teach me."[15]

It seems to me that in the context of the synagogue in which, traditionally, deference is paid to the religious authority of the rabbi and the rabbi's fund of Jewish knowledge, it is not surprising that students prefer to allow the rabbi/teacher to select the text for study. On the other hand, it should be noted that class discussions (i.e., student responses to the content of the text and to one another), as indicated earlier, turned out to be quite freewheeling and unpredictable in nature.

In at least one regard, I was somewhat surprised to find that my determination to provide the most effective level of instruction to my students had impact not only on my interactive teaching activities but also upon my preactive teaching activity.[16] In the past, I had resolutely avoided using Artscroll/Mesorah Press publications because of my discomfort with the fundamentalist religious notions that are explicitly or implicitly present in them. As I undertook the task of preparing for leading the Talmud group sessions, I reviewed the available resource materials that could be of assistance to me in preparing the textual material for my students in the time that I had available. I found that, for the nonspecialist such as myself, the Artscroll/Mesorah Schottenstein Talmud is an essential text. Its great strengths are: a) its helpful style of rephrasing and elaborating upon the Talmud text in English; b) the manner in which it attempts to identify what connects each sentence or paragraph of the talmudic *sugya* to the preceding sentence or paragraph; c) the way in which it states what each paragraph is doing to further the rabbinic deliberation; d) its abundant explanations with citations of the sources from which these explanations are drawn (I often examined these sources and shared them with the students); and e) the full citations and explanations of the relevant biblical and talmudic cross-references. I decided that regular access to this resource would afford me a significant advantage in preparing my lessons. As for protecting my students against the latent ideological bias, I decided that I was capable of identifying it in the course of my preparation, and so could ensure that the students would not be misled by it.

Reading the Hebrew Talmud text was difficult for most students, so it was essential to provide them with an English translation. At first, we tried to study from the Steinsaltz English translation; however, I found the commentary to be excessively lengthy and cumbersome for this group of students, who liked to feel that they were making expeditious progress through the text. Consequently, early in our studies, we began to use the Soncino English/Hebrew Talmud as our primary text[17] and have remained with it. Most students chose to study from the English translation and just a few from the Aramaic/Hebrew text (their choice). The Soncino text was very attractive to the non-Hebrew-reading students because of its brevity and clarity (though at times, Britishisms or legalisms had to be explained or translated into American English). I always shared with the students alternative translations and interpretations not reflected in the Soncino edition that I had come across in the course of my preparation—usually from the Hebrew Steinsaltz, Schottenstein, or Rashi. The brief Soncino footnotes were readily accessible to students inclined to look further into the meaning of the text, and, to my great surprise, most were so inclined. Students loved to read ahead of me in the Soncino text and footnotes so that they knew in advance the answers to the questions that the Talmud text or the teacher was asking.

How Backgrounds and Life Experiences of Group Members Influence the Character of the Learning

Adult-education researchers emphasize that the life experiences of adult learners have a profound impact upon the way that these students participate in classes and affect the way that they construct the material studied for themselves. According to Knowles, "For many kinds of learning the richest resources for learning reside in the adult learners themselves."[18] The students in our group came from a variety of backgrounds: lawyer, doctor, dentist, businessman, social worker, professor of English, a doctoral candidate in Jewish history, and some retirees. Among the ten to twelve regular participants, there were three women. Sixty-five was the average age of the participants. The discussions were enriched by the students' responses to the Talmud text from out of their varied professional expertise and life experiences, often in narrative form. The lawyer commented on the talmudic legal traditions from the point of view of contemporary American law, English common law, and other legal systems. The physician was always ready to comment on medical matters, anthropological issues, and so on.

To cite an example of how students responded from out of their daily experience, here is an excerpt from the discussion surrounding Rabbi Yehuda's comment on *Bava Kamma* 86a, relating to the application of the five types of compensation (*nezek, tzaar, repui, shevet,* and *boshet*) for injury to or by a blind person. Rabbi Yehuda says, *Suma ain lo busha*, i.e., all five types of compensation relating to torts apply to the blind person, with the exception of *busha* (shame/degradation). In the brief talmudic discussion that follows, the Talmud discusses whether this exception applies only to a blind man who has been degraded, or also to a blind man who degrades another person. Upon hearing this, one of the students said:

> This past week, I was driving on 57th Street, approaching the entrance to the 59th Street Bridge. Before I could cross First Avenue to get to the bridge, the light started to change. I did not want to get stuck in the intersection—there was a policeman right there who would have given me a ticket for gridlock—so I stopped, but I was blocking the crosswalk. A blind man with a cane had been waiting to cross 57th Street. He began crossing, waving his cane in front of him. When the cane struck my car, he was outraged and began to curse me with every curse word known to man. I was so embarrassed. I felt sorry for the man, but what was I to do? Don't tell me that a blind man cannot cause shame!

Everyone was ready to respond to the texts that we read out of their life experiences. These comments served to bridge the gap between the ancient text and the lives of the students. If just coming to class week after week places the students in the realm of what Heilman calls "traditioning," here we have entered into the realm of what he refers to as "contemporization," the second of the two seemingly conflicting aspects of the "cultural performance" that Heilman identifies in the Talmud study group.

> There appear to be two main trends of these sorts of cultural performance: "traditioning," and "contemporization.". . . Traditioning allows . . . a group of twentieth-century men [to] seem to sit in the first-century academies of Babylonia or at least the primordial yeshivas of Europe. . . . [Contemporization] involves an imaginative reach back into the world of the Talmud during

which the old words and ideas are swept forward into the contemporary social and psychological cosmos of the *lerner*.[19]

The following summary of a class segment, taken from my journal of significant learning episodes (written from memory after Shabbat), illustrates a somewhat deeper level of students' response to the Talmud text from their personal recollections and experiences (again, in the form of narrative):

> The degree to which group members enrich our studies from their own varied life experience has long been apparent to me—the average age of the group members is probably about sixty-five. However, the course of the discussion that took place this week emphasized the degree to which the text of the Talmud can elicit deeply personal contributions to a degree that I had not hitherto imagined. We read a passage relating to natural disasters on *Taanit* 5a, in which Rabbi Nachman asks Rav Yitzchak to explain a passage from 2 Kings 8:1 in which the people are told that they will suffer drought and famine for seven years. He asks, how can they possibly survive for seven years without supplies of food? Rabbi Yitzchak replies by quoting Rabbi Yochanan, who explains this verse in the following fashion: in the first year, they will eat from the fields; in the second year, they will eat what they have managed to save; in the third year, they will eat their kosher animals; in the fourth year, their *tereifah* animals; in the fifth year, they will eat the insects and reptiles; in the sixth year, they will eat their children; and in the seventh year, they will eat the flesh from their own arms. Thus they will survive.
>
> The first member of the Talmud group to comment on the passage said that this was a horrifying statement: How could Rabbi Yochanan interpret the verse as calling for cannibalism? I explained to the group that such prophecies of cannibalism were actually found in the Torah in the *tochechah* (passages of rebuke). Someone else recalled that such events were mentioned in the biblical Book of Lamentations, which is read on the fast day of Tishah b'Av. Then our physician member recalled a contemporary novel by Piers Paul Read that describes cannibalism by the survivors of an airplane crash in an isolated area.

Then one of the retirees, who, with his wife, came to America from Europe after World War II, said that his wife had recounted to him how the members of her family had been locked into a train by the Russians during the war and sent to Siberia without food. Every so often, they drew lots and killed one of the people in the car for food. Finally, our cantor, who had also survived the Holocaust, reported that family members had told him that in the locked cattle cars on which the Germans shipped doomed Jews eastward to the extermination camps, without food, they ate from the bodies of the Jews who had died.

Over and over again, I found that the Talmud text had the power to elicit such poignant personal expressions. Significantly, though not by design, there almost always was a Holocaust survivor among the participants in our sessions. Among their many helpful contributions to the discussions arising out of the texts that we studied were an authentic knowledge of Jewish life in Eastern Europe; a knowledge of the Yiddish language (many terms that appear in the Talmud are commonly used in Yiddish parlance); and their retelling of unique and meaningful life experiences. Although it certainly would have been possible for us to study Talmud without these in-the-flesh reflections of the Eastern European Jewish ambience, the presence of these survivors added greatly to the authentic and affecting character of our Talmud studies.

Social Aspects of Group Life

Our studies took place around a long table that, later in the afternoon, between the *Minchah* and *Maariv* services, would be utilized for the *se'udah shlishit* (the traditional last Shabbat meal). The *shi'ur* students tended to sit in the same positions around the table each week (e.g., next to the teacher, or at the end of the table) and, as a rule, would not sit in one another's places. Prior to the institution of the *shi'ur*, there was at times a lack of a *minyan* (the quorum of ten men required for services) for the *Minchah* and *Maariv* services. But students in the *shi'ur*, some of whom had previously not attended these services regularly, tended to stay on for the rest of the afternoon.

There was in the class a student who took it upon himself, from the earliest sessions, to bring halvah, licorice, or chocolate bars for refreshments during the class each week. It did not interfere with the studies. In my academic teaching, much as I had become accustomed to the current practice of students bringing all types of nourishment to class, I had been dubious as to whether it abets learning. Here I saw that it contributed significantly to the improvement of the ambience of our learning. Another student was nicknamed "the surgeon," for his facility in dissecting the bars of halvah for convenient eating during class. When one of the students went to Israel, she pledged to bring back some Israeli halvah for the group. The same student who brought the candy also served as our "librarian" and saw to it that the appropriate Talmud texts were ready each week for the use of the students. The student who specialized in slicing up the halvah also took upon himself the responsibility of preparing the study table with a supply of Pentateuchs and prayer books (brought from the synagogue chapel), which would be utilized for reference purposes.

In a chapter of his book entitled "Fellowship," Heilman, in describing his own experience as a participant-observer, draws attention to the manner in which participation in the Talmud *khavruse* generates strong and meaningful social relationships among the members:

> Like the bowler who goes bowling often more to be with the gang than to knock down pins, the card player who joins three others for a rubber of bridge not so much to play cards as to be with friends, . . . I was drawn out of the house to *lern* often because I knew I was expected and when I failed to come, or another insider was missing, that absence was felt.[20]

Heilman's description of the empathetic fashion in which members of one of the Talmud study circles in which he studied responded to a member's death is reminiscent of how our group took the *shi'ur* and the *Minchah/Maariv minyan* to the home of Lou Schwartz (the founder of our group) during the *shivah* for him. Also, when I was sitting *shivah* for my own mother, I was not surprised that the *shi'ur* members came to visit, and, in fact, their presence made it possible for me to have a *minyan* at my home.

> There is nothing that can more certainly ensure that a person will continue to participate in the circle of *lernen* than to have him participate in some other group occupation. That is why all *khavruses* have always found ways to institutionalize such occa-

sions of extended fellowship into their existence—from the *siyum* to the holiday gathering, from the celebrations of birth to the assemblies of mourning.[21]

Of the half-dozen Talmud study groups that Heilman observed, only one failed and was disbanded during the course of his observations. This was the "Jerusalem Social Club Talmud Group."[22] It was the only one of the groups that included non-Orthodox Jews and was the only one that had female participants. Heilman suggests that its failure was due to the presence of the women in this group, which inhibited the social intercourse that he found to be so integral a part of the ambience of Talmud study *khavruses:*

> This mixing of sexes also seemed to inhibit the establishment of fellowship. . . . Missing here was any of the opening banter and sociability that characterized the other groups that I attended. . . . Lacking a sense of fellowship, the people could simply not sustain the experience of *lernen.* As for religious imperatives, these too could not be fulfilled easily in the club setting and in mixed company.[23]

My experience in my own Talmud study group compels me to question whether the presence of women necessarily inhibits the ambience of a Talmud study group, especially when the framework is a non-Orthodox one. The sessions of our own group were fully egalitarian. There was mutual respect and equal readiness among the men and the women to participate by listening as well as by joining into the discussion. While we would not argue with the accuracy of Heilman's observations, as regards this one group, we would wonder whether an asocial man or a group of men might not also have inhibited the type of social intercourse that he sees as so characteristic of Talmud study groups in an Orthodox setting. From observing my students, I saw that in a non-Orthodox Talmud study circle, "religious imperatives" can be as easily fostered in a mixed group as in a single-sex group.

With this exception, I must say that my own experience supports Heilman's conclusion regarding the manner in which the presence of the group enriches the nature of Talmud study.

> Without the *haver* with who one joins to play out the dialogues, debates, and narratives of the text, the Talmud rests in silence,

and Judaism and Jewish feeling remain unexpressed. And yet, once the group of *lerners* comes into being, it has the capacity to go beyond the boundaries of its specific tasks. . . . Together, . . . [the Talmud and the *khavruse*] create something precious and meaningful for all concerned. . . . But what brings the two together? . . . That something is, in a word, "religion." The religious Jew, Orthodox in his orientation, feels a historical and personal religious obligation to *lern* Torah. Out of this felt need he seeks out others who are likewise moved.[24]

Certainly, my own experience supports Heilman's assertion that Talmud study is greatly enriched when carried on within a primary group such as the Talmud *khavruse*. I would only add to his conclusions that it appears that the Talmud study group can be an enriching religious and intellectual experience not just for the Orthodox Jews who study Talmud because it is one of the 613 mitzvot, but also for the non-Orthodox Jews who recognize its significance as one of the foundation texts of Jewish tradition and who understand the enriching nature of lifelong study of classic Jewish texts.

Notes

1. Anyone interested in gaining entry to the literature of the field of action research would do well to start with "The Potential and Practice of Action Research, Part I and Part II," *Peabody Journal of Education* 64, nos. 2–3 (1987); and Marilyn Cochran Smith and Susan L. Lytle, "Research on Teaching and Teacher Research: The Issues That Divide," *Educational Researcher* 19 (March 1990): 2–11. Both sources are extremely rich in substantive as well as bibliographical resources on the topic.

2. Corinne E. Glesne, "Yet Another Role? The Teacher as Researcher," *Action in Teacher Research* 13 (spring 1991): 8.

3. Frank Bruni, "Thousands Celebrate Completion of Talmud Study," *New York Times,* 29 September 1997, sec. B, p. 1. Also see "Special Siyum HaShas Report," *Coalition: News and Views from Agudath Israel of America and the World of Torah Action,* November 1997.

4. See, for example, Adin Steinsaltz, commentator, *The Talmud: The Steinsaltz Edition, Volume I, Tractate Bava Metzia, Part I* (New York: Random House, 1989).

5. Samuel C. Heilman, *The People of the Book: Drama, Fellowship, and Religion* (Chicago: University of Chicago Press, 1983).

6. In the course of this paper, my Talmud study group will be referred to variously

as a class, a circle, or a *shi'ur* (the Yiddish term for "class," which was the nomenclature preferred by the members of this class when they spoke among themselves).

7. Heilman, 235.

8. As regards their not viewing the Talmud as authoritative, I can cite as an example our discussion of the normative statement *Ain maftirin achar hapesach afikoman* (*Pesachim* 10:8), which the Rabbis interpret to mean that seder participants may not eat more after the *afikoman* has been served. Virtually all the students in the class argued that, much as they wanted to follow the laws of the seder, this was not feasible at the seders that they led, since, if the dessert was served before the *afikoman,* the guests would feel free to get up and leave, thereby disrupting the conclusion of the seder. This questioning of or outright rejection of the Talmud's pronouncements is one of the characteristics of our discussions.

9. Susan Imel, "Guidelines for Working with Adult Learners," *ERIC Digest* no. 154. http://www.ed.gov/databases/ERIC_Digests/ed337313.html. Accessed 29 July 1997.

10. Heilman, 234–35.

11. Joseph J. Schwab, "Eros and Education," in *Science, Curriculum, and Liberal Education,* ed. Ian Westbury and Neil J. Wilkof (Chicago: University of Chicago Press, 1978), 109.

12. Heilman, 211.

13. From conversations with a member of that group, Rabbi Jerome Abrams.

14. Malcolm S. Knowles, *The Modern Practice of Adult Education: From Pedagogy to Andragogy* (Chicago: Follet, 1980), 252–53.

15. Ibid., 253.

16. Following the distinction made by Jackson. See Philip W. Jackson, "The Way Teaching Is," in A.S.C.D. Yearbook, *The Way Teaching Is* (Washington, D.C.: National Education Association, 1966), 14–17.

17. For example, Jacob Schachter, H. Freedman, and I. Epstein, eds., *Hebrew-English Edition of the Babylonian Talmud: [Tractate] Sanhedrin* (London: Soncino, 1969).

18. Knowles, 57.

19. Heilman, 62–63.

20. Ibid., 211–12.

21. Ibid., 232.

22. Ibid., 232ff.

23. Ibid., 233, 235.

24. Ibid., 235.

What Do Teachers Need to Know to Teach Torah?*

Gail Zaiman Dorph

O ne cannot teach what one does not know. But we have all had experiences of being in classes with teachers who purportedly knew a lot about their subject matter but could not teach it effectively. So what do teachers need to know about their subjects in order to teach them to students in authentic and meaningful ways? Recent educational research on subject-matter knowledge for teaching offers Jewish educators valuable ways of thinking about this question, though few have applied these ideas to Jewish content. In this paper, I offer a conceptual framework for thinking about subject-matter knowledge for teaching Torah. To illustrate how the different kinds of knowledge that I describe enter into teaching, I begin by bringing an extended example[1] of a Torah lesson taught by an experienced and gifted teacher to eleven- and twelve-year-olds in a supplementary religious-school setting. I start in this way so that the reader has a concrete example of subject-matter teaching to use as a reference point for thinking about the framework offered. I also use the lesson to illustrate how teachers' subject-matter knowledge and beliefs enter into teaching and to build a case for why attention to such knowledge by teacher educators and professional developers is important.

Gail Zaiman Dorph is the director of the Mandel Foundation's Teacher Educator Institute. She was a doctoral student of Professor Joseph Lukinsky at the Jewish Theological Seminary of America.

*An earlier version of this paper was delivered at the Jewish Educational Research Network Conference in Baltimore in 1994.

What's So Bad about Building a City
and a Tower with Its Top in the Sky?

When we enter the class, students are discussing Gen. 11:1–9, the narrative dealing with the Tower of Babel. The teacher, MK, is asking them questions to help clarify their reading of the text.

> MK: So they come to this place and they say, let's do something. What is it that they want to do, Josh?
>
> Josh: They want to get closer to God.
>
> MK: You're telling me an interpretation. I'm asking you a fact question.
>
> Josh: They want to build a big building.
>
> Netanya: And a city. It says [*reading from the Torah text*], "Come, let us build a city and a tower with its top in the sky to make a name for ourselves, else we shall be scattered over the world."
>
> MK: Great, you gave us an interpretation, Josh. And now from Netanya's reading, we know from the text what it is they wanted to do. What were their reasons?
>
> Netanya: [*looking back at the text and reading*] "To make a name for ourselves, else we shall be scattered over the world."

MK writes the following question on the board: "What's so bad about building a city and a tower with its top in the sky? She reminds the students that they knew what was bad about Eve eating the fruit of the tree and Cain murdering Abel, and asks them how they understand the problem here. She elicits the students' ideas, writing them on the board. When it seems that students have generated a variety of answers and have more or less exhausted their ideas for answers, MK offers an interpretation that they have not come up with, a response that she calls an "inside the text" answer. She then asks students questions that require them to read the text carefully.

> MK: One answer that is different from yours: "It's bad to prevent being scattered when they should fill the earth." This is the one I think that you didn't have. What was the command that

God originally gave to Adam and then repeated to Noah after the flood?

Anna: To fill the earth.

Zack: [*reading from text*] "Be fertile and increase and abound on earth."

MK: That's exactly right. What chapter and verse are you reading from, Zack?

Zack: 9:7.

MK: So in chapter 9, verse 7, people were told to spread out and fill the earth. Now they have a great plan as to how they will avoid filling the earth. So maybe if we're looking for an answer that sticks only to things that the Torah tells us, that's what's wrong with what they're doing. That's a real "inside the text" answer. [*MK places a sentence strip on the bottom of the board, which says, "It's bad to prevent being scattered when they should fill up the earth."*]

MK continues to group and label answers, placing them on the board in the shape of a "stepped tower," explaining that she has created the "step-shaped tower" with their answers to represent a ziggurat, a tower that was built in Mesopotamia. Students tell their teacher that they have studied about Mesopotamia in "regular" school, and the teacher comments that Mesopotamians built ziggurats as temples. Then she explains that this is an "outside the text" answer.

MK: Ziggurat is an outside-of-the-Torah-reason answer to: "What's so bad about building the tower?" An outside-of-the-Torah-reason might be: "We don't build ziggurats." We don't think that the right way to communicate with God is by building a tower. You remember this part of the Torah is not about the Jewish people.

Josh: [*looking at the configuration of the board and noticing that there is one "step" that has no answer written in it*] Are there any other reasons?

MK: [*laughing*] You caught on to me. Of course, that's why I left this blank space. Remember, when we were reading the story of Cain and Abel, I introduced you to a midrash. A

midrash is a teaching story or an explanatory story that the
Rabbis wrote when they faced a question such as the one we are
facing here.

MK reads a midrash that offers another angle on understanding what's
so bad about building the tower. After the class discusses its meaning,
she brings the lesson to a close:

> MK: So it's interesting, we started with a simple question. We
> now have four, maybe five, different answers to the question.
> Remember, in chapter 10 we asked, "How come if Adam and
> Eve started it all, there are different languages?" What was the
> answer of chapter 10?
>
> Tracy: It just developed that way. Different families, different
> nations, different languages!
>
> MK: What's the answer of chapter 11—how come there are dif-
> ferent languages?
>
> Eve: It was a punishment cause of how people acted.
>
> Zack: [reads from text] "If with one language for all, this is
> how they begin to act, then nothing they propose to do will be
> out of their reach."
>
> MK: Which answer do you like best? [Class discussion ensues.
> End of transcript]

Conceptual Frameworks for Understanding Subject Matter

Much of the recent educational research that explores issues of subject-
matter knowledge for teaching[2] builds on Schwab's[3] distinction between
substantive and syntactic structures of a given discipline.[4] Schwab defines substantive structures as "conceptual devices, which are used for
defining, bounding, and analyzing the subject matter."[5] The substantive
structure is the determinant of the kind of questions that the scholar of
the discipline asks of the field. According to Schwab, syntactic structures include the canons of evidence that are used by members of the
disciplinary community to guide inquiry in the field. They are the means

by which new knowledge is introduced and accepted into the field.[6] This distinction between substantive and syntactic structures influenced the work of Lee Shulman and his students, who studied how teachers learned and used subject-matter knowledge in teaching and developed a more elaborate set of categories. Their work reinforces the importance of teachers' knowing not only facts and concepts, but also conceptual frameworks, schools of thought, ways of knowing, and canons of evidence.

Schwab's work focused on issues of the subject-matter knowledge and scholarly activity in defining and studying disciplines in general. In his work, Alter[7] suggested three conceptual frameworks, which biblical scholars use to organize, analyze, and study their discipline. These frameworks, traditional biblical exegesis, "excavative" approaches, and modern literary criticism, are actually syntactic structures of the discipline; they are modes of scholarly inquiry in the field. After explaining each, I will use them as tools to analyze MK's lesson.

Subject-Matter Knowledge for Bible: Alter's Categories. Traditional biblical exegesis is built on the assumption that the whole text contains a timeless revelation. It represents a final teaching that is the same in all parts of the Bible. *Hafokh bah v'hapekh bah, d'kholah vah*[8]—"turn it round and round, interpret and reinterpret it, because all is in it." The traditional biblical exegete needs to look at the "book" and find the lessons that are needed in today's world. Commentators, using this approach, need to discover what the divine author had in mind. This process of reading is not a passive reading. It is done through careful examination of and grappling with words in order to interpret the text. The text is broken into units of sentences, phrases, or even words. Words and phrases from one section are connected to words and phrases from other sections. The chronology of the narrative does not preclude linking words, phrases, or verses from earlier or later sections. To the traditional exegete, the Bible is the same throughout. This strategy has taken what could have become a frozen document and turned it into a vessel capable of eternal renewal.

"Excavative" research includes the insights and discoveries of archaeology, comparative Semitic philology, ancient Near Eastern religions, and anthropology. These historical paradigms of Bible study all try to restore the original text.[9] From this point of view, the Bible is conceived as an "intricate set of puzzlements—philological, compositional, historical—that one by one require solutions and with a combination of ingenuity and serendipity will get them."[10] When there is a problem understanding the text, scholars look to archaeological finds, philological clues, and comparative texts emanating from the ancient Near East to help them uncover the meaning of the text. This comparative method maintains that to know the text, one should contrast it with other texts. When there are multiple stories or contradictory statements, scholars using this approach look to the idea of multiple sources of composition to "explain" the problem or incongruity.[11] According to this school of thought, the biblical message is best understood in the light of the time and place in which it was created. For example, the Creation accounts of Genesis can only be understood if read in juxtaposition to the Babylonian creation myth, Enuma Elish.[12]

Recently, biblical scholars (whether they work in anthropology, sociology, rhetoric, or theology) have again been looking at the Bible as a literary whole, just as the "traditionalists" do, analyzing the Bible as a "contained system of structurally related components,"[13] not as separate historical documents. This approach has been characterized as a synchronic approach to the study of the text. It looks at the Torah as an artistic whole. This approach tries to look at the whole literary unit and how it presents itself as the carrier of the message rather than at the chronology and sequence of elements as the embodiment of the message.

These scholars speak of the literary artistry of the biblical "redactor"—an editor who masterfully merged the various sources into their present arrangement. They accept the notion of multiple sources. They are not interested in trying to reconstruct the "original" text from which the Torah was derived. Rather, they are concerned with what the text means, how it expresses its message, and what its message is to us. The redactor has been credited with the pulling together of sources, the patterns of symmetry, repetition, thematic development, and stylistic modulation. When there is a problem in the text, scholars, accepting this approach, would look within the biblical text itself.

Traditional biblical exegesis and modern literary criticism both use hermeneutic principles to explicate the text. However, traditional exegesis of the Bible posits divine authorship of the text and thus, presupposes "solutions" to textual problems. Contemporary literary exegesis, on the other hand, assumes human authorship and "respects the secrecy of the Bible—not by enjoining silence but by articulating an order of commentary that will help readers tune into the multiple reverberations of the secrets."[14]

Beliefs about Torah.[15] Schwab's work did not develop the role of teachers' beliefs about subject matter. Recent research[16] demonstrates that teachers' beliefs about substantive and syntactic knowledge of the subject matter affect both what they choose to teach and how they choose to teach it. According to Greenstein,[17] one's syntactic approach is a function not only of different methodological strategies but also of fundamental differences in assumptions, principles, and beliefs. He suggests that the community of scholars (and, I would add, teachers) would be well served by an open examination of the assumptions underlying each of these approaches. He questions whether the differences are methodological or ideological. One can be committed to reading the Bible as literature and believe in a reader-centered or literary-critical approach. Or one can be committed to reading the Bible in terms of Near Eastern documents that emerged from the same time and geographic space as the Bible. Sometimes, scholars take for granted and fail to articulate the fundamental beliefs that guide their choices.

Beliefs about Torah have unique characteristics that go beyond beliefs having to do with substantive and syntactic issues. Underlying all of them is the nature of the document itself. Is it divine or human in origin? Responding to this question is a matter of what we might call religious or foundational beliefs. There are two basic approaches to beliefs about the authorship of Torah.[18] They can be simplistically characterized as traditional and nontraditional. Traditional beliefs claim divine authorship of the text; nontraditional beliefs imply human authorship. Whichever set of beliefs characterizes the reader (be it teacher, learner, or other reader), it influences how he or she reads and understands the text. Historically speaking, belief in divine authorship precedes the belief in human authorship. Today, each stands at the basis of very different approaches to understanding how the Bible is to be read and understood. Each selects and interprets evidence in order to lend substance to the arguments that serve its ends. These approaches, based on beliefs about the origin of the text, seem at first to be synonymous with the conceptual frameworks explicated above. They are not, however, synonymous. For example, one can believe that the Torah has a divine author and use literary-critical methods or traditional exegetical methods to study it.

Investigating MK's Knowledge of Conceptual Frameworks for Studying Torah and Her Beliefs. From this lesson, what can we learn about MK's knowledge of frameworks such as the one Alter suggests for studying and understanding Torah? She is clearly aware of a variety of approaches for understanding and analyzing the text and is eclectic in her use of them. She creates a lesson that includes information and strategies that derive from the "excavative" and "hermeneutic" approaches to the Torah text. For example, the information about the ziggurat comes from excavative research. The story from the midrash is based on the traditional hermeneutic approach. The notion of reading the text for "inside the text" solutions to the problem (we read "Be fruitful and multiply and fill the earth" in chapter 9) is a classic strategy in traditional biblical exegesis.[19] Because she was teaching students who were eleven years old, she did not use technical terms such as "excavative" or "hermeneutic," but rather, "inside-the-Torah answers" and "outside-the-Torah answers." This was clearly a pedagogic decision.

The questions that MK asked the students, the ways in which she asked the students to attend carefully to the words of the text—these strategies come from a more contemporary approach to literary criticism. MK is actually teaching her students to use one of the syntactical approaches (literary criticism) as they read the text "closely," while sharing the results of the inquiries of other syntactical approaches (when she shares information about the ziggurat, the midrash, and "Be fruitful and multiply").

One of the most interesting features of this lesson is what we can learn about MK's beliefs about how one studies Torah. By creating a lesson in which multiple solutions to the questions raised by the Torah text are generated and no single solution is selected or preferred, she teaches her students that the study of the Torah is an open-ended inquiry. Students leave class understanding that:

- the text holds two different versions of the origin of languages
- there are scholars who understand that these people were building a ziggurat (and that, perhaps, one way to understand the story would be that "we don't build towers in order to reach God")

Pedagogic Content Knowledge

In order to teach, teachers must clearly know more than the subject matter itself. They must have ways of thinking about what is worthwhile and important for learners of different ages to learn as well as about strategies for helping students engage in and learn those things. Teacher must ask themselves questions such as: What do I want my students to learn? Why those things? How will I help them learn? Shulman has referred to this kind of knowledge as "pedagogical-content knowledge" and has defined it as the ability to transform the subject matter based on one's knowledge of learners and learning, of pedagogy and pedagogic process. In his words, it is "the particular form of content knowledge that embodies the aspects of content most germane to its teachability."[20] Four categories of pedagogical-content knowledge drawn from the work of Shulman and others help us begin to describe some of the components of knowledge upon which teachers need to draw to make these decisions.

1. Purposes for Teaching Torah. There are many purposes that one might have for teaching and studying Torah. MK wants her students to know the facts: Genesis, chapters 11 and 12, deals with the origin of languages in two ways. However, that is only the beginning. She wants her students to become readers and interpreters of Torah. She engages them in a direct encounter with the text, which requires them to "read" it in terms of its plain meaning and its multiple interpretations. She introduces them to inside-the-text and outside-the-text interpretations. She shares relevant fruits of scholarly inquiry with them as they are challenged to think about what the Torah means to them. These purposes lead her to frame her lesson around a question that has multiple answers. It leads her to creating a discussion that leaves open the solution to the question: What's so bad about building a city and a tower with its top in the sky? These purposes also lead her to include information such as: They might have been building a ziggurat. Her purposes lead her to choosing an approach to Torah teaching and learning that requires that learners be intellectually and emotionally engaged in the process of reading and making meaning.

2. Students' Conceptions and Possible Misconceptions of Particular Topics in Subject Matter. One issue that students commonly grapple with is "the truth of the Torah." Is it "true"? Is it like science? Is it like history? What kind of "story" is it? In one interchange in the unedited version of the lesson, one girl asks, "What happened to all the men?" Those who teach Torah need to be aware of questions such as these. They need to know what they themselves believe about the nature of the "truth" of the text. They need to realize how students may construe or misconstrue issues relating to literal truth. They need to be ready to engage with students around these questions.

In our transcript, we hear the teacher ask: "Have you learned about ziggurats? Where?" In this interchange, MK tries to take account of students' previous learning—both in religious school and in public school. She tries to help students understand what they are reading in the Torah by building a possible link between what is being studied in religious school and what students are studying elsewhere.

3. Knowledge of Teaching Strategies and Methods. Experienced teachers possess a rich repertoire of instructional strategies that help students understand the substance of Torah and the process by which Torah is studied. MK's lesson does not use a lot of novel strategies in terms of Torah study. It does give us a sense of one very important method that is central to Torah learning for all learners who can read. That method might be called, for want of a better appellation, "close reading of the text."[21]

This approach to Torah teaching and learning requires that learners be intellectually and emotionally engaged in the reading process.[22] They must not only read the words of the Torah literally, but interpretively as well. In her introduction to *Genesis: A New Teacher's Guide*,[23] Zielenziger discusses this approach to the study of Torah text in the following way. Students will be asked: What does the text say (what seems to be its literal meaning?)? What does it mean (how can it be interpreted?)? What does it mean to me (in what ways is it relevant to me and to my life?)? Essentially, this is a technique in which the teacher asks questions that direct students' attention to closely examining the text. It is a strategy that is commonly used in the teaching of all literary documents.

Students were asked not only what the text says and means, but also what it means to them as students of the Torah today. MK encourages a variety of responses to her question. The solutions come from traditional and nontraditional sources. Her students are helped to acquire the variety of skills and understandings that are used within the Jewish tradition to "read Torah," to study it and uncover its meanings. In this particular lesson, students are asked to employ these skills of close reading and interpretation to grapple with a moral problem raised by the text. Why are these people being punished for building a city and a tower with its top in the sky? What is so bad about an action that involves people coming together with a common purpose—

building a city and a tower? Students use their own reading ability to find answers revealed by reading the text closely. Perhaps, "making a name for themselves" is the phrase that holds the clue to the wrongdoing. Perhaps it is the phrase "with its top in the sky." Each seems to say something about the motive of the people that goes beyond what might be acceptable. Each suggestion that learners make is greeted by "Where do you see this in the text?" Learners are helped to distinguish between answers that are stated in the text and those that they infer based on careful reading.

MK teaches students two categorizing techniques. She talks about fact and interpretation questions; she talks about inside- and outside-the-text reasons. She does not talk about explication of text or reader response, but fact and interpretation approaches to reading. She does not distinguish between excavative and hermeneutic approaches to the text, but between outside-the-text and inside-the-text approaches. These categorizations become a shorthand way for them to communicate with one another. They also become tools that students can use as they become independent readers of the Torah text.

Teachers are constantly in the process of constructing and using instructional representations of subject-matter knowledge. "By instructional representations, we mean a wide range of models that may convey something about the subject matter to the learner: activities, questions, examples, and analogies, for instance."[24] In this lesson, the teacher arranges the answers on the board vertically, one answer on top of another, so that she can draw a stepped tower (a ziggurat shape) around them. This visual mnemonic helps learners remember the cognitive content of the lesson.

4. Critical Knowledge of Curricular Materials. Knowledge of curricular material includes familiarity with available curricular materials (as implied by the example above), skill in using published materials, and the knowledge to assess how accurately the materials represent the subject matter. Teachers need to know how to read prepared material and uncover the assumptions that it makes about the subject matter. Developing one's own lesson plans requires a flexible understanding of what is to be learned as well as ideas about how one's students might be helped to learn it. The complexity of this task, even when one has curricular material available, is highly underrated.[25] In this case, MK adapted suggestions from the Melton Research Center's curriculum on Genesis for her setting, a thirty-minute-long public-television slot.

What Does All This Mean
for the Teacher of Torah?

It is clear from MK's lesson that she possesses extensive and complex subject-matter and pedagogic-content knowledge. If we think about her lesson, we begin to understand how content knowledge enters teaching. We learn some of the things that this knowledge helps a teacher do. When we investigate MK's teaching, it is clear that she thought in advance about what facts and ideas she hoped the students in her class would encounter and how they would encounter them. She knew enough about the text, the commentaries, and what might puzzle children to "set up" the lesson so that there was a puzzling question that would hold students' interest as they investigated the verses of the Torah: "What's so bad about building a city and a tower with its top in the sky?" She understood that by juxtaposing the teaching of verses in chapter 10 with verses in chapter 11, she could create a tension and puzzlement that could be a useful pedagogic tool and could also help children learn more about the Torah and how it presents material. By thinking in advance about the questions she would pose and the responses she might receive, she was able to create a graphic representation of students' responses that could help them visually imagine and remember the idea of a ziggurat. Her answers and questions, of course, reflected her knowledge of a variety of possible scholarly "reads" of the text. Her categorization of questions (fact and interpretation) and her categorization of responses (inside the text and outside the text) were not only helpful in terms of this lesson, but helped students build skills for Torah study that reach far beyond this lesson. This analysis only deals with some areas of subject-matter and pedagogical-content knowledge and does not touch at all on other areas of knowledge (such as child development, general pedagogic technique, classroom management, and so on) or on matters of the teacher's personality or disposition.

Thinking about subject-matter knowledge raises serious questions for Jewish education. Research reveals that teachers teaching in our schools have neither the background nor the training that would indicate that they have the breadth or depth of knowledge of an MK. Almost one-third of the teachers in the CIJE studies of Jewish educators received no Jewish education after the age of thirteen. Only 40 percent of teachers reported university degrees in education; 31 percent have a degree in Jewish studies or certification in Jewish education. (In day schools, this number rose to 60 percent.) Only 19 percent have professional training in both education and Jewish studies.[26] While degrees are not an exact representation of what a person knows, they do serve as an indication of the serious lack of schooling in the subject areas that one would assume teachers would need to build their knowledge.

The old paradigm for addressing this problem suggested that we teach teachers Torah (read: any subject area that they need to teach) and pedagogy and assume that they will learn enough about each to apply their knowledge to real-life situations. This way of thinking also assumed that teachers are independently reflective enough and that they will teach long enough to become good at knowing what works and what helps students learn. There are many reasons that this model is flawed; for purposes of this article, suffice it to say that the time that would be needed to make this approach viable is lacking.

Based on my analysis of what experienced teachers such as MK know, I would like to suggest an alternative strategy that addresses the realities of the current state of teacher knowledge and training. I am suggesting that we develop and use subject matter/pedagogical maps such as the one constructed in this paper to help us rethink the preparation and professional development of teachers. The map for the teaching of Torah might include such things as:

- how scholars think about and study Torah
- a range of possible, defensible beliefs about Torah
- a range of purposes for teaching Torah
- ways of thinking about what children might find interesting as well as the questions/problems they might encounter as they learn Torah and ways that they could deal with those problems
- a range of strategies that they could use to teach Torah
- knowledge of curricular materials available to teach Torah to learners of different ages and in different settings

In terms of teacher education for Torah teaching, the conceptual frameworks can be taught in conjunction with text study. Rather than assuming that in preparatory programs, our task is coverage, we might aim for depth and the meta-knowledge of the subject matter gained from understanding the idea of frameworks for studying a discipline. For example, teachers (or students studying to be teachers) could learn several texts in depth, exploring both the meaning of the texts and different scholarly approaches to understanding those texts. They could then discuss the implications of their specific study for learning other texts. Secondary sources for finding different interpretations could be introduced so that teachers would have ideas about the reference library available to them for study and preparation. This approach would allow teachers who may not have deep subject-matter knowledge to at least have what might be called "flexible" subject-matter knowledge. From this kind of study, they would gain a map of the subject. They would develop a sense of the ideological and syntactical positions that they could use as they prepare and as they listen to students' comments and questions.

To help teachers develop pedagogical-content knowledge, we could provide opportunities for teachers to: analyze instances of teaching "live" or on tape; and study curricular materials from a subject-matter perspective.[27] Both opportunities could help teachers develop situated knowledge of content, students, and pedagogy. By analyzing instances of teaching and learning, teachers can learn more about the subject matter itself, what its big ideas are, and what is worth learning. They can gain experience in listening and understanding learners' comments and questions. In addition, they can develop a shared vocabulary to describe, analyze, and reflect on the activities of teaching and learning. By studying curricular materials, teachers can become expert in analyzing and evaluating prepared curriculum materials. They can think more carefully about the variety and appropriateness of the representations of subject matter as understood by curriculum developers. Over time, engaging in these types of analytic strategies would help teachers develop an inquiring, investigative stance toward the activities of teaching and opportunities, think more clearly and carefully about the practices of teaching, and become more able to learn in and from the real practices of teaching.

The issue that this paper has been addressing—What does a teacher need to know about a subject in order to teach it?—is not a new one. In his classic essay "The Child and the Curriculum," Dewey addressed this very question:

> Hence what concerns him as a teacher is: the ways in which that subject may become a part of experience; what there is in the child's present that is usable with reference to it; how such elements are to be used; how his own knowledge of the subject matter may assist in interpreting the child's needs and doings,

and determine the medium in which the child should be properly directed. He is concerned not with subject matter as such but with the subject matter as a related factor in the total and growing experience. Thus to see it is to psychologize it.[28]

This paper on the nature of subject matter for teaching Torah is an attempt to understand and unpack Dewey's pithy phrase "to psychologize the subject matter" with the hope that understanding and unpacking will be a catalyst for experimenting with new approaches to helping people learn to teach.

Notes

1. This transcript is adapted from a videotaped lesson that was part of the Genesis Project, a three-way partnership of the Bureau of Jewish Education of Rhode Island, the Melton Research Center, and the Dimension Cable Television of Rhode Island. The videotaped lessons and MK's lesson plans are available through the Melton Research Center of the Jewish Theological Seminary.

2. Among others, see: Deborah Ball, "Teaching Mathematics for Understanding: What Do Teachers Need to Know about Subject Matter?" in *Teaching Academic Subjects to Diverse Learners*, ed. M. Kennedy (New York: Teachers College Press, 1991), 63–83; Pamela Grossman, Suzanne Wilson, and Lee Shulman, "Teachers of Substance: Subject Matter Knowledge for Teachers," in *Knowledge Base for the Beginning Teacher*, ed. M. C. Reynolds (New York: Pergamon, 1989), 23–36; Lee Shulman, "Knowledge and Teaching: Foundations of the New Reform," *Harvard Educational Review* 57, no. 1 (1987): 1–22; Suzanne Wilson, Lee Shulman, and Anna Richert, " '150 Different Ways of Knowing': Representations of Knowledge in Teaching," in *Exploring Teachers' Thinking*, ed. J. Calderhead (London: Cassell Educational, 1987), 104–24.

3. Joseph Schwab, "Structure of the Disciplines: Meanings and Significance," in *The Structure of Knowledge and the Curriculum*, ed. G. W. Ford and L. Pugno (Chicago: Rand McNally, 1964), 6–30.

4. For a discussion of Schwab's understandings of this issue, see Joseph Lukinsky, "Structure in Educational Theory," pt. 1, *Educational Philosophy and Theory* 2 (November 1970): 15–31, and "Structure in Educational Theory," pt. 2, *Educational Philosophy and Theory* 3 (April 1971): 29–36.

5. Joseph Schwab, "Education and the Structure of the Disciplines," in *Science, Curriculum, and Liberal Education: Selected Essays*, ed. I. Westbury and N. Wilkof (Chicago: University of Chicago Press, 1961; 1978), 246.

6. Applying Gilbert Ryle's (1949) distinction between propositional knowledge (knowing that) and procedural knowledge (knowing how), one might say that knowing the substantive components of a discipline involves propositional

knowledge (knowing about the discipline) and knowing the syntactic components of the discipline implies knowing how to "do it."

7. Robert Alter, "Interpreting the Bible," *Commentary* 89, no. 3 (1990): 52–59.

8. *Pirkei avot*—Ethics of the Fathers, chap. 5: mishnah 25.

9. Edward Greenstein, *Essays on Biblical Method and Translation* (Atlanta: Schol-
    ars, 1989).

10. Robert Alter, *The Art of Biblical Narrative* (New York: Basic, 1981), 143.

11. Assignation of various sections of the Torah text to different authors and times
    is known as the documentary hypothesis. This school of scholarship has as-
    signed authorship of biblical narrative to four major sources, referred to as
    JEPD—a shorthand denoting that J=Yahwistic; E=Elohistic; P=Priestly;
    D=Deuteronomic (perhaps single human authors or schools). These four strands
    were then woven into one document by a redactor, referred to as R. For more
    information, see Richard Friedman, *Who Wrote the Bible?* (New York: Summit,
    1987).

12. For a very specific discussion of this line of reasoning, see Nahum Sarna, *Under-
    standing Genesis* (New York: Jewish Theological Seminary and McGraw Hill,
    1966), 1–11.

13. Edward Greenstein, "The State of Biblical Studies or Biblical Studies in a State,"
    in *The State of Jewish Studies*, ed. S. J. Cohen and E. L. Greenstein (Detroit:
    Wayne State University Press, 1990), 34.

14. Alter, "Interpreting the Bible," 56.

15. For a more extensive discussion of beliefs about Torah and their impact on
    teaching, see Gail Zaiman Dorph, "Conceptions and Misconceptions: A Study
    of Prospective Jewish Educators' Knowledge and Beliefs about Torah" (Ph.D.
    diss., Jewish Theological Seminary, 1993), 67–75.

16. See, for example, Sigmund Gudmundsdottir, "Pedagogical Models of Subject
    Matter," in *Advances in Research on Teaching,* ed. J. Brophy (Greenwich,
    Conn.: JAI, 1991), 2:265–304.

17. Greenstein, "The State of Biblical Studies or Biblical Studies in a State," 68.

18. For a thoughtful discussion of the ways in which one's approach to the Bible in-
    fluences biblical scholarship, see also Greenstein, *Essays on Biblical Method and
    Translation*, and "The State of Biblical Studies or Biblical Studies in a State";
    and Jon Levenson's response to Greenstein in *The State of Jewish Studies*.

19. Michael Fishbane, *The Garments of Torah: Essays in Biblical Hermeneutics*
    (Bloomington: Indiana University Press, 1989).

20. Lee Shulman, "Those Who Understand: Knowledge Growth in Teaching," *Edu-
    cational Researcher* 15, no. 2 (1986): 4–14.

21. Ruth Zielenziger, *Genesis: A New Teacher's Guide* (New York: Melton Re-
    search Center, 1991), vii. She refers to this strategy as biblical inquiry. In *The
    Technology of Making Meaning: A Systematic Inquiry into the Task of Enabling
    the Teaching of Jewish Texts* (Los Angeles: Torah Aura Production, 1988), Joel
    Grishaver describes the act of text study as: (1) isolating phrases where the text

is difficult to understand; (2) clarifying the difficulty; (3) projecting and collecting possible solutions/explanations; and (4) having each learner choose the solutions that work for him/her (p. 3).

22. This is a purpose shared by others as well. For a particularly cogent statement of the purposes of teaching Bible in religious educational settings, see Moshe Greenberg, "On Teaching the Bible in Religious Schools," *Jewish Education* 29, no. 3 (1959): 45–53.

23. Zielenziger, vii–x.

24. G. W. McDiarmid, D. Ball, and C. Anderson, "Why Staying One Chapter Ahead Doesn't Really Work: Subject-Specific Pedagogy," in *Knowledge Base for the Beginning Teacher,* 194.

25. Deborah Ball and Sharon Feiman-Nemser, "Using Textbooks and Teachers' Guides: A Dilemma for Beginning Teachers and Teacher Educators," paper presented at the annual meeting of the American Educational Researchers Association, San Francisco, 1986.

26. See Adam Gamoran et al., *CIJE Policy Brief: Background and Professional Training of Teachers in Jewish Schools* (1994), and *The Teachers Report: A Portrait of Teachers in Jewish Schools* (New York: Council for Initiatives in Jewish Education, 1998).

27. For examples of these strategies from the world of general education, see Magdalene Lampert and Deborah Ball, *Teaching, Multimedia and Mathematics: Investigations of Real Practice* (New York: Teachers College Press, 1998); and Miriam Ben-Peretz, *The Teacher-Curriculum Encounter: Freeing Teachers from the Tyranny of Texts* (Albany: State University of New York Press, 1990).

28. John Dewey, *The Child and the Curriculum* (Chicago: University of Chicago Press, 1902; 1956), 23.

Teaching the Akedah

Neil Gillman

My friend and colleague Joe Lukinsky was responsible for one of the most transforming educational moments I have ever experienced in decades of studying and teaching.

For years, Joe and I have shared an interest in the notion of myth: what myths are, how they work, how they shape communities, and how they give birth to rituals that capture the myth in a concrete and vivid form. Myths can be both secular and religious; for example, I recall with particular delight Joe's extended discussion of the mythic quality of baseball. I first encountered the notion of theological/religious myth (and symbol) in Paul Tillich's *Dynamics of Faith*[1]—a book that played a decisive role in shaping my personal theology to this day. The term "myth" is now omnipresent in the literature of the social sciences and in literary criticism. Of course, by "myth" I do not mean a fiction, legend, or fairy tale, as the term is understood in popular culture; not "myth" as opposed to "the facts" or "the reality," but rather a pattern of meaning. Myths are the various ways in which we connect the discrete data of nature or history so that they become a coherent statement of what the facts mean. Without such a pattern of meaning, we would not even know what the relevant facts are in any single explanatory inquiry. But the patterns—precisely because they are patterns—isolated by a specific myth are far more elusive than any of the specific facts it tries to explain; myths enjoy a singular degree of subjectivity and imagination, which is the source of their strength and their perceived "fictional" quality.

One day some years ago, Joe invited me to attend a workshop on mythic reenactment to be conducted by a friend of his, Professor Sam

Neil Gillman is the Aaron Rabinowitz and Simon H. Rifkind Professor of Jewish Philosophy at the Jewish Theological Seminary of America.

Laeuchli, then affiliated with Temple University, and now retired in Switzerland. Laeuchli had developed a technique of reenacting or dramatizing ancient tales—for example, from ancient Greek literature and from the Bible—in order to probe more deeply into the meaning of these texts.[2] This time, the story to be reenacted was the *akedah,* the binding of Isaac, as narrated in Genesis 22.

I walked into a classroom to find chairs arranged in a circle, with three chairs in the center of the circle. A group of about twenty students had assembled—most of them doctoral students in education from Teachers College, Union Theological Seminary, and the Jewish Theological Seminary. (I was then associate professor of Jewish philosophy at JTS.) Sam spoke briefly at the outset, explaining that he would select three students to play the central characters in the story: Abraham, Isaac, and God. At a signal from him, the three characters would enter into the story and into their roles and begin to talk to one another. There were no intrinsic limitations to the discussion; it could go in whatever direction the characters wished to take it. The point was to fill the many yawning gaps in the biblical narrative. The rest of us were to sit in the circle around them. We could not intervene in the dialogue, but we would have periodic "press conferences" in which we could ask the three participants why they said what they said, what they felt when they said it, and how they understood the story.

Sam snapped his finger and we were off. "God" began, as in the Bible, by commanding Abraham to bring his son to a certain mountain and to bind him as an offering. But contrary to the biblical narrative, our Abraham protested, and our God had to defend his command. Suddenly, I was no longer in a bleak classroom on Broadway. I had entered into a magical realm of mythic space and time, an eternal present, where a primordial, prototypical drama was working itself out. The very spare, bare-bones quality of the biblical narrative, the lack of detail, and the absence of adjectives and of references to feelings—all helped give the proceedings an unreal quality. Unreal, but at the same time, transformative. To say that I was totally absorbed is an understatement; I was transfixed.

The biblical tale is indeed replete with gaps. Where was Sarah? Why doesn't she appear anywhere in this story? What were the "things" (or "words") that preceded God's command to Abraham (in 22:1)? Could they be related to Abraham's expulsion of his concubine, Hagar, and their son, Ishmael, recorded in the chapter immediately preceding this one? Why a three-day journey? What did Abraham feel during these three days? What did Isaac feel? Did they talk to each other, apart from the brief exchange recorded in the text (22:7–8)? Is Abraham's answer to his son a lie, or did he know something that we don't know? Who were the two lads who accompanied the father and son? Why are there two separate angelic speeches at the end? Why angels in the first place, and not God, as at the outset? At the end of the story, we are told where Abraham went, but what happened to Isaac? Isaac doesn't reappear in the biblical narrative until chapters later. And more and more and more. (Recently, in teaching this text, I asked my students to list all the unanswered questions in the narrative. They came up with more than fifty.)[3]

As the drama proceeded, I found myself progressively drawn into the circle, identifying with the personalities, sharing the tension. This was, most emphatically, not like grading a research paper. I was assaulted with waves of emotion, chiefly anger at our "God," a student at Union Theological. When our Abraham challenged God for the sheer cruelty and absurdity of God's demand, this God responded by insisting that he was God, he was omnipotent, he could demand whatever he wished, and Abraham had to obey. Our Abraham simply capitulated and fell silent. This infuriated me, and with a passion that surprised me, I began to feel that this God had it all wrong!

I voiced my anger at this portrayal of God during the press conference. Sam listened quietly, and then responded, "Okay, let's do it again, and this time you [pointing to me] play God." I protested: I am a professor, not a student; I am an observer, not a participant; I came to learn, not to teach, and so on. . . . He simply led me to my chair in the center, and this time, added a fourth chair for Sarah ("Let's make it a little more interesting!"), chose a new Abraham and Isaac, and we began.

Before I (now playing God) could say a word, our Sarah jumped in: "Abraham, it's early in the morning. Where are you and Isaac going?" "To sacrifice our son." "Are you out of your head!?" "It's not my idea. It's his"—pointing to me. Whereupon my Sarah, also from Union, poured forth two thousand years' of accumulated rage at God's (and Christianity's) oppression of women. She must have screamed at me for about ten minutes.

I prayed that Sam would snap his finger so that we could step out of character and so that I could recover and assemble my thoughts before responding. But no such luck. Sarah ended up sobbing, and everyone turned to me. I was terrified. To this day, I'm not completely sure from which level of my being my response came. What I said was something along the following lines: "Look, Sarah. Everybody thinks that I am omnipotent, that I get whatever I want to get here on earth. But in reality, I am a total failure. I have created twenty generations of human beings since Adam, and I have yet to find one human being whose loyalty to me is unquestioned. For the ages, I desperately need to point to one person whose loyalty I was able to win. Please don't stop Abraham. Please let him go on his mission. I need Abraham. Trust me!" I went on in this vein for what seemed to be hours. Mercifully, Sam's finger snapped.

I learned more theology from that moment than from years of reading and reflection. It launched me on an almost decade-long inquiry into the ways in which God is imaged in our classical texts. My methodological assumption is that no human being can grasp God's essential nature in thought or in language. If God is truly God, then God transcends human comprehension. If God is really God, then I, a mere human being, cannot even begin to comprehend God's nature. The alternative, namely, the conviction that God is as God is pictured, is to drift into idolatry. God, then, is not "really," objectively or literally, as God is portrayed in our traditional texts. God is certainly not corporeal, despite the references to God's "mighty arm." God is not literally male or female. God does not have an inner life; God doesn't really get angry. God is also not in space or time. Our options, then, are either idolatry, or worshipful silence in the face of the transcendent mystery, or the recognition that all characterizations of God are—here, pick your terminology—symbols, metaphors, constructs, or myths. The last of these options is the only one that modern students of religion can adopt.

In itself, that assumption is not at all heretical. It is shared by, among others, Maimonides in the very first pages of his *Mishneh Torah* (bk. 1, *Basic Principles of the Torah*, chap. 1, parash. 9–12), who insists that all physical and emotional descriptions of God in Torah are metaphors or analogies. But I probably break with Maimonides in my belief that these images of God were crafted by human beings, here by our ancestors, and that they emerged out of the wide range of human experiences of how God appeared to them, and continues to appear to us in the course of our varied life experiences. My sense is that Maimonides probably believed that God revealed the metaphors. But I believe that our images of God are human projections, our own, very personal fantasies of what God must be like, if we are to account for the feelings that we experience at those moments when God appears most present to us.

Setting aside the epistemological issues involved in the claim that human beings experience God's presence in their lives—a crucially im-

portant issue but one that we will not explore here[4]—my major task is
to collect and trace the evolution of these images throughout our literature, from the Bible, the Talmud and midrash, the classical liturgy, medieval philosophy and the kabbalistic tradition, through to Mordecai
Kaplan, Martin Buber, and Abraham Joshua Heschel. My conclusion is
that our tradition has preserved a wide-ranging, evolving, and fluid system of characterizations of God—fluid because the metaphors come and
go, change, and recur, are abandoned and then reappear or are replaced,
not only within the texts, but also within the liturgical year, and in the
course of a human life. My image of God on Yom Kippur is very different from my Tishah b'Av image. The God I experienced when I was
twenty is different from the God I experienced when I turned sixty. The
images can also be positive or negative, laudatory or condemnatory,
nurturing or abandoning, loving or cruel and capricious; the God of
Psalms 23 or 91 is not the God of the first two chapters of Job, or of
Genesis 22. And there is precious little inner consistency within the system; the metaphors are frequently in tension with one another. Frequently, we can even catch the transformations of a specific metaphor in
later strata of the traditional texts. For example, note the change in Jon.
4:2, of God's self-description in Exod. 34:6–7. Here, the author of
Jonah stands the Exodus image on its head. The process is thoroughly
subversive.[5]

My charge to my students is that they identify the image in a particular text and then enter into the experience, particularly the feeling-
tone, of the person who wrote the text. I ask: What is (or are) the
feeling(s) about God expressed in the text? How does the metaphor capture or express the feelings? Why did they write the story precisely this
way? How else could they have portrayed God? What difference would
this have made in the telling? And then: How does God feel about that
portrayal? How do you feel about it?

My final requirement is that the student write a personal theological
statement reflecting his or her own characteristic image of God. My
point is that we have the right and the responsibility to continue the
centuries-long process of trying to capture how God appears to humans,
now to us, today, in our own cultural and historical context. No footnotes. No bibliography. None of the typical scholarly apparatus. Just a
personal statement of what the writer believes. I have conducted workshops of this kind in school and adult-education settings around the
country, and I have collected dozens of such statements from students of
all ages, rabbis, teachers, laypeople, men and women. How about this

one: "God is Fred Astaire to my Ginger Rogers." Or: "After the Holocaust, God is like a rat caught in a maze. . . . No, better still, after the Holocaust, God is the maze." The first was from a rabbinic colleague, the second from an eleven-year-old! Both led into some of the most fascinating theological discussions I've had in years.

Now, when I teach Genesis 22, I ask my students to retell the story from the perspective of some character in the tale or elsewhere, in some other voice—God, Sarah, Isaac, Abraham, Hagar, Ishmael, the two servants, the donkey, the ram, Job, a Holocaust survivor. (One student chose to tell the story in the voice of the knife!). The results are mind-boggling. My feelings of guilt at how my students frequently stand the biblical story on its head are assuaged by the extraordinarily rich transformations of the biblical tale in the hands of the rabbinic midrashim. If the midrash could insist that Abraham actually killed his son, who was then resurrected by the tears of the angels flowing over his face—all in explicit contradiction of the Bible—then we should be able to tolerate our own modern spins on the text. Midrash also arises out of the gaps in a text. What I want from my students is to write their own, modern midrash on this text.

The image of God that I discern in the *akedah* narrative is vulnerability. That God has a vulnerable side I had learned from my teacher Abraham Joshua Heschel—though that association did not occur to me until well after the workshop. Heschel writes at length of God's "pathos"—God's passionate caring, reaching out, involvement with the world. The divine pathos, Heschel claims, is the ground-tone of all of God's relationship with human beings. But to care for someone is to be vulnerable; we can only be hurt by someone we care about. That's why I was so much opposed to the image of the macho God described by that student. To me, the God of the *akedah* is a desperate, needy, pleading, and vulnerable God. This is a God who has ceded to Abraham the power to make God really God.

This may be a way of "doing theology," but it is a very different way of conducting this inquiry from the ones usually employed in academic circles. For me, it represents the difference between teaching theology to graduate students and to rabbinical students. The former discussion takes place in a classical academic context; the inquiry is detached, objective, historical, and critical. The latter is an existential experience. We may begin with the dispassionate inquiry, but we should then go beyond it into the issue of personal meaning. Now that we know what the text meant to the author, we should ask what it means to us. That's what rabbis today should be asking when they preach the biblical text before their congregants on a Sabbath morning.

That insight impelled me to begin to teach theology to rabbinical students in a very different way. In my early years, I used to teach as I was taught (at JTS in the fifties). The professor stood apart from the text; the text effectively interposed itself between the instructor and the students. From my teachers, I learned everything about the text—its provenance, its setting in ancient Near Eastern culture, its accuracy, its probable dating—everything but what the text meant to my teacher in the most personal way. Or what the text might mean to the rabbinical student. Or how this meaning was to be conveyed to a congregation of lay Jews. Why is this text there in the first place? Why do we read it again and again? How can it change our lives?

Not for a moment do I even want to imply that my education at the Seminary was anything but an intellectually exhilarating experience. My teachers were the greatest scholars of Judaica in the whole world. I gobbled up everything they had to offer and spent six years on a perpetual academic high. But too often, at the end of a class, I was left with, "So what! What am I supposed to do with this text now?" (To be fair, this critique did not apply to all my teachers; certainly, Mordecai Kaplan, Shalom Spiegel, and Heschel himself did address issues of meaning—but they were the exceptions to the rule.) Since I have never served a congregation, I was never forced to deal with these questions, until I began to teach rabbinical students. That's when I began to realize that I was failing them.

What I learned from my experience was to go beyond the text into the living experience that generated the text in the first place. For the very first time, I understood Genesis 22 from God's perspective, not the anonymous narrator's. I had now entered God's persona as I understood it out of my own experience. I have used this method in teaching other texts in our classical literature, and to help my students do the same, so that they in turn may help their students to lift the story off the printed page and into their hearts.

I also realized that if I was going to ask my students to pursue this method, I would have to do it myself, precisely in the classroom, in their presence. That meant putting my self, my own feelings, into the inquiry. If I wanted them to personalize the discussion, I had to set the example and do it myself. It was only much later that I came to the realization that what I was doing stretched the reigning teaching paradigm in our school. I was reshaping what I understood as the school's overemphasis on cognitive learning. I was redressing the balance between the cognitive and the affective. I never demean the cognitive material. We are frequently dealing with students who come to us without any serious background in Judaica and Hebraica, and in five or six years we are expected to transform them into authoritative spokespersons for Judaism. That by itself is an impossible task. But for a rabbi-to-be, the affective issues should have an equal place in the curriculum and in their teaching and preaching. They will have to counsel families on the death of a child, or in preparation for a wedding, or when the primary wage earner is unemployed for an extensive period. How can we ignore the affective dimension of the rabbi's work at such times?

That change of emphasis has a number of critical implications. First, faculty in our schools are hired and promoted according to Western, academic criteria, chief among which is the publication of scholarly books and articles, with footnotes, bibliographies, and the rest. They are not hired for their personal religious sensibilities. The absence of such a sensibility would never disqualify a candidate, but scholarly limitations of some kind always will. I am then questioning the accepted criteria for academic standing in our school. Second, how does one grade a personal theological statement or a modern midrash? Third, most of my courses are cross-registered in both the rabbinical and the graduate schools. Graduate students are not expected to be "religious"—Jews or anything else. (I handle that issue by agreeing to accept a classical research paper from these students in place of the more personal theological statement.) But what I do insist is that the rabbi is not a mini-professor. He or she is to be a religious role model for a congregation of Jews. That role model does demand serious, Western-type learning, but it also demands much more—a grasp of what it means to be a religious Jew and of what it takes to create a congregation of religious Jews.[6]

I have never had the nerve to conduct a reenactment workshop with my own students. In fact, before leaving that workshop, Sam warned us against doing this: "It's much more complicated than it looks." Indeed it is! Serious ethical and psychological implications simmer close to the surface. This is, most emphatically, not an opportunity for group therapy, but it is abundantly clear that role-playing awakens a wide range of private, emotional issues. The leader must be aware of this and act quickly to protect the participant from himself.

That Joe Lukinsky transformed the way I teach theology is probably the least of his many accomplishments. But for that, I owe him my profound gratitude.

Notes

1. Paul Tillich, *Dynamics of Faith* (New York: Harper and Row, 1957).
2. An exposition of Sam Lauechli's theory and method may be found in his "The Expulsion from the Garden and the Hermeneutics of Play," in *Body and Bible: Interpreting and Experiencing Biblical Narratives,* ed. Bjorn Krondorfer (Philadelphia: Trinity Press International, 1992).
3. On the *akedah* narrative itself, particularly on the tradition that Abraham did in fact slaughter his son, see Shalom Spiegel's monumental *The Last Trial* (Woodstock, Vt.: Jewish Lights, 1993); and Jon D. Levenson's *The Death and Resurrection of the Beloved Son* (New Haven: Yale University Press, 1993).
4. On the epistemological issues involved in experiencing God's presence, alluded to above, see this author's "On Knowing God," *Conservative Judaism* 51, no. 2 (winter 1999).
5. A comprehensive study of Jewish approaches to talking about God is in this author's *The Way into Encountering God in Judaism* (Woodstock, Vt.: Jewish Lights, 2000).
6. A more extended discussion of this author's views on rabbinic education can be found in "On the Religious Education of American Rabbis," in *Caring for the Commonweal: Education for Religious and Public Life,* ed. Parker J. Palmer, Barbara G. Wheeler, and James W. Fowler (Macon, Ga.: Mercer University Press, 1990).

Reader Response, Midrash, and Interactive Textual Dialogue

Alvan H. Kaunfer

Struggling with the interpretation of Jewish texts is an age-old Jewish enterprise. I began to appreciate that enterprise over thirty-five years ago, as a young teen studying with Rabbi Joseph Lukinsky in LTF and USY.[1] The example of textual encounter he modeled in his teaching and living has informed my thinking about the significance of textual interpretation and personal readings of Jewish texts. I hope that the approach presented here will help to perpetuate that process.

Texts

Texts are meant to be read. By "text," we refer here largely to narrative texts that attempt to capture the complexities of life, relationships, philosophy, and religious yearnings in literary modes. Although one could argue that legal and scientific texts can also be "read" and can even be "literary" to an extent, narrative texts are unique because they represent a qualitatively different mode of thinking.[2] Jerome Bruner has indicated that the narrative mode is essentially different from the logical, scientific mode, which he calls "paradigmatic." "In logic and in science, you attempt to mean what you say. In narrative, to be successful, you mean more than you say and treat a text or utterance as open to interpretation rather than literally fixed with, so to speak, the 'truth in the text.' "[3]

A narrative text has no single fixed meaning; it has many possible meanings. As an interpretation of the endless subtleties of life itself,

Alvan H. Kaunfer is a rabbi at Temple Emanu-El in Providence, Rhode Island. He was a doctoral student of Professor Joseph Lukinsky at the Jewish Theological Seminary of Amer-

narrative embodies a multiplicity of possibilities. Its ambiguity is its strength; its multivalent quality lends itself to the art of interpretation. As Bruner suggests, this search for multiple meanings in a narrative text stands at the pinnacle of culture: "This method of negotiating and renegotiating meanings by the mediation of narrative interpretation is, it seems to me, one of the crowning achievements of human development."[4]

The nature of the text itself is what makes multiple readings and interpretations possible. As Bruner indicates, narrative texts have the quality of "meaning more than they say" and of being open to "negotiating and renegotiating meanings." The Torah, and indeed the entire Tanakh, have always been viewed by Judaism as a text that is open to multiple interpretations. The Rabbis themselves indicate this by such statements as " 'Is not my word like . . . a hammer that breaks the rock in pieces?' (Jer. 23:29). As the hammer splits the rock into many splinters, so will a scriptural verse yield many meanings."[5] Susan Handelman, in comparing rabbinic hermeneutic to modern literary interpretation, comments:

> The world of time and space is connected to realms beyond time and space through Torah, and every verse, letter, and so on contains, therefore, a plurality of meanings and references, applicable not only to Biblical time and place, but to all time and place. Through proper interpretation, then, the application and meaning appropriate for any contingency is revealed. Thus interpretation is not essentially separate from the text itself—an external act intruded upon it—but rather the *extension* of the text.[6]

In this view of the text, the Bible, by its very nature of being ambiguous, gapped, and multivalent, lends itself to multiple interpretations that themselves become extensions of the text. In this understanding of interpretation, there is no "truth in the text," as Bruner suggests, and the "plain sense of the text" is really its interpreted meaning. As Frank Kermode asserts, "the plain sense depends in larger measure on the imaginative activity of interpreters."[7]

Reader Response

If the texts we read lend themselves to, and are indeed given meaning by, the act of interpretation, then we must return to the role of the reader in this process. The reader is an active participant in this dynamic interaction between text and interpreter. Several literary critics have focused on this interactive reading process under the general rubric of "reader-response criticism." The basic assumption of reader-response criticism is that meaning inheres in the interpretation of the reader rather than in the text itself. The act of "reading" a text is essentially personal and contextual, including what the reader brings to the understanding of the text.

Perhaps one of the most interesting and relevant formulations of reader-response theory is presented by Wolfgang Iser, who claims that the reader acts as a cocreator of the work by supplying what is not written but implied:

> Thus the reader, in establishing these inter-relations . . . actually causes the text to reveal its potential multiplicity of connections. These connections are the product of the reader's mind working on the raw material of the text, though they are not the text itself. . . . The product of this creative activity is what we might call the virtual dimension of the text, which endows it with its reality. This virtual dimension is not the text itself, nor is it the imagination of the reader: it is the coming together of text and imagination.[8]

The raw material of the text is not its meaning. The words of the text are data that are filtered through the mind of the reader. Meaning—the virtual dimension of the text—is created only during the creative act of reading. Iser speaks of the text as being "gapped." It is the reader who fills in these gaps, which may be filled in various ways. Iser concludes:

> For this reason, one text is potentially capable of several realizations, and no reading can ever exhaust the full potential, for each individual reader will fill in the gaps in his own way. . . . [A]s he reads he will make his own decision as to how the gap is to be filled. In this very act the dynamics of reading are revealed.[9]

Iser claims that this process of reading a text is dynamic, interactive, "continually on the move." In addition, the direction of the process is not one way. Not only does the reader have an impact upon the text by creating meaning through interpretation, but the text has an impact upon the reader in turn. "The production of the meaning of literary texts . . . does not merely entail the discovery of the unformulated. . . . [I]t also entails the possibility that we may formulate ourselves and so discover what had previously seemed to elude our consciousness."[10] Creating meaning in reading texts is a highly dynamic and interactive process that results in both the personalized interpretation of the individual reader and the ultimate change in the reader's own perspective on him/herself and reality.

Although reader-response theory may seem to indicate that individuals are acting on their own, some reader-response critics suggest that individual readers may come together into "interpretive communities" in which they approach texts with a common set of strategies.[11] These shared assumptions allow a set of readers of a text to approach that text with common ground rules of interpretation.

Reading and Midrash

This description of the process of reading is reminiscent of the classical reading of Jewish narrative texts: midrash. Midrash can be seen as a rabbinic "reading" of a biblical text, which brings to bear the subjective contexts and consciousness of the rabbi or rabbis who are doing the reading. As Daniel Boyarin states, "We will not read midrash well and richly unless we understand it first and foremost as *reading*, as hermeneutic, as generated by the interaction of rabbinic readers with heterogeneous and difficult text."[12] Boyarin also suggests, as Iser does, that the text that the rabbis are reading is a "gapped text." It is the nature of the biblical text that allows the rabbis to bring their own context to their reading.

> I will imagine the rabbis as readers doing the best they could to make sense of the Bible for themselves and their times and in themselves and their times—in short, as readers. The text of the Torah is gapped and dialogical, and into the gaps the reader slips, interpreting and completing the text in accordance with the codes of his or her culture.[13]

Boyarin describes the rabbis as reading the text through their "ideologically colored eyeglasses." They bring their ideas, philosophies, and concerns of the day to their reading of the text. They are essentially acting as a "community of interpreters" sharing common strategies, assumptions, and approaches to their reading of the text. Thus, when we read the midrash of the rabbis, we really enter the world of their interpretive readings of the texts of the Tanakh.

Interactive Dialogues

If the process of classical midrash itself is a reading of the biblical text by the rabbis, then our own contemporary reading of the biblical text can reflect and continue that midrashic process within the context of a community of readers.

In what setting can that process of textual reading take place? It has been our experience that an extension of a midrashic reading of the biblical text with adults can be achieved in the context of interactive *divrei Torah* (Torah discussions) with congregants.[14] Of late, a number of congregations have introduced interactive *divrei Torah* in place of the classic sermon. This venue provides opportunities for congregants to develop interpretations of the text of the weekly *parashah* (portion). Numerous techniques are being employed in these congregational interactive *divrei Torah*. In addition, a number of approaches have been used with adults to reproduce a "modern midrash" by involving adult participants in role-playing the characters in the biblical drama. Peter Pitzele's work has been notable in this direction.[15]

We suggest a somewhat different approach. Our method differs from the Pitzele model in that it is based on discussion rather than on role-playing. It also differs from some of the other interactive *devar Torah* methods in that it includes reflecting on classical midrashic readings of the text as an integral part of the interactive-dialogue process. First, let us outline the approach in preparing such an interactive textual dialogue. Then we will provide an example set of texts used in an actual synagogue setting.

The Approach

Selecting the Text

As was indicated above, the best type of text for interpretive reading is a narrative text. The text chosen should be one that is inherently ambiguous in its meaning and is "gapped," allowing for multiple interpretations and opportunities for the reader to fill in those gaps in his or her own unique way, as Iser and Boyarin indicate.

Midrashic Readings

The participants should be provided with several midrashic readings of the text. Part of the criteria for selecting the biblical text includes finding appropriately engaging midrashic texts on that section. Employing midrashic texts in the textual dialogue, first of all, initiates the participants into the world of rabbinic midrash as a classic process of reading the biblical text. Participants begin to appreciate the rabbinic approach to the biblical text in which, as Susan Handelman says, "every verse and letter contains a plurality of meanings and references, applicable not only to biblical time and place, but to all time and place." Second, midrashic readings of the biblical text provide models of several possible interpretations of the text being discussed. In the dialogue, those readings can be considered and can spur new alternate readings.

Key Questions

A basic element of this textual-dialogue approach is the discussion facilitator's ability to elicit responses from participants, using key questions. These questions must be open-ended. First, those involved in the dialogue need to probe beyond literal meaning. Open-ended questions allow the reader to delve below the surface of the text. But, in addition, these questions must be able to elicit several possible interpretations. They cannot be a fishing expedition for a particular interpretation or conclusion; that would defeat the purpose of involving participants in a reader-response dialogue. Formulating key questions is perhaps the most challenging educational aspect of this approach. The facilitator must carefully select appropriate key questions before the dialogue. These questions should be on the level that Norris Sanders, based on Bloom's *Taxonomy of Educational Objectives*, calls "evaluation" questions. Applying Sanders and Bloom's category to biblical narratives, Neal Kaunfer suggests that in evaluation questions, "the students are asked to express their own value judgments concerning the actions, statements, and implied attitudes of the biblical personalities."[16]

Yet the most challenging aspect of the questioning comes not so much in the preparation of the key questions as in their implementation in the course of the interactive dialogue itself. The facilitator must be ready to field a number of interpretations offered by participants, to endorse and confirm them, and to help restate and refine those interpretations, while leaving open the possibility for other interpretations to follow. The facilitator must develop both the skill and the art of questioning, reformulating, and devising follow-up questions on the spot.

The key questions may begin either with a general key question about the biblical text itself or with questions that help participants reflect upon the various midrashic readings and apply those possible readings to the biblical text.

Closure

The facilitator must bring the discussion to closure. Closure differs from a conclusion in that it does not aim at a single conclusive interpretation of the text. Rather, in closure, the facilitator must recapitulate the various interpretations offered in the dialogue, articulating the main idea in each and distinguishing one interpretation from another. This, like the presentation and follow-up of key questions, is an art and a skill that the facilitator must develop. The point of closure, as opposed to conclusion, is to demonstrate that multiple valid readings of the text may be offered and that the aim is not toward one particular "correct" interpretation.

An Example Dialogue

Examples of midrashic-style interpretations of biblical texts are often taken from Genesis, where the texts are indeed evocative, ambiguous, gapped, and open to multiple interpretation. The Garden of Eden and *akedah* stories are certainly ripe for developing this method. However, we would like to choose our example from a different section of the Torah in order to suggest that this process can be performed with numerous biblical narratives, not only the most evocative and popular texts of Genesis. The episode we have chosen is "The Smashing of the Tablets." This discussion could be conducted based either on the version of the incident in Exodus (32:19) or on the version in Deuteronomy (9:15–17). We have chosen the version in Deuteronomy, because it is the less well-known version and because the description in the Torah text provides several possible motivations for Moses' actions that are not provided in Exodus. Indeed, the Deuteronomy text may itself be an early interpretation, an "inner-biblical midrash,"[17] on the sparser version in Exodus:

> I started down the mountain, . . . the two Tablets of the Covenant in my two hands. I saw how you had sinned against the Lord your God: You had made yourselves a molten calf; you had been quick to stray from the path that the Lord had enjoined upon you. Thereupon I gripped the two tablets, and flung them away with both my hands, smashing them before your eyes.

In the interactive dialogue, we began with two general questions about the text (though, as indicated above, we might have begun by clarifying the midrashic readings first):

- Why did Moses break the tablets?
- Did Moses do the right thing? Should he have broken the Ten Commandments?

These general key questions left open the possibility of participants dealing with Moses' psychological state—frustrated, angry, fed up with the people. It also allowed them to relate, on the other hand, to the actions of the Israelites and to the enormity of their sin and rejection of God alluded to in the text: "You had made yourselves a molten calf; you had been quick to stray from the path that the Lord had enjoined upon you." Participants might have suggested that the people "didn't deserve" the Ten Commandments, and that is what justified Moses' smashing the tablets. Several transitional questions were then introduced to begin to raise the concerns of the midrash:

- Should Moses have gotten permission from God to smash the tablets?
- Was this a defiance of God's wishes, or did God agree with what he did?
- Were the tablets, made by God, too holy to break?

We then turned the attention of our readers to a set of midrashim from *The Fathers according to Rabbi Nathan.*[18] Interestingly, this chapter contains several alternative readings of the text in terms of understanding why Moses smashed the tablets. We selected some of those midrashic readings:

1. This is but one of the things that Moses did of his own accord. He reasoned by inference, and his judgment agreed with God's. . . . He broke the tablets of the Commandments, and his judgment coincided with God's. [Another version: . . . and God agreed with him (afterward).]

2. Rabbi Yose the Galilean says: I shall tell you a parable, to what may this be compared? To a king of flesh and blood who said to his servant: "Go and betroth me a beautiful and pious maiden of good conduct." The servant went and betrothed her. Afterward, he discovered that she played the harlot with another man. Immediately, of his own accord, he reasoned as follows: If I go ahead and give her the marriage contract, she will be liable for the death penalty and thus will be separated from my master forever. So, too, did Moses reason on his own accord: How shall I give these tablets to Israel? I shall be making them obligated for the major commandments and liable for the death penalty. . . . Rather, I shall take hold of them and break them, and bring Israel back to good conduct.

3. He looked at the tablets and saw that the writing had disappeared from them. How can I give Israel the tablets, which have nothing substantial on them, he thought; better that I take hold of them and break them.

We asked the participants to tell how each of these midrashim justified Moses' actions in breaking the tablets. Several readings of the midrashim themselves are possible. In the first midrash, God actually agrees with Moses' actions, either before the fact or after the fact, depending on which version of the ending you take. That opens up for discussion the whole issue of why God might have agreed. In the second midrash, the parable might demonstrate the covenantal relationship between the people and God, represented by the marriage contract and the Ten Commandments. Here we also have the unusual idea that Moses actually saved the people from a worse fate—death. Had they received the Ten Commandments, they would have been liable for the death penalty. Without receiving the law, they are not obligated to the penalty. The third midrash is a more mythical one with "disappearing" letters.

On this midrash, we asked, "What is the point of the letters disappearing?" One possible suggestion is that the disappearing letters represent the fact that the words of the commandments have no meaning now in light of the people's sin.

After discussing some possible meanings of the three midrashic readings, we turned to a midrash that is rather different from the three in *The Fathers according to Rabbi Nathan*:

4. "Carve out two tablets like the first"—this explains what is written, "Be not hasty to become angry, for anger rests in the bosom of fools" (Eccles. 7:9). And who was it who was angry? It was Moses, as it is said, "and Moses' anger raged, and he flung the tablets" (Exod. 32:19). God said to him: "Ah, Moses, you have vented your anger on the tablets of the Covenant. Would you like me to vent my wrath? You will see then that the world could not endure even for one moment." Moses replied: "And what can I do?" God said: "I will now impose a punishment on you. You have broken the tablets; now you will have to replace them." That is the meaning of the next section: "Carve out two tablets like the first."[19]

We asked:

How is this midrash different from the three we discussed?

This midrash (from a rather different author and collection of midrashim) seems to present a diametrically opposed point of view from the other three. Whereas the midrashim in *The Fathers according to Rabbi Nathan* were all various attempts at justifying Moses' actions, the midrash in *Deuteronomy Rabbah* actually criticizes Moses for smashing the tablets. As one participant put it, "It's like a parent telling a child: 'You want to conduct things in anger, I'll show you anger!'" Moses has to make up for his unjustifiable anger in smashing the tablets by making new ones on his own. This reading evaluates Moses' actions as wrong and takes the beginning of the next chapter, in which Moses carves new tablets, not as a sequel, but as a consequence, a punishment.

Participants were then asked which of the reasons for Moses' actions they thought was the best interpretation of the text. They were encouraged to consider the reasons given in the first part of the discussion when we discussed the biblical text itself as well as the midrashic readings of the text. In the actual dialogue conducted, the group seemed to be split between two positions. There were those who favored the position of the last midrash, which they understood as indicating that Moses "lost his cool," as one participant put it. The rash anger that Moses demonstrated, they thought, was inappropriate for a true leader. Others were fascinated by the imagery of the letters disappearing and thought that that was an apt image for the fact that the people were undeserving to receive the message on the tablets. Moses was therefore justified in smashing the tablets as a dramatic gesture showing that the people had rejected their contents by their behavior. The role of the facilitator at that point was to manage the flow of positions and to recapitulate and organize them into two major stands as closure to the dialogue.

Conclusion

The process of reading narrative texts involves the reader in a dialogue in which the reader, interacting with the text, creates meaning from that textual encounter. This reading process is basic to the reader-response approach to literature and analogous to rabbinic midrash. We can extend that reading process with adults through an interactive-dialogue approach. This approach involves participants in an encounter with a biblical text and midrashic readings of that text. Through a process of textual discussion guided by a facilitator asking key questions, participants develop their own readings based on both the biblical text and its midrashic readings. The dialogue leads not only to individual interpretations of the text, but also to developing a "community of interpreters" with other participants.

Ultimately, the goal of such an interactive textual dialogue is that the participants not only "read" the text, but that the reading transforms their consciousness and perception of themselves and their world. James Fowler, in his explanation of the concept, "Conjunctive Faith," describes his own transformation in reading biblical texts: "Instead of *my reading*, analyzing and extracting the meaning of a biblical text, . . . I began to learn how to let the text *read me* and to let it bring my needs and the Spirit's movements within me to consciousness."[20]

Entering the world of the biblical text is a spiritual venture that changes both the meaning of the text and the inner spiritual life of the reader.

Notes

1. Youth groups of the Conservative movement. Rabbi Lukinsky was a master at teaching and employing textual interpretation in the creative and progressive youth programming that he introduced at Kehillath Israel in Brookline, Mass., in the 1960s.

2. For an approach to law as narrative, see Robert Cover, "Nomos and Narrative," *Harvard Law Review* (1983): 97; and Joseph Lukinsky, "Law in Education: A Reminiscence with Some Footnotes to Robert Cover's 'Nomos and Narrative,' " *Yale Law Journal* 96 (July 1987): 1836.

3. Jerome Bruner, "Narrative and Paradigmatic Modes of Thought," in *84th Yearbook of the National Society for the Study of Education,* ed. E. Eisner (Chicago: University of Chicago Press, 1985), 109.

4. Jerome Bruner, *Acts of Meaning* (Cambridge: Harvard University Press, 1990), 67.

5. *Sanhedrin* 34a. For a similar approach to Jewish legal texts, see Moshe Halbertal, *People of the Book: Canon, Meaning, and Authority* (Cambridge: Harvard University Press, 1997), 53.

6. Susan Handelman, *The Slayers of Moses: The Emergence of Rabbinic Interpretation in Modern Literary Theory* (Albany: State University of New York Press, 1982), 39.

7. Frank Kermode, "The Plain Sense of Things," in *Midrash and Literature,* ed. Sanford Budick and Geoffrey Hartman (New Haven: Yale University Press, 1986), 191.

8. Wolfgang Iser, "The Reading Process: A Phenomenological Approach," in *Reader-Response Criticism,* ed. Jane Tompkins (Baltimore: Johns Hopkins University Press, 1980), 54.

9. Ibid., 55.

10. Ibid., 68.

11. Stanley Fish, "Interpreting the *Variorum,*" in *Reader-Response Criticism,* ed. Tompkins, 182.

12. Daniel Boyarin, *Intertextuality and the Reading of Midrash* (Bloomington: Indiana University Press, 1990), 5.

13. Ibid., 14.

14. Other settings such as adult-education classes, *havurah* discussion groups, and retreats can be equally effective. The author has employed the approach with adults, described below, mainly in the context of a synagogue *devar Torah*. For a discussion of an approach to teaching midrash to children, see the author's "Teaching Midrash in the Conservative Day School" (diss., Jewish Theological Seminary, 1989). A summary of the approach may be found in *Curriculum, Community, and Commitment: Views on the American Jewish Day School,* ed. Daniel Margolis and Elliot Schoenberg (West Orange, N.J.: Behrman, 1992), 110.

15. See Peter Pitzele, *Our Fathers' Wells* (San Francisco: Harper Collins, 1995), and *Scripture Windows: Toward a Practice of Bibliodrama* (Los Angeles: Torah Aura, 1998).

16. See Norris Sanders, *Classroom Questions: What Kinds?* (New York: Harper and Row, 1966), chap. 8; Neal Kaunfer, "A Radical Approach to Teaching the Biblical Narrative in the Hebrew High School," in *1967 Yearbook of the Educators' Assembly*, ed. Eli Grad, 58; and Benjamin Bloom, ed., *Taxonomy of Educational Objectives: Cognitive Domain* (New York: McKay, 1956).

17. See Michael Fishbane, *Biblical Interpretation of Ancient Israel* (Oxford: Clarendon, 1985).

18. Judah Goldin, trans., *The Fathers according to Rabbi Nathan* (New York: Schocken, 1974), 19–21.

19. *Deuteronomy Rabbah* 3:4 (Soncino translation).

20. James Fowler, *Stages of Faith* (San Francisco: Harper and Row, 1981), 186. Italics in text are Fowler's.

A New Look at Old Hebrew Textbooks:
Salient Features and Underlying Principles of Hebrew Textbooks, 1830–1930

Adina A. Ofek

The teaching of Hebrew and its role in Jewish education in America have been, for more than a century, areas of deep conflict and heated debate among Jewish educators and scholars. Why teach Hebrew at all? What kind of Hebrew should be taught, and by what method? These questions remain some of the most poignant ones for educators and community leaders across the spectrum of Jewish religious denominations. Hebrew language textbooks, still the main pedagogic tool in the hands of teachers, have always reflected the social and ideological trends of their era. At the same time, they have provided guidance to Jewish educators, offering them language programs that were rooted in current societal and linguistic trends.

Through analytic descriptions of representative textbooks from the mid-nineteenth century until the 1930s, I will demonstrate how various answers to the aforementioned questions are reflected in these textbooks. During this period, three types of Hebrew language textbooks, each characterized by one of three approaches to language learning, were created. Each was influenced by pedagogic trends in the world of general education as well as in Jewish education, and by prevalent ideologies in Jewish society at large. I will locate the driving forces behind these trends and examine the impact they had on the choice and design of the textbooks.

The first authors of Hebrew textbooks in America were influenced by two main sources: English language spellers; and Hebrew textbooks published in Europe, which were imported, reprinted, or rewritten by author-

Adina A. Ofek is associate professor of Jewish education at the Jewish Theological Seminary and was a doctoral student of Professor Joseph Lukinsky. She specializes in Hebrew language acquisition, teacher professional development and supervision, and the teaching of Hebrew children's literature.

educators who immigrated to America from Europe, so as to adapt them to the new circumstances of American life. Although my description and analysis will focus on the books published in America, I will provide examples from European books as well, to demonstrate their influence on the authors of American textbooks and to show how American textbooks departed from the European examples.[1]

Even a cursory examination of these Hebrew books reveals that the bulk of Hebrew textbooks published in America during the most prolific publishing period of such textbooks (1900 through the 1930s) display a puzzling phenomenon. During this period, two approaches in the teaching of foreign languages prevailed: the Grammar Translation method and the Direct method. Textbooks for teaching all other languages used one approach or the other. In the case of Hebrew in this period, most textbooks used a combination of these two methods. Especially striking is the fact that not only is this phenomenon unique to Hebrew language textbooks—and nonexistent in textbooks of any other language—but these methods have quite different, even contradictory, goals and techniques. I will argue that this unique choice of "hybrid" textbooks was not an accident. Rather, it was an attempt to resolve a sharp contradiction between Jewish educators' belief in the goal of teaching Hebrew, on the one hand, and their pedagogic convictions regarding the "right" way of teaching a foreign language, on the other.

What follows is a description of the three approaches reflected in the textbooks: the Grammar Translation method (GT); the Direct method (DM), also termed the Natural method; and a combination of the two in the "hybrid" texts. I will describe and analyze these methods against the background of the historical and sociological conditions of the Jews in America at the time of their publication, showing what impact these circumstances had on the development of the texts.

The History and Development of the Grammar Translation Method

The teaching of languages (mostly Latin and Greek) had for centuries been connected with studies in religion or classics. The teaching method was characterized by reading from a classic text in the target language and learning it through translating the text into the native tongue. Gradually, the first English readers compiled by Noah Webster, "spellers," began to serve as language textbooks. Their format followed a consistent pattern: it began with the alphabet, followed by meaningless word fragments, followed by three-letter words, and culminating in short sentences containing moral lessons, hymns, and catechisms.[2] From the seventeenth century onward, the study of grammar was added to translation and quickly became the main purpose of study. Students were exposed to endless paradigms and grammar rules that were drilled mechanically.

The teaching of Hebrew developed along parallel lines. For centuries, textbooks for Jewish children were the classic sources: the Bible, the prayer book, and the Talmud. Mastering these texts was the highest goal of study. The alphabet, reading, and writing were acquired as by-products of the study of Torah and the use of the prayer book. With the beginning of the Haskalah (Enlightenment) in Europe, a new era began in Jewish education, characterized by a revised choice of cultural treasures that constituted the content of Jewish education, reflecting various new sets of values and new goals. One of these changes was a revision in the attitude toward the Hebrew language and textbooks, reflecting the inclusion of new text materials or radical editing of the religious sources.[3] For the first time, writers published textbooks specifically prepared for teaching the Hebrew language to children. Some of the greatest luminaries of Hebrew literature, such as Abraham Mapu, Judah Leib Gordon, Hayyim Nahman Bialik, and Jacob Fichman, were among the first authors of such textbooks in Europe.[4]

Most of the Hebrew textbooks published in Europe during this era were designed in the GT method and also represent, from a pedagogic point of view, what scholars of education refer to as the subject-matter-centered approach.[5] This approach is characterized by a total emphasis on the subject matter at hand, disregarding all other aspects involved in the didactic situation. It does not take into consideration the specific characteristics of the learners, their age, gender, aptitude, or motivation, nor the time allocated for the subject or its level of difficulty. This approach was applied to all subject-matter fields, but it fit especially well into the theoretical components of the GT method in language teaching, which remained popular until the end of the nineteenth century.

A typical example is one of the earliest and most widespread textbooks for children: Judah Leib Ben Ze'ev's *Bet hasefer,* a reader in two volumes. Volume 1, *Mesilat halimud,* published in Vienna in 1802, appeared as a response to the need for textbooks for the new Haskalah schools. These schools were established (among other reasons) to respond to the demand for a more graded curriculum in Hebrew that would ease the students' path into the Bible and difficult talmudic texts. *Bet hasefer* was subject-matter-centered and thus included long and detailed complex explanations on the structure of the language. It became very popular, was translated into Russian and other languages, and was published in nine editions.[6]

At the beginning of the twentieth century, a new, more subjective psychological/pedagogical approach in designing educational materials emerged. Here the focus shifted to the learner, who determined, at least in theory, the quantity of the material presented, its content, and its pace. As for teaching materials, this shift signified a limited quantity of low-difficulty materials in the beginning stages, gradually increasing in quantity and difficulty as the learning proceeded, as well as other learner-centered components, to be discussed later.[7]

Textbooks Replace Classic Religious Texts

In tandem with the development of English language textbooks in America and the Haskalah movement in Europe, Hebrew language textbooks were replacing primary religious sources. The chief goal of teaching Hebrew in America in the late eighteenth century and in the nineteenth century was to prepare students to read the Bible. For that reason, textbook authors followed the models of the spellers and of classics readers when they produced textbooks for university students (mostly non-Jewish). These were short volumes, starting with the alphabet, some short biblical phrases with English translation, and grammar rules. These books, along with others published by non-Jews, mostly for adult students, were apparently used to teach Jewish children as well, for lack of more suitable materials.[8] The first Hebrew textbook for children published in America was influenced by Ben Ze'ev: Isaac Leeser's *Moreh Derech: The Spelling Book*. In his preface, Leeser states that he wrote the book to assist a good friend (the famous Rebecca Gratz) in her newly opened Sunday school in Philadelphia. In his words:

> I wrote this little book to fulfill a promise I gave to a dear friend, to use in the school she has just opened. This will be my modest contribution to help her spread the knowledge of the ancient language to our children. Books such as this one appeared long ago in Ashkenaz, and one was first written by the scholar grammarian Ben Ze'ev, but until today I have not seen one that will suit children whose native tongue is English.[9]

GT Remains Dominant despite Expressions of Discontent

A milestone was reached in 1868 with *A Practical Grammar of the Hebrew Language for Schools and Colleges,* by Bernhard Felsenthal. Although he titled his book as a grammar book, in his preface Felsenthal stated:

> This book is intended to ease the study of the Hebrew language. We say the study of the *Hebrew language* and not the study of *Hebrew grammar* [emphasis in the original], because grammar is not the student's goal but rather fluency in the language. . . . Although the book is based on the Grammar method, we tried to give only the basic rules . . . but we are aware that we still sinned by giving more room to grammar than we should have.[10]

Because of his Reform rabbinic education and his being a teacher, Felsenthal must have understood intuitively that it was not useful to teach young learners only the grammar rules; even though he designed the book in the then-popular style, he expressed his reservations and tried as best as he could to give it a new direction. His goal in teaching Hebrew was still the biblical language (as was that of his contemporaries), but nevertheless he suggested that a course in reading should be added, so that the student would acquire a real sense for the language (*Sprachgefühl,* in German).[11]

Beginning in the 1880s, when Eastern European Jews immigrated in large numbers to the United States and more Jewish schools were needed, immigrant Jewish educators introduced Hebrew textbooks that they had used in the restructured European schools known as *hadarim metukanim.* The Maskilim, now teaching in the Talmud Torahs in America, used the same books and methods for teaching Hebrew as they had used in Europe. The method that they imported was the GT method, which was suitable for the target population and for the goals that teachers were aiming to achieve at the time. The Talmud Torahs were a voluntary Jewish education system, which children attended after a full day in public school. The Jewish school was in session in the afternoon for five days, three days, or, later, even just one day a week. The goal was to learn to read Hebrew as quickly as possible so that children could read the Bible. The books were designed accordingly— introducing the alphabet and meaningless syllables, then isolated words,

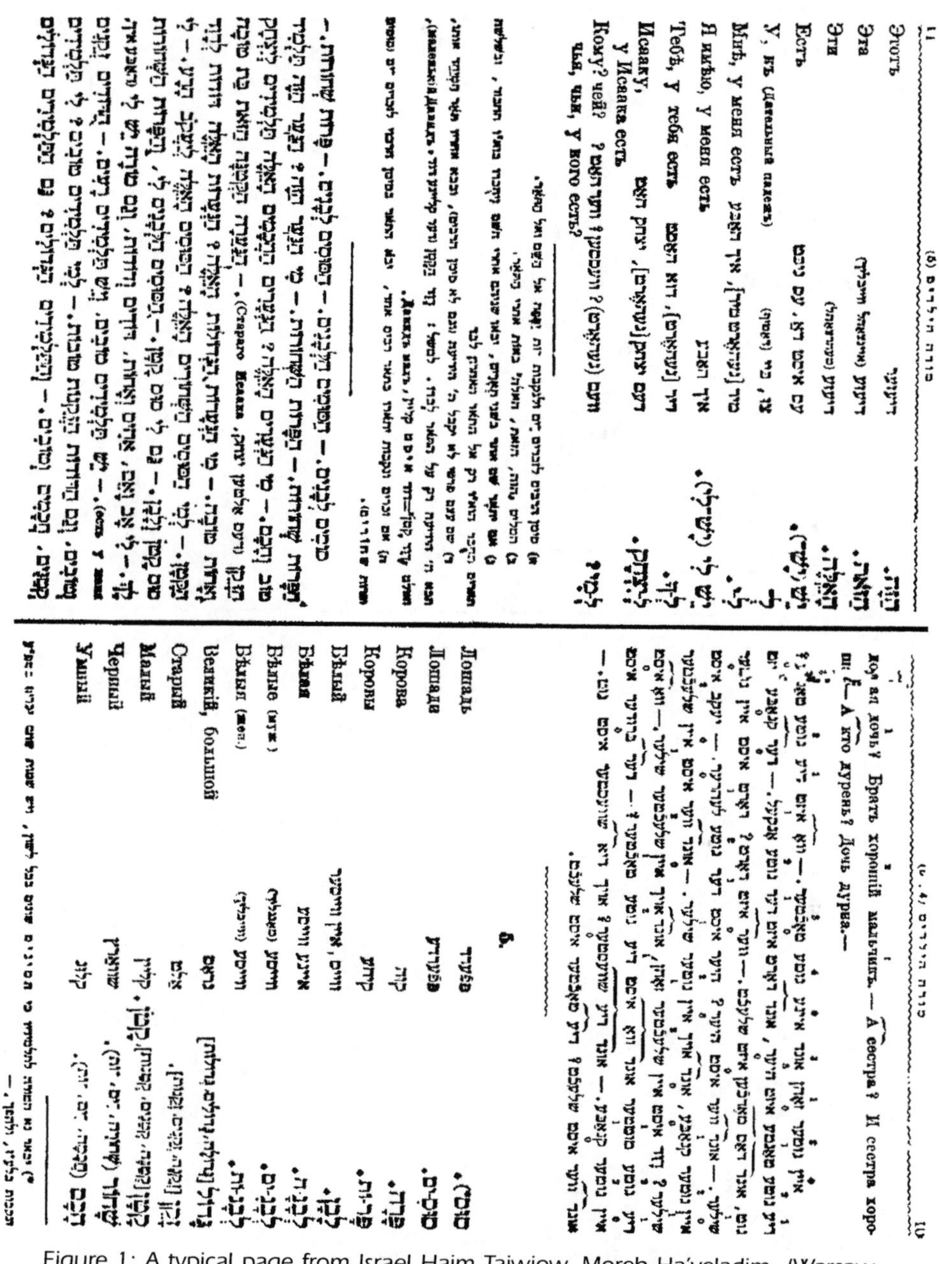

Figure 1: A typical page from Israel Haim Taiwiow, Moreh Ha'yeladim, (Warsaw, 1903). Features of the GT method are: The text at the bottom of the left hand page consists of isolated sentences illustrating the grammar rules and vocabulary that appears above the text. In the vocabulary list, the Hebrew words are on the right, German translations (transliterated into Hebrew letters) in the center, and Russian translations on the left.

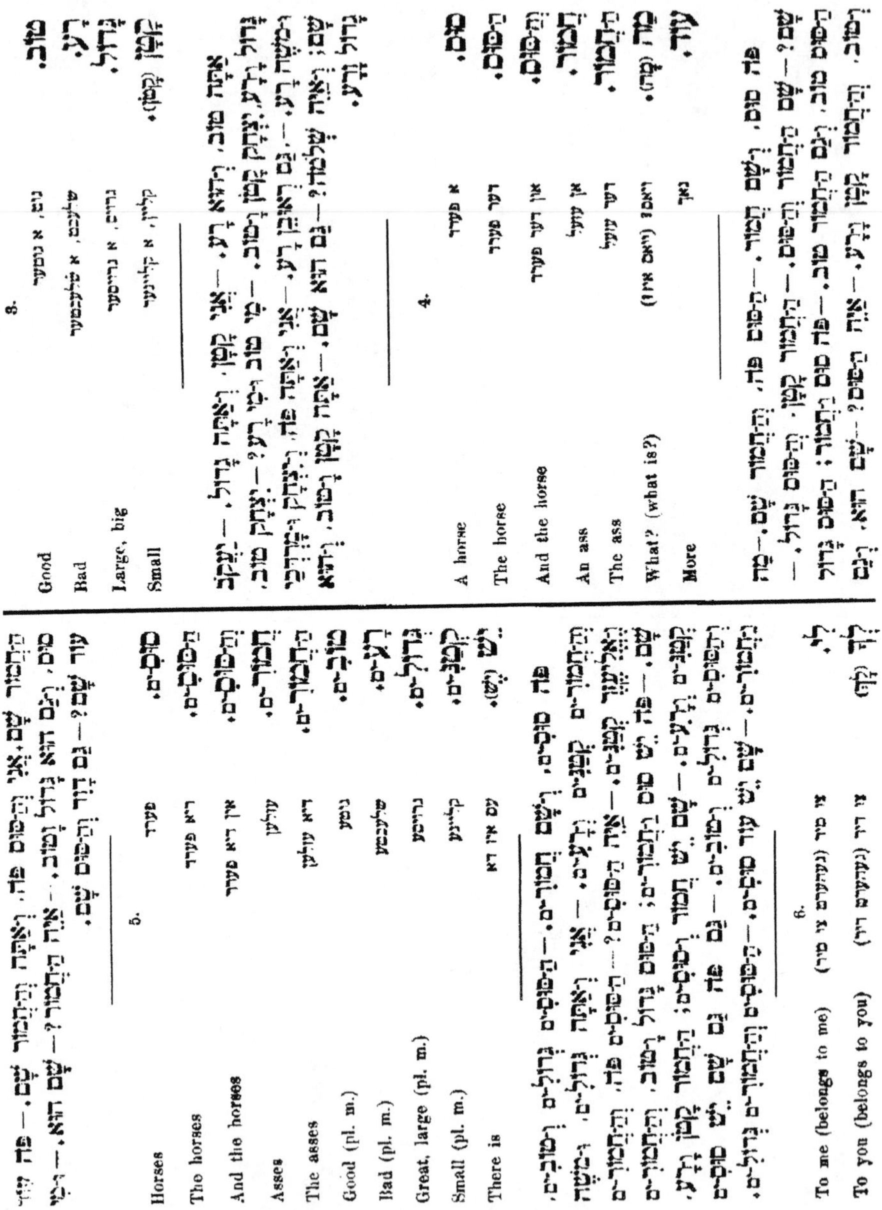

8.

Good
Bad
Large, big
Small

4.

A horse
The horse
And the horse
An ass
The ass
What? (what is?)
More

— 7 —

5.

Horses
The horses
And the horses
Asses
The asses
Good (pl. m.)
Bad (pl. m.)
Great, large (pl. m.)
Small (pl. m.)
There is

6.

To me (belongs to me)
To you (belongs to you)

Figure 2: Tawiow revised Moreh ha'yeladim for use in America, where it was called Ha'mechin. (New York: Hebrew Publishing Co., 1919) These pages (6 and 7) correspond to the pages from Moreh Ha'yeladim in figure 1. He uses the same method of presentation: Hebrew vocabulary lists are translated into English and Yiddish. The detailed grammar rules from the earlier edition have been eliminated.

disconnected sentences to be translated, and basic grammar rules, and moving quickly to readings of a high level of difficulty that students were required to translate.

Zevi Scharfstein presents the textbooks prepared by Israel Hayyim Tawiow as a typical example of the GT method. Tawiow was a prolific translator in Europe and wrote several Hebrew textbooks, including *Moreh hayeladim* (1898) and *Hamekhin* (1899), of which thousands of copies were published and widely used. In his preface to *Moreh hayeladim,* Tawiow explains his method in presenting the translations with numbers above the words to make it easier for children to follow the different word order. He included all the grammar rules, conjugations, and even vocalization rules, yet claimed to have corrected the "evil in our methods, the ridiculous readings . . . without humor or good sense." He goes on to say that "his readings contain clever ideas and are fun to read." (See Figure 1.)

In 1909, Tawiow's *Hamekhin,* with English and Yiddish translations, was published in America and became very popular. According to Scharfstein, thousands of copies were published in many editions. The lessons in the book moved ahead at a fast pace, with eight words and their translations and conjugations taught in the first two lessons, immediately followed by phrases using these words in translation exercises. In the fourth lesson, the infinitive is explained; in the fifth, singular and plural; and in the eighth, the adjective. There are no illustrations in the book, and all exercises consist of unrelated, often nonsensical, sentences, none really speaking to a young child's interest. One wonders, as Scharfstein did, "what made this talented author create something so boring and unsuited to children." He concludes that "it must have been the method of the time." (See Figure 2.)

Another American author who published in the same method and style was Hillel Malachovsky, in *Hanisayon harishon.* This book, for first-year students, contains 100 pages divided into sixty-three short chapters, each with a list of vocabulary with translations into English and Yiddish, and isolated disconnected sentences. In his introduction, the author claims to have included lovely, heartwarming stories and poems, all original. While reading these, the learner acquires a wide range of Hebrew style and grammar in an easy and fun way.[12] (See Figure 3.)

The GT method remained popular throughout the nineteenth century and even into the twentieth century, despite strong opposition to the method and attempts by several prominent language teachers and scholars to introduce new methods.

.10

		Honey
		A forest
		A field (1)

אֵיזֶה

	A tree
	A wall
	A roof
	A pigeon (1)
	A bee
	A Stork
	A hive
	· Cattle
	A beast

Figure 3: These are two pages from chapter 10 in Ha'nisayon Ha'rishon by Hillel Malachovsky (New York: Hebrew Publishing Co., 1908). Here we see Hebrew vocabulary lists with Yiddish and English translations, isolated Hebrew sentences and one of Malachovsky's "heartwarming" poems.

144

The Direct Method

Toward the end of the nineteenth and at the beginning of the twentieth century, the Direct method (or Natural method) was advancing rapidly in Europe and in America. Variations on the natural approach (i.e., to follow the way a child learns the language, repeating the names of objects in his immediate environment first) to language teaching became popular from the mid-nineteenth century onward. One such example was G. Henness's private school for languages in New Haven. The approach that Henness described in a book in 1867 was the Natural method. At that time, C. Marcel published a book on language teaching in which he suggested abandoning the translation and grammar rules in teaching language. Instead, he advised starting with a long period of listening, then reading easy and familiar material, speaking, and writing. However, these attempts (as earlier ones) remained sporadic and local. The real revolution came with the publication of a book by W. Vietor, *Der Sprachunteritcht muss umkehren* (Leipzig, 1882), as cited in Haramati.[13]

As the twentieth century began, knowing spoken languages proved useful in fostering new trade relations among countries, and increasingly more common, travel abroad. In Jewish circles, the Natural method came to be known as Ivrit be'Ivrit (Hebrew in Hebrew). In Hebrew, as in other languages, this method came as a reaction to low achievement and apathy among students as well as dissatisfaction with their level of Hebrew achievement by educators and parents. The failure of the Talmud Torah system is attributed to many factors, but a common criticism shared by most was the nature of textbooks and their method of teaching Hebrew. The main flaws found in the GT method are summarized well in Scharfstein's early book *Horaat halashon ha'Ivrit*.[14]

Scharfstein points out that the GT begins with grammar rules. He asks what use the rules are to a student who does not know the language. All books in the GT method are full of exercises that are really isolated sentences serving as illustrations of grammar rules. How could one remember these strange, disconnected sentences? A language is not single words, continues Scharfstein, and translating word by word will not convey the real meaning of the sentence. A language is learned by using it and not by talking about it in the native tongue. "Here young students are asked to apply abstract thinking, comparisons, and the manipulation of rules to disconnected sentences. But . . . children learn by using all their senses—seeing, hearing, touching—this is how knowledge is imprinted in children's minds. . . . No teacher can create interest in his students through these dry rules and isolated, boring sentences."[15]

The results of the GT method are devastating, as pointed out by A. Perlberg in the 1927 *Hadoar* yearbook:

> Hebrew teachers have been complaining that the books that come from Europe are not suitable for the children in America. Indeed, they are correct. However, I would add that these books were not suitable for the children in Europe, either. It seems as if all the authors have united just to make it difficult for children to learn Hebrew. . . . I can attest that very few students, and only the very best among them, really move from the first book to the next level. Most children in the class, upon finishing the first book, need to go back to another book at the same beginning level.[16]

The method that replaced the GT in almost all modern language teaching was the Direct method (DM). According to the *Longman Dictionary*, its basic features are:

> Only the target language should be used in class; meaning should be communicated "directly" by associating speech forms with actions, objects, mime, gestures, and situations. Speaking should be taught first and then reading and writing, [and] grammar should only be taught inductively. Grammar rules should not be taught. This method is a culmination of various Natural approaches that preceded it.[17]

Toward the end of the nineteenth century, as Hebrew was becoming a living language in Eretz Yisrael and the Zionist movement was growing stronger, three outstanding and influential teachers, working mainly out of Palestine, developed the Ivrit be'Ivrit method, with variations (Yitzhak Epstein, David Yellin, and Yehuda Grazovsky).[18] According to various sources, Epstein was the most original of the three, and it was his article in 1899, and later his book, that created the revolution in language teaching in the *hadarim metukanim* in Europe.[19]

In Epstein's method, learning is based on all the senses and adapted to the active nature of children. Since children like moving around, playing, and running, teaching is done through these activities. Such methods also justify teaching language to very young children (starting at age four, as mentioned in the title of his book; see n. 19). The organization of the teaching material will be natural, even in the artificial situation of the classroom, if, according to Epstein, teachers present a meaningful text instead of disconnected sentences. The sentences that they teach would accompany activities and objects that have a logical, natural connection or order. Attention should also be paid to the progression and organization of the material from one lesson to another, beginning with objects and activities in the immediate environment of the child, both external and internal (what interests a child at a certain age). Epstein also advocated abandoning the excessive emphasis on wordiness, replacing it with a concrete and direct connection with nature. In his words: "Read to them every day, even if only a few lines, from the big living book of the universe."[20]

Speaking, he suggested, should be the basis for reading and writing, and should precede it. He expressed his hope that this would bring about a natural way of using Hebrew as it was being revived. He also claimed, as did many teachers after him, that teaching with this approach enables children at the age of six to begin reading the Bible. (Note that even as Epstein advocates a direct, natural method of teaching Hebrew, his vital goal is still to quickly reach a level of language proficiency that would enable children to study the Bible in a meaningful way.) All in all, he considers the method to be much more efficient, since the target language is the only language being used, and thus the entire study period is spent using it.

The DM was obviously embraced with enthusiasm by Zionists and advocates of the Hebrew revival movement in Europe and in America—but not only by them. There was a complex set of factors that impelled American Jewish educators during that period, schooled as they were in the Grammar Translation method, toward the inclusion of the newer natural method: Ivrit be'Ivrit.

Reasons for Adoption of the DM in America

Modern spoken Hebrew was intrinsic to the Zionist culture imported to Palestine by Eastern European Zionists at the end of the nineteenth century. They saw no reason why teachers should not teach spoken Hebrew through Hebrew, giving rise in Palestine to the Ivrit be'Ivrit method for teaching the Hebrew language—a method that was equivalent to the Direct method of teaching foreign languages that had developed in Europe (though some Zionists were unfamiliar with that pedagogic development). Jewish educators in Europe subsequently adopted the Ivrit be'Ivrit method, and those who came to America brought that approach with them as an integral part of their collection of teaching strategies.

The rise of the Direct method in the teaching of other languages also smoothed the way to its use in Hebrew instruction. Created in Europe, the method was imported to America in the nineteenth century and widely accepted for foreign language instruction. The progressive educators who dominated educational scholarship during this period embraced the Direct method of teaching foreign languages. As the field of Jewish education developed in North America, progressive educators, especially those Jewish educators who studied at Columbia University Teachers College and other universities where progressive education was regnant, came to believe that the Direct method was appropriate for Jewish education as well.[21]

Hybrid Hebrew Textbooks

If the pressures to adopt the DM were so strong in the United States, why, then, did this newer method not simply replace the Grammar Translation method in the teaching of Hebrew in America, as it did in the teaching of other languages? Part of the explanation is surely that while Jewish educators were drawn to the Ivrit be'Ivrit method, faithful to the classic tradition of Jewish education, their main goal remained that of teaching students Bible and siddur. Their chief aim was not to teach fluency in spoken Hebrew. Even those Maskilim who favored the Natural method and who, given their ideological preferences, would have liked to teach for fluency in Hebrew, bowed to the pressure to compromise the DM for the sake of the goal of teaching Bible.[22]

Clash between Learning Bible and the DM

The conflict between the goal of teaching children Bible and using the DM results from fundamental features of the method. To begin with, the DM insists on teaching psychologically suitable material, taken from the daily environment of the child. That would mean stories and poems much like those that students read in public school. While these materials may make sense for the goal of learning a language, they drain the

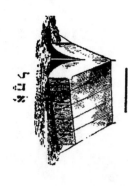

Figure 4: This figure shows two pages from the textbook Shaharit, by M. M. Tomarov, B. Hirsh, and S. Stein (Boston: Sifra Publishing). Page 31 on the right, titled "Family," shows how the early lessons provide a language foundation for later lessons like page 95 on the left, titled "Cain and Hevel," which is more complex language but still easier than the original biblical language.

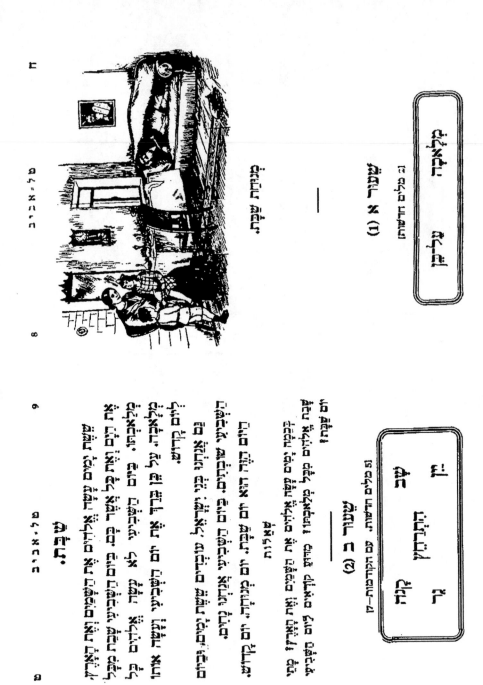

Figure 5: On this and the facing page are four pages from K. Whiteman, Tal Aviv (New York, 1925), a textbook that begins with pictures and single words (see page 8) and narratives in simple Hebrew with biblical content

(see page 9). It moves quickly to stories in Biblical Hebrew. Pages 57–58 are typical examples of a non-biblical story told in biblical language as preparation for bible study.

Jewish content out of the curriculum of the Jewish school. The Jewish content was, after all, the *raison d'être* for Jewish schools.

What is more, teaching Ivrit be'Ivrit would mean a long period of dealing with very simple words reflecting objects and actions that a child would be likely to encounter. There is a significant disjunction between such a simple vocabulary and the language of the Bible. The DM also involves the gradation of the material presented: simple words, ideas, and sentences only slowly lead to more complex language. How long would it take until the students would be introduced to vocabulary and language structures similar to those in the Bible?

Perlberg, in his 1927 paper, describes both these problems in adopting pure DM textbooks for Hebrew teaching. He states serious problems with the new DM textbooks:

> The commonly accepted opinion is that we are obligated psychologically to supply the Jewish child with general material that is age-appropriate. In the Jewish school, this approach is wrong for true psychological reasons—namely, that the child is a Hebrew child. When he comes to Hebrew school, he expects that special delights will be prepared for him there. Many teachers admit the fact that real excitement is injected into the classroom during the holidays, when we teach them stories that are taken from our own Jewish tradition. Most of the books for young children that were published in the last twenty years typically aim to supply the Jewish child with general childish stories that have very little Jewish content in them.[23]

For Perlberg, not only do the DM textbooks fail to meet the goal of Jewish content for Jewish education; they are not effective because they do not speak to the child's Jewish self. In addition, Perlberg sees another set of problems created by the fact that these textbooks move quickly to very difficult, complex, GT-style material. He argues:

> The most important reason [for the failure of the DM Hebrew textbooks] is the difficulty of the language and the eagerness to put in idioms and complex language construction. This is really a pedagogical and a moral sin toward the child. Often this attitude will set up hidden hatred in the child's heart toward this difficult, tiring language. . . . In addition, the leaps from one level to another are confusing and surprising, and often a whole year is needed to close the gap that exists between volume 1 and volume 2.[24]

Conflict of Methods and Goals
Yields Hybrid Textbooks

Perlberg explains why the textbooks move so quickly and unrealistically to more complex language. If we read his analysis carefully, we see that he identifies that it is the goal of getting students to read the Bible that requires such an accelerated series of lessons. As an example of a hybrid text that to some degree avoids, but still suffers from, this problem, he cites the textbook *Shacharit:*

> The book by Tomarov, Hirsh, and Stein, *Shacharit,* published for the first time in 1916, excelled in terms of the easy language, sentence structure, and Jewish content, although it still lacks the constant repetition of words and sentences, which the Direct method requires. . . . This book and others like it [unfortunately] have one thing in common—they aim to get the Jewish child as quickly as possible to the goal of reading the Bible.[25] (See Figure 4.)

The gap between educators' pedagogic beliefs about how best to teach languages and their commitment to teach the Bible finds expression in the prefaces of their textbooks. Many, if not most, agree that the Ivrit be'Ivrit method is the correct approach. Concerned that students will not reach the level that will enable them to read the Bible, they decide to begin the book with the method, but quickly move on to much more complex, difficult texts. As a result, by the end of the 1930s hardly any material was being published in the "pure" Ivrit be'Ivrit method. The arguments in the prefaces of the books and in periodicals during that period are mostly of two kinds. First, there are those whose main purpose is fluency in Hebrew, but they succumb to the pressure to prepare the students to read the Bible and thus claim that even if reading is all you want to teach, the fastest way to reach this goal will be though speaking first. Second, there are those who primarily believe in preparing for the Bible, but would also like the students to become fluent in the language. They believe that beginning with Ivrit be'Ivrit will also make their students better readers of the Bible.[26] Yet even those who offer little more than lip service to the DM feel that they cannot afford to present themselves in opposition to Ivrit be'Ivrit. They admit that Ivrit be'Ivrit is good, but because class time is so limited, they must rely on more efficient methods.[27]

The results of both views are textbooks that use a hybrid of the two methods. Typically, the books begin with very simple pictures and words but quickly move on to supplying translations, complex texts, and even grammar. The reliance on such complex texts is a hallmark of Grammar Translation!

Conclusion

The conclusion reached in the analysis of these books clearly documents a shift in emphasis over time toward the teaching of modern Hebrew in the Talmud Torah and synagogue school. This was a result of the Zionist movement and the settlement of Jews in Eretz Yisrael and modern and progressive educational trends in Western society. The decreased amount of time available in supplementary Jewish school programs, however, has raised, in earlier decades and in recent years, serious questions as to whether teaching spoken Hebrew is feasible, and if so, whether it can prepare students to achieve the main goal of these schools: the ability to read the Bible and prayer book in a meaningful fashion.

This preliminary examination of one aspect of the old Hebrew textbooks opens up many other questions relating to those textbooks, some to which I have alluded.[28] Among those questions are: (1) What kind of society is reflected in the content and the illustrations in these books? (2) What kind of values do they promote? (3) To what extent were these authors influenced by commercial considerations, and what drove them to write and their publishers to publish these books? (4) How user-friendly were these books to the students and to the teachers? (5) What kind of guidance was offered to the teachers? (5) How much consideration was given to the developmental stage of the intended student? (6) What thought was given to aesthetic considerations in the preparation of these books?

Answers to these and similar questions may help illuminate the issues that we face in Hebrew instruction in contemporary Jewish education.

Notes

1. A comprehensive list of textbooks in all Judaica subjects published in America can be found in Aaron Klein, "The Development of Hebrew Textbooks for Jewish Schools in America" (Ph.D. diss., Jewish Theological Seminary, 1955).
2. Clifton Johnson, *Old-Time Schools* (New York: Macmillan, 1917). The first

spellers were illustrated with wood-block carvings—some of the very same carvings that could later be found in early Hebrew textbooks. See also Elizabeth Baker Withmore, *The Development of Elementary English Language Textbooks in the United States* (Nashville: Peabody College, 1929).

3. Rachel Dror-Elboim, *Changes in Education and in Jewish Society* (Jerusalem: Yad Ben Zvi, 1986), 47.

4. Uriel Ofek, *Hebrew Children's Literature: 1900–1948* (in Hebrew) (Tel Aviv: Dvir, 1988).

5. See Joseph Schwab, "The Practical: Translation into Curriculum," in *From the Scholar to the Classroom,* ed. S. Fox and G. Rosenfeld (New York: Melton Research Center, 1980).

6. Zevi Scharfstein, "Textbooks and Social Trends," in *Yearbook for the Jews in America* (1939), 260–75. Scharfstein describes this textbook as unique, with its wide range of topics that included science, world literature, geography, and more, all in addition to teaching the basics of Hebrew and prayer.

7. Shlomo Haramati,*Mapu the Hebrew Teacher* (in Hebrew) (Jerusalem: Council on Teaching Hebrew, 1972).

8. This is implied in Leeser's preface to the Hebrew textbook that he prepared for children; see n. 9.

9. Isaac Leeser, *Moreh Derech: The Spelling Book* (Philadelphia: Haswell, Barrington & Haswell, 1838).

10. Bernhard Felsenthal, *A Practical Grammar of the Hebrew Language for Schools and Colleges* (New York: L. H. Frank, 1868).

11. To this short list of the very first Hebrew textbooks for young learners we should add a unique and original attempt by R. A. Sonn, *Or hadash* (Cincinnati: Bloch, 1885). In the preface, the author complains that children leave the Sabbath school without the ability to read. In his opinion, we should blame the method. So he wrote a book on the "analytic synthetic" method, in which children learn the technique of reading through the English word. The students learn English words written in Hebrew transliteration.

12. Hillel Malachovsky,*Hanisayon harishon* (New York: Hebrew Publishing, 1908). Others in the same style include Dov Aryeh Fridman, *Sefer mikra kodesh: Rashit hahinukh leyaldei Yisrael* (New York and Warsaw: Hebrew Publishing, 1890); and Goldin and Silkner,*Ivrit shanah rishona* (New York: S. Drukerman, 1908).

13. Shlomo Haramati, "Hadash veyashan behoraat leshonot," in *Studies in Education,* ed. A. Cohen (Haifa: University of Haifa Press, 1975); see also Zevi Scharfstein, *Ways of Teaching Our Language* (New York: Shilo, 1940).

14. Zevi Scharfstein, *The Teaching of the Hebrew Language* (in Hebrew) (New York: Jewish Theological Seminary, 1934).

15. Ibid., 9–13.

16. A. Perlberg, "Hebrew Textbooks in America," in *Hadoar Jubilee Volume,* ed. M. Ribolow (New York: Hadoar, 1927). Perlberg studied at Teachers College,

Columbia University, and was a teacher in the New York area until he moved to Israel, where he taught education. See also the periodical *Shevilei hahinukh,* 1925–27.

17. *Longman Dictionary of Language Teaching and Applied Linguistics,* ed. Jack Richards, John Platt, and Heidi Platt (London: Longman, 1992), 109.

18. Shlomo Haramati, *Three First Teachers* (in Hebrew) (Jerusalem: Yad Ben Zvi, 1984).

19. Yitzhak Epstein, "Ivrit be'Ivrit: Hashita hativit bereshit limudei sfat ever," *Hashiloah* (4 Heshvan 1899); and later his book, *Hebrew in Hebrew: The Beginning of Learning Hebrew according to the Natural Method, for Teachers and Fathers Who Teach Hebrew to Children from the Age of Four Years and Up* (Warsaw: Achiasaf, 1901).

20. Yitzhak Epstein, *Studies in the Psychology of Language* (in Hebrew) (Jerusalem: n.p., 1947), 5.

21. Progressive education was associated in the minds of American Jews with Americanization. For this reason, American Jewish educators readily adopted such key features of progressive education as the natural approach to teaching foreign languages.

22. Another, perhaps less important, explanation was that while other foreign languages being taught by the DM were fully living languages, with established cultures and nation-states, Hebrew was in the process of being revived as a living language.

23. Perlberg, *Sefer hayovel* (New York: Histadrut Ivrit of America, 1927), 299.

24. Ibid.

25. Ibid.

26. See, for example, the prefaces to textbooks for beginners: H. P. Bergman and S. H. Berkuz, *Sfat yeladim* (New York: Hebrew Publishing, 1905); Z. Scharfstein, *Sefer hatalmid* (New York: Bureau of Jewish Education of the Jewish Community, 1913); Fishman, Lieberman, et al., *Safa hayya* (Riga, 1898; New York: Hebrew Publishing, 1902).

27. Some were less apologetic about deviating from the DM. Bialik, for example, argued that teachers should not stoop down to children, but raise them up. Children have to get used to difficult words even if they do not understand everything; they need to understand the context. In Uriel Ofek, *Gumot hen* (Dimples) (in Hebrew) (Tel Aviv: Dvir, 1984), 106–7.

28. This study represents one aspect of my larger research project on the development of Hebrew textbooks and curricula over the past century.

The Emerging Role of Jewish Women as Providers and Recipients of Education:
1840–1920

Eduardo Rauch

The experience of Jewish women from 1840 to 1920 in America, as well as their role as providers and recipients of education, is an area that has emerged prominently in Jewish social-science research only in the last twenty-five years. Before then, the study of the roles of Jewish women was mostly neglected. In 1983, Ellen Condliffe Lageman stated:

> Women's history grew out of an interest in recovering an over-looked aspect of human experience, and it is not only and should not always be approached as the study of a female 'sphere.' . . . Implicit in women's history is a possibility for promoting greater awareness of the need to develop more accurate and encompassing histories of all people and for identifying the kinds of questions that must be asked if such histories are to appear.[1]

What emerges from the research picture in terms of gender is a Jewish middle class and an upper middle class composed mostly of Jewish women of German origin on the one hand, and an ever-growing number of impoverished girls and women arriving from Eastern Europe, on the other. Most of the established population of women lived very comfortable lives amid a community dedicated to family. It was not common, or in any way acceptable, that women should work for profit in the marketplace. However, there was among them an increasing interest in study, education, and voluntary service, and they began organizing around bodies such as the National Council of Jewish Women, Hadassah, and others.

Eduardo Rauch is an educator working at the Jewish Theological Seminary of America.

157

By 1870, 11,000 immigrant and American women were enrolled in institutions of higher education; by 1900, the figure had climbed to 85,000; and by 1910, to 140,000. As in the Jewish community, some of these women were merely interested in acquiring the refinement of an advanced education. A larger number, however, intended to enter the labor market as self-supporting wage earners, much unlike middle-class Jewish women.[2]

In German Jewish society, a single woman was pitied or even derided. Because of the social mores of the time, the few Jewish women who decided to dedicate their lives to public service and enter the job market generally never married. Such is the case of Julia Richman, an outstanding educator who was active both within and outside the Jewish community and acted as a bridge between the two realms.[3] Other women in this category were: Rebecca Gratz; Rose Sommerfeld, director of the Clara de Hirsch Home for Working Girls (see below); and Henrietta Szold, one of the founders of Hadassah.[4]

Women who arrived in America from Eastern Europe came from a world where education for young girls—except for a smattering of Yiddish so that they could read the women's Bible—had generally been discouraged. This situation changed a bit after 1900 in the Austro-Hungarian Empire, where school attendance became compulsory and free.[5] Parents often felt that too much education might make girls less interested in domestic duties and less desirable as brides. Nonetheless, toward the end of the century, there was an intense awakening of interest among Jewish women to acquire more education, while liberating changes had begun to occur in the surrounding culture. Because religious learning was closed to women, girls focused their interest on secular education, which was becoming increasingly acceptable to parents.[6] By the 1920s, the entire body of Jewish parents had come around to encourage secular education at all levels for all their children.[7]

With a free public school system and free college education in America, these girls and women found a very different world and attitude toward education. Studies have indicated that Eastern European Jewish girls embraced these new opportunities with unqualified enthusiasm. Moreover, secular education in America created true opportunities to enter the job market and for the pursuit of careers. Even among Orthodox Jews, girls often made their way to public schools and found decreasing resistance among their traditional fathers. This growing interest for education among girls soon extended to college training. Fathers often were unable to understand this interest but came to accept it as time passed. Mothers tended to be more sympathetic, especially when their own desire for education had been unrealized.[8] The socialist daily *Forward,* the most influential and popular newspaper among the immigrant community, enthusiastically encouraged education for all.[9]

Vocational courses in dressmaking, sewing, and other subjects were very popular. The learning of English and becoming more Americanized also aroused great interest among young Jewish women. Public lectures, extremely popular on the Lower East Side of New York City, attracted young Jewish working women in droves. These lectures, on an amazing variety of topics, satisfied the learning hunger of many immigrants who had no other way to fill this need. Most cared little what the topics of the lectures were, as long as they could expand their horizons. In 1903–4, more than a million immigrants attended lectures with titles as disparate as "Hegel's Dialectic," "Pictures from Hindu Life," and "How to Breathe." The sponsors of these lectures were the Workmen's Circle, socialists, Zionists, the unions, and many other organizations.[10]

By 1898, there were sixty-one evening elementary schools and four high schools run by the New York City Board of Education.[11] Generally, girls left school before boys during periods of intense immigration and great poverty. Families needed the income of whatever work that these girls could perform. By 1908, there were 100,000 immigrants attending schools in New York City—primary, secondary, and Americanization classes. Forty percent of the female students were Jewish women.[12] Women tried hard to continue their education once that they started working, by attending evening classes; many registered, but attendance was often erratic.[13]

On occasion, women organized themselves in the workplace around educational pursuits, which they attended at night. Some young people who lived together in a commune were among the students who attended the Jewish Workers University, founded by workers who wanted their students to develop a class consciousness. This university encouraged the study of American language and culture as well as of Jewish culture.[14] A much more dramatic demonstration of the sophistication and the political mentality characteristic of the immigrant women was the kosher meat boycott of 1902. The high price of food gave immigrant housewives a vehicle for political organization. They used both traditional and modern tactics in the context of a neighborhood network to stage a successful three-week boycott of kosher meat shops.[15]

Individual teachers were often credited for stimulating the love of learning among immigrant girls. But often, the price to pay was leaving behind all external signs of being Jewish, such as persistent accents, and embrace America and its culture unabashedly.[16] Formal education remained an unreachable goal for many immigrant women, but not so for their children. Yet no other immigrant group had as many sons and daughters in school as did the Jewish community had, and they remained there longer than anyone else.

As the nineteenth century came to an end, German Jewish women launched themselves into an era of unprecedented involvement. The agenda of the benevolent women, mostly of the upper middle class, went beyond self-support and included ideals that were characteristic of nineteenth-century American womanhood. In 1893, in conjunction with the Chicago World's Columbian Exposition, Jewish women held their first congress in an atmosphere of unbridled enthusiasm.[17] Inspired by the innovative work of Rebecca Gratz and Henrietta Szold, the Congress launched an agenda based on three pillars: religion, philanthropy, and education. The organizational outgrowth of the Congress was the National Council of Jewish Women (NCJW).[18] Although the Council never represented the interests of all Jewish women, it did gain a foothold among the middle-class German Jewish community. The NCJW went from ninety-three members at its founding to more than fifty thousand members in 1925.[19] "The Chicago chapter of the Council . . . established a Sabbath school for girls to fill the void left by the traditional Talmud Torah's rejection of religious training for young women. Three hundred girls enrolled immediately."[20] In fact, the NCJW established schools in twenty-nine cities between 1893 and 1896. These schools mainly served immigrant communities, many of them taking in both girls and boys.[21]

While Jewish women had long acted as nurturers, this impulse now evolved into a sophisticated volunteer movement.[22] With plenty of leisure time for charitable work, they founded the first female Jewish benevolent societies and women's clubs. Funds were contributed to education projects, such as kindergartens and night schools. By the 1890s, American women had created for themselves a new stage of life: young womanhood. Jewish women also were part of this new consciousness and searched for useful roles and functions on which to concentrate. At first, membership consisted of young married women, taking care of one another and their own. Later, unmarried ladies were permitted to join. Immigrants, first treated as friends, later became "cases" that had to go through committees for help. Eventually, efforts to "uplift" immigrants were increasingly shot through with condescension. The concept of nurturant benevolence was replaced by more specialized institutions. Selfless charity frequently became unfair moralistic supervision.

With the passage of time, women's clubs moved from instinctive to educated nurturing, offering professionalized nurture not only beyond their social class, but beyond the ethnic community. Women learned how to conduct meetings and study the scientific literature on issues such as education and public health. They were bringing new ideas and organizational skills to the nurture function, partially redefining the relationship of the community to the widening secular world.[23]

New immigrants became a special interest of German Jewish women. They were especially concerned with the problems of the single young working girl.[24] The "immigrant girl problem," as it was called at the time, included prostitution, white slavery, delinquency, "immorality," and father desertion. Homes for working girls were created by rich benefactors. These homes combined boardinghouse and vocational school. Imitating Protestant benevolent women's reform activities, these women were motivated by Jewish communal responsibility, middle-class social control, and sisterhood. They felt that charity and education were their special responsibilities.[25] A more complex analysis of the German Jewish motives argues that "German Jews also took advantage of Americanization and used it as a tool to gain acceptance for themselves."[26]

The Clara de Hirsch Home for Working Girls in New York City, founded in 1897, is illustrative of the reformers' work. The infrastructure was built at a good distance from what these charitable women perceived as the backward and ignorant immigrant community. It was directed by Rose Sommerfeld, a model female settlement-house worker of the late nineteenth century: middle-class, unmarried, and motivated by religious conviction as well as scientific optimism.[27] Jewish girls were trained to enter the marketplace, and this was a great success, according to internal reports. The schedule was rigorous, starting at 6:00 A.M. and ending at 6:30 in the evening. The needle trades provided natural employment for these girls, and they were trained for that profession, but they were also prepared for household duties, expressing the ultimate hopes of the women benefactors who saw piety, purity, domesticity, and submissiveness as the central tenets of true womanhood.[28] There is no question that these homes could often be deeply patronizing. Anzia Yezierska, a great American Jewish writer, lived in the Clara de Hirsch Home for some time. When she mentioned her desire to become a writer to "uptown" German Jewish benefactress Sara Olesheimer, she was discouraged to follow that path and urged instead to train as a cook.[29]

Education in the domestic arts became more prevalent with growing industrialization, even as more women were drawn into the wage-earning workforce. This trend was supported by progressive reformers, educators such as John Dewey, and settlement-house workers. By 1910, support for the professionalization of domestic education had led to strong support for mandatory home economics in the public schools. There was a strong feeling that most women were no longer prepared for the rigors of housewifery.

At a time of increasing shortage of domestic servants in the marketplace, German Jewish women became interested in training Jewish immigrant girls and women for the tasks of household management. Not only could this resolve a big problem, but could also inculcate in the immigrant population the "domestic virtues" that the benefactors thought that they were not acquiring in the tenement environment.[30]

This training was also a subtle method of controlling the sexuality of immigrant females. The German Jewish reformers feared the environment of the sweatshop and garment factory, believing it to be immoral and physically damaging. They were not totally wrong about this. These concerns with sexuality were also expressed in many other ways in the programs at the homes. Girls were given their own individual rooms and were individually supervised. Sex hygiene lectures were also introduced, and strict curfews were enforced. Sex was rarely directly mentioned. Instead, terms such as "moral lapse," "moral resistance," and "immorality" were used. An emphasis on the quality of social life was seen as helpful, thus keeping the girls from seeking pleasure elsewhere.

Leisure activities at the homes included participation in the Girl Scouts, chaperoned visits to museums, concerts, and the theater, physical culture classes, and house productions. The home also offered an alternative to the public dance halls by sponsoring Sunday evening dances. Even during the summer months, an intensive calendar of activities was programmed by the homes, including summer camps, picnics, and campfires, all of which were strictly chaperoned.

Other virtues strongly encouraged by the homes were thrift, diligence, and charity, all encouraged by specific programs. Piety remained an important value in these programs, despite the increasing secularization of Jewish life. Food at the homes was always kosher, despite the fact that German Jews did not live by or understand the laws of kashrut. Most Jewish holidays were observed, and Sabbath was observed in ways comfortable to Reform Judaism. Religious education nonetheless played a minor role in the homes. Some education took place in the nearby Reform synagogues, and the girls did attend High Holiday services. On Saturday mornings, the homes encouraged Bible study.

Domestic service was also a way of struggling against the real dangers of prostitution, a rising issue from the mid-nineteenth century into the immigration period. German Jewish women were instrumental in this struggle. However, this whole effort in education and training toward domestic service was to fail precipitously. Jewish girls overwhelmingly preferred the manufacturing trades because of their independence from social control and higher remunerations.[31]

Despite their commitment to self-support, these German Jewish women reformers deeply believed that work in the marketplace was to be temporary for women, only until the day they got married. The acquisition of skills was seen as the beginning of these girls' ascent out of the working class. Certain tensions persisted in the homes between the objectives of parents who wanted their girls to get to the workplace as soon as possible, and the German reformers who saw the advantages of delaying work for a better education and as a form of controlling sexuality.

Whatever the problems, these homes were a source of security and stability. The German Jewish reformers often acted as substitute families for the girls during this period of adjustment. The good results of this work were shown by well-attended reunions and the return of a number of former trainees and boarders as volunteers in later years. Ultimately, as affluent German Jews sought social integration into the society of their Protestant peers, they imparted "proper" middle-class American womanhood values to their Eastern European kin.[32]

Because they had begun to develop interests and commitments beyond their own homes, in later years Jewish women were to be accused by certain circles of being the cause of the growing tide of assimilation. These accusations reached a feverish pitch during the first quarter of the twentieth century, when club women were expanding their activities most intensely.[33]

Notes

1. Ellen Condliffe Lageman, "Looking at Gender: Women's History," in *Historical Inquiry in Education: A Research Agenda,* ed. John Hardin Best (Washington, D.C.: American Educational Research Association, 1983), 251.

2. Bette Wenek, "Social and Cultural Stratification in Women's Higher Education: Barnard College and Teachers College, 1898–1912," *History of Education Quarterly* 31, no. 1 (spring 1991); Barbara M. Solomon, *In the Company of*

Educated Women: A History of Women and Higher Education in America (New Haven: Yale University Press, 1985), 84.

3. See Selma Berrol, "When Uptown Met Downtown: Julia Richman's Work in the Jewish Community of New York, 1880–1912," *American Jewish History* 70, no. 1 (September 1980).

4. June Sochen, "Some Observations on the Role of American Jewish Women as Communal Volunteers," *American Jewish History* 70, no. 1 (September 1980).

5. Stephan F. Brumberg, *Going to America, Going to School: The Jewish Immigrant Public School Encounter in Turn-of-the-Century New York City* (New York: Praeger, 1986), 47.

6. Sydney Stahl Weinberg, "Longing to Learn: The Education of Jewish Immigrant Women in New York City, 1900–1934," *Journal of American Ethnic History* 8, no. 2 (spring 1989): 109.

7. For example, see Maxine Seller, "The Education of Immigrant Children in Buffalo, New York," *New York History* 62 (April 1976): 198–99.

8. Weinberg, "Longing to Learn," 117.

9. Charlotte Baum, Paula Hyman, and Sonya Michel, *The Jewish Woman in America* (New York: Dial, 1975), 126.

10. Ibid., 121.

11. Selma Berrol, "From Compensatory Education to Adult Education: The New York City Evening Schools, 1825–1935," *Adult Education Quarterly* 26 (summer 1976): 210.

12. Baum et al., *The Jewish Woman in America*, 129.

13. Berrol, "From Compensatory Education to Adult Education," 212.

14. Minnie Fisher, *Born One Year before the Twentieth Century: An Oral History* (New York: Community Documentation Workshop, 1976), 20–25.

15. Paula E. Hyman, "Immigrant Women and the Consumer Protest: The New York City Kosher Meat Boycott of 1902," in *The American Jewish Experience*, ed. Jonathan D. Sarna (New York: Holmes and Meier, 1986), 195.

16. Charles E. Silberman, *A Certain People: American Jews and Their Lives Today* (New York: Summit, 1985), chap. 2, passim.

17. Deborah Grand Golomb, "The 1893 Congress of Jewish Women: Evolution or Revolution in American Jewish Women's History?" *American Jewish History* 70, no. 1 (September 1980): 52.

18. *The American Jewess*, a magazine of short but fruitful life, established in conjunction with the Council, is a good place to follow the developments, ideologies, and daily life of the NCJW and its members during its early years. See Selma Berrol, "Class or Ethnicity: The Americanized German Jewish Woman and Her Middle-Class Sisters in 1895," *Jewish Social Studies* 47, no. 1 (winter 1985).

19. Rebekah Kohut, "Jewish Women's Organizations in the United States," *American Jewish Year Book, 1931–32* (Philadelphia, 1933), 178. By 1895, seven German Jewish women founded the Atlanta chapter of the NCJW, the first Atlanta

women's organization to affiliate nationally. The Council worked in aiding the newly arrived immigrants with educational programs, provisions of food and clothing, and financial assistance. See Beth S. Wenger, "Jewish Women of the Club: The Changing Public Role of Atlanta's Jewish Women (1870–1930)," *American Jewish History* 76, no. 3 (March 1987): 314–15.

20. Sochen, "Some Observations on the Role of American Jewish Women as Communal Volunteers," 26.

21. Faith Rogow, *Gone to Another Meeting: The National Council of Jewish Women, 1893–1993* (Tuscaloosa, Ala.: University of Alabama Press, 1993), 258 n. 133.

22. Beth S. Wenger, "Jewish Women and Voluntarism: Beyond the Myth of Enablers," *American Jewish History* 79, no. 1 (autumn 1989): 16–17.

23. William Toll, "A Quiet Revolution: Jewish Women's Clubs and the Widening Female Sphere, 1870–1920," *American Jewish Archives* 4, no. 1 (spring/summer 1989): 7–26.

24. Nancy B. Sinkoff, "Educating for 'Proper' Jewish Womanhood: A Case Study in Domesticity and Vocational Training, 1897–1926," *American Jewish History* 77, no. 4 (June 1988): 572–73.

25. Wenger, "Jewish Women of the Club," 314–15.

26. Seth Korelitz, " 'A Magnificent Piece of Work': The Americanization Work of the National Council of Jewish Women," *American Jewish History* 83, no. 2 (June 1995): 201.

27. Allen F. Davis, *Spearheads for Reform: The Social Settlements and the Progressive Movement, 1890–1914* (New York: Oxford University Press, 1967), 34.

28. Barbara Welter, "The Cult of True Womanhood: 1820–1860," in *The American Family in Social Historical Perspective,* ed. Michael Gordon (New York: St. Martin's, 1973), 224–50.

29. Mary V. Dearborn, "Anzia Yezierska and the Making of an Ethnic American Self," in *The Invention of Ethnicity,* ed. Werner Sollors (New York: Oxford University Press, 1989), 110.

30. Sinkoff, "Educating for 'Proper' Jewish Womanhood," 583.

31. Alice Kessler-Harris, *Out to Work: A History of Wage-Earning Women in the United States* (New York: Oxford University Press, 1982), 127.

32. Sinkoff, "Educating for 'Proper' Jewish Womanhood," 597–98.

33. Paula Hyman, "The Modern Jewish Family: Image and Reality," in *The Jewish Family: Metaphor and Memory,* ed. David Kraemer (New York: Holmes and Meier, 1986), 188–90.

A Military Model of Jewish Education*

David Resnick

> There is a war to wage against the vulgar, against the glorification of the absurd, a war that is incessant, universal. Loyal to the presence of the ultimate in the common, we may be able to make it clear that man is more than man, that in doing the finite he may perceive the infinite.
>
> *A. J. Heschel*[1]

Writing when the wounds of World War II were still raw, Heschel transmutes the clash of combatants to a struggle between worldviews. Viewing life as a battle has a hoary lineage, from the Book of Psalms to Hamlet's "slings and arrows of outrageous fortune." Among the most ancient Jewish metaphors is God as warrior (Exod. 15:3) and the Jewish people as His troops (Exod. 12:41).[2] The metaphor is not relegated to the margins of Jewish thought; the observant Jew confronts it as a central part of each morning's prayer, with echoes throughout the daily liturgy. In trying to make sense of Jewish life in the contemporary world, pursuing the image of the Jewish people as an army may yield unusual insights with educational implications. This exploration is

David Resnick is Senior Lecturer in the School of Education at Bar Ilan University.

*I have not had the privilege of serving in the armed forces. Therefore, much of what I have written here has been cherry-picked from hither and yon. Inspiration for the model came from my son's experience during his Israeli Navy officers' training course. As always, the assistance of Professor Michael Rosenak was invaluable.

based on Ramsey's[3] analysis of theological models and Scheffler's[4] of educational metaphors. Scheffler maintains that metaphors are akin to educational theories and are an invitation to search for meaning, rather than a forthright statement of those meanings. Ramsey points out that models of God help us grasp complex realities, and therefore—particularly for theological issues—a single model will not suffice. Thus, I have elsewhere proposed additional models for Jewish education.[5]

While a military metaphor may seem far-fetched or even distasteful, the reality of wars and armies is still with us, and the usefulness of a metaphor is judged by the insights it can yield, not its initial appeal. As for unease with the image of God as warrior, even in ancient times the metaphor grated. Hence Rashi's comment (drawn from the Mekhilta) on verse 15:3b ("God is a Warrior, *God is His name*"): "Even when He avenges and battles His enemies, He cleaves to His tendency to have mercy on His creatures and to sustain all of earth's inhabitants. Not like earthly kings, who when engaged in war divert themselves from all other pursuits, lacking the capacity to pursue both." Samson Raphael Hirsch, perhaps also troubled, puts the metaphor in the best possible light:

> God, the One who sees to it that a new, better future shall come for mankind, is on that very account a man of war. He fights down every social force in humanity that stands in the way of His plan for this better future. . . . The path that leads to the ultimate happy solution to the problem of life can only lead via destruction of the bad and evil.

In exploring a military model of Jewish life, I am not promoting a militaristic[6] Judaism. I am searching for parallels in human culture that can shed light on our current situation, with implications for education. A military model may be apt precisely because life is a struggle: "Life is lived on a spiritual battlefield. Man must constantly struggle with 'the evil drive,' for man is like unto a rope, one end of which is pulled by God and the other end by Satan."[7]

The military has recently been rehabilitated in the popular media (e.g., the film *Saving Private Ryan*), after a generation of antiwar films based on the Vietnam experience (*Platoon, The Deer Slayer, Apocalypse Now,* and others). The rehabilitation is not happenstance. Perhaps contemporary culture has become dissatisfied with unbounded individual-

ism, seeking instead models of pride in service to others, even of martyr-
dom. Indeed, *Ryan* is a film framed by a pilgrimage to the grave of a
World War II martyr. The Gulf War and Kosovo action are also widely
regarded as justified military interventions and have restored some balance to the discussion of war and related issues.

The Parallel

The basic situation of armies and of the Jewish people strikes me as similar. Each is an artificial organization created (Isa. 43:21) to have an impact on the real world in arenas largely beyond its control. Like most
organizations, each is defined by its goal, which, in this case, is securing
and maintaining life and peace. An army's means is violence, actual or
threatened. Yet military goals are usually restorative or status quo, except in cases of outright aggression. Western religions can also be aggressive, seeking to redeem the world through faith and works
("Onward Christian soldiers marching as to war"), regaining some
Edenic state.

   The biblical portrayal of the founding of the Jewish people fits this
paradigm, both for its overall goal and for the life of the individual "soldier." Abram's response to his initial commission by God is silent obedience (Gen. 12:4). He is told that the new nation will be a blessing to
humanity, but is given no specifics. The paradoxical goal of the nation
emerges in Abraham's contestation with God over the destruction of
Sodom: "For I have singled him out, that he may command [!] his children and his posterity to keep the way of the Lord by doing what is just
and right" (Gen. 18:19a). Abraham is obedient in the face of adversity,
yet the moral nature of his divine commission impels him to challenge
God itself. Thus, he is the heroic archetype of the loyal soldier who is
also willing to question the orders of his superiors on moral grounds.

   For Judaism to realize its moral goals and for an army to achieve its
strategic goals, both utilize a comprehensive culture to unify and motivate their adherents: frequent ritual, uniforms (mutual identification
and marking-off from other units and armies), hierarchic leadership, education, and ceremonies to build loyalty based on tradition (*Semper Fi-
delis*). Indeed, Abraham's remonstration with God is immediately
preceded by a double-edged circumcision: to create a covenant with
God is to separate oneself physically from the other nations among

whom one will do "what is just and right." Yet when a conflict arises between the ritual means to group cohesion and the moral goal of Jewish life, ritual almost always yields to morality. Moreover, contemporary anthropological analysis of Jewish ritual (e.g., Mary Douglas on kashrut) shows that it reinforces core religious values, rather than being merely an arbitrary system of building in-group identity at the expense of an out-group.

The formative desert experience of the Jewish people was a military one. The desert camp is set up on a military model, and the frequent censuses are for the purpose of a draft.[8] Yet the Levites are exempted from fighting, even as they are counted and conscripted to a higher service:

> Why did the tribe of Levi not merit a portion in the Land of Israel and in the spoils of its conquest with the other tribes? Because they were separated to serve God and to teach His upright ways and righteous laws to the multitudes. As the verse states: "They shall teach your laws to Jacob and your statutes to Israel" (Deut. 33:10). Therefore, they are separated from the ways of the world. They do not wage war like the rest of the tribes nor do they acquire a portion in the land or provide for their own sustenance. Rather they are the army of God, as the verse states: "God will bless His army" (Deut. 33:11). God provides for them, as it states: "I am your portion and inheritance" (Num. 18:20). (Rambam, *Mishneh Torah*, Shemitta and Yovel, 13:12)

The Rambam here is positing two parallel Jewish armies: one of the body and one of the spirit. What characterizes both is loyalty and dedication, even unto death. Walzer explores the implication of the Levites as a vanguard: "The people, dreaming of milk and honey, are materialists; Moses and the Levites, dreaming of holiness, are idealists."[9] He goes on to show that the Levites represent a very this-worldly spirituality, one in which economic comfort can only result from social and political justice (the redeeming of the world mentioned above). Moreover, the long-term goal is to turn the entire people into a nation of priests. The social and educational challenges of an army segmented into masses and elites is an issue to which we will return below.

The common ground between armies and the Jewish people includes not only their origins and current operation, but also their distant futures. Isaiah's hope (2:4) for total military disarmament is one of the defining visions of the end of days. Disarmament follows on the heels of a universal acknowledgment of God's kingship (45:23), which also has consequences for the Jewish people. The Jews become one among a family of blessed nations (19:23–25), and there is movement to restore the unified humanity of primeval times (Zeph. 3:9). Some rabbinic sources envision the cancellation of holidays that celebrate the uniqueness of Jewish history (cf. *Torah Temima* to Esther 9:28). Utopian strains of Jewish messianic thought entertain the abolishment of other positive commandments,[10] as a new reality obviates the need for a separate Jewish vanguard.

This thumbnail sketch of the common ground between the Jewish people and a military organization points to the challenge facing Jewish life in the modern, self-centered world, summarized in the query, "Why bother to join a particularist group that imposes uncomfortable obligations on me when its utopian goal (were I to accept it) might better be achieved by a more universal, less demanding regimen?" This is the query with which recruiters (for the Jewish community and the military) must contend, though their appeals to past group glory and current personal benefits are only partly successful.

Surprising Insights

Methodologically, the value of the modeling method is the surprising insights generated by the playing out of the *mashal*. I shall explore three such instances: the high-alert squad; the problem of authority (and related issues); and the experience of organizational life.

The High-Alert Squad

A regular part of army life is the high-alert squad. In every base and bivouac, one group is designated to be on high alert, to respond to surprise attack. The squad is briefed on likely threats and then assumes the (uncomfortable) readiness stance (e.g., sleeping fully dressed, including boots). The notion of "being ready for anything" is fictional, as troops are trained and focused for particular kinds of action. To a large degree, we perceive that which we are primed to perceive,[11] and military disasters (e.g., the Yom Kippur War) sometimes arise from disregarding signals that do not conform to expectations.

We have already seen that the Jewish people understand themselves to be a high-alert squad: to act justly and morally in the world. They have committed themselves in advance to act in situations when others might not. What constitutes the briefing of this Jewish squad, the priming for perception and appropriate action? One part of the daily morning prayers appears to fulfill that function:

> These are the things whose fruits a person enjoys in this world, while the principal remains for him in the world to come, namely: honoring father and mother, practice of kindness, early attendance at the *beit midrash* morning and evening, hospitality to strangers, visiting the sick, dowering the bride, attending the dead to the grave, devotion in prayer, and making peace between people. But the study of Torah equals them all. (Mishnah *Pe'ah* 1:1)

The recitation of this list early each day places the individual Jew on high alert to key areas of personal responsibility. Moreover, within the communities of the committed, each Jew can look to others to help in the fulfillment of these shared tasks. The challenge of remaining on high alert for long periods of time (known in perceptual psychology as the problem of vigilance; see n. 11) is itself included in the briefing list in an almost ironic way: devotion in prayer.

The Problem of Authority

Armies are surely the prime example of "top-down" institutions. Classical Judaism, too, is hierarchical. While ultimate authority rests in God, the tradition is mediated through authoritative texts, rabbinic leaders, or (at a minimum) local custom. Yet the modern spirit of individualism undercuts traditional social organizations such as religions, and also ushered in the era of the volunteer army. Thus, some contemporary streams of Judaism have made individual choice their hallmark, and army recruitment puts the emphasis on self-fulfillment ("Be all you can be") rather than dedicated service. Practically speaking, all Jews in the modern world are liberated, with whatever religious authority exists being self-imposed. While that may be salutary for individual religious sentiment, it is problematic for effective group life. In terms of demographics, individualism has allowed Jews to opt out of the Jewish community, just as the volunteer army has left the military understaffed. Both groups have responded to shrinking numbers by lowering standards, further compromising their effectiveness.

Related to the issue of authority are subsidiary issues of: leadership and group structure; motivation and initiative; and autonomy and individual responsibility.

Leadership and group structure. The old saw that "generals always fight the previous war" highlights the irrelevance—even harm—of traditional leadership out of touch with the demands of contemporary life. Yet experienced leadership means precisely mastery of prior challenges. From a social-science point of view, Campbell[12] asserts that classical religions are the best equipped—because they are the most experienced—to deal with enduring personal and social dilemmas. But that does not ensure their ability to deal effectively with future challenges. Hence, the dilemma of wise leadership is how to preserve the best of the past in the service of the present and future. The era of nuclear weapons and ICBMs might have done away with training troops for traditional infantry and air combat. Current "brush wars" demonstrate the need for preserving traditional skills while developing new capabilities.

Leadership implies functioning in group settings. Indeed, effective human endeavor requires group action. Yet the current Zeitgeist is anti-group, radically individualistic. Even military movies are made from an individualistic point of view, promoting the mistaken notion of a "one-man army" (the Rambo and Schwarzenegger archetypes). There is a profound need to reeducate for the value of group living, even as it compromises individualism to a certain degree. There is a paradoxical loss of individual freedom for those who struggle to guarantee group freedom: "The soldiers who do the fighting . . . lose the rights they are supposedly defending. . . . Whatever their private hopes and intentions, they have lost their title to life and liberty, and they have lost it even though, unlike aggressor states, they have committed no crime."[13] This is precisely the situation of the Jewish people, though it does not sit well with modern sensibilities: "For they are my servants, whom I freed from the land of Egypt; they may not give themselves over into servitude" (Lev. 25:42)—not to others or to themselves. The same paradox of freedom exists in most social (including educational) contexts, where some freedom is traded away in order to gain protection from coercion.[14]

The expected—indeed, demanded—self-sacrifice of soldiers to fulfill their mission is a *sine qua non* of military life. "It is not by chance that we define completing the mission as the ultimate value, and preserving the lives of the soldiers as second in importance. Otherwise, why ever take the offensive? Why endanger life at all?"[15] The religious parallel is the *akedah*, the fundamental acknowledgment that human life is meaningful only when it is, at least potentially, sacrificed for the highest good, *al kiddush hashem*. What can redress the imbalance of excess individualism is the realization that even individual fulfillment requires a group setting and values that transcend the individual. In other words, education for commitment to extra-personal values may be the only ultimate basis for individual meaning.[16]

Motivation. With individualism and volunteerism compromising both hierarchic leadership models and group cohesion, the problem of motivation is a key concern in the army, especially the volunteer army. Ordinarily, we assume that soldiers are motivated by the carrots of loyalty and honor, and the stick of coercion. General Yom Tov Samya,[17] discussing motivation in the Israeli army, asserted that loyalty to broad ideals and slogans may be useful in the regular course of military life, but motivation in combat is based on cohesion with one's own unit and officers.

So, too, in Jewish life. "We Are One" and broad slogans are fine for ceremonial occasions, but compelling loyalty in the day-to-day demands of Judaism are rooted in the network of family, rebbe, and congregation (or perhaps even more effectively, the *havurah*). "We do not wage war with evil in the name of an abstract concept of duty. We do the good not because it is a value or because of expediency, but because we owe it to God."[18] While Heschel articulates the highest level of religious commitment, Joseph Lukinsky once remarked that the theology we talk at the grass-roots level is Reconstructionist, i.e., socially based. But the very engine of motivation from intimate subunits contains within it the seeds of narrow loyalties and interservice rivalries. This is an issue to which we shall return.

Autonomy and individual responsibility. In an age that believes that individual autonomy is the highest moral value, it follows that the heroes of military films are those who challenge the chain of command (*Crimson Tide, Outbreak*); and the victims, those who do not (*A Few Good Men*). The conflict between autonomy and social duty is well summarized in Berger's analysis of "the obsolescence of the concept of honor":

The social location of honor lies in a world of relatively intact, stable institutions, a world in which individuals can with subjective certainty attach their identities to the institutional roles that society assigns to them. The disintegration of this world as a result of the forces of modernity has not only made honor an increasingly meaningless notion, but has served as the occasion for a redefinition of identity and its intrinsic dignity apart from and often against the institutional roles through which the individual expresses himself in society. . . . Institutions cease to be the "home" of the self; instead they become oppressive realities that distort and estrange the self.[19]

No wonder that military and religious institutions find themselves irrelevant to daily life. "At best, honor and chastity are seen as ideological leftovers in the consciousness of obsolete classes, such as military officers or ethnic grandmothers."[20]

In this post-Holocaust era, we are rightfully sensitive to the dangers of "just following orders." On the other hand, what armies are all about is following orders, and feeling honorable for having done so. In rabbinic terms: "Said Rabbi Hanina: more worthy is the person who is commanded and acts than the person who is not commanded and acts" (*Kiddushin* 31a). This complex issue is analyzed in detail in Walzer's *Just and Unjust Wars* (especially chapter 19, on war crimes) with one detail especially relevant to our situation: "Ignorance is the common lot of the common soldier."[21] We usually make individual acts meaningful by placing them in a larger framework, but the ordinary soldier (and honorable individual) must often take the framework on faith.

The problem of individual responsibility in a hierarchic system has its parallel in religious life. Reform Judaism has resolved the problem by abolishing the hierarchy. Orthodox life has a tendency to defer individual responsibility to the ruling of a rebbe or a *gadol*. Both extremes are misguided. While this kind of top-down mentality seems to fit army life, no individual can forfeit his personal responsibility, nor can a "blindered" organization long endure.

The Experience of Army Life

Up to this point, the analysis has been from an institutional point of view, and the central issue has been how individuals can be persuaded (educated) to serve the needs of the larger organization. Thus, military education is primarily socialization, leading soldiers to emulate, or at least obey, their superiors. The well-being of the soldiers is not an intrinsic value, except as it affects performance. The Israeli army does articulate to concerned parents that it appreciates having been entrusted with the parents' most prized possession. But as the army makes clear to its soldiers, the mission comes first; soldiers' welfare, second. The purpose of basic training is to unlearn the habits of civilian life—to break down the individual—in order to create fighting units. The genre of boot-camp movies well illustrates this process (GI Jane).

Likewise, criticism of the dehumanizing effect of educational settings has been a central part of contemporary educational literature. Education and Ecstasy[22] is merely the update of Dickens's Hard Times. Hand-wringing over violence in high schools is evenly divided between those who see it rooted in the inhumanity of the schools themselves, and those who see it imported from the surrounding culture. In a disturbing parallel, the failure of school or army to sustain individuals often results in violent deaths, and because of easy access to firearms, we have mass killings in high schools and suicide in the army.

Two educational challenges arise from the problematic place of individuals in army life. First, in the long run, armies do not want soldiers who are robots. Certainly at the officer level, they want what is known in the Israeli army as rosh gadol: the willingness and ability to be proactive; to modify a battle plan in light of changed conditions; and to show initiative. This cluster of traits is essentially identical to Rosenak's[23] "language/literature" distinction, in which preserving classical values requires adapting them to new circumstances, but only by those who have thoroughly internalized the value structure.

Second, there is the challenge of the "peacetime army." This issue has many ramifications, mostly in terms of motivation. Soldiers may be willing to learn skills that they do not actually use, especially if the price of using them is risking their lives in combat. If they are draftees, their army service is a passing phase in their life, understood to be unrelated to real, civilian life. Much of contemporary educational thought grapples with the problems arising from the disjuncture of institutionalized education from "real life." For schoolchildren, the disjuncture is doubled, as they are both isolated from outside daily life and "segregated" in their youth culture. For religious education, the situation is even more severe. The attempt to teach information and skills (let alone "values") that are irrelevant to real life all but dooms the enterprise to disaster from the outset.[24] Thus, recent attempts at improving Jewish education have moved in the direction of bridging the gap between school and life.[25]

One final, critical aspect of the experiential parallel is the degree to which the individual student/soldier can come to feel pride in service. "Pride in one's unit" is standard army fare, with the understanding that it involves more giving than taking. In Jewish education, mere "belonging" may not be enough. Dedication to goals that transcend the self are what make group life sustainable and self-reinforcing, without which individual life, too, soon withers.

The Educational Challenge

Battlefield imagery of education ("back to the trenches"; "combat pay") "conveys a sense that conflict, hostility, and aggressive action are a normal and expected part of school and classroom life."[26] I have already mentioned the deleterious effects of authoritarian models of school life drawn from the worst of military life. (The British film *If . . .* includes them both.) But I prefer to focus on constructive insights that might be gleaned from the comparison.

Loyalty and Dedication

Jewish education has an inescapable dimension of group life and identity. Indeed, some have defined the creation of *kehillot kodesh* as the essential goal of Jewish life and education. Thus, a slogan such as "war on Jewish illiteracy" or campaigns to "save the Jewish people" ring true. Behind them stands the military notion of *devekut bamesima* ("total commitment to the task"), which has its literal parallel in the religious term *devekut* ("clinging") (cf. the parallel in the liturgy, "but you who *held fast* to the Lord your God, are all alive today," Deut. 4:4). The ability to "rally the troops" in service of a worthy goal, thereby creating enduring interpersonal bonds, is the key to success in most educational work, formal and informal. While the Lubavitch approach of "the armies of the Lord" (replete with mitzvah tanks) is often regarded with derision, no one gainsays their absolute devotion to the cause of Jewish education and their admirable sense of urgency.

Likewise, Jewish education will be preoccupied with inculcating loyalty and dedication to ways of Jewish life that can inspire and motivate, especially because it is a variety of minority education. In this regard, the differences between Jewish ways and other ways need not be minimized, so a conflict model (e.g., versus cults) does hold to a certain extent. While we may phrase our educational goals in the positive ("Renaissance," continuity), unless we can mark off our differences from other groups, we will cease to exist. Our saving grace is that while we value maintaining our separateness, we also acknowledge that our corps is just one division in the army of the Lord. How to balance these conflicting demands is the issue to which I now turn.

In/Out Groups

A military approach also has educational downsides. I have already indicated that generating in-group loyalty is often at the expense of solidarity with other units. In the Israeli army, combat troops regard noncombat *jobnikim* with near-derision, and there are differential benefits for combat soldiers. This conflict is inherent whenever a social organization relies on elites, as all must to some extent. Education for tolerance, to see the contribution that all make to the common cause, is a clear consequence of this situation. "Have we not all one father? Did not one God create us? Why do we break faith with one another, profaning the covenant of our fathers?" (Mal. 2:10). The same need for tolerance holds for those groups in opposition to us. The tendency in war is to demonize the enemy. The biblical response (at least, after the dust has settled) is: "You shall not abhor an Egyptian, for you were a stranger in his land" (Deut. 23:8). In sum, the real-life pressures of military/religious education may lead to indoctrinatory practices, as Rosenak[27] has shown. But education for loyalty *and* tolerance ought to be possible, even if difficult.

The dilemma of creating vanguards has already been mentioned in the context of intra-group tension. Framing a meaningful role for those who cannot be part of the vanguard is the consequent challenge. Perhaps the notion of "weekend warriors" is apposite, akin to the army reserve who do their share in a scaled-down way. There should also be adjunct formats for people who are unable (or unwilling) to make a full-time commitment to Jewish community but are looking for a meaningful way to identify with and contribute to the cause. The various soldier-support organizations (USO, *Va'ad Lema'an Hachayal*) come to mind.

Breakdown of the Analogy

At some point, every analogy breaks down, and it is important to note the differences between Jewish living and army life. This applies especially to the essential nature of the two groups. "But the army is an organization, not a community, and the communion of ordinary soldiers is shaped by the character and purposes of the organization, not by their private commitments. . . . [U]nity is reflexive, not intentional or premeditated."[28] Army life is characterized by a loss of freedom and constrained responsibility. In arguing for the importance of group religious life and the sacrifices it requires, I have so far omitted a key factor that characterized Jewish life from the beginning of the covenant at Sinai: it was a covenant accepted by free agents, which continued to rely on free agents to implement it.

Likewise, I have stressed the need for loyalty to the group as it strives to achieve its goals. But for Judaism, there is a value higher than group loyalty, and that is the quest to realize God's goodness on earth. The case of the *zaken mamreh* (Deut. 17:12) well illustrates this tension, where freedom of conscience is guaranteed, even if not full freedom to act on that conviction. "Loyalty versus quest for the good introduced an unresolvable tension into life. But the awareness of the good as such and the desire to possess it are priceless humanizing acquisitions."[29] In Jewish life, that unresolvable tension is the prophetic tradition, calling not for the dissolving of group life, but for its reform. Restoring loyalty to the group (with the caveats just mentioned) and the quest for the good may well be the two overarching goals for modern Jewish education.

Finally, the analogy breaks down because "warrior" is only one among many metaphors for God in the Bible. Some are more pacific ("shepherd"); others, more stern ("Judge of all the earth"). Ramsey cites nineteen biblical metaphors for God and analyzes them.

Afterword in Appreciation of Joe

I hope that this analysis of Jewish education has some resonance with Joe's own experience as an army chaplain. From what he has shared with me, his role was very much one of trying to preserve individual dignity in the face of the military machine, which is a problem that I acknowledged for this model. At an early point in my career, Joe helped redirect my work in the paths that it has subsequently taken. As always, he was much more shepherd than sergeant.

Notes

1. Abraham Joshua Heschel, closing words of *The Earth Is the Lord's* (New York: Harper, 1962).
2. The phrase "the troops [or "ranks," NJPS] of the Lord" applied to the Jewish people, rather than the heavenly host, is a rare one. The Lubavitch appropriation of the rare usage warrants further study.
3. Ian Ramsey, "Talking about God: Models, Ancient and Modern," in *Myth and Symbol,* ed. F. W. Dillistone (London: SPCK, 1966).
4. Israel Scheffler, *The Language of Education* (Springfield, Ill.: Charles Thomas, 1966).
5. See David Resnick, "Jewish Education as Third World Education," in *Proceedings of the 12th World Congress of Jewish Studies,* 1997, Division E (2001): 115–22.
6. There have been periods in history when Jews longed for the warrior God to appear. To ask, "Where was God at Auschwitz?" means, in part, where was the warrior God to bomb railway tracks or—better—rout the Nazis outright, as He did the Egyptians. The heartrending *kinah* for Tishah b'Av (*Amarti sh'u*) by Kolonymous Bar Yehuda, who witnessed the slaughter of European Jews in 1096, cries out, "Thus you are called 'man of war'/Your foes to destroy and on them to wreak revenge/God who revenges and is angered." The psalm for Wednesdays (94) echoes the same sentiment: "God of vengeance, Lord, God of vengeance, appear!/Rise up, judge of the earth, give the arrogant their deserts!"
7. Abraham Joshua Heschel, *God in Search of Man* (New York: Harper, 1955), 366.
8. Jacob Milgrom, *Numbers* (Philadelphia: Jewish Publication Society, 1990).
9. Michael Walzer, *Exodus and Revolution* (New York: Basic, 1985), 103.
10. Gershom Scholem, *The Messianic Idea in Judaism* (New York: Schocken, 1974).
11. Howard Egeth and Steven Yantis, "Visual Attention," in *Annual Review of Psychology* 48 (1997): 269–97.
12. See Donald Campbell, "On the Conflicts between Biological and Social Evolution and between Psychology and Moral Tradition," *American Psychologist* 30 (1975): 1103–26.
13. See Michael Walzer, *Just and Unjust Wars* (New York: Basic, 1977), 136.
14. R. S. Peters, *Ethics and Education* (London: George Allen, 1970).
15. Gadi Eizenkot, *Haaretz Magazine,* 10 September 1999, 32 (in Hebrew).
16. Charles Taylor, *The Ethics of Authenticity* (Cambridge: Harvard University Press, 1991).

17. Yom Tov Samya, lecture at Bar Ilan University, 11 May 1999.

18. Heschel, *God in Search of Man,* 376.

19. Peter Berger et al., *The Homeless Mind* (New York: Random House, 1973), 93.

20. Ibid., 83.

21. Walzer, *Just and Unjust Wars,* 312.

22. George Leonard, *Education and Ecstasy* (New York: Delta, 1968).

23. Michael Rosenak, *Roads to the Palace* (Providence: Berghahn, 1995), 246–47.

24. John D'Amato, "The Belly of the Beast: On Cultural Differences, Castelike Status, and the Politics of School Life," *Anthropology & Education Quarterly* 18 (1987): 357–60.

25. Isa Aron et al., *A Congregation of Learners: Transforming the Synagogue into a Learning Community* (New York: UAHC, 1995).

26. See Phillip Schlechty and Anne Joslin, "Images of schools," *Teachers College Record* 86 (1984): 160.

27. Michael Rosenak, "Jewish Religious Education and Indoctrination," *Studies in Jewish Education* 1 (1983): 117–38.

28. Walzer, *Just and Unjust Wars,* 15.

29. Allan Bloom, *The Closing of the American Mind* (New York: Simon and Schuster, 1987), 38.

Rabbi Eliyahu E. Dessler:
A Philosopher of Haredi Education

Michael Rosenak

Must Contemporary Jews Be Modern?

It is surprising that ultraorthodox thinkers have been so thoroughly ignored by Jewish educational scholars, and this despite the phenomenal growth of *haredi* education, in Israel and in the Diaspora. This may be attributed in part to a modern distaste for the hagiographical style of much ultraorthodox biography and the subsequent inclination to view the subjects of such treatment as themselves unworthy of attention.[1] But this neglect reflects substantive prejudgments as well; such writings are deemed too irrelevant, or discomforting to be of interest to the academic community and to the mainstream Jewish communities that are the significant frames of reference of these academicians.

This neglect of interest seems unjustified. *Haredi* beliefs, religious practices, and social norms unambiguously shape the Jewish education of increasing numbers of Jews. These beliefs and norms and the educational approaches (hasidic, Lithuanian-yeshiva-oriented, and others) that flow from them have been astoundingly successful in achieving their stated aims, certainly in comparison with other, more moderate, ideologically modern ones. It is true that many of the premises of this *haredi* worldview and many of the policies that translate it into practice are specifically and polemically directed against modernity and modern Jews. But scholars who pride themselves on their academic perspective can hardly decline to study them on the grounds that they are offended by them.

Michael Rosenak is the Mandel Professor of Jewish Education Emeritus at the School of Education, the Hebrew University of Jerusalem.

Moreover, from a strictly programmatic perspective, the educational Jewish world cannot afford to neglect *haredi* thought. It seems sensible to relate seriously, even if critically, to all available models for Jewish education—perhaps to discover that there is something to be learned from them, perhaps only to understand why, and to whom, they are unacceptable. Certainly, *haredi* thought, no less than that of thinkers such as Buber, Kaplan, Soloveitchik, and Rosenzweig, arises out of Jewish experience and reflection. The *haredi* antimodern ideology, then, should be studied to enable modern Jews to better understand their own commitments and to provide them with a lever for useful self-criticism.

All *haredi* thought makes fundamental assumptions that sets it off from what is termed "modern" consciousness and sensibility. Among these fundamental assumptions:

a) The liberation of most aspects of life (work, love, art, social relations, interests, and private pursuits) from their former subjection to the comprehensive and exclusive rule of religion should be understood not as a process leading to beneficial change or enlightenment, but as a rebellion against the sovereign reign of God.[2] This rebellion is a valuative decision on the part of modern people to replace the sovereignty of God with idolatrous substitutes such as the state or the individual; this "throwing off the yoke of the kingdom of Heaven" is the source and substance of modern culture. Hence, modernity as such is a negative and spiritually nocuous phenomenon, antagonistic to the service of God (religion) in principle. At best, the philosophers and other architects of modernity have permitted religion to take a ceremonial place *beside* culture. More commonly, they have constructed cultures that simply chained religion and made it into a pathetically reduced, "harmless" adjunct of culture itself.

This liberation of culture from religion must be confronted and combated at every turn. The loyal Jewish community, to which the teaching to serve God alone was originally revealed, must be rebuilt, strengthened, and, generally, segregated. Where the rule of Torah (halakhah, rabbinic authority, study of Torah in line with the curriculum set by authorities) obtains, there is no need for compartmentalization (between the holy and the profane) or inte-

gration (between the world of Torah and culture). The profane (i.e., non-Torah) studies should be elementary and instrumental. Promising scholars will, at the discretion of
their teachers, study what these mentors deem useful for
those who are destined for leadership.[3] Integration is inad-
missible to begin with, for culture corrodes Torah, and that
must be kept away from the faithful.

b) All real wisdom resides in the words of the Sages, for their
teachings wholly articulate the divine Torah. This wisdom is
absolute and unchanging. Hence, when it is profoundly understood, even by latter-day sages, it remains what it always
was: eternal truth. Even contemporary sages are therefore
endowed with the authority of the talmudic Sages, though
they exercise appropriate modesty in considering themselves
much inferior to the former ones. All other (alleged) manifestations of wisdom are either pretentious foolishness or
pedagogically useful reformulations of the wisdom expressed by the Sages. The reformulations may indeed make
use of contemporary theories and conceptions, if rabbinic
authorities find them congenial to Torah.

The need for (sometimes belligerent) confrontation of
Jewish truth with foolishness, on the one hand, and for the
qualified use of modern rhetoric, on the other hand, both
follow from the fact that authentic Jewish life in modern society is actually and always at war with secularism. This is a
commanded war, for secular culture is ultimately the modern manifestation of idolatry. Wishing to win, or at least to
hold its own, the Jewish (i.e., *haredi*) side may use weapons
from the enemy's arsenal at the discretion of its leadership,
and employed according to its precise instructions.

c) All attempts to take non-Torah realms that are in conflict
with Torah seriously and to synthesize them with Torah are
mistaken and dangerous, for they are based on the admission, whether through confusion or perversity, that the
enemy is partly right, that there is genuine value beyond the
comprehensive and absolute truth of Torah. This applies
even to such notions as *Torah im derekh eretz*. These are, at
best, pedagogical devices for saving what can be saved in
specific historical situations (*hora'at sha'a*).[4] At worst, they
are insidious denials of rabbinic authority and leadership.

d) Jewish life is ideally organic, with the highest rungs in the social hierarchy reserved for scholars of the Torah, whose highest institutional reflection is the yeshiva and its world. In this organic society, the individual is judged by his or her ability to accept the social order and to learn how to live happily and spiritually within it.

Of course, the hypothetical acceptance of each or any of these premises by mainstream Jewish education would significantly change and undo its modern thrust and agenda. This education is constantly preoccupied with the issue of integration (between Jewish tradition and modernity). It takes worldly wisdom with utmost seriousness and sees higher education as an entry into profound understanding as well as worthy competence. It invests heavily in change, which is generally viewed as the self-understood way to solve problems that inevitably arise in life, presenting challenges to ingenuity and inviting inquiry by persons of diverse competencies. And the organic character of premodern life, the Jewish included, is constantly being tempered or phased out; hence the ongoing efforts to achieve equality between the sexes, to rethink Jewish-Gentile relations, and to replace institutional authority with autonomy and the demands of conscience.

Our subject here is one central aspect of the educational thinking of Rabbi Eliyahu Eliezer Dessler, a prominent teacher and spiritual leader within the ultraorthodox world of the first half of the twentieth century. R. Dessler emigrated in the late 1920s from his native Lithuania to London, where he served several communities as rabbi, developing a coterie of students who became his ardent disciples. During World War II, he built the *kollel* (graduate study program) of the Gateshead yeshiva in northern England, helping to make Gateshead a center of Orthodox learning and life. After the war, he accepted a call to serve as *mashgiah ruhani* (spiritual guide) at the Ponovicz yeshiva, by then situated in B'nai Brak, Israel. In the years before his death, his fame as a thinker of the yeshiva world and of the contemporary *mussar* movement grew apace.[5] As Schweid has shown,[6] Rabbi Dessler's thought and educational activity constituted an explicit response to the Holocaust, a single-minded attempt to rebuild the shattered world of Eastern European Jewish learning and, in effect, a refusal to accept that the yeshiva world had been irreversibly destroyed.

R. Dessler's activities included constant traveling (to raise funds for the Gateshead institutions, including the Girls' Teacher Seminary) and his teaching in London, Manchester, and elsewhere. Some of his important letters and essays were written on trains as he was traveling, throughout the war years, from northern England to London and back, a route he seems to have traveled almost every week.

What we have of Rabbi Dessler's writings was collected by several disciples—most prominently, Rabbi Aryeh Carmell, now of Jerusalem. The Hebrew collections of his writings are entitled *Michtav Me'eliyahu*. Three volumes in English, entitled *Strive for Truth* (henceforth, *S.T.*), edited by R. Carmell, correspond to the first volume of *Michtav Me'eliyahu*, containing renditions of Dessler's work "as he might have written it had he written in English" (*S.T.*, 1:22). Much of the material is admittedly written up from notes of the master, but the first volume of *Michtav Me'eliyahu* (henceforth, *M.E.*) consists of essays and reflections that, we are told, were published as he himself formulated them.[7]

Two Educational Responsa

R. Dessler's writings are all directly relevant to education. However, in the very last section of *Michtav me'eliyahu*, volume 3, we find a section devoted to letters that are specifically focused on educational matters. We shall deal with two of these educational responsum-type letters first, for they articulate basic principles that will accompany us as we move into a discussion of R. Dessler's philosophical and psychological conception of human personality and explore his essay "On Choice" to locate educational ground rules and guidelines.

The first letter, entitled, "On Striking Children" (*M.E.*, 3:360–62), responds to a query: how to relate to the strictures of "innovative researchers" who counsel against hitting children because the children "will learn to imitate the acts of their parents, hitting those who act against their will." (Can they be right despite the traditional practice?)

R. Dessler categorically pronounces his support for striking children to train their characters, for this is the teaching of the Sages. The view of the "innovators," he explains, is based on two errors: first, they believe people come into the world without attributes, holding the view that personality traits, *middot*, are learned only from their environment. But this, we learn from the Torah and *Hazal*, is not so.

[And the prooftexts are in what God said to Cain:] "Sin lies in wait at the door" (*Bereshit* 4:7) and . . . [what] our Sages said about Esau—that when [pregnant] Rebecca passed houses of idolatry, he struggled to get out. . . . [This shows that] the qualities of a person are created with him.

Not sparing the rod falls into the paradigm of all genuine education that, first and foremost, is intent on breaking the power of the evil impulse that comes into the world with the child. The fear of heaven, which protects one against the evil impulse, arises in the human being only when he or she learns fear. Those who believe that corporal punishment is unjustified and counterproductive would do well to learn about it from the Torah, which is the source of all truth about God, the world, and human nature.

Second, the modern psychological theory that children learn aggressiveness from being punished is based on the erroneous assumptions that children must be guided toward autonomy and that parents and educators should befriend children and pupils. However, our tradition teaches us that autonomy is nothing but a term that confers honorable status to the desire to overthrow the rule of the good impulse that induces to the service of God and to follow the advice of the evil impulse. To ostensibly do what you want, but actually, to do what the *yetzer hara* ("the evil impulse") wants, is natural to humankind. The aggression that modern innovators are afraid of is part of autonomy, for one becomes aggressive when thinking that one deserves whatever one wants and may do anything to get it. In R. Dessler's words:

[Modern educational theorists] think that one has to cultivate independence in children, and this is a great mistake. It is not independence [autonomy] that must be developed, but submission. [For] even when [the child] is taught humility and submission, he will [by himself] learn pride and killing. But to teach him [the doctrine of] "Only I [count] and none besides me" is the doctrine of Edom, the doctrine of murder and robbery.

Children whose pride has been broken will not learn from corporal punishment to strike others. Just as it would not occur to the servant to strike the king, so the child's reverence for the parent will overcome any tendency to imitate aggressiveness. The latter is only possible if the child is taught the evil educational ideal to see him or her as a "friend." The parent is charged with taming the natural evil in the human heart, making him or her good, not making children *feel* good about themselves.

Judaism, then, understands the nature of the human being, and an appropriate education neutralizes the evil in the human heart and helps people conquer it. As for the "innovative researchers": it is not only their errors that must be exposed, but their own submission to the wiles of the evil impulse that is evident in their theories:

> In their search for novelty and [their desire] to destroy the foundations that even the Gentiles know to be true, whose source is God's Torah and the prophets, [they] have concocted new inventions [i.e., theories] that turn all the roots upside down and educate impudent little Hitlers.

From all this, R. Dessler, concludes, we see how careful that one must be in examining every psychological and educational innovation, scrupulously examining whether there is in these theories anything that contradicts the words of the Sages and their interpreters, or customs of Israel that are themselves in the category of Torah. If indeed there is such a contradiction, one must throw out these defiled innovations and not adopt them in any way. Several basic assumptions of R. Dessler are evident from this letter:

a) Midrashic passages teach true doctrine no less than any other traditional source. No traditional texts may be ignored in deciding on the correct course of action.

b) Human beings are naturally corrupt, i.e., under the influence of the wily *yetzer hara*. It not only entices embryos in the direction of pagan temples, but leads "innovative researchers" to mistakes that reveal the extent of their own enslavement to the *yetzer.*

c) Falsehood, then, has its source in evil, even as truth is synonymous with good. The source of truth and goodness is the Torah, i.e., all that the Sages and their interpreters have said. The idea that one can distinguish between facts and values, i.e., between the objectively true and the morally good, is a false idea, for it leads to the overturning of the Torah. It is, as Dessler intimates in our second educational correspondence, the doctrine of the university.

Between Frankfurt and the Yeshiva World

In correspondence with rabbinical leaders who wish to set up a teachers' seminary attached to their yeshiva that would enable yeshiva students to study education and pedagogy while simultaneously working toward a B.A. at a university (*M.E.*, 3:355–60), we find R. Dessler, though always respectful and courteous, adamantly opposed. He cannot accept the rabbis' argument that only those yeshiva students who would otherwise leave the path of Judaism would be accepted to the program and that "real" yeshiva men will (naturally!) stay and study Torah exclusively, at most taking some non-degree-granting courses of the yeshiva itself in pedagogy. The proposed seminary, states Dessler categorically, will draw even excellent students of Torah, tempted (by the *yetzer*) to get a university degree. Hence, they will not become great scholars of Torah, which is the highest stage of Jewish self-development and the greatest need of the Jewish people.

Dessler admits that in modern times there were two approaches to the university: that of Frankfurt, i.e., the *Torah im derekh eretz* movement; and the yeshiva approach. The former kept Jews within the fold of observing the commandments, some even punctiliously so. Yet this approach created almost no great scholars of Torah and even a small deficiency (*ketzat likui*) in the purity of the Frankfurt worldview with regard to the absolute truth of the way of the holy Torah wherever science contradicted it, leading to a peculiar partnership that posited the possibility of welding together in one heart an actual contradiction.

The other way, that of the *yeshivot*,[8] looked upon pure Torah study as the optimal state of affairs. True, some were incapable of it, and yeshiva leaders would help them find another way in life, as long as it did not involve academic training or a "real" profession. Such pursuits as running a store, which required no preparation and did not draw the heart, were suitable alternatives for simple, but pious people. But those who wished to learn a profession, all the more those who chose for themselves an academic profession, these the yeshiva world did not help at all to move in the direction of their desires in order not to ruin the others. The upshot is that the teachers' seminary, established to "save" the weak, who are incapable of genuine Torah study, will ultimately corrupt the strong and entice them to desire a B.A. degree. The rabbis at that yeshiva are therefore elegantly yet firmly told that their plan is not acceptable.[9]

One may well ask how it is that a teacher of devotion and apparent genuine love for others—especially for his students and his children (to whom he writes with authority yet with affection and tenderness)—and who states that teachers who get angry at pupils are unqualified to teach (S.T., 1:84) should counsel hitting children. Likewise, why would R. Dessler, with his broad knowledge of psychological principles and literature, declare so firmly against the world of the university? Let us briefly analyze the principles operative in his decisions.

a) In both Cain and Esau, "natural badness" is evident. Cain, as R. Dessler reminds us elsewhere (S.T., 2:229), had everything. So why should he offer a second-rate sacrifice? What possible reason but that he could not get himself to give anything first-rate? As for Esau, no environment had made him evil. In wishing to join in idol-worship, even while an embryo, he was expressing human nature, which is naturally in the clutches of the evil impulse. One may ask why Dessler does not mention that same midrash's description of Jacob wishing to get out of the womb to study at the yeshiva of Shem and Eber.[10] But it appears that the righteous are few and immeasurably above all that we are or can aspire to (S.T., 2:191–207). We are Cain and Esau! It is as such that we must be educated, i.e., liberated from the yetzer.

b) The distinction generally made between truth and falsehood, on the one hand, and good and bad, on the other, is unacceptable to R. Dessler. Note: the educational innovators who decry striking children are not only wrong, but they are intent on "novelty . . . [to] destroy the foundations that *even the Gentiles know to be true* . . . [to concoct] new inventions that turn all the roots upside down." Novelty, of course, is a device of Satan.

c) The animosity toward the university, too, requires explanation. Why does acceptance of academic learning as legitimate cast a shadow even upon the pious of Frankfurt? Why would yeshiva men, immersed in Torah study, which is supremely valuable, be tempted by it? What is enticing about it, and what is wrong with it?

How Negi'ah Deceives the Intellect

R. Dessler's conception of human personality is elucidated in his essay "The Roots of *Mussar*" (*S.T.*, 1:160–72). Here he posits that all human inclinations and actions are rooted in prior interest, *negi'ah*, which determines how the matter at hand touches or affects the person, i.e., myself. What my interest is, is rooted in the *will*. What I *desire* (to begin with) is presented to the intellect for (ostensible) decision making and operative guidelines. The intellect is charged with the task of achieving what the prior interest, the *negi'ah*, demands. This is not the case with technical problems. With regard to these, the intellect is permitted to work matters out for itself (how to do this; how to get from here to there). But where decisions are valuative (is this good for me or not? is this where I ought to be going?), the intellect is the tool and slave of the will.

To illustrate, R. Dessler notes that one usually consults the *Shulhan Arukh* on the permissibility or otherwise of playing chess on Shabbat if one already wants to play chess. If we assume, then, that it is not the intellect that poses questions but that it actually learns of their existence and urgency only from the will and from prior interest, we are led to the question: To what extent is the intellect capable or incapable of arriving at true decisions? May we ever rely on our intellect to give us true conclusions in any matter that is not purely technical?

R. Dessler's pedagogic style generally involves, first, examples from everyday life (e.g., playing chess on Shabbat, noticing every detail of a stamp if we are ardent philatelists), and then it shows how the theory being presented is rooted in rabbinic sources, for "the Sages of the Torah are familiar with the depth of the human psyche." Here, the prooftexts are halakhot and aggadot about accepting bribes, which "blind the eyes of the righteous" (*Devorim* 16:19):

> Rava said: What is the reason [for the prohibition of] bribery? Why is it forbidden to take a bribe even with the sincere intention of declaring the innocent party innocent and the guilty party guilty? Once [the judge] has taken a bribe from [one party], he becomes close to him his mind: he becomes identified with him. And [the fact is that] *no one can see anything to his own disadvantage.* (*Ketubot* 105b)

Since it is interest that arouses thought, which in turn gives us tools for judgment, interest "is not likely to prompt the intellect to produce arguments that conflict with itself"; on the contrary, it will do its best to suppress them. In the words of Rabbi Yehuda Lowe, the Maharal of Prague, the phrase "blinds the eyes of the wise" means that the correct argument will not occur to him. " 'And distorts the words of the righteous' [i.e., 'the righteous words,' Rashi]—this means that even if his attention is drawn to the correct view, he will distort it." R. Dessler also cites the Maharal that it is forbidden to hear the argument of one side before the other party has arrived (in court), for in such a case, one has already been drawn to the arguments of the first party and hears the second party less attentively and favorably.

Since we are all judges, called upon to pass judgment on the correctness of our actions and the truth of our views, we must consider the extent of the distorting influences that are brought to bear on our minds, influences no less injurious to truth than bribes offered to court judges. We must admit that "the intellect is powerless to produce reliable results in any moral problem." The heart must be cleaned of bias before any case is presented to the judge (the intellect).

That the bias of the heart is subtle and pervasive is attested to by the case of the twelve spies who thought that their desire to spy out the land was truthfully expressed in their stating their case to Moses. According to a midrash in *Yalkut Shimoni* (*Bamidbar* 13–14):

> When Israel first suggested sending spies into the land of Canaan, Moshe asked why (implying that before the deterioration in spiritual climate brought about by the sin of the spies, it was understood that independent effort of this kind was uncalled for). They replied: The Holy One, blessed be He, promised us that we would find treasures of all kinds. . . . But the Canaanites will have heard that we are about to enter. . . . If they hide their property . . . and we will not find anything, it will seem as if God's promise has not been kept. . . . Therefore let spies go (to find the hiding places).

R. Dessler posits that the spies, all originally righteous men, were not deliberately deceiving Moshe, and indeed, Moses himself fell into this trap, as it says, "And the matter seemed good to me." He, too, believed, as the spies did, that the motive was purely one of *kiddush hashem*, sanctifying God's name by making sure that no one would suspect that He could not carry out what He had promised.

Such is the power of *negi'ah*. To be in its clutches is to be ruled by the evil impulse. And it is not the intellect that can save one, for it merely thinks through what has been presented to it by the will of the person. How, then, is the will purified? R. Dessler insists that God, in His mercy, has given us an inkling of truth that does not completely desert us even when caught in the web of biases. Somehow, we know when we have chosen evil. No less important, the community and, to an extent, every individual have instruments of enlightenment ready for their use. R. Dessler presents a talmudic story that is reminiscent, in the converse, of John Dewey's famous parable of "finding one's way at the branching of the road," for which previous crossroads provide no sure guidance.[11] R. Dessler's story is taken from *Sotah* 21a:

> What is a human being like in this world? Like a man wandering in an impenetrable forest in the deepest darkness of the night. He is in danger from thorns and briars, ditches and pitfalls, from bandits and wild animals, and, furthermore, he does not know in which direction to go. He happens upon a torch that he can light. Now he is safe from the thorns and briars, ditches and pitfalls, but he is still in danger from the bandits and wild animals, and he still does not know in which direction to go. The sun comes up. He is now safe from the bandits and wild animals, too, but he still does not know in which direction to go. When he reaches the crossroads and sees the signpost, he is saved from them all.

The torch is interpreted to symbolize mitzvot: the sun, study of Torah, and the crossroads, as the day of death when the *talmid hakham*, who continues his learning, sees the way out. Such a one has reached purity of heart and has liberated himself from biases (*negi'ot*) to the largest possible extent. His intellect serves a pure intention that desires only to do God's will.

The ramifications for our educational texts are clear, and we can proceed to examine the questions posed previously: if the originally righteous spies, and even Moses himself, fell into the trap of deliberating and deciding on the basis of the smallest *negi'ah*, namely, hidden fear of what they would find in the land and hence, lack of deep faith in Providence, allowing the evil impulse to disguise itself as the *yetzer hatov,* obviously every other person, certainly in our age, is in a far worse predicament. It is true that there are superhuman persons whose *yetzer hatov* is extremely great, such as Jacob, or the other patriarchs and matriarchs, but these personages instruct us only about the ideal destination of every human soul, not about the soul's natural state. We may not compare ourselves to such ideal figures nor may we question them, for both the comparisons and the criticism are based on our intellects, which have been fed by our tainted desires and biases. The human being, as such, is like Esau, not Jacob.

If the intellect is given access to any subject only when it is presented by the (tainted) will, we may understand why truth and goodness are synonymous, as are evil and falsehood. All truth is processed by the intellect only after a good will has made it available; likewise, a bad will will present matters in a biased way, leading the intellect to inadequate or distorted conclusions. This is the reason that one cannot academically distinguish between goodness (moral values) and truth (the result of research). Thus, the university, which is founded on this distinction, leads even pious Frankfurt persons to think that the distinction is possible and leads them to perdition. The only exception that R. Dessler suggests: those technical matters in which the "how to do it" question has already been rooted in a valuative "what to do" decision.

Who can make these decisions? The talmudic crossroads parable offers a clear—and hierarchical—answer. All those who observe the commandments have some illumination granted to them, but ultimately, it is the study of Torah that corresponds to the sun itself and only *talmide hakhamim* who have devoted their entire lives to Torah study deserve the mantle of leadership. They alone know where to turn. Professors, even of moral philosophy, see no need to make their learning correspond to the halakhah; indeed, as they proceed in their careers, their theories offer them increasing rationalization for obeying the evil impulse. They become increasingly expert and "scholarly" in explaining their *yetzer*-driven decisions, even philosophically.

R. Dessler's point of view is operatively most evident in a concept that he espoused fervently and that, because of the popularity of his writings even among non-*haredi* religious youth, gained widespread endorsement, even in national-religious circles, namely, *emunat hakhamim.* According to this doctrine, one may not question Torah luminaries, not even those of our impoverished generation. Their intellects alone process a will that is as closely attuned to the divine will as is humanly possible. Conversely, all the intelligence and deliberation marshaled against their decisions is based on *negi'ot*. For example, if Jews criticize rabbinic leaders for not doing everything to remove Jews from Europe before the Holocaust, this criticism is a subterfuge for the sin, the *negi'ah*, of insolence, a veritable rebellion against the Torah (*S.T.*, 1:217–25).

Free Will: "Becoming" and "Being"

The concept of personality that underlies R. Dessler's assumptions and commitments involves two major distinctions: a) between free will and causality; and b) between "being" and "having." The first is a philosophical distinction;[12] the second is more explicitly moralistic (*S.T.*, 3:173–217).

> There were and still are great philosophers who . . . have denied the reality of free will and human responsibility. They assert that man is but a plaything in the hands of natural causes and that any idea he may have of claiming credit for his actions is purely illusionary. But at the same time, the same person [who makes this claim] will, in the most egoistic manner possible, take pride in his intellectual achievements and claim credit for his professional success. . . . How can the thinker have forgotten so soon that he has just demonstrated . . . that man is nothing but a machine, a stimulus-response mechanism? Can a machine claim credit for its predetermined activities? This only goes to show how people dominated by their negi'ot[13] cannot be trusted. Their unconscious bias determines their opinions; truth takes second place. . . .

> This attitude is . . . by no means confined to philosophers. If a person does something for which others applaud him, he will have no hesitation in taking all the glory for himself. But if he commits a crime and is found out, his ego suddenly takes a backseat. If all else fails, he will try to avoid responsibility by hiding behind a deterministic shield. That is how philosophic problems can be used to promote a permissive lifestyle. And, of course, with characteristic inconsistency, the same person will claim credit for his "discovery," which . . . will be applauded by all likeminded people.

R. Dessler's solution to the dilemma: determinism, or "cause and effect," is deduced from external observation, while free will is the result of inner perception: "We experience within ourselves the power and the freedom to act or to desist, as we wish." These two perceptions "are distinct aspects of the human mind." Moreover, the attempt to refute one mode by reference to the other is as absurd as the argument of the blind philosopher who insisted that the sense of vision was unreal because he could not experience it by the sense of touch. As for the intellect, while it serves both modes of perception (the sense of selfhood, on the one hand, and causal sense perception on the other), it does not grasp the essence of either of them, but only its own mental constructs (e.g., triangles). Each, then, has its place, with selfhood related to service of God, and in general, obligation and responsibility (which require free will).

On the other hand, our senses perceive causes. But even this perceived world should make the servant of God see the hand of God behind them (not with the intellect, but with the inner perception). Thus, the result for the righteous person is that even the world of sense perception leads to modesty. In the words of the Psalmist, "When I see your heaven, the work of your hands . . . what is man that you should take note of him?"

Here, as in the interpretation of *Yalkut Shimoni* on the twelve spies, we have an intimation that the world of causality is unreal. Just as the spies should have understood that no effort was required on their part in the conquest of the land, so must we understand that causality is a screen, an illusion. Actually, all comes from God (the absolute free being), and making an effort in material matters—including the effort to make a living—is good only if these efforts protect us from misused leisure. The appearance of causality is a test for the righteous. Yet even the righteous should do some work, make some effort, lest they conclude (prematurely and arrogantly) that they are deserving of God's unmediated care. This view of causality as merely apparent has clear and far-flung ramifications for the importance and legitimacy of exclusive Torah study for those who are deserving. It underlies a much-used polemic in favor of exemption from army service for *b'nai yeshivot*. This deserves discussion that is beyond the scope of this brief study (see *S.T.*, 2:263–311).

b) Being and having: All that we call "life" can be summarized in the distinction between ego consciousness, an awareness of our being; and awareness of the ego's relationship with the world outside itself.

This second awareness takes three forms: awareness of what we lack or need, awareness of an urge to fulfill our need, and awareness of the actual fulfillment of our need. The first of these constitutes "being," and the second, "having." Together, these perceptions are life itself.

> What a person yearns for *is* his life. If his yearning is for vanities of this world, his life itself is vanity; if for spiritual things (the world to come), his life partakes of the nature of the spiritual world.

All spiritual acquisitions become part of our being, while all mundane acquisitions remain in the realm of having. But spiritual acquisitions do not include spiritual concepts that we grasp with our intellect. Detached knowledge is not part of our inner selves. Thus, while mundane matters always belong to having, spiritual matters may be either having or being. It is knowledge that was stored or "had" that is appropriated by, or "returned to the heart" that enters the world of being. This corresponds to self-making. The Torah of God, that is, the Torah outside the self (an objective, even theological datum), becomes the learner's (own) Torah that lives within the individual, to which he is committed in a manner that it constitutes the basic building blocks of being, identity. When that happens, Torah knowledge moves from being an intellectual accomplishment to a veritable change of the ego, of the personality itself. It is, even now, even in this world, a "share in the world to come."

Having touched above on focal assumptions, beliefs, and paradigms in Rabbi Dessler's language of Judaism, we may now hope to understand R. Dessler's discourse on free will, which is a central statement in his educational philosophy, a kind of conception of the educated Jew (*S.T.*, 1:48–64).

Choosing Truth

As is his wont, R. Dessler begins with a case familiar to many readers from their own experience: the cigarette smoker who can't kick the habit and correspondingly wakes up at night with severe chest pains. While in pain, he decides not to smoke the next day, come what may. In the morning, he craves tobacco and decides to smoke just this one: "One cigarette can't hurt me." Shortly thereafter, he tells himself, "Just one more cigarette can't do any harm." And so it goes the whole day long, with the chest pains at night. Why does he deceive himself in this manner?

Clearly, we have two conflicting wills here: the desire to smoke; and the desire, much more cogent, not to have chest pains. Yet by subterfuge, the weaker prevails. The person himself, the chooser, must decide between the two wills. In this case, though he knows where right lies, he continues to deceive himself; he deliberately ignores the truth. Instead of choosing life and blessing, as the Torah commands, he chooses curse and death—and convinces himself that he can't help it and has no control over it.

But as we have seen with regard to the concepts of causality and freedom, the latter functions in the world of the spirit, of obligation and responsibility, where no causal external factors operate. Hence:

> *Behira* [free choice] depends on the person alone. There is no outside cause involved. The prime[14] cause is the person himself. This is well known to anyone who has ever exercised his *behira* and conquered his evil inclination. Such a person feels with utmost clarity that he has relinquished illusion and opted for truth.

Those who immediately give in to the will, i.e., the *yetzer hara,* are easily convinced that their actions are determined by external forces. Having made a bad choice, they lose all choice; having never exercised *behira,* they have none. R. Dessler declares that their "philosophy is merely a reflection of their own heart(s). You deny free will because you are, in fact, unfree; you have enslaved yourself to the evil within you." Isn't this, too, a *behira?* This "having no behira" is also a choice, a choice of nothingness.

This becomes clear when the moral teaching of "choice" is translated into theology. The essence of good *behira* is to "recognize the unique and indivisible nature of truth; and this, in effect, is to recognize the Creator." Bad choices, which present themselves as non-choices, accept the falsehood of duality. As the rabbis taught, whoever listens to his *yetzer* is like an idolater.

Yet we have seen that external factors do seem to determine much in our lives—at least, so it is in the lives of those who have not yet approached perfection. Yet how can we choose what is seemingly determined? This perceived problem provides the existential and philosophical framework for this essay's central analogy:

When two armies are locked in battle, fighting takes place only at the battlefront. Territory behind the lines of one army is under that army's control, and little or no resistance can be expected there. A similar situation prevails with respect to territory behind the lines of the other army. If one side gains a victory at the front and pushes the enemy back, the position of the battlefront will have changed. In fact, therefore, fighting takes place only at one location, though potentially the line could be drawn anywhere in the territories of the two contending countries.[15]

Behira, ideally, is an advance of the *yetzer hatov*'s lines. But we note that it cannot happen "behind the lines," i.e., where external forces prevail. Where good and evil (e.g., truth and falsehood) are unreflective and taken for granted, determined by education, environment, or habit, they do not present themselves for choice.

Many of a person's actions may happen to coincide with what is objectively right because he has been brought up that way and it does not occur to him to do otherwise, and many bad and false decisions may be taken simply because a person does not realize that they are bad. In such cases, no valid *behira*, or choice, has been made. Free choice is exercised and a valid *behira* made only on the borderline between the forces of good and the forces of evil within that person.

To illustrate what being at the "*behira* point" means: many observant Jews who would never dream of desecrating the Sabbath will freely gossip and speak *lashon hara* without realizing that it is a grave sin. Why? Because this particular forbidden behavior is "behind the enemy lines." Similarly, for some of those who observe the commandments diligently, the *behira* will involve whether to observe them with a pious intention or not. Conversely, for one brought up among thieves and robbers, whether or not to steal "does not present any *behira* at all: his *behira* point might be on the question of shooting his way out when discovered. . . . This is where for him the forces of good and evil, truth and untruth, are evenly balanced."

Education, the environment, and even heredity will place the *behira* point differently for different people. And what you have been educated to, for good or evil, determines where you are confronted: what is self-understood for you, either for good or for evil, does not count for or against you. Thus, Lot, who risked his life to practice hospitality toward the two men who came to remove him and his family from Sodom, deserved no credit for that; everyone raised in Abraham's household was intensely and successfully educated about hospitality. For them, hospitality was well behind the lines of the *yetzer hatov*. Yet he deserved to be saved because, overhearing Abraham refer to Sarah as his sister, he did not divulge the secret; he did not betray his uncle. Despite the greed for material possessions that led him to settle in Sodom, he withstood the temptation to be rewarded for betrayal.

The aim of *behira* is to conquer the evil impulse, to start from the point that education and environment have left you, to take over more and more of the *yetzer*'s territory, at the ever new *behira* points brought into view by prior decisions, for freedom is found only at those points. Those who plod along, rather than move along at their *behira* points, do not use the freedom that is the purpose and optimal goal of human existence.

One who moves more and more aspects of life into the realm of the good paradoxically finds in himself or herself a sense of compulsion. For not only are the matters that are moved behind the lines no longer matters of choice (unless the *behira* point is moved back, by transgression), but the individual discovers that the choice between good and evil was really no choice at all, for evil is the service of idols, and idols have no existence. "Truth is reality, and falsehood is nothing; it is surely no valid choice but simple error to consider 'nothing' as 'something.' " In this sense, the mitzvot, while chosen, are decreed upon us from above.

At a yet higher level, the sense of compulsion, too, fades away. Compulsion bespeaks resistance, but a point comes when one acts out of love.

> At this point, the human being becomes truly free, finding no resistance within him to the good that he loves. This is the state to which our Rabbis referred when they said, "No one is free but he who occupies himself with the Torah.". . . This man of the spirit is the truly liberated man.

The concept of *behira* is doubtlessly consistent with other concepts that we have located in R. Dessler's thought, which together point to an educational agenda, on the basis of articulated principles of an educational philosophy. Let us state certain aspects of it explicitly.

The purpose of education is to give each individual the best possible starting point for "self-making" through *behira*. Moving from point to point, the person is engaged in lifelong character education. Education for values is not a peripheral affair; it is the enterprise of self-making, of becoming righteous—hence, wise. The congruence of value and wisdom is, of course, based on a clear knowledge on the part of those whom Plato would call the "philosophers," as to what constitutes the good, the real, and the aim of human life. In R. Dessler's educational philosophy, those who know what is good and therefore true are the Sages—of the Talmud and of each generation. Their point of departure for the knowledge of the truth is not the intellect, but the will; their achievement is a will attuned completely to the truth and goodness that is the will of God as found in His Torah. What this divine will is, is lucidly revealed only to those who have rid themselves of all *negi'ot*, moving beyond the illusion that there is a real choice to be made between good and evil and finding perfect freedom in their love of truth.

Their insights are flawless, and they speak with the voice of authority. They brook no compromise between good and evil. They teach that only within the life of the community that they head is there salvation and individual movement toward truth (*S.T.*, 2:67–73). Responsible for all who live in their community and who are besieged by secular culture, they are knowledgeable even about the non-Torah world and are permitted and qualified to use such knowledge because, at its best, it reflects the Torah that they have appropriated and that is part of their being.

While their outlooks and aims are absolute, they are educationally nonjudgmental. They understand that each has his or her *behira* point for which they are, at least at first, not to blame. It is the purpose of education to place young people at the highest possible level to begin with. Providence has given Jewish education and life special character-building opportunities. Israel, through the multitude of mitzvot, has more *behira* points than others, and only Israel has a community headed by leader-philosophers, *talmide hakhamim*, the highest representatives of the academy, that is, the world of the yeshiva. Only they know what the highest level of human self-actualization is, for they live in the world of truth, spiritually unaffected by the philosophies of modern culture.

The world portrayed by R. Dessler combines a generally pessimistic understanding of humankind with hope and even anticipation of happiness and salvation. Everyone knows who to look up to, and no one need feel lost or estranged. Society is firm and visible. Each is expected to find—and accept—his or her place in the order of things.

For R. Dessler, the first-order knowledge of commitment, taught within the rhythms of initiation and participation, is the only one that really matters; hence, the antagonism to the detached methods and the academic notion of knowledge that characterize the university. All those who believe, with him, that education is fundamentally character education, and that all the rest is mere instruction, will have to confront that position and ask: Is there, in the modern era, an alternative way to take Torah seriously, one that respects objective research and knowledge?

The non-*haredi* educator will ultimately part ways with R. Dessler on the issues of authoritarianism and corporate community life. R. Dessler's views, while helping us to criticize aspects of modernity, also help us to appreciate its gifts, which we wish to incorporate into our understanding of Judaism and into Jewish education. Our modern sensibilities raise two groups of questions:

1) If learning is the key to self-actualization and to the service of God in the highest sense, why do only men learn Torah? Why can't even yeshiva men decide for themselves whether the university is dangerous for them? Perhaps the university itself is designed to remove certain *negi'ot* from its students? Perhaps its professors are also searchers for truth? Are philosophically valuative decisions never to be made by anyone who is not a sage?[16]

2) How are the *negi'ot* of sages themselves to be exposed and moved, from *behira* point to *behira* point, so that insensitivity, blindness to genuine differences between people, and the assumption that all absolute truth has been appropriated will be moved behind the enemy's lines, becoming unheard of for the *talmid hakham*, so that the evil impulse can be kept from using the *yetzer hatov* in the alleged service of Torah?[17]

Perhaps the paradigm of the battlefield on which *behira* points are located characterizes the distinction between modern Jewish and *haredi* education. The individual is educated to choose at a high level between what appears to him or her as a choice between good and evil: between defending Eretz Yisrael though not (yet!) observing the mitzvot; between observing commandments with a pious intention or not; between studying Torah every spare hour on Shabbat or playing chess (assuming that it is permissible to do so on Shabbat).

The assumption, at each point of *behira,* is that there is a right way, leading upward, and a wrong way, drawing the line back into enemy territory. But in fact, valuative decisions are not always, or even usually, of that kind. The distinction between right and wrong is essential and important. But riding on the backs of the absolute and existential opposites of good and bad are valuative problems wherein the choice is not to be made between these absolutes, but rather between what is possibly better and more worthy in a given situation and what is possibly worse and less worthy. In such choices, there is no clear distinction between value and anti-value, but a dilemma, involving a conflict between values. In the first case, obedience, loyalty, and character are at stake; in the second case, sensitivity, responsibility, and deliberation are on the line.

For example, in a given situation, it may be more compassionate, sensible, and even righteous to play chess than to study Torah. In certain situations, chess may bring cheer into someone's life (perhaps even my own!) and cement relationships, while study will be an evasion, a retreat from what the situation demands. What to do in such situations? Is the battlefield and its drawn lines between good and evil an adequate analogy for what is going on?

R. Dessler might say that the presentation of dilemmas to consciousness testifies to the wiles of the evil impulse that wishes to keep us from choosing the good. For once an issue is seen as a dilemma that invites deliberation, one readily finds good reasons not to act as the Sages have proscribed. An educated Jew, according to the battlefield model, will therefore shun the conceptual field of dilemmas. Rather, he or she will perceive what is going on as a difficult question that must be brought to the attention of a *posek,* one who rules on halakhic questions. The latter will consider the case carefully, and without *negi'ot,* and will return it to the questioner with a decision of what must be done: what is good and what is bad in the particular situation.

Ordinary people, then, must be protected from dilemmas. Yet what kind of educated person is it who has no dilemmas? What problems, moral and existential, will such a person fail to perceive? What kind of inner freedom can he or she have? R. Dessler believes that the Torah must be protected against innovators. This requires making matters absolutely clear: don't befriend your child, because it will make him or her impudent. Don't set up a teachers' seminary that will tempt yeshiva learners to seek university training. Don't send your child to a school that teaches Torah and science, for it will make him, at best, into a dabbler in Judaism (*M.E.*, 3:337–40). R. Dessler's fears, while dogmatically delivered, are not unfounded. The influence of modern culture, with its pagan assumptions that self-gratification and upward mobility are the height of self-actualization, does sometimes turn the study of some Torah into a handmaiden of secular culture. Torah, then, becomes a religion of private values, ceremonial skills, and ethnic aesthetics: raisins in a secular pie.

Yet is there no intermediate path? Does befriending a child rule out all discipline? Don't some children thrive on, and desperately need, great warmth, while others are content with a love that, being certain, is also challenging? What about the child who can be a scientist and wants to be a good one? Is that out of bounds for all good Jews?

Even when we disagree with R. Dessler's premises and policies, there is much to be learned from him. He can teach us a great deal about the limitations of objective knowledge. His translation of theological concepts (the world to come, Satan, and so on) into existential and philosophical ones readily enlightens and instructs, for we never fear that the translations are reductionistic or that they diminish Torah rather than illuminating it. He warns us about the special pleading to which we are prone in the name of truth and values. He portrays religious life as a spiritual challenge, rather than as a path to peace of mind. If R. Dessler's disciples wished to discuss Judaism and Jewish education with us, not only to convert us to a premodern sensibility but to listen as well as to speak, we would probably have as much to learn as to say.

Notes

1. See the discussion on *gedolim* books in Jacob J. Schacter, "Facing the Truths of History," *Torah Umada Journal* 8 (1998–99): 200–273, esp. 213.
2. For this development, see Ernst Akiva Simon, "Are We Israelis Still Jews?" in Arthur Cohen, *Arguments and Context: A Reader of Jewish Thinking in the Aftermath of the Holocaust* (New York: Harper and Row, 1970), 388–401.
3. R. Dessler himself, as Rabbi Aryeh Carmell writes, studied Russian and other subjects. *Strive for Truth*, 1:9 (see n. 5 below). R. Carmell wrote a brief biography of his teacher in the *haredi* newspaper *Yated ne'eman* (24 Tevet 5754), in which he disclosed that Dessler was taught, in addition to Torah and *mussar*, what a *ba'al habayit* would need for success (his father hoped to see him, like

himself, a pious and learned businessman). So, "true to the principles of his rebbe, R. Simcha Zissel, the boy's father, included [in his education, which took place at home] general studies . . . [including] some classics of world literature in Russian translation. One of them (so Rabbi Dessler told me) was *Uncle Tom's Cabin,*" Schacter, "Facing the Truths of History," 200.

4. Rabbi Samson Raphael Hirsch, the founder of neo-Orthodoxy (*Torah im Derekh Eretz*) in nineteenth-century Germany, figures often in *haredi* literature as having acted as he did only to meet the demands of the historical situation. From this, it is concluded that he, too, considered his approach unacceptable for other places and times. See Schacter, "Facing the Truths of History," 216–17.

5. We summarize here from the introductions to the two collections of R. Dessler's writings upon which our discussion in based: *Michtav Me'eliyahu,* ed. Aryeh Carmell and Alter Halpern, 3 vols., 9th ed. (B'nai Brak: Committee for the Publication of the Writings of Rabbi E. E. Dessler, 1964 [5734]); and *Strive for Truth,* trans. and annotated by Aryeh Carmell (Jerusalem and New York: Feldheim, 1978 [vol. 1], 1985 [vol. 2], 1989 [vol. 3]). I make use primarily of *Strive for Truth* except where I cite from or refer to the 2d and 3d vols. of *Michtav Me'eliyahu.* On the origins and development of the *mussar* movement and its educational features and ramifications, see Immanuel Etkis, *Rabbi Yisrael Salanter and the Beginning of the Mussar Movement* (in Hebrew) (Jerusalem: Magnes, 1982), esp. chaps. 2 and 17, in which the concepts of the "unconscious," the role of the evil impulse, and "fear" are developed. These concepts give a historical context for many of the central ideas of R. Dessler, such as *negi'ot,* biases of the soul, to be discussed below.

6. Eliezer Schweid, *Bein hurban l'yeshuah: Teguvot shel hagut haredit lashoa b'zmana* (Tel Aviv: Kibbutz Hameuchad, 1994), chap. 7.

7. Rabbi Carmell informed me by telephone that 90 percent of the material in this volume appears as R. Dessler formulated it.

8. In the letter, the formulation is *aval, shitat hayeshivot,* "but, the yeshiva way." I venture that the *aval* ("but") possibly makes a literary allusion to the liturgical poem of the High Holidays, "Ma'ase eloheinu" ("the acts of our God"), which, in the poem, are juxtaposed to the "acts of the human" (that are lowly and pitiful). After the latter *ma'ase enosh* are noted, the poet again returns to "the acts of our God," with a flourish: *Aval* ma'ase eloheinu!

9. R. Dessler does not relent even when the inquiring rabbis inform him (in response) that they have made commitments that morally oblige them to establish the seminary. He tells them of having consulted, upon receiving their second letter, with the luminaries of the generation, Rabbi Cahaniman, head of the Ponovcz yeshiva, and even with the Hazon Ish, who were both unequivocal in their opposition.

10. Shem and Eber are the son and grandson of Noah, who, the midrash assumes, had been keeping alive the torch of revelation, "Torah," in the generations since Noah. The rabbis envision them as having established a yeshiva in which Jacob,

the tent dweller, himself studied Torah. For what was his "dwelling in tents" but "dwelling in the tents of Torah"?

11. John Dewey, *How We Think: A Restatement of Reflective Thinking to the Educative Process* (Boston: Health, 1933), 13.

12. See Carmell's discussion on this point (*S.T.*, 3:172–73). He notes that R. Dessler's approach "bears a striking resemblance, in its basic approach, to that proposed by Immanuel Kant," though he does not believe that the master actually studied Kant's writings.

13. Though Carmell uses the word *middot* ("attributes") in *Strive for Truth*, the Hebrew text in *M.E.* refers to *negi'ot*.

14. Rather, on the basis of the Hebrew, and the idea that the "ego" is actually free, it might be better to translate the Hebrew *rishoni* as the "first cause," suggesting that no other causes come into play to begin with.

15. R. Carmell reminds the reader that the master's reference is to the way that wars were *formerly* waged, a touching act of respect to the rebbe.

16. It is advisable for modern Jewish educators to explore classic sources that present even "simple people" acting and reacting independently. Professor Uriel Simon of Bar Ilan university has pointed to the neglected example of Samson's mother, as related in *Shoftim* 13. There are many examples of "not asking the rabbi" in our sources.

17. The reader is referred to the story of R. Elazar b.R. Shimon and his encounter with an ugly man (*Ta'anit* 20 a–b).

Knowledge Outline of Jewish Education:
A Model for the Design of the Field

Chaim Zins

This study originated in a frustrating experience while searching the World Wide Web for information on Jewish education. The search, in which I used major Internet resources, unexpectedly resulted in the "stunning success" of hundreds of useless results—much ado about nothing. The few significant sites that I managed to locate did indeed lead me to invaluable information. Nevertheless, most of the major Web resources are organized in a way that compels users to retrieve the needed information in an exploratory trial-and-error method, rather than a systematic one.

For example, at the Web site of the Jewish Theological Seminary of America (JTS), the courses are organized in ascending order based on their alphanumeric code. This order complicates the search process by compelling the person searching for courses on a specific topic to browse through the entire list. By contrast, a systematic subject structure improves the search by enabling the searcher to focus on a specific aspect. Generally, subject structuring is aimed at facilitating an efficient information retrieval in a well-defined subject domain. But it requires two necessary conditions: systematization and comprehensiveness.

This study is aimed at developing a systematic and comprehensive knowledge outline of Jewish education, based on solid scientific foundations. One hopes that this outline will be used as an exemplary model for the design and evaluation of Jewish education studies in the academic milieu, as well as for information-system development.

Chaim Zins is a lecturer at the University of Haifa. He was a doctoral student of Professor Joseph Lukinsky at the Jewish Theological Seminary of America.

Subject Classification Schemes of Jewish Education

The concept of "knowledge outline" in this study refers to the structured classification scheme of the subject domain, with its main divisions and subdivisions. To avoid a situation of "reinventing the wheel," it is crucial to explore existing schemes. Therefore, in a pilot study I explored twenty information resources that were expected to include subject-classification schemes of the field. These resources are divided into five groups.

The first group comprises two leading library classification schemes: the Library of Congress Classification (LCC)[1] and the Dewey Decimal Classification (DDC).[2] The LCC is probably the most common scheme in the academic world because of the leading position of the Library of Congress Classification system in academic libraries. The DDC is the most common classification system in public libraries and school libraries. Besides the printed versions of the classification schemes, I reviewed two related Internet classification projects: CyberStacks,[3] which utilizes the LCC, and CyberDewey,[4] which utilizes the DDC.

The second group of resources comprises five Internet classified directories and portals. These are major Internet gateways, among them Britannica Internet Guide,[5] Excite,[6] LookSmart,[7] WWW Virtual Library,[8] and Yahoo.[9]

The third group comprises two classification schemes that were developed especially for classifying bibliographic materials on Jewish education: *Bibliography of Jewish Education in the United States*[10] and *A Classification System for Libraries of Judaica*.[11]

The fourth group comprises six Web resources that specialize in Jewish education and Judaic resources: CAJE: Coalition for the Advancement of Jewish Education,[12] JESNA: Jewish Education Service of North America,[13] Jewishnet: Global Jewish Information Network,[14] The Pedagogic Center,[15] Shamash,[16] and Virtual Jerusalem.[17]

The fifth group of resources is composed of the Web sites of five academic institutions in the United States that offer an academic degree—B.A., M.A., or Ph.D.—in the field of Jewish education. These are Gratz College,[18] Hebrew Union College,[19] Jewish Theological Seminary,[20] Spertus College,[21] and Yeshiva University.[22]

The first two types of resources—namely, the two library classification schemes and the five Web portals—are general outlines of human knowledge and do not provide a classification scheme of Jewish education. The last three groups of resources are specialized resources on Jewish education. Unexpectedly, the five academic institutions, listed in the fifth group, do not list their courses by an explicit subject classification. Still, the eight resources listed in the third and the fourth groups do present eight classification schemes of Jewish education. Of all eight schemes, Drachler's[23] is the most detailed and systematic. Nevertheless, none of the eight schemes seems to reflect a systematic structuring that is based either on a conceptual analysis of the concept of "Jewish education," or on a scientifically valid research methodology.

Methodology

It is assumed that the scientific validity of the knowledge outline is based on the scientific validity of the structuring methodology. Here the structuring followed a qualitative three-phase research methodology. The first phase was a conceptual structuring based on a phenomenological analysis—an analysis of the studied phenomenon for its basic characteristics—of Jewish education. The conceptual skeleton was then elaborated and adjusted to the field of Jewish education by a grounded theory methodology. This is a general research methodology for developing theory—in this case, model structuring, which is grounded in data systematically gathered and analyzed.[24] The data used for grounding the structuring were the eight classification schemes mentioned above. Finally, the model was tested and refined by a classification of all the courses listed in the course list of the Davidson School of Education at the Jewish Theological Seminary in three successive years: 1997–98, 1998–99, and 1999–2000.[25]

The Model

The three-phase research methodology produced a hierarchical three-level knowledge outline. This means that usually the model presents three levels of subject classification, except in those instances where the level of topical subdivision is different. The first level and the infrastructure of the classification is composed of seven sections: (1) foundations (meta-knowledge), (2) educator, (3) environment, (4) organization, (5) content, (6) teaching method, and (7) student.

The first part, meta-knowledge, is unique in its grounding its rationale on philosophical foundations rather than on the phenomenological analysis of Jewish education, as is the case with sections 2–7. The necessity of the meta-knowledge section is derived from Gödel's "incompleteness theorem."[26] The philosophical implication of this theorem, which was formulated by the mathematician Kurt Gödel in 1931, indicates that it is logically impossible to form an axiomatic system without assuming additional postulates. By accepting this implication, we realize that theoretically, it is impossible to formulate a sufficient explanation that is exclusively based on the phenomenological analysis of Jewish education. Consequently, the additional meta-knowledge section is a necessary foundation in the knowledge construction of Jewish education, as is the case with any phenomenologically based subject-domain structuring.

As noted, sections 2–7 are based on the phenomenological analysis of Jewish education. Education is, in its essence, a social service. I have identified six key elements common to all social services:[27] the provider, the recipient, the environment, the organization, the need, and the type of service. Every service is an interaction between the provider and the recipient effectuated through four media: the environment, the organizational framework, the needs addressed by the service, and the type of service. By adjusting the generic terminology to the context of Jewish education, one can define six basics essential for characterizing the educational phenomenon. These are the educator, the educational environment, the organization, the content, the teaching method, and the student. Every educational activity is an interaction between the educator and the student, effectuated through four media: the environment, the organization, the content, and the teaching method. These relations are shown in Figure 1.

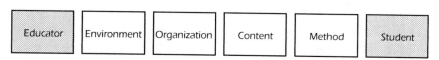

Figure 1: Six basics of the (Jewish) education phenomenon

Foundations (Meta-Knowledge)

The meta-knowledge section of the model is composed of five subsections: theory, history, research, evaluation, and education.

Theory. The theoretical background of Jewish education combines five bodies of disciplinary knowledge: philosophy, religion, sociology, education, and Judaism. These are the five theoretical foundations of the field. The philosophy foundation is centered in the rationale of Jewish education in the modern era (or the postmodern era), especially in light of the conceptual confusion regarding its key concepts: identity, humanity, Judaism, nationality, religion, modernity, and education.

The religion foundation is rooted in the fact that Judaism is primarily a religion. The sociology foundation deals with the sociological and communal characteristics of Jewish education. Jewish education in the global context is essentially a communal response of local Jewish communities to specific Jewish as well as non-Jewish environmental conditions. Finally, education and Judaism are apparently the most significant foundations of the field. Note that in the American milieu, Jewish education is part of religious education.

History. The history of Jewish education is divided here into four major periods: ancient Judaism, premodern period, pre-Holocaust, and post-Holocaust Jewish education. The first two categories refer to the premodern era. Ancient Judaism refers to the biblical and talmudic periods. Premodern period refers mainly to the Middle Ages and the pre-Emancipation period. The last two categories, pre-Holocaust and post-Holocaust, refer to the modern era. Note that the historical classification of a subject domain is determined by the ideological weight of historical events. Hence, in addition to the successful struggle for emancipation, there are at least five other seminal developments in modern Jewish history that significantly affected Jewish education in the global context: the Enlightenment, secularization, religious reform movements, the Zionist movement, and the establishment of the State of Israel. These five developments may be used as a basis for alternative classifications of the history of the field.

Research. Jewish education research is characterized by its methodology. Basically, there are two types of educational research: a theoretical and conceptual type; and an empirical type. Empirical research is divided into two categories—quantitative and qualitative.

Evaluation. Evaluation and assessment are essential for planning the educational activity and measuring its effectiveness.

Education. The education section refers to academic Jewish education studies—the professional education of scholars and practitioners in the field of Jewish education. Jewish education studies comprises two key components, theory and praxis, i.e., teaching the theoretical background and providing practical training.

Educator

The educator section of the model addresses the educator's personality traits, value orientation, theoretical knowledge, and teaching experience. Without discussing the value orientation of the Jewish educator, one can say that it is expected that he or she internalize the goal of maintaining the continuation of the Jewish people.

The educator's theoretical knowledge. The subcategory "theoretical knowledge" refers to the theoretical knowledge of the specific educator and what he or she should know. It differs from the "theory" subcategory in the Meta-Knowledge section, which refers to disciplinary foundations of the field of Jewish education. The educator's theoretical knowledge consists of four elements: general humanistic knowledge, basic knowledge on Judaism, disciplinary knowledge in the field of expertise (i.e., Bible, history, literature), and pedagogical knowledge.

Environment

The environment section refers to social, political, or religious perspectives, regarding the legal conditions, norms, values, and goals of the specific educational community in the societal realm. There are two major environmental elements relevant to Jewish education: national conditions (e.g., Argentina, Israel, United States); and religious inclination (e.g., Conservative, Orthodox, Reform, secular).

Recently, we have witnessed the formation of a new arena: the international, boundless milieu of cyber Jewish education. It is too early to assess the long-term implications of virtual education for shaping the nature of the Jewish people, as we live in the real world and are bound to the social conditions of its communities. Nevertheless, the phenomenon is too significant to be ignored. The term "international cyber education" refers here mainly to academic cyber courses designed for an international audience. It is not addressed to the common utilization of the Internet as a mere venue for communication among members of local communities.

Organization

Most educational activities are performed by established organizations. Sociologists in the field of organizational theory have suggested several models to classify organizations.[28] One of the most common classifications divides organizations into three sectors: the government sector, the private or business sector, and the public sector. The public sector includes nongovernmental nonprofit organizations. It is also known as the "third sector." Jewish education is executed by public and private organizations, with one exception—Israel, which is the only country where most Jewish education is sponsored and supervised by the government. The organizational affiliation has significant administrative and managerial implications. The Jewish Theological Seminary even offers its students a course entitled "Executive Leadership for Nonprofit Jewish Organizations: Theory and Practice."

Nevertheless, I followed an alternative classification of educational organizations, common in the realm of education. In the model suggested here, the organization section is composed of two main categories: formal education and informal education. Formal education refers to principal schooling. This comprises all kinds of established full-day schools, from kindergartens through primary schools, secondary schools, and high schools to higher education. Informal Jewish education is composed of five subcategories: community centers and synagogues, summer camps, supplementary religious schools (e.g., Sunday schools, Talmud Torah, and so on), youth movements, and educational organizations. The educational-organizations subcategory includes all other nonprofit, as well as for-profit, private organizations that activate Jewish cultural or educational informal activities, such as distant learning and the like.

Content

Since any educational activity is primarily aimed at causing a change in the students, the content of the activity becomes the most substantial part of the educational phenomenon. Generally, Jewish education is focused on changing prospective students in three major dimensions—intellectual, emotional, and behavioral. The intellectual dimension culminates in mastering Jewish literacy. The emotional dimension culminates in internalizing Jewish identity. The behavioral dimension culminates in adopting Jewish moral values. In religious educational settings, the behavioral dimension is also implemented in the practice of religious practices. In the educational context, it is assumed that the behavioral dimension is controlled by volition. Consequently, the content section is divided here into three main categories: intellect, emotion, and volition.

Teaching Method

The teaching-method section was not structured. The educational and teaching methods used in various Jewish educational settings are not unique to the field of Jewish education. Educators in the field utilize lectures, text readings, dilemma discussions, tours, trigger films, information technology, and the like. However, all these methods are common to other areas of education. A tour to the death camps in Poland, for instance, is considered as a unique Jewish educational activity, by virtue of its content, not its methodology, since travel is implemented in Christian education as well. A *havruta* session is a common practice in the realm of the *yeshivot*. However, what makes it a unique Jewish educational experience is its "Jewish" content rather than its Socratic dialogue technique.

Student

The seventh and last section, the student section, is divided according to two criteria: age group and target group. The age-group category is composed of three subcategories: childhood, adolescence, and adulthood. The target-group category includes three groups: individuals, families, and communities. Individuals relates to individual teaching—namely, teaching the other, and to self-education. The concept of self-education has two interchangeable perspectives—self-teaching and self-learning. Including self-education in the student section stresses the self-learning perspective of self-education. The hierarchical three-level model is presented in Figure 2.

Model Validation

As noted above, in the last phase of the structuring, the model was tested and validated by classifying the courses in the course list of the Davidson School of Education at the Jewish Theological Seminary in

1. **Foundations (Meta-Knowledge)**
A. *Theory*
  1. Philosophy
  2. Religion
  3. Sociology
  4. Education
  5. Judaism
B. *History*
  1. Ancient Judaism
  2. Premodern
  3. Pre-Holocaust
  4. Post-Holocaust
C. *Research*
  1. Methodology
    a. Theoretical and conceptual
    b. Empirical
      1. Quantitative
      2. Qualitative
D. *Evaluation*
E. *Education*
  1. Theoretical education
  2. Practical training

2. **Educator**
A. *Personality Traits*
B. *Value Orientation*
C. *Theoretical Knowledge*
  1. General humanistic
  2. Basic Jewish
  3. Disciplinary (e.g., history)
  4. Pedagogical
D. *Teaching Experience*

3. **Environment**
A. *Real Community*
  1. National conditions
  2. Religious inclination
B. *Virtual Community*
  (international cyber education)

4. **Organization**
A. *Formal Education*
  (principal schools)
  1. Kindergartens
  2. Primary (elementary) schools
  3. Secondary schools
  4. High schools
  5. Higher education
B. *Informal Education*
  1. Community centers and
    synagogues
  2. Summer camps
  3. Supplementary religious
    schools
  4. Youth movements
  5. Educational organizations

5. **Content**
A. *Intellect (knowledge)*
  1. Judaic studies (by subject)
  2. Hebrew language
B. *Emotion (feelings)*
  1. Jewish identity
C. *Volition (behavior)*
  1. Moral education (values)
  2. Religious practices

6. **Teaching Method**

7. **Student**
A. *Age Group*
  1. Childhood
  2. Adolescence
  3. Adulthood
B. *Target Group*
  1. Individuals
    a. Individual teaching
    b. Self-education
  2. Families
  3. Communities

Figure 2: A knowledge outline of Jewish education

three successive academic years: 1997–98, 1998–99, and 1999–2000. The classification was based on a content analysis of the course descriptions. The descriptions were published at the JTS Web site.[29] The forty-seven distinct courses are listed in Appendix A. Each course was classified in the most relevant categories. The result is presented in Figure 3.

Discussion and Conclusion

The knowledge outline of the field of Jewish education is based on a three-step research methodology. The first step was a conceptual modeling based on a phenomenological analysis of the various phenomena of Jewish education. The structuring was rooted in the conception of Jewish education as a social interaction between the educator and the student. The analysis resulted in seven key categories. The seven-category model was then elaborated following a grounded structuring methodology. The materials used for grounding the structuring were eight subject-classification schemes that have been utilized in eight major bibliographic and Web reference resources. The third and last step was the testing and the validating of the three-level model by classifying forty-seven courses listed on the course list of JTS in the last three academic years.

The classification of courses at JTS was aimed at refining and validating the model. Still, it exemplifies an important application of the systematic knowledge outline as a tool for designing and evaluating Jewish education studies. As it is reflected in Figure 3, the program at JTS extensively covers the theoretical background of Jewish education, focusing on the fields of education and Judaism. It is also focused on integrating Jewish subjects in educational settings (i.e., the Judaic studies category in the content section) and in the practical aspects of teaching methods and techniques (i.e., the teaching-method section). In addition, the program offers numerous courses aimed at enriching the pedagogical knowledge of its students and developing their teaching skills. There are at least eight courses of supervised practicum and internship in the field (5140, 5475, 5513, 5514, 5521, 5560, 7401, and 7402) and at least four courses that are focused on the pedagogical personal knowledge of the participants (5031, 5559, 7401, and 7402). It should be noted that Figure 3 does not necessarily reflect the knowledge coverage

Foundations (Meta-Knowledge)	Theory		General theory courses: 5127
		Philosophy	5127
		Religion	8326; 9548
		Sociology	8610
		Education	5127; 5549; 8326; 9535; 9537; 9548
		Judaism	5036; 5127; 5323; 5525; 5547; 5548; 9535; 9537
	History	Ancient Judaism	
		Premodern	
		Pre-Holocaust	
		Post-Holocaust	5684
	Research	Methodology	5314; 5315; 9505; 9506
	Evaluation		9423
	Education	Theoretical education	
		Practical training	
Educator	Personality Traits		5642
	Value Orientation		5642
	Theoretical Knowledge	General humanistic	
		Basic Jewish	
		Disciplinary	
		Pedagogical	5031; 5559; 7401; 7402
	Teaching Experience		5140; 5475; 5513; 5514; 5521; 5560; 7401; 7402
Environment	Real Community	National conditions	
		Religious inclination	
	Virtual Community		
Organization	Formal Education	Kindergarten	
		Primary school	5312; 5313; 8610; 8611
		Secondary school	
		High school	
		Higher education	
	Informal Education	Community centers & synagogues	General courses: 5213; 5513; 5514; 8610; 8611 Courses on summer camps: 5139; 5140
		Summer camps	
		Supplementary religious schools	
		Youth movements	
		Educational organizations	
Content	Intellect (knowledge)	Judaic studies (by subject)	5011; 5036; 5038; 5059; 5158; 5425; 5525
		Hebrew language	5159
	Emotion (feelings)	Jewish identity	
	Volition (behavior)	Moral education	5547; 5548; 5549
		Religious practices	5055
Teaching Method			5031; 5055; 5765; 7124; 7401; 7402; 7412
Student	Age Group	Childhood	5116
		Adolescence	5115
		Adulthood	5135
	Target Group	Individuals	
		Families	
		Communities	

Figure 3: Subject classification of courses at the Jewish Theological Seminary

of the JTS program. Evaluating the program requires a thorough study of academic requirements, including courses that students are required to take in other departments at JTS. This thorough study exceeds the framework of this paper. However, the knowledge outline, as presented in Figure 3, provides a tool for planning and evaluating the course of study of individual students.

Developing the model proved its feasibility. Still, the model should be evaluated on the basis of its advantages and limitations. The model is systematic, comprehensive, updated, and scientifically valid; however, it cannot escape an essential limitation common to any knowledge structuring: it reflects philosophical, professional, and ideological tenets. Nevertheless, the subjective interpretations, which are inherent in phenomenological analysis as well as in grounded-theory research, do not imply that the model is arbitrary and irrational. Its scientific validity lies in the systematic modeling methodology. Yet it is an optional model— not the ultimate model. Furthermore, it is incomplete. Three levels of subclassification seem to be insufficient in some parts. The diversified interpretations are expected to affect future refining of at least two key categories, Judaism in the meta-knowledge section, and Judaic studies in the content section.

Despite these difficulties, the suggested systematic knowledge outline enables scholars and practitioners to map accumulated knowledge in the field and to specify the basic components of the key concepts. Apparently, it prepares the theoretical ground for academic education design, determines a prospective agenda for future research, and will facilitate quick access to relevant information if it is implemented in information systems and Web resources.

Appendix A

Combined List of Courses at the Jewish Theological Seminary in Academic Years 1997–98, 1998–99, and 1999–2000

EDU 5011   Jewish Education and Judaica: The Bridge Course (Bible)
EDU 5031   Skills for Teaching
EDU 5036   The Parashat *Hashavua* as a Construct of Jewish Time and
           Consciousness II
EDU 5038   Teaching the Jewish Holidays
EDU 5055   Methods of Teaching Prayer

EDU 5059   Jewish Education and Judaica: The Bridge Course (Liturgy)
EDU 5115   Developmental Issues in Jewish Education: Adolescence
EDU 5116   Developmental Issues in Jewish Education: Childhood
EDU 5127   Foundations and Current Issues in Jewish Education
EDU 5135   Themes in Adulthood and Adult Education
EDU 5139   Camping as a Resource for Jewish Education
EDU 5140   Seminar for Summer Camp Leadership Interns
EDU 5158   Curriculum and Instruction in Jewish Educational Settings: Introduction
EDU 5159   Curriculum and Instruction in Jewish Educational Settings: Hebrew Language Instruction Approaches
EDU 5213   Informal Jewish Education
EDU 5312   Practicum in Jewish Education: The Day School (I)
EDU 5313   Practicum in Jewish Education: The Day School (II)
EDU 5314   Methods of Research in Jewish Education I
EDU 5315   Methods of Research in Jewish Education II
EDU 5323   Redefinition of Jewish Identity in the Modern World
EDU 5425   Judaism and Creation: An Introduction to Ecology and Its Implications for Education
EDU 5475   Supervised Field Work
EDU 5513   Practicum in Jewish Education: The Afternoon School and Informal Educational Settings (I)
EDU 5514   Practicum in Jewish Education: The Synagogue and Other Educational Settings (II)
EDU 5521   Internship in a Jewish Teachers' Center Day School or Other Educational Setting
EDU 5525   Translating Jewish Theology for Educational Settings
EDU 5547   Perspectives on Religious Education I
EDU 5548   Perspectives on Religious Education II
EDU 5549   Moral Education and the Jewish School
EDU 5559   Staff Development and Supervision in Jewish Educational Settings
EDU 5560   Supervised Internship in Jewish Education
EDU 5642   Portraits of Teachers
EDU 5684   Jewish Education in Nonreligious Frameworks in the State of Israel
EDU 5765   Practices of Teachers
EDU 7124   Teaching Texts to Adolescents and Adults
EDU 7401   Practicum for Rabbinic Education Interns
EDU 7402   Practicum for Rabbinic Education Interns
EDU 7412   Exploring Experiential Learning Techniques
EDU 8326   Education, Religious Education and Jewish Education

EDU 8610   Executive Leadership for Nonprofit Jewish Organizations:
            Theory and Practice
EDU 8611   The Art and Practice of Educational Administration in the
            Jewish School
EDU 9423   Program Evaluation in Jewish Education
EDU 9505   Doctoral Seminar
EDU 9506   Doctoral Seminar
EDU 9535   The Educational Implications of Jewish Thought I
EDU 9537   The Educational Implications of Jewish Thought II
EDU 9548   Studies in Religion and Education

Notes

1. Library of Congress Classification (Littleton, Colo.: F. B. Rothman, 1998).
2. M. Dewey, Dewey Decimal Classification and Relative Index, ed. J. S. Mitchell et al., 21st ed. (Albany: Forest, 1996).
3. CyberStacks (WWW document, accessed July 1999), URL: http://www.public.iastate.edu/~CYBERSTACKS/homepage.html
4. CyberDewey (WWW document, accessed July 1999), URL: http://ivory.lm.com/~mundie/DDHC/CyberDewey.html
5. Britannica Internet Guide (WWW document, accessed July 1999), URL: http://www.britannica.com
6. Excite (WWW document, accessed July 1999), URL: http://www.excite.com
7. LookSmart (WWW document, accessed July 1999), URL: http://www.looksmart.com
8. WWW Virtual Library (WWW document, accessed July 1999), URL: http://vlib.org
9. Yahoo (WWW document, accessed July 1999), URL: http://www.yahoo.com
10. N. Drachler, ed., A Bibliography of Jewish Education in the United States (Detroit: Wayne State University Press, 1996).
11. D. H. Elazar and D. J. Elazar, A Classification System for Libraries of Judaica (Northvale, N.J.: Jason Aronson, 1997).
12. CAJE: Coalition for the Advancement of Jewish Education (WWW document, accessed September 1999), URL: http://www.caje.org/index.htm
13. JESNA: Jewish Education Service of North America (WWW document, accessed September 1999), URL: http://www.jesna.org
14. Jewishnet: Global Jewish Information Network (WWW document, accessed September 1999), URL: http://www.jewishnet.net/subjects/educa.htm
15. The Pedagogic Center (Department for Jewish Zionist Education, the Jewish Agency for Israel) (WWW document, accessed September 1999), URL: http://www.jajz-ed.org.il/index1.html

16. Shamash (WWW document, accessed September 1999), URL: http://www.
    shamash.org
17. Virtual Jerusalem (WWW document, accessed September 1999), URL:
    http://www.virtual.co.il/vjindex.htm
18. Gratz College (WWW document, accessed July 1999), URL: http://www.gratz-
    college.edu/college
19. Hebrew Union College (WWW document, accessed July 1999), URL:
    http://huc.edu
20. Jewish Theological Seminary (WWW document, accessed July 1999), URL:
    http://www.jtsa.edu
21. Spertus College (WWW document, accessed July 1999), URL: http://www.sper-
    tus.edu
22. Yeshiva University, Azrieli Graduate School of Jewish Education and Adminis-
    tration (WWW document, accessed July 1999), URL: http://www.yu.edu/
    azrieli, and Yeshiva University, Stern College for Women (WWW document,
    accessed July 1999), URL: http://www.yu.edu/stern
23. See n. 10 above.
24. A. Strauss and J. Corbin, "Grounded Theory Methodology," in *Handbook of
    Qualitative Research,* ed. N. K. Denzin and Y. S. Lincoln (Thousand Oaks,
    Calif.: Sage, 1994).
25. The courses are listed on the Web site of JTS. See n. 20 above.
26. K. Gödel, "On Formally Undecidable Propositions of Principia Mathematica
    and Related System I," in *Collected Works,* 1929–36 (New York: Oxford Uni-
    versity Press, 1986), 1:145–95.
27. C. Zins, "Issues and Considerations for Designing Human Services Studies in
    Israel," in *Social Security: Journal of Welfare and Social Security Studies* 55
    (1999): 83–101 (in Hebrew).
28. Y. Samuel, *Organizations: Features, Structures, Processes,* 2d ed. (Tel Aviv:
    Haifa University Press, 1996).
29. See n. 20 above.

JUDAISM AS A RESOURCE
FOR GENERAL EDUCATION

A Modern/Ancient Encounter with Text:
Talmudic Format in Secular Contexts

Stephen I. Brown

> Get yourself a teacher and find a study partner.
>
> —*Pirkei Avot*

When President Kennedy invited Nobel laureates to the White House for dinner, he was reputed to have said, "At no time in the history of mankind has so much brain power been gathered in so small a region—save when Thomas Jefferson dined alone." With only a modicum of hyperbole, so it is today with technology and its pedagogical promise in relation to the Talmud. With CD-ROM, hypertext, interactive Internet modes, and the like, at no time in the history of education have we gathered so much material that has the potential to transform the concept of educational text—save when the Talmud was created a couple of millennia ago.[1]

For a number of years, I have been seeking ways to transform the concept of text in the education of teachers so that it is seen as a more vibrant, intellectually enticing, and aesthetically appealing resource. My goal has been to encourage readers to come to grips with their (frequently unarticulated) beliefs about the nature of education, subject matter, and self. Using a talmudic format is my latest effort—one that derives from my cherished association with Joseph Lukinsky for over three decades.

Stephen I. Brown is professor emeritus of philosophy of education and mathematics education at the Graduate School of Education at the State University of New York at Buffalo.

The Lukinsky Connection

Initial Influence

Joseph Lukinsky and I met as doctoral students in the late 1960s at the Harvard Graduate School of Education. He had received his rabbinical degree several years earlier, and was studying philosophy of education; my primary affiliation was with mathematics education. Many forces drew us together.

Influenced by Dewey's view of progressive education, we were both seeking ways to enable students to appreciate that knowledge at its most sophisticated level is not unconnected with their own intuitive experiences. We both incorporated elements of popular culture into our teaching. Thus in the education of teachers, Lukinsky looked toward such art forms as theater and dance, and I found connections with comedy and metaphorical thinking.

But there was more that fueled our friendship. We discovered that each of us had been an alter ego of sorts for the other. I disclosed to him that, though my training was in mathematics, I had had earlier fantasies of becoming a rabbi. He revealed to me that he had been enticed by the prospect of becoming a mathematician—assuming that he could not make it as a professional baseball player.

Upon completing our doctoral programs, Lukinsky joined the faculty at Brandeis University, and I the Harvard Graduate School of Education. We team-taught a course that was cross-registered for students at both institutions. The course was entitled "Math and Morality," and we investigated what those fields had in common. At the beginning, some students believed that they had virtually nothing in common, since one was obviously an abstract system unrelated to people and focused primarily on logic, while the other was concerned primarily with the intricacies of human behavior. Others claimed that the fields were obviously quite similar, since they both were rule-driven: one being mathematical rules; and the other, rules of human interaction. The course involved a whittling away at this dichotomy and resulted in our all coming to understand more substantial commonalties and differences in the two fields. An important legacy that our collaboration has achieved is that it inspired me to think more creatively about what it means to relate any two fields of inquiry.

Lukinsky and the Secular Talmud

A sacred text, the Talmud is considered to be second only to the Bible in Jewish tradition. It consists of two main sources: the Mishnah and the Gemara. The Mishnah was produced in the second century A.D. and is an attempt to codify religious traditions. The Gemara, produced in the fifth and sixth centuries, is commentary on the Mishnah—an effort to locate the problem or set of problems that the Mishnah assumes as a "given." They both deal not only with abstract principles of action but with the most detailed discussion and analysis of everyday practical problems. One of the most interesting qualities of the Talmud as an educational text is its nonlinear format. It is assumed that anyone who begins to study the thousands of pages of the Talmud is already familiar with the entire collection—a refreshing counterpoint to the belief that students' lives provide them with no clue about important intellectual issues unless they have been spelled out in progressively greater detail.

I was first attracted to the possibility of creating secular texts via talmudic format upon reading an essay by Lukinsky.[2] Commenting on the Talmud's deliberative, nonlinear style of exposition, he states:

> Modern books are linear and present the perspective of the individual author. The author's inner deliberation is for the most part buried and implicit in the smoothed-out reasoned argument that is published or presented orally. If another view is presented at all it is usually refuted or incorporated, not given a fair presentation. . . . On those occasions when another view is fully stated, the same problem arises. That perspective, too, appears in a polished and unequivocal guise. The reader or listener is left to his own devices to put the argument together. . . . The framework and presuppositions of the authors are hidden in the editing, and they may seem to be speaking past each other.[3]

Steinsaltz, in his ongoing project to produce commentary for an English translation of the Talmud, explains one reason for the style Lukinsky describes:

> The arrangement of the Talmud is not systematic, nor does it follow familiar didactic principles. It does not proceed from the simple to the complex, or from the general to the particular. . . . Textbooks deal with specific material, and it is therefore easy to

present that material in a clearly defined order. The Talmud, by contrast, deals with an overwhelmingly broad subject—the nature of all things according to the Torah. Therefore its contours are a reflection of life itself.[4]

What makes the talmudic page particularly appropriate as a study of the evolution of ideas is not only that it orchestrates the dialogical Gemara with the more rule-bound Mishnah, but that text is surrounded by commentary of scholars as well as anonymous critics whose reactions span hundreds of years. To engage the Talmud is to experience an emotional and intellectual adventure across centuries as if one is actually a participant in the dialogue. On each page, we find not only comments and reflections upon comments, but as Lukinsky summarizes:

> It is a vast anthology of centuries of legal argument, religious speculation, scriptural exegesis, historical and quasi-historical sources, personal legends, specific facts, fantastic imaginings, and more. The editing is associative. One point leads to another. A legal discussion leads to a story, a spiritual interpretation, a fanciful piece of imagery.[5]

Furthermore, even when the discourse is problem-oriented, it is not unusual for a carefully reasoned debate with conflicting points of view to end with the statement: *Tie*. Neither side has provided a definitive enough argument, and it is left to the reader to decide.

If this kind of activity sounds overly elitist, it is worth remembering that not only rabbis and aspiring scholars, but all members of the community (more recently, including those who are of the same gender persuasion as Barbra Streisand—as anyone who has seen the movie *Yentl* can attest) engaged in talmudic study on a daily basis. Such study was integrally connected with how one lives a life. In addition, the study is a collaborative act done in pairs—perhaps one of the earliest forms of cooperative learning.

Lukinsky sketches the ways in which we can use the talmudic experience in a variety of fields, from law and the study of the constitution to popular culture, as in the famous "pine tar" debate in baseball.[6] Figure 1 is a revised schematic of a typical talmudic page.[7]

Before turning to the potential of the talmudic format as text in mathematics education, we provide a whirlwind account of some developments in the foundations of mathematics as a discipline.

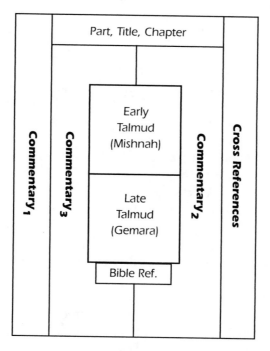

Figure 1: Schematic of Talmudic page

A Changing View of the Nature of Mathematics

More than any other area, mathematics education has been dominated by mischievous epistemological views. Mathematics is portrayed popularly as a discipline that is impervious to doubt and scornful of the realization that what is considered relevant knowledge is a social construction. In educational embodiments, we have been reluctant to appreciate its history of controversy or debate, disinclined to honor nonlinear unraveling of ideas, and slow in acknowledging that cognition and emotionality are inextricably intertwined.

It is only within the past seventy years or so that the resistance of classical mathematical problems to solution has been viewed in a new light—one that places it closer to the camp of the humanities than had heretofore been imagined. We think of literature, for example, as a genre that at best suggests partial answers to questions that are continually being reframed. The groundbreaking work of the Austrian logician/philosopher Kurt Gödel in the 1930s demonstrated that the existence of problems that are simply stated but remain unsolved for hundreds of years (such as, How many consecutive odd numbers are there such that both of them are prime?) is not necessarily a temporary setback that awaits the brilliance of a genius to unlock. Rather, it is an indication of some deep recalcitrance within the discipline itself.[8]

For reasons of this sort and others, the philosophy of mathematics began to take on a new complexion. There has been a transformation from a long-standing inquiry into foundational interests associated with competing "isms," such as logic*ism*, intuition*ism*, and formal*ism*—schools that attempted to establish the bedrock of mathematical certainty in different ways. They differed in a number of ways, but they were all concerned with the question of seeking a foundation from which everything else might flow. As Van Bendegem points out, philosophical analysis has begun to shift toward questions related to how the discipline is practiced. Some scholars, for example, are concerned with a nontrivial analysis of why it is that accepted proofs are subsequently refuted.[9]

We have barely begun to raise some of the interesting philosophical issues that challenge the standard view of mathematics as fixed and uncontroversial. Despite recent rejuvenation of the field via documents and programs associated with *The Standards,* there has been little in the way of text material that conveys the nature of mathematics as a controversial and debatable field of inquiry.[10] It is as if we have totally lost sight of the fact that the very names that have been bequeathed to number systems testify to the labor pains experienced during their long and difficult birth. It is no mere coincidence that the number systems studied in much of high school are referred to as "rational," "irrational," "imaginary," "complex," "negative," and the like.

Talmudic Format in Mathematics Education

Prior to incorporating the talmudic format, I had made use of another alternative style designed to correct some of the entrenched epistemological attitudes—that of storytelling and novel as mathematical text. In my own novella, *Posing Mathematically,* the protagonists are two teachers who jointly teach a course to high school students, and they stumble upon problem posing as an idea to explore. They wonder about how to organize their emerging ideas and how to make them accessible to their colleagues.[11] At one point, the protagonists organize a conference by selecting a panel in which five competing views are presented regarding the nature and educational value of problem posing. The roots of each of these positions as well as the educational implications are hinted at but not fully developed. The two teachers explore the different rationales for problem posing, attempt to apply some of the associated strategies in their teaching, and engage in a variety of problem-posing activities per se. The reader is enticed to elaborate upon, criticize, and make sense of these different perspectives. In appropriate self-referential fashion, the protagonists eventually decide to write a novel as a way of disseminating their idea.

There are parts of *Posing Mathematically* that are expository in nature and others that just tell a story. As I moved from thinking about the novel as text to developing a talmudic format, I began to think not only about intertwining the two epistemological styles in a more deliberate manner, but about the different functions served by storytelling and explaining. In my course work with teachers, we experimented with narrative versus expository voices to try to figure out the differences in their stance toward the concepts of truth and reality as well as their effect upon fellow students in the class and upon others who had not been part of the talmudic experience. In creating talmudic-style text, we found it helpful to think of the Mishnah as describing a content-oriented or pedagogical situation that seemed straightforward and noncontroversial, almost inconsequential. Eventually, as the many different voices in the Gemara and associated commentary respond to that situation, the talmudic text becomes alive and the supposedly simple beginning unfolds into a spectacular chorus with accompanying cacophony as well.

An Example: Setting the Context

An example of an early talmudic effort of mine is depicted in Figures 2, 3, and 4 below.

In the Mishnah (Figure 2), "The House of Shamai and the House of Hillel" refer to two sects that have historical talmudic relevance. Their discussion is about a very simple calculation that all of us do unflinchingly—adding numbers that end in zero by first ignoring the zeros and then appending them to the answer.[12]

Having begun with a relatively benign situation, the associated Gemara then explores many different reasons for why the "zero shortcut" might work (Figure 3). We are then sidetracked by a number of

Mishnah
Shortcuts

The House of Shamai and the House of Hillel return from purchasing corn seeds. They promise to pay the corn-seed merchant in a month with the money that they will receive from the father-in-law of the House of Shamai. Together they will be building a new barn for him, and he has promised to pay their total expenses for their corn seed as soon as they have framed the structure. The corn-seed merchant has told the House of Shamai and the House of Hillel that he has figured out how much they owe, based on the information they have given him for each of the two plots of land that they will be sowing. He has said that the House of Shamai owes 470 shekels and the House of Hillel owes 220 shekels. They each calculate separately the amount of money that they will have to request from the father-in-law of the House of Shamai.

The House of Hillel does his calculation in the sand and figures out that it will be 690 shekels altogether. He did the addition as follows:

$$470$$
$$+220$$
$$\overline{}$$
$$690$$

The House of Shamai also figured out the sum, and it is indeed 690, but it is possible to do so without moving around so much sand on the ground. He says that it should be done as follows:

$$47$$
$$+22$$
$$\overline{}$$
$$69$$

And then the House of Shamai says that you should just tag on a zero at the end and make the answer 690.

The House of Hillel says that this is a trick that seems to work in this case, but that it is not the way to do addition. He asks: If the sum were 475 and 225 shekels, would you do the same thing? He shows the two procedures:

475	47
$+225$	$+22$
$\overline{}$	$\overline{}$
700	69

Then if you tag along the common 5, the answer would have to be 695, when you know it is really 700.

Figure 2: First Mishnah: The zero-adding shortcut

tangentially related issues: How do these different reason-giving activities relate to one another? Have we been duped into thinking that it makes sense to think of zero as a placeholder? If we think beyond the activity of trying to *prove* why things work in adding numbers ending in zero, we are inclined to ask what might have motivated anyone to engage in the "dropping the zeros shortcut" many years ago. Eventually, the Gemara returns to the very concept of shortcut, revealing that the idea is not as trivial as it may seem. In the midst of these "diversions," the Gemara stops its analytical development and, out of the blue, recalls a dream that would enable one of the characters, Reb Estaban, to predict the gender of his unborn grandchild.

He dreams that he is whisked away in a chariot and visits a different land that is in every way like his own, except for the fact that time and space are contracted. Everyone is considerably smaller, and events are played out in a small fraction of the time it would take in his "real world" (Figure 4). The upshot, of course is that the potential exists for him to learn the gender (before the days of ultrasound or amniocentesis) of his grandchild in a few seconds rather than having to wait for the better part of nine months.

As the text unfolds, diverse commentary appears in the Gemara margin. Issues such as the following are raised: What is the connection between the rather simpleminded shortcut of adding numbers ending in zero and Reb Estaban's story of the gender of his unborn grandchild? Several attempts to understand the relationship of the original situation and the story are revealed. Eventually, a case is made that the story, by establishing a "mapping" between the real world and the dream world, is talking about a structure that is analogous to the shortcut used in the arithmetic of the Mishnah. As the tractate develops, one of the most fundamental mathematical concepts is seen as lurking beneath the surface. Like a ripple that develops into a tidal wave, the concept of isomorphic structure is revealed as a link between the mathematical shortcut and the story of Reb Estaban's unborn grandchild.

What had begun as an arithmetic issue turns into a philosophical/pedagogical one. Eventually, my students began to embellish the Gemara and created their own comments in the margin. One experienced teacher, assuming the role of the confused pupil, wondered why it is difficult to understand the issues being raised and how they might be made more accessible by visual schemes. On the contrary, another explored the value of intentionally misunderstanding the idea of isomorphism—thus investigating the ways in which errors can be productive. Yet another voice soft-

Gemara

Reb Burton tries many examples of adding pairs of numbers, each of which ends in zero. Indeed, the procedure of the House of Shamai—ignoring the zeros for each pair at the beginning and then appending a zero at the end—works in all cases that he has tried. He believes that it will work always.

[1] Reb Vilson points out that Reb Burton, Reb Adina, and Reb Luke are each looking at proof in a different way. One is trying to establish the generalization based on an empirical mode by trying many cases; one is coming up with a proof that works for all such cases. That proof, however, makes use of an algorithm or a procedure, and though it proves somthing, it does have a blind quality to it—unless one already understands the positional notation on which the algorithm depends. The third proof gets at the meaning of the notation, at least in part. Reb Vilson wonders if there are other proofs that might be even more revealing. He wonders what kinds of things a proof might be expected to reveal in general, other than merely showing that something is true.[2]

[2] Reb Tamara looks again at the three different proofs and wonders what role zero is playing, even apart from the proof. She has heard people say that zero is not a number but a placeholder. She wonders which of these two conceptions is being revealed through the notations being used.[3]

Reb Adina realizes that there is a simple reason that the procedure works with zeros at the end of each pair. She observes that if you follow the standard algorithms for adding numbers, then if you start at the most right-hand corner of each pair, and if each member of the pair ends in zero, then you are just adding zero plus zero and, of course, you end up with zero as the sum.

Reb Luke claims that in order to make sense out of the procedure, it is necessary to appreciate what the little zero is doing at the end of each of the numbers. It is not just adding a little zero to each of the numbers of the original pair. What, for example, is the relationship between 47 and 470? What is the relationship between 22 and 220? He points out that 470 is really 10 times 47; and 220 is really 10 times 22. When you look at the sum, 690 is really 10 times 69. Thus, what we really have is the following:

[3] Reb Putzik thinks of something that she had not thought about before: it is one thing to understand the meaning of the positional notation used in numbers and even to be able to prove things with such notation; but how is it that anyone ever was motivated to come up with the idea of positional notation? What must have been used to represent numbers before it was fully developed?

$$47 \times 10$$
$$+\ 22 \times 10$$
$$\overline{69 \times 10^1}$$

Reb Estaban points out that Reb Luke is not wrong, but that not everything isfitting into place. For one thing, the problem does not begin with finding the sum of 47 and 22, but rather the sum of 470 and 220. He knows that what Reb Luke has done is relevant, but despite the fact that everything looks so simple, he wonders if there might be something beneath the surface that is missing. He is tired and lies down to rest in the field next to his farm. As he lies down, the last thing he recalls is the good news that he has just heard from his daughter-that she is in her first trimester of pregnancy. He dreams about his forthcoming grandchild and wonders if it will be a boy or a girl.

Figure 3: Beginning of the Gemara for the Mishnah of Figure 2

Gemara

Reb Estaban dreams about his forthcoming grandchild and wonders if it will be a boy or a girl. If it is a girl, his son-in-law will have to think about how to prepare a proper dowry in about twenty years. Reb Estaban wonders if he himself might be able to contribute to that dowry by passing along some of his land, which he imagines will be rich in corn in years to come. He should only live so long. If it is a son, he imagines that the boy will accompany his son-in-law and him to services every Sabbath. He should only live so long. It crosses his mind that he might also like to have a granddaughter accompany them to services, but no one in his shtetl ever heard of such a thing. Of course, he then smiles as he imagines that one day, men might have to come to the family of their prospective wives with a dowry. He is imagining what the child might look like, whom it might resemble, what its first words might be, when suddenly he sees a brightly colored horse-drawn carriage and an old woman with emerald beads on her blouse and skirt. She beckons him to step up to the seat beside her on the carriage. He is shy and does not feel comfortable sitting next to a strange woman, but he steps aboard as she whispers that she has mysteries to reveal. They chat away about the weather for a while. Suddenly, the horse begins to take flight, hovering only a few feet above the ground at first, but eventually he can just barely see his farm from the air. After a period of time that seems interminable, he begins to see stars from a distance. They are covered with a thin veil of tightly crocheted yellow lacy curtains—the sort that his wife had made for his daughter when she was a baby, to protect her carriage from flies as the family walked to town in the summer. He hears the voices of his daughter and son-in-law—barely audible but still coming from the direction of his hometown. They are telling him that he is in for an adventure and that he should go with the flow and not resist in the way that he resisted the last time that he got a massage and was supposed to try to relax. He begins to fear that he will never return. He then hears his daughter and son-in-law singing, but their voices are no longer coming from his farm. They seem to be coming from a strange land that is miles away from his village. The horse stops abruptly and lands on a piece of earth. At first, it looks as though he has returned to his own village. He sees the farmhouse in the distance, the plot of land on which he will plant corn, and he sees several people coming toward him from the distance. He embraces his wife, his daughter, and his son-in-law. They seem to be the same as when he left on his horse-drawn adventure. They have the same clothing, the same smells, and they talk the same; but something is peculiar. As he is hugging them, he realizes that he is lifting each of them up into the air. They are about four feet above the ground. Why is that? Suddenly, he realizes that though they all have the same features, they are about one-tenth their normal size. His daughter—whom he is hugging—hits the ground with a thump, and he realizes that he, too, has begun to shrink in size. His wife has prepared a picnic of his favorite gefilte fish and matzos. They toast his joyful return with some wine used only for special occasions. Reb Estaban wipes the dripping wine from his lips with his shirt sleeve and is preparing to tell them about his adventure, when suddenly his wife calls him in from the field for dinner. He is just completing dinner when she tells him that they are ready to eat breakfast before going to visit her family in the next village.

Figure 4: A story in the first Gemara

ened the concept of isomorphism and began to wonder about the meaning of the more general concept of "same" and "different" as it applies to a variety of mathematical and human encounters. Another voice spoke about how the particular problem reveals something interesting about the nature of mind and of mathematics.

In Figures 2–4, we display excerpts from the talmudic text that we have just described.

Revealing a Larger Mathematical Picture

The first major mathematical focus is revealed in Reb Luke's formulation when he observes the following:

$$
\begin{array}{r}
47 \times 10 \\
+22 \times 10 \\
\hline
69 \times 10
\end{array}
$$

It is an instance of a fundamental property of numbers that is used intuitively in many of the arithmetic shortcuts that we employ with little explicit reflection. Figure 5 below suggests one way of mentally calculating the product of 15 and 23.

One way of seeing what is behind both the dropping of the zeros and the shortcut in Figure 5 is that they are instances of the distributive property—one formulation of which is: $(a \cdot b) + (c \cdot b) = (a + c) \cdot b$.

What makes the distributive property particularly interesting among the many arithmetical properties (the axioms) is that it is the only one that explicitly connects two operations of arithmetic: addition and multiplication. The others (for example, the commutative property that essentially asserts that when two numbers are added, the result is not

Figure 5: An intuitive application of the distributive property

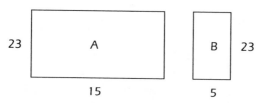

Figure 6: Geometric version of the distributive property

affected by their order) involve only one of the two operations for each property. That is only a beginning, however. Its algebraic formulation has a geometric counterpart, as suggested in Figure 6 above. That is, in order to find the total areas of two rectangles $[(23 \cdot 15) + (23 \cdot 5)]$ with one common dimension, we need not calculate each separately, but can join them along an edge with a common length and can calculate the sum mentally $(23 \cdot 20)$.

Starting with the above rather modest observations, I embarked on a program of writing a tractate on the distributive property in talmudic format for mathematics teachers that challenged the narrow way in which we tend to define "progress" in the development of mathematics and especially in mathematics education. That is, progress is usually conceived of as covering more and more content by plastering or layering one new mathematical concept on another.

This realization led me to design a unit in which I was motivated by the following question: Would it be possible and worthwhile to choose *one* mathematical property as a centerpiece for the purpose of illuminating and exploring a large number of issues regarding the nature of mathematics as a discipline and of self in relation to the discipline?

Educational Matters

The Distributive Property as a Peephole

My point of view is well captured by the following poem by William Blake:

To see the world in a grain of sand
And heaven in a wild flower,

To hold infinity in the palm of your hand
And eternity in an hour.

That is, I was essentially asking whether I could use the talmudic format on the distributive property, not as a building block to create new and more magnificent mathematical structures per se, but rather as a peephole into the nature of mathematics and mind.

Below are some of the issues that contributed to the peephole concept of the distributive property.

a) What are the many different ways in which we might characterize what the distributive property asserts? What are some interesting mathematical misconceptions that are associated with this abstraction [$(a + b)^2 = a^2 + b^2$ might be one such example]? What are some "real world" nonmathematical illustrations of the property? How, for example, does the concept of "(x) *loving* (y) *and* (z)" operate in the real world distributively? In what ways is the use of love revealing? Problematic?

b) The concept of "same" and "different" is a fundamental human concept and is built into how we think and act. It is, as a matter of fact, one that may "do us in" as a species one day. It is also one that has evolutionary value as lower organisms define "friend" and "foe." How is the concept of isomorphism described in the talmudic text associated with the distributive property dependent upon the notion of "same" and "different"? To what extent can we characterize mathematical thought as an effort to capture what is the same about what is different, and vice versa? How do we define "same" and "different" in ways that are helpful? Harmful?

c) We showed two mathematical versions of the distributive property above—an algebraic and a geometric interpretation. How do algebraic and geometric ways of thinking about this particular property compare? Are each of the renditions revealing the same concept? If you try to generalize from the algebra versus the geometry, do you end up with the same sort of generalization? What do we make of the fact that Euclid was able to grasp such concepts as the distributive property geometrically, but not algebraically at all? Algebra is frequently associated with a linguistic formulation, and geometry with something essentially visual. Is this distinction valid? Helpful? How are we influenced by the two different modes of presentation?

d) I have come across several appearances of the distributive property that have led to results that are surprising and counterintuitive. Sometimes, the surprise can be overcome and a "better" intuition reestablished once we understand why we were surprised in the first place. Sometimes, no matter how cogent an explanation, we continue to remain surprised by the result. What role does surprise play in the evolution of new ideas in mathematics? In other aspects of our lives? To what extent are we unnerved by surprise? Why?

Stepping Back: Voices in the Margin

I have taught several courses to teachers in which I have used the talmudic format. There are numerous ways to incorporate that text style in a secular education, but it is important to appreciate that the structure has been suggestive rather than a model to be adopted in its entirety. In the spirit of modifying the Talmud for secular uses, I have, in collaboration with my students, identified a number of types of voices that make for powerful commentary in the margins, including:

A *pseudo-history voice:* In developing a mathematical idea, I have found it helpful to ask students not to do research of a historical nature, but rather to imagine what *might have been* the predecessor of a concept that is now well entrenched. What might the idea have looked like, for example, prior to the existence of present-day language to describe it? As in the case of the distributive property, they are to imagine what non-algebraic formulations there could have been to express the concept.

The philosophical voice: What does this idea mean? What views of mind, emotion, and personhood are expressed by them? What contradictions are there in this idea as it is expressed? How compatible is it with other ideas expressed so far?

The voice of the recalcitrant student: Why is this worth thinking about? How does it relate to anything that is important in one's life?

The voice that strives for clarity and minimizing confusion: What is ambiguous or vague about this concept?

The voice of the muddifier: How can we transform something that appears to be clear and settled into an idea that has enough confusion so that it opens up fresh ways to explore?

The explanation/storytelling skeptic voice: This voice looks at the style in which text was expressed and wonders whether what was offered as an explanation should have been a story (or vice versa) and why.

An Epilogue and a Prologue

With only minimal suggestion by me, each class found ways of elaborating upon the commentary categories described above as well as the manner of interrelating Mishnah and Gemara. In one of the most interesting embellishments, students created a weekly diary that spoke about how the talmudic experience was affecting their perception of themselves as teachers, friends, students, and parents (and how it was enabling them to dissolve what many had heretofore seen as the divide among those many roles), and they not only invited the reaction of fellow students but also stipulated a range of marginal voices that would be particularly welcome. Thus, they created a talmudic format to enable them to understand what the talmudic format was all about.

    Surely the two-thousand-year-old talmudic tradition is much richer and more complicated than I have described. It involves many ways of thinking and feeling that I am just beginning to understand. Since I have been using it primarily for the purpose of challenging accepted epistemological views, however, my students and I have not considered adaptations to be a sacrilegious act. Nevertheless, it has provided me with a new set of lenses with which to understand myself as a teacher and as a student as well. As I try to measure the impact of such an orientation on my own students, I am awestruck by the extent to which it has created an attitude that blurs some commonly held distinctions—such as that between teaching and therapy or that between learning a discipline and self-understanding.

    Below is a comment made by one of my students in a secular Talmud course. He was a private person, who had just begun to teach and loved nothing more than solving mathematical problems, and who, before engaging in the talmudic experience, detested the prospect of writing essays, especially ones that were introspective. I offer his reaction not for self-serving purposes, but to sensitize my colleagues to the frequently hidden desire that many of our students have to see themselves in relation to subject matter even when they would have us believe otherwise.

> This is truly a sad time, yet still a time to rejoice. The semester is over. Yet so much has to be done. I am trying to think back to what I have immediately learned, and accepting that in the future, I will inevitably see more. One of the most peculiar things I have begun to develop, and for which I credit this class, is a better sense of humor and love of life in general. I had mentioned to Dr. Brown about laughing until crying and bodily convulsions set in. Some of the critical-analysis skills I have picked up in this course have opened up these venues of humor. This course is titled for mathematics education, and I feel I have learned a lot of ways to improve upon my mathematics teaching. But I feel that most of what I learned was how to be a better person. . . . I feel that what this course has done is keep the playful spirit of the child in our education, and reminded us to keep it in our classrooms and our lives.

I do not think that we had explicitly spoken of the child within each of us. Though I cherish humor, I do not recall exhibiting an unusual degree of humor, nor having made that an explicit part of the curriculum. I do believe, however, that the talmudic experience invited students not only to experience deliberation and to uncover multiple perspectives on a variety of issues, but to listen to new and previously hidden voices within each of them and to engage in the risky behavior of uncovering and incorporating aspects of their lives that had previously been seen as isolated and protected.

I close with a moving story about a rabbi who approached a member of his congregation, a world-famous physicist, and asked her what the legacy was that Einstein had left. The physicist told him that Einstein had not only created relativity theory in which he looked at energy, space, and time in ways that had never been imagined before, but had also devised "mind experiments," which were subsequently verified by laborious empirical methods. She then pointed out that Einstein made the concept of relativity a metaphor in everyday discourse for virtually everyone on this planet. The rabbi replied, "What a *shandah*. Imagine how much better off the world would have been if he had only studied the Talmud instead."

If the rabbi had inquired about a famous educator rather than a physicist, he might have learned of the power of "constructivism," or of the concept of "empowerment," or of "assessment" in relation to testing. With only a modicum of hyperbole, he then might have replied, "What a *shandah*. Imagine how much better educated our culture would be if that educator had engaged his students in the study of secular Talmud instead."

Notes

1. For a kinder view of the relationship of the Internet to the Talmud, see Jonathan Rosen, *The Talmud and the Internet: A Journey between Worlds* (New York: Farrar, Straus & Giroux, 2000). Complicating this claim is the fact that not only the Bible, but the Talmud itself (comprising both the early Hebrew Aramaic and more recently translated English version) is now produced on CD-ROM. See *The Soncino Talmud, The CD-ROM Judaic Classics Library* (New York: Institute for Computers in Jewish Life and Davka Corporation and Judaic Press, 1991–93).

2. Joseph Lukinsky, "Law in Education: A Reminiscence with Some Footnotes to Robert Cover's 'Nomos and Narrative,' " *Yale Law Journal* 96, no. 8 (1987): 1836–59.

3. Ibid., 1843.

4. Adin Steinsaltz, commentator, *The Talmud*, English translation; Israel V. Berman, senior translator and ed., introductory vol. (New York: Random House, 1989), 7.

5. Lukinsky, 1838–39.

6. Ibid., 1855.

7. Ibid., 1842; permission to modify and use is granted by the Yale Law Journal Co. and Fred B. Rothman & Co. from *Yale Law Journal* 96 (1987): 1836–59.

8. For discussions of the work of Gödel that are relatively nontechnical, see James Nagel and James Newman, *Gödel's Proof* (New York: New York University Press, 1958); and John W. Dawson, "Gödel and the Limits of Logic," *Scientific American* 280, no. 6 (1999): 76–81.

9. Jean Paul Van Bendegem, "Foundations of Mathematics or Mathematical Practice: Is One Forced to Choose?" in *Math Worlds: Philosophical and Social Studies of Mathematics and Mathematics Education,* ed. S. Restivo, J. P. Van Bendegem, and R. Fisher (Albany: State University of New York Press, 1993), 21–38.

10. Three documents published by the National Council of Teachers of Mathematics (Reston, Va.) constitute what is known as *The Standards*. Entitled "Curriculum and Evaluation Standards for School Mathematics" (1989), "Professional Standards for Teaching Mathematics" (1991), and "Assessment Standards for School Mathematics" (1995), they focus on curriculum, teacher education, and assessment, respectively. The latest, entitled "Principles and Standards for School Mathematics" (2000), takes into consideration more recent research on learning and teaching as well as the practical experience of living with the original three documents.

11. Stephen I. Brown, *Posing Mathematically* (Portsmouth, N.H.: Heinemann, 1996).

12. I have maintained much of the religious language and even the specific talmudic references (such as the two sects mentioned in this Mishnah) in this tractate. It was done as a heuristic for holding the talmudic spirit in mind, but will be modified in future secular incarnations. The secular Talmud that appears later in this section is a modified version of what I wrote in *Reconstructing School Mathematics: Problems with Problems and the Real World* (New York: Peter Lang, 2001). The publisher has granted permission to reproduce that material for this essay.

Enhancing Religious Education through Collegial Teaching

William Bean Kennedy

During my fifteen years on the faculty at Union Theological Seminary, the experience in the Joint Program in Religion and Education with Teachers College and the Jewish Theological Seminary of America contributed substantially to my overall understanding of religious education. Joseph Lukinsky from JTS, Douglas Sloan from TC, and I from UTS formed a team working with doctoral students of all three institutions. Regular seminars gave us opportunities to help students with their research and studies of educational theory and practice and to focus with them on a series of issues about religion and education.

The names used in our program included the particularistic terms "Jewish education" and "Christian education," as well as the broader "religious education." The one we preferred, however, was either "religion and education" or "education and religion," depending upon which institution was using it. I preferred the latter two names, because the other terms imply education within a religious community.

But religion also acts beyond particular religious communities as a major force in society. When one religious tradition becomes too dominant and tries to influence or force all citizens to conform to it, serious conflict occurs for those who belong to other religious traditions. Jews living in the midst of Christian, Muslim, or other majority religions are keenly aware of those problems. Where so-called secularism threatens to undercut religious traditions, the issue involves both education and religion. Our joint program, unlike most other doctoral programs in religious education, put religion both outside as well as within particular

William Bean Kennedy is the Skinner and McAlpin Professor Emeritus of Practical Theology at the Union Theological Seminary.

242

religious traditions and therefore treated the issues as societal and global as well as particularistic toward specific traditions. We tried constantly to attend to both dimensions.

Before 1979, my contacts with Judaism and Jewish education had been haphazard. My grandfather, for whom I was named, used to read for family devotions from the Hebrew text in his polyglot Bible. My mother was once kept as a baby by a Jewish neighbor through a dangerous epidemic. In my hometown of Spartanburg, South Carolina, our youth group visited the synagogue in order to learn something of different religious communities in town. In college, I became aware of how requiring attendance at Christian chapel services caused a problem for the few Jewish students.

My first personal relationship with a Jewish person came in the navy at the end of World War II, when I became friends with Harold Rafalowitz (later changed to Rafson). A visit to his home in Jamaica, New York, gave me my first taste of a home-cooked Jewish meal. Many years later, the Lukinskys shared their seder meal with my wife and me. Joe's interpretation made it special.

In my doctoral work at Yale in the mid-1950s, Marshall Sklare's sociological study *Conservative Judaism*[1] fascinated me with his descriptions and analysis of distinctive characteristics of Jewish life and faith. My awareness of the Holocaust and its impact upon us all came gradually as the stories and horrors became more generally known. Bruno Bettelheim's description of his experiences in a concentration camp[2] prepared me for Elie Wiesel's sensitive writing.

So when I came to New York in 1979 and discovered the rich experience I was able to share with Joe in the Joint Program and the life of the Jewish Theological Seminary, my interest and fascination moved into more focused learning. I shall comment on that learning in three parts: the world of Judaism, Jewish education, and ongoing questions about Christian education from those experiences.

Getting to Know the World of Judaism

We rotated the seminar among the three schools, so every third semester the class met at JTS, where we all felt the hospitality and ambience of that institution. Often we three met over lunch in the cafeteria and sometimes joined in the celebrations of Jewish holidays.

The seminars included students from all three institutions, and the quality and diversity of those from JTS added immeasurably to what we were learning. Through an Israeli student who worked in a peace center, we learned about the substantial proportion of the population in Israel who were working for peaceful solutions. That student cited as the greatest moment of his life the arrival of Egyptian president Anwar Sadat's plane on the Israeli runway. Through others, we were introduced to the complex religious and educational problems in Israel and some of the different reflections on its political life.

An American Jewish student who worked in the educational department of the Jewish Museum in New York took the class to the museum and engaged us in a probing discussion of ways to educate people through Holocaust exhibits. Through another's educational analysis of her work as a chaplain in a Jewish old folks' home in New York, we gained insight into the importance of repetitive ritual activities, such as lighting the candles at dusk.

Literature from the work of Jewish educators became part of seminar assignments and discussion. Particularly memorable was our study of Michael Rosenak's *Commandments and Concerns*,[3] which challenged us all—Jewish, Protestant and Catholic Christians, and others—to rethink the philosophy and practice of religious education in our own traditions. Issues of the *Melton Journal* regularly contributed to our research and discussions.

Visiting colleagues such as Chancellor Ismar Schorsch, in a seminar dialogue with Donald W. Shriver, president of Union Theological Seminary, witnessed to their commitment to cooperation in theological education between the two schools. Occasional joint faculty dinners deepened our sense of common interests. During my early years at Union, Professors Schorsch and Lukinsky had study offices near mine at Union, and frequent casual meetings deepened our friendships. Neil Gillman's life story brought alive the history of one Jewish educator's pilgrimage to his work at JTS. Eduardo Rauch, Burton Cohen, and others joined the seminar for special occasions. My learning was enriched in those inter-institutional activities.

More systematic investigation into Jewish education came with my oral history project with religious educators. Joe was a member of the small advisory team that helped me shape my oral history project. It included the life stories of fourteen religious educators from various faith traditions. With his guidance, I did interviews with Sylvia Ettenberg, Seymour Fox, and Alvin Schiff. Those transcripts[4] present the life stories of those three outstanding representatives of different dimensions of Jewish education in the United States and beyond. Through the laborious work of editing those transcripts, I remembered again and again the deep insights I gained from talking with them about their lives and work.

My earlier years in the Office of Education of the World Council of Churches (WCC) in Geneva, Switzerland, had brought me into the worlds of Eastern, Russian, and Greek Orthodox Christianity. After centuries of religious life in stable villages in many places, those traditions were forced by the upheavals and diaspora situations of the last several centuries to rethink their ways of doing their educational work. Facing similar situations in many countries, Jewish educators were seeking ways to address new challenges to their educational work in the new world of diaspora and "secularism."

The research activities in the seminars and the involvement in JTS continually stimulated and enriched my search for effective ways of understanding and doing religious education in different faith communities in modern societies.

Learning from Jewish Education

From reflection on those experiences, I can summarize some important understandings I gained about education and religion:

1. Jewish education is basic, very important, to Judaism. Some Christian traditions do not ascribe such significance to religious education, but participating in Jewish education quickly teaches one that education is essential to the being, continuity, and well-being of that religious community. Those who educate are revered and honored, and their work is held up as vital. Those who are being educated as children and young people are assumed to be serious about it. Adults affirm the importance of ongoing learning for themselves, and that serious commitment to learning can be felt in the entire community.

2. Jewish education builds on a long history of interpretation of their sacred texts. From the biblical texts themselves, and through the rabbinical commentaries, Jewish studies take seriously the continuing interpretation of the texts as different periods and settings have

affected the lives of Jewish people. From our work together, I learned to use an "exegetical circle" around a text that graphically pictures that ongoing interpretation. The text is written in the center of the page. Then circling around it may be commentaries from various centuries and places. Most important, there is one blank space for contemporary scholars and students to write in their own commentary. The person today is invited into the history of reading the text, along with the collection of previous and varied commentaries. Such a method avoids the temptation of many religious groups, including many Christians, to leapfrog from today back to the sacred text and "find" an authoritative word for today's world. That process does not have built into it the insights from different historical situations that call forth pertinent meanings that contribute to a broader and deeper understanding of the text.

3. Jewish education affirms the importance of language. The challenge to keep teaching and using Hebrew in various diaspora contexts sees Hebrew language as the doorway into the special community of the past, present, and future. Central in worship and study, Hebrew language continues to be an essential carrier of the tradition. Because diaspora realities abbreviate the time and limit the occasions when young Jews can master that "mother tongue," Jewish educators have developed a variety of efforts to help them make at least minimal usage of Hebrew and thus be exposed to the culture of which Hebrew is a major carrier. Alvin Schiff helped me understand the vital importance of this effort and the many types of aids to learning that are continually produced.

4. Closely tied to the language is the community with its culture. The Ramah Camp programs and the periodic experiences in Israel bring young Jews into a serious Jewish context where the language is spoken and ritual activities are observed. Such programs are designed to provide immersion in Judaism as a way to strengthen the nurture of the home, the synagogues, and the community context. In those locations, members are influenced by the leaders and others whose regular participation in worship and home ritual activities keeps the focus of everybody on these carriers of the tradition.

5. Unlike so-called mainline Christian denominations in the United States, which for centuries have simply assumed that they were centrally important in the total society and which never had a doubt about their safety or their historical continuity, the Jewish community through centuries of persecution and the experience of the

Holocaust recognizes the importance of education for survival. A Presbyterian document in the 1940s was entitled "The Church Must Teach or Die!"[5] Often in my involvement with Jewish educators, I would think of how that sense of the absolute importance of education contributes to the seriousness with which they work on their educational activities.

6. These various "learnings" gained from participating in Jewish education no doubt show my partial and inadequate understanding of all that is involved in their work. For them, the diaspora is far more a living experience in our country and around the world than the general increasing degree of diversity that we all share. From them, I gained an ongoing sense of explicit and deeper study of that historical continuity. The current American interest in genealogical study of one's family lineage does not match the Jewish recital that "Abraham was my father." As a Christian educator, I wish that our sense of the origins of our traditions were as deep within us all as is the *Shema* for Jews.

Ongoing Questions

I came to these warm and enlightening experiences with Joe Lukinsky and JTS as an ecumenical Christian. My six years in the Office of Education in the World Council of Churches in Geneva had exposed me to cultural, linguistic, and religious diversities far beyond my southern Presbyterian beginnings. Those years were a difficult course in broadening my perspective on the world and God's work in it.

The WCC's work in "dialogue with persons and groups of other faiths and ideologies" challenged me constantly to rethink my theological commitments in a larger context. One WCC program dealt with the particular significance of Christian relations with the Jews, and although I did not work closely with that office, the issues it addressed were always present in our thinking. When one nation would not guarantee entry passports to all WCC delegates to a world meeting, and specifically the Jewish participants, the WCC changed its plans and went to another location where such guarantees were in place.

During that period, the Christian community could not—and cannot now—ignore the relation of the Jews to the nation of Israel. With long-standing aid efforts to help the dispossessed, Christian bodies worked in the refugee camps with Arab and Palestinian Christians and others who suffered in the Middle East in this century. So I was among those Christians who sought to understand the politics of the Middle East, with only relative success.

We rarely discussed the politics of Israel and the surrounding nations in our seminars, and, looking back, I wish we had done such study. We were made aware of the variety of opinions and movements within Israel and among the Jewish population in the United States. My oral history interview with Seymour Fox, taped in New York on one of his trips from his institutional base in Israel, opened up a broader understanding of the strong efforts in Israel to do good Jewish education and leadership development there and around the world. From many such experiences, I gained insight into the religious divisions in Israel and the complications of using a singular expression for "Jewish community" or "Jewish education." The Lukinskys' summer trips to Israel brought me closer to the deep pain over the assassination of Prime Minister Yitzhak Rabin and the continuing violence in the Middle East. I have tried to keep up with events there and have read with appreciation Chancellor Schorsch's efforts in that regard.

We once had an Arab Christian religious educator in our program, who in the seminar became acquainted with Ruth Zielenziger. Ruth was then developing study materials on Genesis and Exodus. To both women, the opportunity to work together on Bible study was appealing, and they became good friends. They met with some regularity, with profit to both.

One additional insight that comes from all these experiences, and especially the Israeli situation, is that American Jews seem to have a kind of double focus on the world. For many Christians, the international context is a simplistic blend of "inside the twelve-mile limit" chauvinism and a romantic memory of foreign missionary church programs, so for them a sense of the whole world and the whole of humankind must be developed. To a greater degree, Jewish identity seems historically to have been broader. Through the centuries, Jewish culture has sustained itself in many places with a common culture that bridged political divisions. No doubt there are Jews who tend also to focus so strongly on the particular chosen people of their tradition that dealing with the whole human race requires special educational attention. For this Christian colleague, it was often a pleasure to sense their broader identity.

One of our TC students, Stuart Polly, wrote "The Portrayal of Jews and Judaism in Current Protestant Teaching Materials: A Content

Analysis."[6] I was his adviser and worked with him for several years through the difficult issues that his research addressed. Again, it was an experience that in retrospect I wish we had shared more directly in the doctoral seminar.

When I was at Yale in my doctoral program, a fellow student, Bernhard Olson, was working on the same issue as Polly. He had a roomful of Christian curriculum materials and books on that subject, and he produced a similar study, "Faith and Prejudice: Intergroup Problems in Protestant Curricula."[7] Sadly, Polly's study showed that little progress had been made in the intervening thirty years toward less prejudicial treatment of the issue. Both showed a distressing lack of attention to the history of the Jews in the last two millennia and to the role of organized Christianity in the persecution of the Jews.

Both those writers addressed the issue of supersessionism, the view that after Jesus the Christian Church came to believe that Christians had superseded the Jews as God's chosen people. In recent years, Christian theology has attempted to address this interpretation and to work positively at the puzzle of how two world religious traditions that use the same historical texts and share in some way a common tradition can relate to each other. Since Vatican II, the Catholic Church and many Protestant denominations have been working to overcome historical prejudices and develop a better understanding. But the effect of two thousand years of that persistent belief has contributed to the persecution of the Jews and to the ready acceptance by Christians and others of many of the prejudices that contributed to the Holocaust. These are serious problems, and such studies as those of Olson and Polly are seeking to overcome those prejudices. The issue is not past, nor is it being ignored. I wish that we had addressed such questions more directly in our program.

So thank you, Joe, for welcoming me into the fascinating world of Judaism and Jewish education and into your collegial institution with its students and scholars. I miss those days and remember with gratitude the excitement of the learning we shared.

Notes

1. *Conservative Judaism: An American Religious Movement* (Glencoe, Ill.: Free Press, 1955).
2. *Surviving and Other Essays* (New York: Knopf, 1979).
3. Michael Rosenak, *Commandments and Concerns: Jewish Religious Concerns in Secular Society* (Philadelphia: Jewish Publication Society, 1987).

4. Available at JTS, UTS, Columbia University, the Claremont School of Theology, and Union Theological Seminary/Presbyterian School of Christian Education in Richmond.

5. In the *Faith and Life* curriculum series. See William B. Kennedy, "Neo-Orthodoxy Goes to Sunday School: The Christian Faith and Life Curriculum," in *Journal of Presbyterian History* 58, no. 4 (winter 1980): 347.

6. Stuart Polly, "The Portrayal of Jews and Judaism in Current Protestant Teaching Materials: A Content Analysis" (diss., Teachers College, Columbia University, 1992; University Microfilms International, Ann Arbor, Mich.).

7. Bernhard Olson, "Faith and Prejudice: Intergroup Problems in Protestant Curricula" (diss., Yale University, 1963).

Jewish Perspectives
on American Education

David E. Purpel

This paper is focused on the feasibility and desirability of engaging in a Jewish critique of current educational policies in America. I take the position that it is not only proper that Jews "as Jews" actively engage in a critique of American society and culture, but that such a process would be to the benefit of all Americans. I accept this as a general maxim, but it seems that currently we are in an especially propitious and critical time for this engagement to be intensified. I have in mind the conjunction of several phenomena: the rise of multiculturalism, the strength of the Jewish community, and the moral crises of American culture.

Multiculturalism and the Jews

By multiculturalism, I mean the movement to reenergize the process by which all social and cultural groups have the opportunity to express their own aspirations and to participate in the process of creating a more inclusive, cohesive, and integrated America. The attempt has both a critical and constructive dimension. On the one hand, there has been the discourse of uncovering and revealing the political nature of the dominant culture in its Eurocentric, Christocentric, sexist, and racist biases masked as essential and objective truth. There is, concurrently, a renewed and invigorating interest in the recovery, construction, and affirmation of particular social and cultural identities, e.g., among

David E. Purpel is professor of education at the University of North Carolina at Greensboro.

women, people of color, those of varying sexual orientations, ethnic groups, religious orientations—groups that have been marginalized, if not written off, by the dominant culture.

The multicultural movement has been, and surely will continue to be, a highly problematic project, for it has forced us to reexamine a number of troubling fundamental issues. We have had to confront issues on several levels—personal, communal, and national as well as in several dimensions, e.g., our tolerance of others, the nature and intensity of our multiple, often conflicting, identities, and our visions of American society. It is a healthy and valuable debate, for it has required us to confront inequity, injustice, and arrogance while affording us the opportunity to re-create ourselves closer to our highest moral and spiritual standards. It also provides an exciting and potentially liberating challenge, one that requires goodwill, wide and deep participation, creativity, compassion, and understanding. In other words, it is an aspect of our continuing responsibility to participate in the creation of a more just and loving community.

Obviously, Jews have as much right and have equal responsibility as any other group to participate actively in this process. However, it is not at all clear what the basic form and foundation of that participation should be. One of the most revealing results of the multicultural debate has been the realization that Jews are typically not listed among the various minority groups, aggrieved or not. This is in very sharp contrast to a time, not so long ago, when Jews (and, to some extent, Catholics) were considered a minority, much discriminated against. It was perhaps only a generation ago when anti-Semitism was a serious social problem in America, and when, although there certainly were no pogroms, there was considerable discrimination, harassment, and violence. There was a great deal of stigma attached to being Jewish, reflected in job discrimination, college admission quotas, and restrictive housing covenants.

This situation has dramatically changed for the better. Although there is still a reservoir of anti-Semitism in the land, Jews have largely won the struggles of the early and mid-twentieth century: they are among the most prosperous and successful of all immigrant groups; they are widely accepted and admired by the dominant culture; and they are overrepresented in many prestigious fields such as academia, science, medicine, and law. With those accomplishments, however, has come the question of what the cost has been. Has part of the price been a thoroughgoing assimilation such that Jewish success has, ironically enough, made Jewish survival in America a genuine concern? Have Jews in their pursuit of integration lost some of the edge that comes with marginality and provides them with the capacity to be critical of the status quo? Is it true that Jews have become "white" and/or *goyim* and hence, less likely to champion equal rights for all?

Although the issue of the relationship of Jews and Judaism to the larger "host" societies is complex and controversial, we are not without wisdom and insight in these matters. First of all, Jewish history provides a great deal of experience in dealing with issues of identity, particularity, and integration. Jews have also had to struggle theologically with the problematics of their status as a chosen people in a world inhabited by other, often dominant, nations. In addition, as a diaspora, they have been continuously challenged with the threats and realities of assimilation and destruction by the larger society. Much of this concern is of a defensive or negative consideration, i.e., how to prevent assimilation, contamination, idolatry, and destruction. This paper, however, focuses on the questions of the universality of Jewish ethical principles and the more positive responsibility of Jews to promote those principles among non-Jews.

Basic to consideration of this matter is the formulation of the Noahide laws, an ethical code designed to apply to non-Jews as well as to Jews. This code signifies that Jews recognize that God has both general ethical expectations for all peoples as well as particular requirements for Israel. Moreover, it seems that Jews are to be involved in both sets of expectations. David Novak puts it this way:

> It is beyond dispute that Classical Judaism in both its scriptural and rabbinic developments has been concerned with what God requires of the gentiles as what God requires of the Jews, albeit not equally. . . . Our relationship with American Christians concerns what God requires here and now of our respective communities and how and why these demands do indeed coincide on crucial public issues more often than not.

I would add that these concerns should also include Americans of other religious traditions as well as agnostics and atheists. As instances of this relationship, Novak describes a nineteenth-century movement called "The Mission of Israel": a concept originating in German Liberal Judaism and later extended and applied in America. Its central idea was that "Judaism not only is not a particularist ethnic 'fossil' . . . but is the true vanguard of the universal culture that the modern world proclaimed." Although Novak is critical of some specific manifestations of the movement, he is basically sympathetic to it:

> One need not be a Liberal Jew in any sense of that term to admire the project as the first real attempt to define a Jewish religious participation in American life, existentially concerned with both Judaism and the United States as a society in which Jews need no longer abandon Judaism in order to be true participants.[1]

This would seem to be a good time to express a number of disclaimers. I am certainly not positing any essentialist notion of what it means to be Jewish or what would constitute a Jewish consciousness. I also do not want to argue that all Jews should define themselves as primarily Jewish and that they must act in accordance with Jewish traditions. Nor do I wish to make a case for the necessity that Jews should act in concert with one another in order to have a greater political impact.

Jewish identity is a highly problematic term, and there are any number of ways in which people identify themselves and others as Jews. And there are many varying, often conflicting, Jewish traditions and serious and legitimate differences of opinion within those traditions. What I am arguing is that those who do identify themselves with certain Jewish traditions and perspectives ought to feel free to bring those perspectives to bear on larger political and social debates. Moreover, I would also urge that people do this not only because they have the right to do so but because these perspectives would constitute a significant contribution to the broader debate and discourse. Indeed, the very diversity and richness of varying Jewish traditions and perspectives is an important element of the effort of the society to be genuinely inclusive, instead of being co-optive.

A Jewish Critique of American Culture:
The Case of Public Education

Public education is a social and cultural phenomenon, as well as an integral ingredient of democratic forms. As such, it requires thorough public and professional scrutiny and critique. It is an institution that affects us all, and we have a responsibility to respond to it, not only in technical matters (e.g., class size, teacher salaries, and instructional techniques), but in moral terms, i.e., to what degree do the schools foster a just and loving community? Jews as citizens have the responsibility to participate in general educational discourses, and Jews as Jews have a special contribution to make to both the technical and moral discourses of schooling.

The State of the Schools and the Schools of the State

Fundamentally, present public educational policies and practices are directed toward facilitating a system of meritocracy, global economics, bourgeois morality, and personal materialism. The public education system has come to be seen as the training ground for providing a pool of compliant, highly productive workers and managers required in an increasingly technological and competitive economy. It is an economy that is grounded in the possibility of the acquisition of immense wealth for some, even if it comes with the price of poverty and privation for others.

The ethical mantle that is placed on this impersonal and cruel vision is not the quest for a just and compassionate community but rather the creation of a society built on the principle of equality of opportunity (often popularized as "leveling the playing field"). This ethic of opportunity, of course, privileges the strong and the talented as it punishes the weak and less talented, thereby trumping justice with functionality. The opportunity allows for so-called fair competition in which only the contestants can be responsible for the outcome, i.e., they deserve or earn their rewards or defeats. In a society that measures human worth by achievement, this displaces an ethic of equal dignity for all with one in which dignity is a scarce commodity, to be rationed out to the most deserving.

In this vision, the educational process involves hard and disciplined work, a strong character, and the acquisition of basic skills with emphasis on mathematics, science, and technology. It requires a consciousness that legitimates aggression, competition, and hierarchy while desensitizing our impulses for peace, equality, and intimacy. It necessitates a professional staff of demanding educators with "high standards" who will insist that their students do as they are told, spend a lot of time on homework, study hard, and score high.

This is an educational orientation that represents a grotesque blending of eighteenth-century Puritan piety with the cruelty of nineteenth-

century social Darwinism and the cutthroat competition of the twenti-
eth-century global economy. No one has encapsulated this ideology of
triumphant capitalism and self-aggrandizement better than former president Bill Clinton in his 1994 State of the Union address, in which he acknowledged and lent support to policies designed "to empower local
school districts to experiment in chartering their schools . . . or having
more public school choice, to do whatever they wish *as long as we measure every school by one high standard: Are our children learning what
they need to know to compete and win in the global economy?*" (emphasis mine).

Elements of a Jewish Critique of American Education

I want to suggest what might be entailed in a critical examination of
public education from certain Jewish perspectives. My purpose is only
to illustrate the possibilities of such a project by briefly and broadly discussing three general issues from my Jewish viewpoint in the hope that
others would offer their own interpretations.

The issue of justice. The issue of justice is clearly central to Jewish traditions, and, as such, we are required to carefully examine the implications
of current policies and practices of public education for social justice. I see
a terrible and cruel irony operating here. On the one hand, Jewish students are generally advantaged by these meritocratic policies, since they
typically perform well on standardized tests and tend to achieve high
grades in school while Jewish families are more likely to be actively involved in their children's education. To the degree, then, that schooling
serves the function of providing opportunities for social and economic advancement, it would be fair to say that current educational policies provide an edge to American Jews, given their overrepresentation of
high-achieving students. Indeed, Jews have traditionally and legitimately
fought for the use of merit in university admissions and employment policies as a way of dealing with anti-Semitic discrimination.

However, this newly achieved edge means that others now have less
of an edge. I see this as a serious violation of Jewish traditions that de-
plore personal gain at the expense of others and a violation of principles
that affirm justice and dignity for all. The current testing and evaluation
mania is simply another instance of the moral tragedy of an educational
and social system that requires winners and losers and is no less a moral
tragedy when Jews are among the winners. Indeed, it would behoove

the winners to witness the anguish and pain that comes from being successful in such a sordid and demeaning endeavor.

Although I am prepared to passionately defend my stand on the basis of Jewish values, I realize that it can and has been contested from other Jewish perspectives. I cannot be so arrogant as to call my viewpoint the truly Jewish one, however much I hoped it were. However, I have confidence that traditional Jewish modes of reflection and dialogue can further the cause of justice. It seems evident that there is much in Jewish traditions that can help the process by which we can all shed light on this tangled and volatile issue. There are significant topics for discussion here that can help elucidate both Jewish thought and American practice. How does, in fact, meritocracy jibe with traditional Jewish notions of justice? Are the talented more deserving of social benefits than the less able? Is it possible to reconcile the social need for differential recognition with the moral requirement of dignity for all?

This process is not a simpleminded case of mechanically applying so-called Jewish principles to an issue; rather, I am suggesting that Jews can contribute to the public discourse by addressing these matters from various perspectives of Jewish thought. To address the meaning of justice in the context I have described is, for example, clearly within the rabbinic tradition of the need for continuous study of the dialectic between Torah and changing historical conditions. Are there not, also, Hasidic teachings that can provide insights into the dilemma? Surely the writings of the Prophets and Psalmists will shed light on the tangle; and are there not relevant precedents that are discussed in the Talmud? Indeed, there are many other strong and vibrant Jewish traditions (cultural Zionism and kabbalah, to mention only two) that clearly can be sources of wisdom and clarity for these difficult issues.

Such an examination is very likely to clarify both Jewish teachings and American politics and to elucidate similarities and differences between them. I am not speaking of any such things as "Jewish solutions," but of insights, perspectives, and practices that come out of Jewish traditions and experience.

Epistemology and pedagogy. Is it good for the Jews to live in a culture where most schoolchildren are subjected to primitive positivism and didactic pedagogy? How good can it be for anyone if truth comes to be defined as fragmented bits of knowledge that can be attained only in textbooks and encyclopedias? Surely, it is not good for any person or group when the educational process is crassly reduced to doing well on tests.

Part of the tragedy of the current school scene is the erosion of attractive alternative approaches that have been available and utilized by generations of American educators. I have in mind such concepts as progressive education, the discovery approach, group process, experiential education, and education as play and creative experience. It is not merely that in some situations, these traditions have been explicitly rejected, but perhaps even worse, their very memory is being lost in the wake of our triumphant pedagogy of de-contextualized knowledge. In a word, we live in an era when public discourse on serious pedagogical issues is essentially uncritical and largely devoid of compelling and competing alternative orientations.

Interestingly, many of our neglected, if not abandoned, educational approaches are resonant with certain Jewish educational traditions. The pedagogy of the seder, with its emphasis on discovery and the signal importance of encouraging and valuing questioning has been and continues to be an implicit model for progressive educators. The educative possibilities of the Sabbath (and the sabbatical), with its emphasis on contemplation and reflection, stand in sharp contrast to the frantic competitive pace of modern schools, public and private. There are other tenets of Jewish education that offer serious challenges and alternatives to existing approaches in American schools. One important illustration is the stress on communal learning as reflected in the institution of *hevruta,* a technique that assumes that deeper learning is more likely to occur in a cooperative and symbiotic relationship. Further, the extraordinary emphasis on multiple, often conflicting, interpretations in Torah and Talmud study is a profound affirmation of both accepting uncertainty and the necessity, nonetheless, to pursue truth. Study in this tradition is not only about studying and coming to know certain things. At its best, it is also concerned with encouraging students to be active participants and contributors in the creative process rather than passive recipients of right answers.

Jewish experience and thought offer alternative notions of truth and alternative conceptions of learning and teaching, as well as competing ideas of the purposes of education. In a society bereft of a serious educational discourse, it would be most ungenerous to withhold imaginative, bold, and provocative ideas. In a culture bent on an educational orientation grounded in greed and domination, it would be irresponsible to do so.

This is certainly not to suggest that American schools can or should become yeshivas, but only that the introduction of these alternative perspectives can, at minimum, provide nourishing food for thought to the current tasteless and empty diet of educational discourse. It remains to be seen which, if any, of these and other Jewish educational traditions could be readily absorbed and integrated into mainstream educational practice. Such a process, however, must begin with the willingness of the Jews to offer these ideas as well as the readiness of the larger community to be receptive to them.

Education for meaning and redemption. Public education in America is plagued with an inability to ground itself in a set of larger moral and spiritual aspirations. Indeed, within the profession, there has been a determined effort to substitute a technical and bureaucratic discourse for a moral and political one. Much of the profession has staked out a realm in which education is seen as an apolitical process for which social-science discourse is the most appropriate mode of analysis.

The preoccupation by the profession with the conceptual tools of social-science research has created a moral and political vacuum that the far right and corporate America have been only too eager to fill. The schools have been accused of fostering moral laxity and academic flabbiness and failing to provide the skilled workforce that is required if America is to maintain its dominant military and economic position. It surely is not the case that public education has, overnight, been kidnapped and politicized, since public education has always been, inherently and inevitably, a political institution. What has occurred is that the public schools have been overwhelmed by a particular ideology, one that involves the legitimatization of economic greed and moral propriety, in which the promiscuous practices of the free market cohabit with the straitlaced pieties of conventional morality.

I cannot speak with any authority to the range of practice in Jewish education, but I assume that it also suffers from the difficulties of competing and ambiguous goals. Indeed, I am sure that educators, parents, and children involved with Jewish schools also struggle with the conflicts between the demands of the secular society and the requirements of Jewish traditions. However, the historically close integration of Jewish education, with its cultural and religious traditions, is an invaluable and readily available safeguard against the reification and fragmentation of the educational process. Moreover, these traditions provide powerful frameworks of meaning and redemption that are meant to infuse all aspects of life, including education.

However many the various modes of Jewish expression may be, it is inconceivable that any would engender an educational policy focused on "competing and winning in the global economy." Jewish traditions are directed at connection and integration rather than detachment and self-absorption, emphasizing the joy rather than the utility of learning, focusing on spiritual rather than material growth. These traditions insist that we remember the plight of the "other," that we take social responsibility for them rather than rationalizing indifference to their suffering, and that we focus on the importance of community rather than the centrality of the individual. This tradition of meshing the struggle for meaning, joy, community, and spirituality with education could be of immense help in an American society awash in alienation and thirsting for spiritual meaning.

You Don't Have to Be Jewish

The promise of a multicultural American society is one in which toleration and harmony are not threatened by diversity, one in which difference is an enriching rather than divisive process. It is important to remember that, to a very large degree, our culture already reflects the vibrancy that can emerge from tapping into the creative roots of various groups and communities, as reflected, for example, in music, dance, and the arts. Moreover, in acting on its commitments to protect the civil rights of all, American society has often responded forcefully and vigorously. Although the advances we have made in these areas are real and substantial, they must, however, be seen as partial, and the efforts to grow and improve must be seen as continuous and ceaseless. Hence, our society and culture need more, not fewer, of the diverse ideas and insights that emerge from the multiple perspectives of the many peoples and communities that constitute our nation.

Public education, as a particularly important social and cultural institution, requires an intense and informed public discourse, but it currently is in a state of intellectual and moral bankruptcy. The introduction of various aspects of Jewish thought into that discourse would make a particularly significant contribution to the development of a more thoughtful and textured public debate on education.

My suggestions have focused on how Jewish thought could inform issues of the relationship between education and justice, on classroom pedagogy, and on education and meaning. One certainly doesn't have to be Jewish to share the views and perspectives that I have expressed, since they are part of the thinking of many people of varying traditions. However, those who are committed to expressing themselves in the form and substance of Jewish thought have the opportunity and the responsibility to enrich Jewish life and American society by working for a meaningful educational system rooted in the quest for justice and loving-kindness.

Notes

1. David Novak, *Jewish Social Ethics* (New York: Oxford University Press, 1992), 228–29.

EDUCATION IN ISRAEL

The Jewish Education of Teachers for Israeli State Schools

Walter I. Ackerman

There has hardly been a time in the history of Zionist national education that has not been marked by criticism of the schools dedicated
to the education of the "New Jew": "healthy, stands erect, strong, brave
and industrious . . . loves [the] homeland, joyfully works its land, risks
life in its defense, [and is] honest, modest, loyal, trustworthy, and seeks
justice."[1] The "Jewishness," variously defined over the years, of the
products of these schools, first in the *Yishuv* and then in the State of Israel, has been an unending source of debate and discontent.

At the beginning of the twentieth century, Joseph Klausner, then editor of the influential and prestigious journal *Hashiloah,* complained
about the narrow nationalism of the "Young Hebrew"—a designation
intended to convey disjunction with the past—whose schooling was centered on the language and the land to the virtual exclusion of religion
and all other manifestations of the national ethos and spirit.[2] A half century later, Ben-Gurion noted that "our young people are seriously defi-
cient in Jewish consciousness, in recognition of our historical heritage
and moral identification with world Jewry. We should strive to develop
a curriculum that will correct this deficiency."[3] And as recently as 1991,
Israel's minister of education, Zevulun Hammer, appointed a committee
to examine "the standing of Jewish studies in the state school and to
offer recommendations regarding approaches and goals, curricula and
other initiatives capable of advancing Jewish education in Israel."[4]

While there are many reasons for this lack of interest in—and sometimes, hostility toward—Jewish studies and other things Jewish, there

Walter I. Ackerman is the Shane Family Professor of Education Emeritus at Ben Gurion
University and the dean for the Center for Jewish Education at the Schechter Institute of
Jewish Studies in Jerusalem.

can be no doubt that Zionism itself was a contributing factor. The Zionist analysis of the Jewish condition was clearly influenced by ideas regnant in Central and Western Europe during the latter half of the
nineteenth century. It was a time when an increasing number of people
began to believe that "what was inherited from the past was an irksome
burden to be escaped from as soon as possible."[5] The belief in the supe-
riority of the new so clearly explicit in the idea of progress and the inheritance of the moral naturalism of the Enlightenment and its emphasis
on science and reason—together with a celebration of individuality that
taught that personal realization was possible only when the self was free
of the encumbrance of the past—necessitated a reevaluation of the
meaning and place of the religious traditions of Judaism in the nascent
secular society. The national Zionist school, among other agencies, undertook the task of creating a "civil religion—ceremonies, creeds,
myths, and symbols that would legitimize the new social order. The holy
language became Hebrew . . . [and] the Holy Land became Eretz Yisrael
. . . [and] the holy writ became Tanakh."[6]

Whatever the intellectual underpinnings of the attempt to adapt a
religious tradition to the demands of modern times, nonreligious
schools in the *Yishuv* and in the State of Israel contend with circumstances created by the unique experience of the Jewish people:

> The national school in this country has had to contend with a
> number of educational contradictions since its very beginning.
> How to educate youngsters here for loyalty to the Jewish people,
> when the overwhelming majority of Jews are in other places?
> How to implant in youngsters here a feeling of being part of
> Jewish history, when half of that history took place outside the
> Land of Israel? How to inculcate Jewish consciousness in Israeli
> youth, when Israel consciousness and the revolution it demanded
> deny the legitimacy of exile and dispersion? How to educate Is-
> raeli youth who receive their education in a nonreligious school
> to appreciate the cultural heritage of the Jewish people, which
> for most of its time, has been suffused with religion?[7]

Whatever the ability of schools to change deep-seated societal attitudes, it is clear that the task is virtually hopeless without teachers
keenly committed to the particular ideal. The members of the Teachers
Assembly, the first effort to form a professional organization in the
Yishuv, understood this very well. In discussing the criteria for member-

ship, it was decided that the fledgling association would be open only to teachers "whose activities and way of life are appropriate to our goals, [which are to] . . . work for the revival of the Hebrew language . . . [and to] encourage the use of Hebrew in the family."[8] The members of the Assembly even considered denying membership to teachers who taught other languages[9] because their work was "inimical to our purpose of making Hebrew a spoken language."[10]

The emphasis on Hebrew was a signal characteristic of nonreligious Zionist schools. Less than a decade before the founding of the state, Eliezer Rieger, a prominent figure in the educational establishment, stated: "The process of reviving the Hebrew language is far from finished. . . . People who speak Hebrew with a Ukrainian or a German accent are not fit to be teachers."[11] At the same time, Rieger called upon teacher-training institutions to intensify their efforts to bring students closer to Jewish sources through the study of Hebrew literature, Jewish history, and the geography[12] of Israel. The importance assigned Hebrew literature in this proposal and others cannot be overestimated. "Cultural" Zionists approached the subject with an awe formerly reserved for sacred Scripture.

As might be expected, the baggage considered essential to the work of teachers in nonreligious Zionist schools changed over time. In the early days of the modern Jewish school in the *Yishuv,* many teachers had studied in European *yeshivot;* they were steeped in traditional Jewish learning and often knew Hebrew well, but frequently lacked general education. That balance was inverted over the years as native-born teachers entered the schools.[13]

Teacher training in Israel today, as in the past, takes place in two settings: universities and teachers' colleges. The former prepare students for high school and junior high; the latter are concerned with personnel for the preschool, elementary, and junior high schools. In the nature of things, the colleges are less prestigious than the universities,[14] and even though a process of "academization" has accredited many of them to grant a first degree (bachelor of education), their standing still falls below the status enjoyed by the universities. This structure, considered outmoded by many, reflects a hierarchical conception of the process of education in which the lower levels are seemingly less important, or less intellectually demanding, than those above them.

Candidates for a teacher's certificate[15] from the university are enrolled in a department or school of education as well as a subject-matter department. Occasional attempts notwithstanding, there is next to no contact between the two. The demands of the discipline and a research orientation determine the course of study in the subject. Neither the needs of students who intend to become teachers nor the demands of the high school curriculum play a role in ordering programs in the disciplines. While themes such as Jewish identity, patterns of Jewish life, and Jewish continuity may be part of a study of a particular genre in Hebrew literature or a course in some aspect of the history of the Jewish people, the critical factor in determining the sequence of courses that lead to a degree is a conception that draws its authority from the structure of the discipline and its distinctive mode of inquiry. Several promising attempts to bridge the divide were abandoned when the Ministry of Education withdrew support from programs inspired by the recommendations of the Shenhar Committee.[16]

We know little about the way in which courses in any or all of the traditional subjects of Jewish studies—Bible, Hebrew literature, history of the Jewish people, Jewish thought—affect student attitudes and behavior. Whether or not university faculty—like their peers in American colleges and universities—think it part of their responsibility as scholars and teachers to help students define a personal identity or shape a worldview is a moot question.[17]

The excerpts that follow are probably somewhat overdrawn, but they do tell us a great deal about the way in which Bible is taught in the university and in the high school:

> For the non-Orthodox schools, the problem is that the Bible itself—with the possible exceptions of the Scroll of Esther and the Song of Songs—talks about the most embarrassing aspect of Judaism's biblical heritage, namely, God, who is treated in contemporary Israel as the monopoly of the Orthodox. Now, if you cannot talk about God as the source of right and wrong, you cannot seriously teach pentateuchal law, which continually asserts its divine origin. If you cannot talk about God, you cannot discuss the prophetic experience—i.e., the close encounters of the third kind experienced by an unusual group of men and women portrayed in the early and later prophets—men who claimed to have dialogued with God. If you cannot talk intelligently about God, you cannot seriously discuss that great gem of Hebrew Scripture, the Book of Job, which is an argument with God about the most basic of human truths, namely, undeserved suffering. Consequently, notwithstanding all the hours of

so-called biblical study, many Israeli students arrive at the university fully convinced that the problem of undeserved suffering first rose to challenge Jewish Orthodoxy in the 1940s C.E. . . .

[S]tudents enrolled in the departments of Bible in Israeli universities spend relatively little time studying a biblical text—to find out what [it] can tell us about itself or about life or about theology. The bulk of their time is spent avoiding the Bible: courses are offered in ancient inscriptions of the ancient Near East, ancient languages, bibliography of biblical research, text criticism of the Bible (all the possible mistakes in the Bible arising from letters that were misread in antiquity), the history of biblical criticism, medieval commentaries, and history of the biblical world.[18]

The logic of curriculum design for the teacher-training institutions draws its authority from a different source. Even though subject-matter courses—a significant portion of the course of study—are rooted in the disciplines, the guiding principle is outside the disciplines themselves; it is, rather, some idea of what it is that a teacher *ought* to know. Discussions about the details of a curriculum—the relative emphasis of certain periods in the history of the Jewish people as opposed to others or a recommended list of readings in Hebrew literature—are often stymied, if not altogether brought to a dead halt by the claim that "it is inconceivable that a teacher not know."

That approach is clearly evident in the recommendations of a committee established in 1942 for the purpose of designing a curriculum for the four nonreligious teacher-training schools—in reality, little more than high schools—then in existence. The program of studies requires that students "cover" all the Tanakh; study twenty to thirty pages of Talmud, including the *Mishnayot;* and acquire a knowledge of the "basic material" in the first volumes of *Sefer Ha'aggadah.*[19] Altogether, Jewish studies[20] constituted some 25 percent of the course of study.

These requirements, along with others, stretch far beyond the material that constitutes the curriculum of the elementary school, now and even then. As clearly noted, the idea of what a teacher ought to know seems here to be guided by an image of an "educated Jew" rather than by some conception of what "knowledge is most worth" for an elementary school teacher.

Approximately a decade after the establishment of the state, the Ministry of Education and Culture initiated a program in state schools intended to deepen the Jewish consciousness of pupils. The idea of the program generated wide debate and discussion, particularly among those who considered it "religious coercion" in disguise. The range of opinions regarding the meaning of "Jewish consciousness" did not prevent the then minister of education, Zalman Aranne, from providing and implementing a guiding principle—"Were I asked to define the essence of Jewish-Israeli consciousness, I would reply: the acknowledgment of the young Israeli generation of its responsibility to the continued existence of the Jewish people all over the world."[21] The centrality of the collective in Aranne's conception stems from a basic tenet of Zionist and other nationalist ideologies—individual fulfillment is attainable only through complete identification with the nation's striving for self-realization.[22]

A directive of the ministry in early 1958 called the attention of teachers in teacher-training institutions, particularly those who taught "Hebrew subjects," to the topics that were central to the new program. The history of the Jews in the Diaspora (*golah*) and Jewish culture were given primacy. The former was to be taught in such a manner as to "provide an accurate picture of our people's past and to instill in pupils a love of our people (*Ahavat Yisrael*) and an attitude of respect and honor toward its moral strength in the struggle for survival . . . [and the understanding] that religion and tradition together with the longing for redemption strengthened our people's unity and sense of uniqueness."[23] These and similar motifs in the guidelines for teaching history represent a significant departure from the once regnant ideology of the negation of the Diaspora (*shlilat hagolah*).

The curriculum unit called "The National Tradition: Knowledge of Jewish Religious Practice" included prayers and practices of the Sabbath and holidays, selections from the *parashah*, rituals such as washing the hands before eating, expressions such as *baruch hashem* and *b'ezrat hashem*, and objects such as tallit, tefillin, *sefer Torah*, and mezuzah. It is difficult to discern the principle of selection, i.e., why teachers in training were expected to know some things and not others.

This particular aspect of the attempt to foster Jewish consciousness, both in teachers' colleges and in schools, caused wide opposition and criticism. The ministry was accused of using a seemingly neutral and generally acceptable idea as a vehicle for the introduction of religion into schools defined by law as secular and chosen by parents for that reason. Indeed, complaints of religious coercion were so persistent that the Ministry of Education and Culture thought it necessary to publish a public disclaimer: "The program is not intended in any way to change the state school from its essential character as a national school. Just as that school does not and will not offer religious instruction, so it has not and will not offer antireligious instruction."[24]

The rhetoric that shaped the thinking about the largely ineffective effort to nurture Jewish consciousness does not altogether disappear in the necessarily continued efforts to deal with the Jewishness of teachers in Israel's elementary schools. Some twenty years later, the introduction to the report of the coordinator of Jewish studies in state teachers' colleges exhorts students to understand that "before the young teacher can teach Judaism to others, he must first understand his own Jewishness and learn the idea and ideals of Judaism and their expression in a way of life, its ethical principles, and concern for human relations."[25] The details of the report provide a summary of courses, programs, and activities related to Judaism and the Jewish people.[26]

The details of the report inform us that the major areas of study of Jews and Judaism in the colleges are Bible, Hebrew literature, history, Jewish thought, and the catchall, Jewish culture. More specifically, courses were offered in problems of the Jewish people and the State of Israel, holidays and celebrations, history of the *Yishuv*, Eretz Yisrael, legends of Eretz Yisrael, the Diaspora, Zionism, and the Labor movement. One institution reported that during the year in review, all students were required to take four credits in Bible and four credits in Oral Law. Electives in the third and fourth years included: a topic in Bible, approaches to biblical interpretation, holidays and traditions, anti-Semitism in modern times, Jewish folk literature, selections from the midrash, and selections from kabbalistic literature. This institution established the Center for the Development of Jewish Studies, whose major function was to create materials and experiment with methods for teaching Judaism. In addition, the school sponsored a series of "study days"(*yom iyun*), each dedicated to an approaching holiday. Regular classes were canceled, and students spent those days studying texts chosen for the occasion and participated in experiential activities.

While statements of goals and objectives do not always tell us what actually goes on in classrooms, no matter at what level, they do indicate what those responsible for the conduct of schools think *ought* to be learned. The recommendations of several subject-matter committees appointed at this time are important for an understanding of what teachers, supervisors, and academicians hoped that the teachers' colleges might achieve. The committee on Bible, committed to the national

Zionist principle that the Bible is the basis of the age-old Jewish heritage, suggests that a graduate of a teachers' college should have acquired a knowledge of the different aspects of the canonical text—historical, linguistic, social, and cultural. One hopes that a student will be able to continue independent study to acquire a deeper knowledge and greater appreciation of biblical values. The committee advises instructors to organize the study of text around specific themes—God and Creation, revelation and prophecy, free will, and man and the universe. It should be remembered that students in teachers' colleges had studied Bible in one form or another during all twelve years of their elementary and secondary school.

The committee on Jewish history (*Toldot Yisrael*) proposed that the study of that subject should lead students to "an interest and concern for the survival of the Jewish people." Selected aspects of the history of the nation were intended to provide a knowledge and appreciation of the varieties of Jewish lifestyles, models of leadership, and expressions of creativity. Suggested topics for study include: the idea of community in Judaism, the place of Eretz Yisrael in the life of the people, modern anti-Semitism, religion and nationalism in Zionist thought, and varieties of Jewish historiography.

Instructors in teachers' colleges, no less than students, were encouraged to expand their knowledge in areas of Jewish studies. A one-day conference sponsored by the ministry of education early in 1981 is an example. The program of the day included lectures with topics such as: the siddur as a source for teaching Jewish thought, the central idea of the *Amidah,* and the languages and thought of the siddur.[27]

The significance of all that has been brought here is best weighed when we consider that the requirement of Jewish studies for all students consists altogether of six credits out of the ninety, and even more are needed for graduation and the teacher's certificate. There is almost something wistful in the hope that the "colleges breathe Jewishness and that students preparing for careers as teachers be infused with Jewish spirit."[28]

There is no available evidence that might help us understand whether the efforts described here, and many others, have had any discernible effect on the attitudes and beliefs of young people enrolled in state teachers' colleges. We do, however, have findings about the Jewish-Israeli identity of a sample of 564 students enrolled in teacher-training institutions—state and state religious—at the beginning of the 1990s. Participants were divided into four categories: nonreligious (secular); traditional (positive orientation toward religious tradition); national, religious (Zionist); and ultraorthodox (non-Zionist). Religious identification, it appears, is the most significant factor affecting Jewish-Israeli identity. The nonreligious students considered themselves more Israeli than Jewish, did not feel themselves part of the Jewish people in any meaningful way, and thought that the most important events in Jewish history were those related to the State of Israel—the Holocaust, the establishment of the state, and the country's wars. The findings also indicate that the Israeli component of their identity tends to weaken as Jewish elements become more pronounced. The more religious a student, the stronger the identification with the Jewish people and all periods of its history.[29]

It is instructive to compare the earlier efforts referred to here with the recommendations for teacher training proposed by the Shenhar Committee, appointed in 1991 to "examine the standing of Jewish studies in state schools and to offer recommendations regarding approaches and goals, curricula, and other initiatives capable of advancing Jewish education in Israel."[30] The report of the committee, published in 1994, is informed by a view of Judaism as "a national culture in a continuous state of development."[31] An acquaintance with Jewish culture in all its expressions during the many years of its history is an essential element in the development of the identity and the shaping of the spiritual and ethical world of the Israeli youngster. The centrality of the idea of personal identity in the thinking of the committee represents a significant shift away from the collective in the direction of the individual. The stance of the committee is at one with the patterns that characterize the larger society of the time.

The committee's proposals for achieving changes in attitudes and behavior place Jewish studies in the broader framework of the humanities. They call for the development of curricula and other materials that encourage dialogue and critical inquiry, emphasize the importance of an interdisciplinary approach, and enlist the media and other public forums to create a climate that is supportive of the efforts of the school.

The sweep of the report of the Shenhar Committee extends also to teacher training, both pre-service and in-service. It calls for a thorough review of the programs in teachers' colleges and the introduction of changes that reflect the ideas of the committee. Teachers of the future not only will have achieved expertise in a particular discipline but will also be acquainted with all the disciplines of Jewish studies and the humanities. Even teachers who do not specialize in Jewish studies, particularly elementary school teachers, should acquire a broad knowledge of the holidays, the life cycle, Jewish-Israeli identity, issues in modern Jewish history, and the history of Zionism and the State of Israel. Because the study of Jews and Judaism as recommended by the committee will revolve around Jewish culture, Hebrew, Zionism, and Eretz Yisrael, teachers should become well versed in these areas and their adumbrations. The ideas of interdisciplinary or interactive teaching and learning run through all these suggestions; they are particularly evident in the weight assigned to teaching and learning *tarbut Yisrael* (culture of Israel).

The proposals for in-service training, perhaps because of the greater freedom available for play in this setting, provide an even closer fit to the assumptions of the committee. In-service courses should engage experienced teachers in exploring the relationships between various areas of Jewish studies, integrating Jewish and general history, examining cultural contacts between Jews and other peoples, using the arts in the teaching of Judaism, learning about contemporary Jewry and the various trends in modern Judaism, and analyzing the dilemmas confronting Jews, individually and collectively, in our time.

The National Center for In-Service Training in Jewish Studies for Educational Personnel, located in Beersheva, is perhaps the most visible institutional expression of the recommendations of the Shenhar Committee. The stated purposes of the center are: to develop material and methods based on an interdisciplinary approach to Jewish studies; to examine various aspects of secular Jewish identity; and to expand and deepen knowledge in the various disciplines of Jewish studies.[32] Since its opening in early 1995, the Center has provided an integrated educational experience to more than ten thousand teachers, principals, and supervisors who work in the elementary schools of the state school system.

The program of the center is framed by the possibilities of four- or five-day seminars built around a central theme treated from the vantage point of the several disciplines of Jewish studies and its expression in various art forms. It is an intensive experience that encourages participants to think about Jews and Judaism in a way not previously encountered. Over the years, the themes have included: "We and They—Israel and the Diaspora"; readings from Rambam; free will and determinism; the idea of Klal Yisrael; Jewish culture in a changing world; the world of aggadah; "Judaism and Democracy—Do They Go Together?"; fifty years of the State of Israel; history—the new curriculum; respect and the limits of freedom; "Old Terms and New Contents."

An evaluation of the work of the center discloses that it has engaged primarily in transmitting knowledge and information. Participants expressed a high degree of satisfaction with the program and thought that they had been personally enriched. Only a small minority, however, felt that the experience had in any way influenced their work in the classroom. Overall, there was a sense that the seminar had not provided tools for translating the newly acquired knowledge into practice. One teacher, perhaps speaking for many, thought that "a window had been opened" but did not yet feel herself ready to teach the material: "There is too much missing."[33]

Like their peers in most countries around the world, elementary school teachers in Israel teach the full range of subjects of the curriculum, teachers of specialties notwithstanding. The course of study in teacher-training institutions—in those accredited to award the degree of bachelor of education as well as those that have not achieved this status—is based on the structural artifact of the self-contained classroom. The four-year program in the accredited institutions requires that all students complete 48 credits—approximately half the total required for graduation—in subject-matter courses, from a minimum of 6 to a maximum of 24 in any of the subjects taught in the elementary school. The specific requirements in Jewish studies vary from school to school. In one case, the minimum requirements of all students include: Introduction to Oral Law (2); Israel's Holidays (1); Introduction to the History of Jewish Thought (2); and the Biblical Narrative (2). In the same institution, a "concentration" requires Bible (6); Oral Law (6); Jewish Thought (6); and Integrated Studies (6). In another institution, students may elect either the minimum or the maximum from a list of courses that includes: Prayer and the Modern Man; Modern Jewish Philosophy; Male and Female in Judaism; Bible and Jewish Culture; Holidays; Basic Ideas in Judaism; The Growth of the Modern Jew—Trends and Movements; and the Birth of Israel. The rationale for a "major" in *tarbut Yisrael* in yet another institution is illustrative of an emerging pattern "to encourage our students to understand themselves, their heritage, and to ask serious questions about their cultural identity in the framework of an evolving Israeli reality," according to the catalog of the institution. The course list includes: Jewish Identity and Its Expressions in Hebrew Literature; Introduction to Jewish Art; Who Needs Ethical Rules? Secularism and Religion; Exodus; Teaching the Bible; and Selected Reading from Medieval Poetry and the Prayer Book. In addition to formal course work, students are able to participate in workshops devoted to special topics. They can also take advantage of other activities conducted by the college that are intended to enhance the teaching and learning of Jewish subjects. The character and style of these activities vary from institution to institution.

Considering the importance of the Shoah in the collective consciousness of the society, it is surprising to discern that the subject occupies relatively little space in the curriculum of the teachers' colleges. The most systematic of the approaches seems to be that of the institution that requires all students, regardless of their specialization, to participate in a one-credit course (Educational Engagement with the History of the Shoah) in the first year and follow that with a three-day seminar in the second year (Consciousness of the Shoah), and round out the sequence with one day in the third year devoted to methods of teaching the Shoah.

The various programs mentioned here are in large measure a reflection of the curriculum of the state elementary school. The almost universal inclusion of courses dealing with holidays and aggadah is the most prominent example. It is difficult to imagine a state elementary school in Israel that does not teach and observe the major holidays. The role that Jewish studies and cognate activities play in the overall work of teacher-training institutions remains a matter of concern. The "forum" of coordinators of Jewish studies in the teachers' colleges recently complained that there is little understanding of what they try to do, and that despite all their efforts, they have not succeeded in convincing their colleagues that Jewish studies is not religious studies, a perception that is hardly helpful.[34]

School systems, perhaps more than any other agency of government, generally reflect the values and ideals of the society that sponsors them. While individual schools may, and often do, function outside the boundaries created by conventional norms, the framework that serves the overwhelming majority of children is essentially the society writ small. The debate concerning the place of Jewish studies in the curriculum of state teacher-training institutions is the localization of the larger issue that is today at the heart of public discourse in Israel: the nature of the Jewishness of the sovereign state established by Jews.[35]

As I was writing this paper, I kept asking myself what questions that Joe might ask about what I've put together. I think that they might go something like this: Is this the *kind* of knowledge that elementary school teachers in Israel ought to have about Jews and Judaism? Do they know what to do with what they have learned? Does what they know and do cohere into a clear vision of the state school as a place that "provides pupils with options?[36] This form of pointed inquiry has enriched the practice of Jewish education in the United States in our time. My certainty of Joe's approach rests on three sources: my reading and understanding of papers that he has written; contact over the years with his students; and my image of him created by that group of unusual young men and women with whom we both worked, but in different settings, in Boston of long ago, at a time when neither of us could possibly imagine that we would one day grow old. Even though we never really worked together, it was always good to know that Joe was there. His presence has enriched Jewish education in the United States beyond measure.

Notes

1. See Marc J. Rosenstein, "The New Jew: The Place of Jewish Tradition in General Zionist Secondary Education in Palestine from Its Beginnings until the Establishment of the State" (in Hebrew) (Ph.D. diss., Hebrew University, 1985), ix.

2. Joseph Klausner, "The Young Hebrew" (in Hebrew), *Hashiloah* 20 (1909): 401–5.

3. Ben-Gurion, 11 November 1955, as given in Chaim Navon, "Jewish Consciousness in State Education" (in Hebrew) (master's thesis, Bar Ilan University, 1982), 123.

4. *A People and the World: Jewish Culture in a Changing World* (in Hebrew) (Jerusalem: Ministry of Education and Culture, 1994), 1.

5. Edward Shils, *Tradition* (Chicago: University of Chicago Press, 1983), 2.

6. David C'nani, *The Second Aliyah and Its Attitude to Religion and Tradition* (in Hebrew) (Tel Aviv: Sifriat Hapoalim, 1976), 13.

7. *Proceedings of the Knesset*, 15 June 1959 (in Hebrew).

8. A. Drayanov, *Documents in the History of Hibbat Zion and the Settlement of Eretz Yisrael* (in Hebrew), (Odessa, 1932), 3:988–89.

9. The reference is to teachers working in schools sponsored by Jewish organizations in Europe whose language of instruction was also that of the country of the organization's origin. The most noteworthy were the Alliance Israélite Universelle (French) and the Hilfsverein der deutschen Juden (German).

10. Drayanov, 3:988–89.

11. Eliezer Rieger, *Hebrew Education in Eretz Yisrael* (in Hebrew) (Tel Aviv: Dvir, 1940), 2:279.

12. The Hebrew *yediat ha'aretz* connotes much more than is apparent in its translation to "geography." See Yoram Bar-Gal, *The Motherland and Geography in a Hundred Years of Zionist Education* (in Hebrew) (Tel Aviv: Am Oved, 1993).

13. Yaffa Sikli, "A Portrait of the Hebrew Teacher in the Colonies of the First Aliyah, 1984–1904" (in Hebrew), *Cathedra* 84 (1997): 143–74.

14. The very term "college" has, until very recently, connoted a level of instruction and status inferior to that of the university.

15. The Ministry of Education awards the license.

16. So called after its chair, Prof. Aliza Shenhar, then rector of Haifa University. See the report of the committee, A People and the World: Jewish Culture in a Changing World (n. 4 above).

17. This may be one of the major distinctions between a university and a yeshiva; the latter has no question about its obligation to inculcate a hashkafah.

18. Mayer I. Gruber, "Reflections on the Teaching of Bible in Israel," in Judaism and Education, ed. Haim Marantz (Beersheva: Ben Gurion University Press, 1998), 209–10.

19. As given in Yosef Yonai, "The Committee for Designing the Curriculum of Teacher-Training Institutions, 1942–1944" (in Hebrew), Dapim 16 (1993): 7–28.

20. Bible, Hebrew, rabbinic literature, history, Zionism.

21. Zalman Aranne, Pangs of Education (in Hebrew) (Jerusalem: Ministry of Education and Culture, 1947), 103.

22. Asher Ginzberg (Ahad Ha'am), "Shinui ha'arachim" (in Hebrew), in Kol kitvei Ahad Ha'Am (Tel Aviv: Dvir, 1947), 154–59.

23. Bulletin of the Director General, A Curriculum Proposal for Teacher-Training Institutions (in Hebrew) (Jerusalem: Ministry of Education, February 1958).

24. Davar, 19 November 1957 (in Hebrew).

25. Jewish Education in State Teachers' Colleges (in Hebrew) (Jerusalem: Ministry of Education and Culture, Dept. for Training Educational Personnel, 1978), 6.

26. Another report bearing the same title was published in 1979. The material that follows is drawn from both documents.

27. Ministry of Education and Culture, Dept. for Training Educational Personnel (in Hebrew), 28 Dec. 1980.

28. Jewish Education in State Teachers' Colleges, 11.

29. Yair Auron, "Jewish Israel Identity among Israel's Future Teachers," as reported in Jerusalem Letter/Viewpoints, no. 334, 1996.

30. A People and the World: Jewish Culture in a Changing World, 1.

31. Ibid., 5.

32. Bulletin of the Director General (in Hebrew) (Jerusalem, Ministry of Education and Culture, April 1995).

33. The Center for In-Service Training in Jewish Studies for Educational Personnel (in Hebrew) (Jerusalem: Dept. of Evaluation, Ministry of Education and Culture, 1997).

34. Chaim Licht, "Discussion of the Forum of Coordinators of Jewish Studies" (in Hebrew), Dapim 13 (1991): 97–99.

35. Rochelle Furstenberg, Post-Zionism: The Challenge to Israel (New York and Ramat Gan: American Jewish Committee and the Argov Center of Bar Ilan University, 1997).

36. A People and the World: Jewish Culture in a Changing World, 6.

A Mifgash in the Context
of the Israel Experience

Yehuda Bar-Shalom

O ver the last two decades, the "Israel experience" has evolved into an industry that brings thousands of Jewish teenagers from the Diaspora to Israel each year, with the goal of deepening their commitment to Israel. However, years of practical experience and anecdotal evidence, as well as a growing body of research, have pointed to weaknesses in the effectiveness of the Israel experience as an educational tool.

One of the sharpest criticisms has been that it does not allow "real" contact with Israel. Ethnographic studies by Goldberg and by Heilman illustrated that North American groups travel through Israel in a very selective and restricted way, as their reality is mediated by the groups' directors, educators, and *madrichim* (guides/counselors).[1] Furthermore, despite their possible emotional ties to and preexisting identification with the State of Israel, Diaspora teenagers are also tourists[2] being exposed to a new country, usually for the first time. As tourists, they suffer from culture shock[3] and require a period of adaptation before they can function successfully in the visited culture. Out of necessity, they judge and interpret the host society according to their own frame of reference, processing events within their own group context, reflecting upon their own narrative with their own compatriots.[4] This, critics believe, amounts to seeing Israel from inside an artificial bubble, having essentially an "American"[5] experience in a foreign country.

Moreover, a good number of visiting teens come away from their Israel experience with a very positive view of the country and of the trip, but with negative feelings toward Israelis. This often occurs when visi-

Yehuda Bar-Shalom is a teacher in the education and adult-education departments at the David Yellin College of Education in Jerusalem. He was a doctoral student of Professor Joseph Lukinsky at the Jewish Theological Seminary of America.

tors do not have the opportunity to interact with Israeli peers; rather, they develop an image of Israelis based only on their chance meetings with "people who chase them trying to sell them things," "rude bus drivers," or "rude guys who try to pick up our girls."[6]

Mifgashim (the Hebrew word mifgash means "encounter") are a response to this problem. Mifgashim are one of the newest and perhaps the fastest-growing components of the Israel experience program, providing opportunities for Jewish teenagers from all over the world to interact with their Israeli counterparts in a structured environment, thus creating a more representative encounter with Israel. In describing the importance of the mifgash, one Israeli educator explained, "We want the participants to experience not only the stones of Israel, but also the people of Israel." Organizers of mifgashim typically believe that:

- the mifgash reduces the number of stereotypes about Israelis that are created by the casual encounters cited above;
- the mifgash enables both the Israeli and Diaspora participants to grow emotionally and socially;
- the mifgash enables both sides to expand their Jewish horizons by learning to appreciate each other's different perceptions of Jewishness.

The Mifgash and the Contact Hypothesis

A successful mifgash cannot be achieved by merely throwing a group of non-Israeli teenagers together with a group of Israelis and hoping for the best. Researchers such as Amir tested the hypothesis that merely bringing people together will improve cross-cultural understanding. Amir states that if conditions for contact are favorable, there is indeed a chance of forging positive intergroup relations; if conditions are unfavorable, the negative aspects of contact and prejudices will only be magnified. Spontaneous contact tends to occur mainly under unfavorable conditions.[7] A successful encounter includes the following conditions:

- All participants in the encounter are treated equally within the encounter.
- The contact is between members of a majority group and members of the higher stratum of a minority group.
- The social climate promotes favorable contact.
- The contact is intimate rather than group-based.

- The contact is pleasant or rewarding.
- The members of the group interact in functionally important activities while developing shared goals.[8]

Mifgashim programs attempt to break this tourist "bubble" by enabling meaningful encounters between Diaspora Jewish youth (non-Israelis) and the local Israelis.

Still, it is important to remember that the encounter between Diaspora and Israeli youth is not a standard cross-cultural encounter. It is complicated by the fact that the two participating populations share some common myths, rituals, and history, yet interpret them differently, either as members of a minority living in a pluralistic society, or as members of a majority in a Jewish state. In some aspects, these two populations are even in conflict.[9] A *mifgash* between them must take into account these differences.

Previous Findings

In his research on *mifgashim* in 1994–95, Cohen[10] found that all participants were quite satisfied with the program and felt that they gained a better understanding of the other side, but more Israelis than Americans would recommend the program to others. Horenczyk and Bekerman[11] found that the *mifgash* caused American participants to perceive Israelis as more similar to themselves, but as less positive from a Jewish point of view.

The Szold Institute[12] conducted an in-depth study of three *mifgashim*. In one, most participants enjoyed the experience and rated the home-hospitality element as positive, exciting, and successful. The two other *mifgashim*, neither of which included home hospitality, seemed to be less successful.

The Purpose of This Study

In this study, commissioned by the Charles Bronfman *Mifgashim* Centre in Jerusalem. I conducted a qualitative inquiry across a wider number of groups. I evaluated fifteen groups, constituting approximately 15 percent of all *mifgash* populations, utilizing several techniques, including individual interviews, focus groups, and observations. My objective was to test and gain a more profound understanding of the quantitative data of past studies, as well as to add new dimensions and identify new directions relative to the previous case studies.

Faithful to the qualitative approach, I went into the field with broad questions but remained open to surprises and new questions that arose during the collection of data. The use of multiple techniques and my ongoing consultation with members of the research committee[13] and other experts during collation of the material contributed to the triangulation of the data.[14] The reliability of the case study is judged according to its relatability to other practitioners working in similar conditions or facing similar problems.[15]

Intended Audience

This paper is intended primarily for those involved in the field of Israel and Jewish education or who already have basic knowledge about the Israel experience. One hopes that it will serve practitioners and leaders of organizations in their practice as well as their decision making regarding *mifgashim*. The research exposes complex issues and problems as well as possible solutions and creative ideas as they emerged from actual *mifgashim* in the summer of 1997. This paper may also be of interest and relevance to researchers studying intercultural communication, particularly in an internal Jewish context, and to those interested in the differences and similarities between Israeli Jews and Jews from Western countries.

The Research Method

Out of a total of ninety-five *mifgashim* modules on record during the summer of 1997, I had access to fifteen. In addition to observing activities in the field, I held focus-group discussions with Israeli and non-Israeli participants before, during, and after the *mifgashim* and conducted numerous in-depth interviews with senior personnel of some of the sponsoring organizations, *mafgishim* (persons who facilitate the *mifgash*), group tour guides, and experts. A research committee, composed of Professor Steven M. Cohen of the Hebrew University, Bronfman Centre director Elan Ezrachi, and myself, developed the framework and format of the project before field research began.

What Is a Mifgash?

Before moving to the actual study, it is important to have in mind a composite picture of a *mifgash* and the various models that exist. As noted above, the simple definition of *mifgash* is "encounter," but in the context of the Israel experience, a *mifgash* is a prearranged encounter with a planned agenda between Israeli and Diaspora Jewish youth. Three major types of *mifgashim* can be identified:

1. *Stationary.* The non-Israelis and the Israelis are brought to a "neutral" site, such as a youth village or a resort camp, where they stay for the bulk of their encounter. In many cases, at the culmination of the *mifgash,* the Israelis invite their new friends from abroad to their homes for a weekend. The *mifgash* staff often arranges the lodging in such a way that members of both groups share rooms, in the belief that this abets community building.
2. *Home Hospitality/Mobile.* During the day, the entire group engages in joint activities at various sites, and almost every night Israelis host one or two of the non-Israeli teens in their homes. Hiking, walking, swimming, and other activities are usually combined with educational assignments at selected sites. The group often has one outdoor overnight on the beach or at a campground.
3. *Kibbutz.* In this model, the teenage kibbutz members act as hosts. Some activities take place on a kibbutz, and others are held on sites in the vicinity of the kibbutz. In some cases, the guests stay in separate quarters; in others, they stay with the kibbutz families in their homes.

Some Things That Happen during a Mifgash

Studies of group work have shown that participants experience many anxieties when they are tossed into a new group situation, e.g., "Do I belong here?" "Do I want to be here?" "Am I safe here?" Some of these feelings are rooted deep in every person's subconscious, perhaps as traces from our infant world.[16] The *mifgash* differs from a "new group" situation in that the compatriots know one another (the in-group) but not the others (the out-group), and at the same time the two groups share a symbolic bond, i.e., Jewishness. Nonetheless, both populations tend to enter the *mifgash* with anticipation and suspicion.

The role of the facilitator in a new group is to enable the members to work through their anxieties and eventually feel comfortable enough to express themselves freely. The *mafgish* usually begins with activities defined as "icebreakers," in which the participants are encouraged to share a part of themselves with the rest of the group (e.g., my favorite color, what makes me nervous). In other activities, participants share their qualities as a group (e.g., an Israeli answers a question written anonymously by a member of the non-Israeli group, such as, "Why are you so shy?" "Why do you hug each other all the time?" "Do you like us?"). These activities convey to all participants that they can safely express themselves and take risks in this environment.

Both sides come to the *mifgash* with preconceptions. In almost all cases, the non-Israelis had developed some negative attitudes toward Israelis:

> You can be walking down the street and they try to hit on you, or whistle. I'm not used to this [*laughter*]. Or people honking. In Montreal, you never hear that. It was annoying.

> They are rude; they seem not to like foreigners. I picked this up here and there. They are trying to become Westerners, but they hate Westerners.

The *mifgash* dramatically reduces negative projections against Israelis that are often created by impersonal encounters with Israeli individuals whose main objective is to earn a profit, pick up a girl, or in some way take advantage of foreigners. One American participant commented, "It was great to spend time with kids our age. We didn't like the Israelis we met before, but after the *mifgash,* and especially after hanging out with them, home hospitality, seeing where they live, we realized that they are basically the same as us."

The Israelis come with prejudices of their own. Unlike their counterparts, who have been touring a foreign country for some time, witnessing new things and formulating ideas within a group context, the Israeli teens develop stereotypical images drawn from global culture: television, magazines, movies, and so on. Accordingly, they believe that the non-Israelis are:

- very rich, because they are Americans
- not religious; they are cool
- the same as us, like youth all over the world
- weak and soft

The Israelis, too, gain more realistic insights from a *mifgash*, learning that not all Diaspora youth are spoiled, rich, soft, or cool. Rather, in many ways, they are similar to Israeli teens. "Despite the fact that they don't plan to live here or serve in the army, we have many things in common with them: first of all, they are Jewish. Second, they are teenagers like us, with almost the same taste in everything."

The *mifgash* enables the participants from both sides to test the perceived differences between the groups and between individuals. While on many levels, both sides discover similarities, profound differences emerge in terms of how they interpret Jewishness (see below).

We Are All One

We have often heard the phrase "we are all one" describing the connection that Jews have with one another, but it may be that the source of our unity is more than a common religious heritage. It appears that contemporary global culture, promulgated by modern technology and instant communication, has provided its own common language among ever broadening populations.

In the *mifgashim* that we examined, the symbols that connected Israeli youth with the Diaspora population and caused them to identify with each other were drawn from Western culture. *Mifgashim* use these common denominators as starting points because they provide a certain degree of comfort among the participants and allow them to relate easily. The more substantive issues, such as Judaism, Zionism, and Israel-Diaspora relations, are usually more divisive. Sensing that the *mifgash* has a higher chance of success in the informal areas, some staff tend to minimize the more formal content of the encounter, steering clear of potential conflict. While global culture brings youths together, Judaism pulls them apart. In the participants' own words:

> *Non-Israeli:* They are very friendly. We have things in common, like music and stuff. We thought that they would be more behind. None of them had bar mitzvahs—that was a big surprise. I thought that they would be more religious. It was a bit weird not having a traditional kabbalat Shabbat.

> *Israeli:* The *mifgash* is fun because these are youth. We talk with them about what youth speak about all over the world. In the activities, the *mafgishim* tried to push Judaism.

YBS: Would it matter if they weren't Jewish?

Israelis: No. [*consensus*]

Israeli: We talk about movies, MTV.

Non-Israeli: We met loads of people. It was good to change, to rest. All Israelis are very similar. They like the same sports; they smoke the same cigarettes. We like the same music as the Israelis do. Most of them are not very religious; most don't even fast on Yom Kippur.

It was often difficult for me and many other *madrichim* and educators to differentiate between the Israeli teens and those from abroad. In one instance, while observing a *mifgash* activity in the north of Israel, I noticed one of the Americans playing rock music—Elton John, George Michael, James Taylor—creating a nice ambience. A colleague sitting next to me asked if I thought that the music was planned. It was a good question, so I asked the musician. To my amazement, the "American" musician turned out to be one of the Israeli participants—the son of a Moroccan father and a Rumanian mother, whose only experience abroad was one week in London. Six other educators who had came to lead the activity on Jewish identity, most of them *olim* (immigrants to Israel who make aliyah) themselves from English-speaking countries, were amazed that this guy was an Israeli. The singer told me that the music was indeed planned in advance and that he "just loves Barbra Streisand." When I asked him why he did not sing Israeli songs, he said that he was trying to "adapt himself to the atmosphere."

Those educators who see the *mifgash* as an opportunity for both sides to grow Jewishly by learning about the other's Jewishness may be disappointed to realize that the shared "global" language, which in many cases makes it easy for the *mifgash* to succeed socially, tends also to deprive the *mifgash* of its Jewish content. For many Israelis, the non-Israelis are just "Americans," "Canadians," and so on. For many of the visitors, Israel is just another country. When asked why they wanted to take part in the *mifgash,* some Israelis replied: "To see other habits, to see how people live in another country. To meet new people, to improve my English, and to prepare for my own trip abroad." I asked a non-Israeli participant what was special about the bench that his group was building for a local synagogue as a community project, and he replied: "I think that it does make a difference. We leave part of us in another country, another place; our creation will be somewhere." Another non-Israeli: "Compared to the other parts of our trip, the *mifgash* is better, because you get to meet people like you in a different country, and you see how they are similar to the way that you are."

Part of the success of the *mifgash*, then, depends on the ability of both sides to understand and communicate in the global, Western language. This is easy for the non-Israelis, who usually come from English-speaking, Western countries. What about the Israelis? In all the groups I observed, there was a process of selection through which the sponsoring organizations tried to match populations. Usually, they recruited middle-class teens who speak English quite well and who are generally in touch with Western culture. It seems that a large segment of Israeli youth who may be less Western, more traditional, and from working-class families is not represented in the *mifgash* world. Limited as it may be, the cross-section of populations from both sides still yields a wide spectrum of ideas and attitudes within each national group and within the *mifgash* group as a whole.

Jewishness in the Mifgash

We know that Jewishness is perceived and defined differently in Israel from the way it is in the Diaspora. The relationship between Israel and Diaspora communities has often been problematic, with many emotional conflicts and misunderstandings. These burning issues are usually discussed not by the average citizen but are addressed by the intellectual and power elite from both sides, those with a deeper understanding of the issues at stake. These people can be defined as "initiated" and may include American Jews who have spent much time in Israel, Israelis who were successful *shlichim* (World Zionist Organization cultural emissaries from Israel to the Diaspora), and other individuals who have had extensive exposure to both cultures.

In a way, the *mifgash* is an attempt to initiate the uninitiated. Although the success of the *mifgashim* that we observed was most apparent on the level of global culture, there was not a single *mifgash* that did not deal with some aspect of the participants' Jewishness, Israeliness, Zionism, or commitment to Israel. While the level of intensity varied, all *mifgashim* included at least one dimension of "initiation."

Prior to meeting the Israelis, the Diaspora teens tend to project their own standards or ideal of Jewishness onto them. Take the example of this group of Reform teens on the second day of their trip, three weeks before the *mifgash:*

> *YBS (before the Reform teens have met the Israelis):* How are the Israelis Jewish?
>
> Some are the same as me; some are more religious.
>
> *YBS:* What do you think is going to happen during home hospitality?
>
> They are going to accept us because we are Jewish. We are going to have Shabbat services—we almost always do Shabbat at home—and a family dinner.
>
> I don't know; I've never done a Shabbat in Israel. I guess there is going to be a kiddush cup, challah.
>
> I don't care, as long as they are a warm family.
>
> I think that Shabbat is going to be family-style, mellow.
>
> *YBS:* How do you think it is at a secular home on Shabbat?
>
> I'm sure that in Israel, everyone kind of mellows out on Friday night, whether they are Orthodox or secular.
>
> I'm sure that they light candles and do kiddush, but that not many go to services.
>
> There are many that do nothing—they're Orthodox or nothing.
>
> It doesn't matter what you do, but how you feel.

The *mifgash,* particularly the home-hospitality element, brings the Diaspora teens to the realization that Israelis' Jewishness is very different from their own. However prepared the visiting groups may be, however thorough the orientation, there are still big surprises, as attested to in these comments:

> We split up into groups and discussed what it means to be Jewish, and it turned out that it's the Israelis who did not feel that they were particularly Jewish; they were just Israelis. In America, if you are Jewish, you know it, because most people aren't.
>
> One told me that he considers himself first an Israeli and then a Jew, and that sort of surprised me, because if you live in Israel,

why not take advantage of all the opportunities? There are a variety of things. But he considers himself an Israeli who happens to be Jewish.

The Israelis, on the other hand, are surprised to find a group of people their age who feel very Jewish and express it so differently. The non-Israelis are traditional in ways that are unknown to the majority of Israelis, who may not be Orthodox but tend to accept the Orthodox standard of Jewish religious practice.[17] Some Israelis react very positively to the new forms of practice that they observe, but others find it difficult, especially the unfamiliar songs and prayers that combine English lyrics with Hebrew text, such as Reform camp songs. One Israeli staff person reported an encounter involving Reform Jewish youth and Israelis:

> The song leader simply gave up. She said that the Israelis were not ready to listen to American songs, and especially not to NFTY [Reform youth movement] songs, but the Americans came with open minds to Israeli music. The Israelis kept yelling that they wanted Israeli music.

Still, there were many instances in which Israelis actually joined in the songs and blessings. When the *mifgash* was successful in forming a more or less unified community with a warm, safe environment, participants felt secure enough to take social risks, such as engaging in new ritual behaviors.

During a NFTY *mifgash* in the north, the entire group went inside the Baram ancient synagogue. The *madricha* asked questions such as, "In what way is the place Jewish?" Most people in the group were attentive. She then transferred the authority to the group educator, Saul, who explained what a Reform service was, as they were about to conduct one. After explaining, he called on Ziva, an Israeli *madricha*, who spoke about how she had felt when she had been exposed to a Reform service at a summer camp in the United States. Saul explained, "In Reform Judaism, we emphasize the issue of choice; therefore, everyone will do what they feel like." The Israelis were invited to participate, or to sit and observe. The service was entirely in Hebrew. Those Israelis who were scattered among the non-Israelis participated; those who were sitting together remained seated during the whole service. At the end of the service, the Israelis commented on the experience:

It was nice, but strange.

I liked the singing; it was like a prayer with David Broza [an Israeli rock singer] music.

I couldn't do it. I can't do something that I do not believe in.

Saul: And you don't have to do it; that is our ideology. [*Non-Israelis nod in agreement.*]

Saul then told the group that he had recently received his rabbinical ordination.

Israeli: You don't look like a rabbi.

Saul: What does a rabbi look like?

Israeli: I don't know; different hair, different hat, different clothes.

The use of personal narratives, such as those of the young rabbi and the Israeli *madricha,* are often effective in opening the Israelis up to the liberal religious experience. In the case cited above, it may also be that those Israelis who reached a higher level of intimacy with their non-Israeli friends were more open to take the social risk of participation in the service.

In another *mifgash* that I observed, the Israelis were given the option to pray with the Americans, but none chose to do so. The Americans were offended when all the Israelis left the room where the service was to be held. In retrospect, it would have been constructive if the staff had urged the Israelis to remain at the service so that they could formulate an opinion of it. "They could have at least stayed in the same room," said one American sadly. Later in this *mifgash,* one Israeli girl cried after being told by one of the Americans that she was "not really Jewish."

Israel-Diaspora Relations

Becoming aware of the various understandings of Judaism leads the participants to deliberate on Israel-Diaspora relations. Inevitably, the Israeli participants steer this discussion toward what they often perceive as the most important and meaningful thing that they do as Jews: serve in the Israeli army. Their underlying message to the non-Israelis is that because they physically defend their country, they have more Jewish "rights" than non-Israelis. Some of their comments about serving in the Israel Defense Forces:

> *Israeli:* They can think whatever they want—that if you don't believe in God, you are not Jewish—but I'm the one who's going to the army. How can he tell me that when he lives over there?
>
> *Non-Israeli:* The Israelis are very patriotic. For us, that's difficult to understand, because in Canada, nobody gives a shit. [*laughter*]
>
> *Non-Israeli:* The main issue was that they were sixteen, and so were we. We were planning our college future, and they were going to the army.

The emphasis on army service reflects not only the Israelis' need to respond to the non-Israelis' professed feelings of Jewishness, but their attempt to process the non-Israelis' declared loyalty to both Judaism and their mother countries, something that Israelis find very difficult to understand. The discussions tend to be long. The non-Israelis frequently inject into the conversation examples of how their lives have been threatened because of their Jewishness. One *mafgish* told me:

> Often, they talk about hard and difficult experiences, such as an Israeli girl who told about her brother dying in Lebanon, and she is just sixteen. The non-Israelis understand that this is not CNN. Then there was a sixteen-year-old non-Israeli girl sitting with them who told them about a terrible case of anti-Semitism in her school.[18]
>
> *YBS:* Doesn't this reflect young people's tendency to talk about death and related issues?
>
> No, I think it is more of a Jewish thing. We tend to concentrate on the negative, especially the Israelis. We always remember persecutions, the bad parts that define Jews and Jewishness.

This is an example of how, whatever the subject, the *mafgish* uses an inclusive narrative to frame the experience, usually emphasizing that, despite material differences, the participants share many similar emotional reactions. Still, the fact that many *mifgashim* participants from both sides offer examples of negative Jewish experiences (e.g., anti-Semitism, persecution) makes us wonder about the considerable weight that these myths have on Jewish youth everywhere. A common enemy, or another "other" is often critical to forming a bond between different populations. There are even programs, such as the March of the Living, that use common negative historical experiences as the crux of their curriculum. Yet in an era when peace agreements are being negotiated between Israel and its neighbors and when most Jews in the world are not persecuted or in physical danger, perhaps more emphasis should be placed on issues of partnership, mutual creativity, and constructive reasons to be Jewish. The *mifgash* could be exploited as an opportunity to neutralize negative Jewish myths and reactive ideologies that rely on an eternal negative force and to enable participants to explore new common bonds.

Summary and Conclusions

The *mifgash*, which was created—among other reasons—to enable positive contact between Diaspora youth and Israelis, seems to succeed in creating a better image of Israelis among visiting Diaspora youth. In some cases, the *mifgash* experience also offers a serious opportunity for both sides to discuss, and perhaps to accept, the differences in Jewishness reflected in the process. Still, in many cases the *mafgishim*, sensing that the global level makes the *mifgash* comfortable and socially successful, leave it at that point, reducing the explicit Jewish components.

While the global culture unites both sides, Jewishness often creates conflicts and misunderstandings. Non-Israelis are surprised to find youth who are very patriotic and nonreligious. The Israelis, who expect to meet "just Americans," are surprised at the display of nonorthodox forms of Jewish religious practice. In some cases, the Israelis are prepared to take the social risk of participating in such practices during the *mifgash*.

Many times, unity between the two groups is achieved by employing negative memories of persecution and anti-Semitism. Perhaps in the future, more positive and creative myths should be explored instead of negative and reactive ones, for symmetry fits well into the emerging trend of partnership in the Israel-Diaspora relationship. Partnership is a positive myth that needs to be explored and reinforced. Successful *mif-*

gashim have the potential to reduce the needs of Jews everywhere to rely on external and negative factors, such as crises, to unify them. In this new era of peace talks and conflict resolution, we should engage in partnership not against a common enemy, but toward a positive and creative future.

Notes

1. H. E. Goldberg, "A Summer on a NFTY Safari: An Ethnographic Perspective" (Hebrew University, 1994); S. C. Heilman, "A Young Judaea Israel Discovery Tour: The View from Inside" (Hebrew University, 1994).
2. Machlis and Burch define the encounter between tourist and host as "an interaction between strangers." This interaction leads to many misunderstandings, and the *mifgash* experience must be studied from this perspective. G. E. Machlis and W. R. Burch, "Relations between Strangers: Cycles of Structure and Meaning in Tourist Systems," *Sociological Review* 31 (1983): 666–92.
3. Pearce points out that tourists tend to suffer more of a culture shock than other sojourners because of the limited period of time spent in the new country, compatriots' support for negative reactions to the new culture, and physical restrictions of the tour that limit chances of extensive encounters with locals. Heilman and Goldberg address this phenomenon within the Israel experience context (see above). H. P. L. Pearce, "Tourists and Their Hosts: Some Social and Psychological Effects of Inter-Cultural Contact," in *Cultures in Contact: Studies in Cross-Cultural Interaction,* ed. S. Bochner (Oxford: Pergamon, 1982). For more on the culture-shock phenomenon, see Richard Brislin and Tomoko Yoshida, *Intercultural Training: An Introduction* (Thousand Oaks, Calif.: Sage, 1994), 77–79.
4. Because we are examining teenagers, we should note what Erikson defines as the natural tendency to seek sameness within the peer group as a defense against the confusion of autonomous identity forming. See E. H. Erikson, *Identity, Youth and Crisis* (New York: W. W. Norton, 1975), 128.
5. Or a Canadian experience, or an English experience, etc.
6. These are typical of the remarks I heard during my research. See also Erik Cohen's survey on attitudes toward Israelis, showing that spontaneous encounters with Israelis were far from satisfactory for participants in the Israel experience. In a survey conducted in 1993 after the end of the program, "73 percent of the participants viewed the encounter with young Israelis as the best means of improving the quality and the impact of summer programs." Findings such as these led the Youth and Hechalutz Department of the WZO to extend the *mifgashim* program in following years. E. H. Cohen, *The 1994–95 Mifgashim Programs: Questionnaires & Survey* (Jerusalem, 1996).
7. Y. Amir, "Contact Hypothesis in Ethnic Relations," *Psychological Bulletin* 71 (1969): 319–41.

8. Paul Pedersen, *A Handbook for Developing Multicultural Awareness,* 2d ed. (Alexandria, Va.: ACA, 1994), 108.

9. For a detailed account of the differences emerging between American and Israeli Judaism, see C. S. Liebman and S. M. Cohen, *Two Worlds of Judaism: The Israeli and American Experiences* (New Haven: Yale University Press, 1990), 163–65. See also E. Ezrachi, "Encounters between American Jews and Israelis: Israelis in American Summer Camps" (Ph.D. diss., Jewish Theological Seminary, 1993).

10. Cohen, *The 1994–95 Mifgashim Programs.*

11. G. Horenczyk and Z. Bekerman, "The Effects of Intercultural Acquaintance and Structured Intergroup Interaction on In-group, Out-group, and Reflected In-group Stereotypes," *International Journal of Intercultural Relations* 21, no. 1 (1996): 71–83.

12. L. Findling-Andy and A. Spector, *Mifgashim in the Israel Experience: Encounters of Diaspora Youth with Israeli Youth* (Jerusalem: Szold Institute, 1997).

13. As another method of triangulation (see n. 14 below) and data validation, I presented the categories and findings as they emerged to the research committee: Professor Steven M. Cohen and Dr. Elan Ezrachi, as well as to experts from the Bronfman Centre, and others.

14. "Triangulation" refers to the "need to gather more data from a variety of sources before drawing any conclusions." See Vicky Kubler Labosky, "Case Investigations," in Judith H. Shulman, *Case Methods in Teacher Education* (New York: Teachers College Press, 1992), 178. See also John Elliot, *Action Research for Educational Change* (Philadelphia: Open University Press, 1991), 80–83.

15. M. Bassey, "Pedagogic Research: On the Relative Merits of Search for Generalization and Study of Single Events," in *Oxford Review of Education* 7, no. 1 (1981): 85.

16. Melanie Klein, "Our Adult World and Its Roots in Infancy," in *Group Relations Reader,* ed. D. Coleman and M. H. Geller (Washington, D.C.: A. K. Rice Institute, 1985), 2:5–19.

17. See Liebman and Cohen, 163–65.

18. I recall Professor Jack Wertheimer at the Jewish Theological Seminary quoting research showing that American Jews believe that there is more anti-Semitism than they actually encounter.

Art in Cultural Education

Zvi Bekerman

"A rt is a quality of doing and of what is done."[1] This short statement is an attempt to say something relevant regarding the use
of art in education. My concern is art with a small "a," art that is not
seen necessarily as a finished product but that can help us overcome
modern thought/experience, mind/body dichotomies. By education, I
mean not just education, for general purposes, but those institutional
educational efforts that are made to socialize our youth into our people's meaning matrices, interpretative schemes, and communal settings.
Any short statement, especially when regarding such broad issues as art
and education, will not allow everything to be said. The reader should
be aware of this and at the same time be kind; indeed, much will be left
unsaid, hoping that the little said can in some way become significant.

When considering our present situation, there is something paradoxical about the biblical description of the artisan Bezalel in Exod.
31:3 as one filled "with the spirit of God, in wisdom, and in understanding, and in knowledge, and in all manner of workmanship." This
description has little in common with our modern perceptions of art as
that which, given certain socio-historical contexts, is appropriated by
particular people as cultural goods, i.e., that which today is consumed
by the bourgeoisie. Bezalel's art is not the autonomous act of a Carte-
sian-imprisoned individual self, nor is his art set at work so as to severe
its bonds from society. Bezalel's portrayal runs contrary to the modern
conception of art as the best of human creativity[2] and the Kantian view
on aesthetics, which strove to distinguish what pleases from what grati-

Zvi Bekerman teaches anthropology of education at the School of Education and at the
Melton Centre for Jewish Education, the Hebrew University of Jerusalem. He was a
doctoral student of Professor Joseph Lukinsky at the Jewish Theological Seminary of
America.

fies.[3] The description of Bezalel connotes art in its more traditional sense, as that which pleases and is serviceable to the community.

Unfortunately, present educational attitudes, particularly those in formal schooling, reflect both the triumph of the Cartesian paradigm in Western philosophy[4] and Kantian perspectives of high aesthetics as solely the practice of reflection. These attitudes become explicit when educators' central aim becomes the improvement of intellectual tools geared toward the development of the mind's imprisoned self. They are also reflected when cultural affiliation is envisioned as that hierarchical and compartmentalized knowledge, linear and causal in nature, that has to be imparted to the absorbing minds of passive individuals.

Educational institutions are not to be blamed for this. As has always been the case, institutionalized learning has for the most part reflected societal trends. Since the sixteenth century, with the dawn of the scientific/rational revolution in the West, we have all been set on the path of opposition to mythical thought. Myth, that enchanted device that had allowed for coherence and proximity between past and future, always adapting itself to new circumstances and allowing sense to be produced out of the fluidity and complexity of present reality,[5] was replaced by reductionistic scientific research. Scientific reductionism has its positive side: it helped humans conquer a world. But at the same time, it seems to have its down sides: meaning is being lost. Modernity seems to have bonded a strong fit between individuality, rationality, science, and literacy and has placed all these in opposition to the mythological and the primitive.[6]

In this essay, I will address three subjects central to traditional forms of education in our Western society: educators' conventional perception of who their students are (their students' self and identity); educators' traditional understanding of culture as subject matter and content; and the potentially damaging strategies used in ethnic cultural education for the dominant educational goal of creating a literate society. Only a radical shift in our conventions regarding these issues will help us revitalize educational processes directed toward strengthening ethnic cultural identity. The arts, when properly understood, might hold a partial answer to these problems.

First, let us consider two major modern premises that guide the work of our educational institutions toward cultural continuity: the incontestable existence of an inner self; and the unquestionable existence, or preexistence, of culture. Accordingly, all involved in the educational struggle for continuity believe that our culture is a "thing" to be carried by a "self."

Abandoning these positivistic perspectives might help reconceptualize our present situation, and if the term "abandoning" sounds too strong, then at least education should seriously consider, and eventually incorporate, understanding offered by more recent developments in the fields of cultural studies, literacy, literary criticism, anthropology, and cultural psychology influenced by strong hermeneutical and pragmatic leanings.[7] Within these current views, older conceptualizations of cultures as coherent and discrete meaning systems, common to all members, have been undermined.

The cultural practices of a group of people are no longer seen as representing the essential character of a culture, nor can they automatically reproduce its members. Rather than positioning culture a priori, culture is located in social communicative ways as the actual patterning of given interactive processes themselves.[8] Culture is neither "out" nor "in," but in between—managed and constructed continuously in social concert. Together with the disruption of an understanding of culture as preexisting, congruous, and harmonious, a new view of self has been envisioned. This self of high modernity[9] or postmodernity[10] is not any more essential or necessarily consistent or integrated, but rather, multiple and, at times, ephemeral. The self still develops but does not become conclusive; the self is now historically and locally situated in social interactional events, where it becomes in dialogue with coparticipants, taking many forms and expressions.[11]

Concerning the potentially damaging strategies adopted in ethnic cultural education—a product of the dominant educational goal of creating a literate society—it is worth recalling that presently within our educational institutions, writing has become the central mediational means through which language and physical systems are represented. In so doing, and in line with the historical development of schooling,[12] our educational institutions have became detached from contexts of practical activity, have compartmentalized experience, and have, as well, became places in which cognitive learning is conducted by strangers and not kin.

Though undoubtedly a strong precursor of scientific (logical/rational), specialized, and compartmentalized knowledge, the invention of writing and, with it, the development of a literate society with particular modes of perception, might have influenced human cognition in negative ways. The process of literate education has become a matter of absorbing mediated abstract knowledge through teachers who are strangers or books. The use of writing also provoked a schism between

"the arts" and "knowledge," the former still dependent on outside inspiration, and the latter disassociated from natural contexts and constrained to "book" learning. Regarding modes of information
transmission and transformation, written culture mediates knowledge
demanding its static recording and its proper organization, thus creating
the conditions for slow development and change. As such, written culture loses the creative, circular, ever evolving weaving (the traditional
meaning of text) of cultural fabrics characteristic of oral traditions.
These cognitive changes, product of the evolution of writing, were slow
in conquering our society. Only toward the end of the Middle Ages did
Europe function on the basis of written premises, and only toward the
end of the industrial revolution can we speak of a world dominated by
literate modes of perception. Today, inexorably, we have finally chained
culture to misunderstood texts kept in bookshelves.

The dangers of fully surrendering education to written culture and
schooling are presently being discussed.[13] Though schools' traditional
approach to teaching (sustained by an understanding of subject matter
as scientific stuff to be transmitted and learned) has undeniable merit, it
might be on its way to stagnating powerful human resources. Given
these indications of the dangers of our present educational efforts in advancing the acquisition of basic skills, how much more careful we
should be when these efforts are geared toward the strengthening and
development of cultural ethnic education. Cultural acquisition—its production and development—seems to stand in strict opposition to most
of the characteristics of schooling as presented in this paper. Cultural acquisition and production are strongly related to social and historical
contexts. Culture is produced in practical everyday activity, especially
those activities closely connected to kinship networks. Culture, by definition, does not compartmentalize factual knowledge, but connects webs
of personal and social meaning. In other words, culture seems to relate
better to oral practices, procedures, and style than to written modes of
perception. What I am calling for is not a return to "primordial" oral
culture or the denial of the benefits of written perception. When seriously considering the interface between the written and the oral, we
might choose to recapture some of our lost oral tradition—a step that
might help us revive our ailing educational institutions.

The arts might help us advance in this direction. I am not pointing
to the need to teach the history and products of the arts, but rather
am referring to art as a concrete activity. Though some knowledge
could be gained by attending the arts in the narrow modern sense, this

is not what the arts are all about. In a world already too polluted by endless bits of knowledge and information, more knowledge cannot ever be considered a solution, not even for the most ignorant among us. Any such consideration of arts as a remedy for ignorance, while fitting modern times, would place us back into the conceptual fallacy of considering culture to be a thing to be known by the mind. Ethnicity and culture are, at their worst, a set of vanishing memories and, at their best, a connecting hermeneutical pattern in the present, achieved through concrete human interaction, which helps us make particular sense of our particular reality. Culture is the narrative of "why" and "what for." Thus, ethnicity and culture as art cannot be exposed or exhibited for them to be acknowledged, judged, or known. The problem that we confront is not a problem of literacy, but of meaning. Regrettably, the world is being filled with the management of knowledge.

The greatest bureaucracies, as we have shown is the case for institutional education, exist so as to organize knowledge hierarchically and compartmentalize it. We have become attuned to these developments, and our minds have become unidirectional in direct opposition to art forms that are multidirectional, circular, and redundant by design. As such, the arts might guard secrets relevant to the ethnic, cultural, and educational enterprise. Art is holistic; it creates webs of relationships; it has healing power. Functionally, art attacks compartmentalization, detachment, and indifference. Art's design is an invitation to renegotiate meaning in concert.[14] Art echoes history and is created through it—not the scientific history, but the mythical one. By feeding and reviving myth, art might help us rediscover and nourish our oral perception so as to better sustain our cultural ethos. The revitalization of ethnic cultural education implies the need to rediscover the healing power of our oral condition in all its artful forms, not denying rationality, but affirming the need to locate self and society once again in mythical space and time.

For Gregory Bateson,[15] art was the clue for human integration and consequently for the attainment of grace. Grace can only be achieved when the reasons of the heart are integrated with the reasons of the reason, when human sensibilities are reunited with human rationality. This point by itself should be enough to encourage all of us to further the use of art in education. Though through modernity, with its rationality and scientism, we seem to have reached the outer limits of man's world domination, we seem at the same time to have lost meaning and a sense of communion. If, as Bateson and others[16] would have us believe, art codes information about psychic integration, then art might become a partial remedy for the perceived modern disintegration and fragmentation of our ailing community education.

Notes

1. J. Dewey, *Art as Experience* (New York: Perigee, 1938), 214.
2. Wendy Griswold, *Cultures and Societies in a Changing World* (Thousand Oaks, Calif.: Pine Forge, 1994).
3. P. Bourdieu, *Distinction: A Social Critique of the Judgment of Taste,* trans. R. Nice (Cambridge: Harvard University Press, 1984).
4. R. A. Shweder, "Cultural Psychology—What Is It?" in *Cultural Psychology,* ed. J. W. Stigler, R. A. Shweder, and G. Herdt (Cambridge: Cambridge University Press, 1990), 24–55.
5. C. Levi-Strauss, *Myth and Meaning* (New York: Schocken, 1978).
6. J. Goody, *The Interface between the Written and the Oral* (Cambridge: Cambridge University Press, 1987).
7. S. Greenblatt, "Culture," in *Critical Terms for Literary Study,* ed. F. Lentricchia and T. McLaughlin (Chicago: University of Chicago Press, 1990), 75–81; M. Moerman, *Talking Culture: Ethnography and Conversation Analysis* (Philadelphia: University of Pennsylvania Press, 1988).
8. Donal Carbaugh, *Situating Selves: The Communication of Social Identities in American Scenes* (Albany: State University of New York Press, 1996).
9. A. Giddens, *Modernity and Self-Identity* (Stanford, Calif.: Stanford University Press, 1991).
10. K. J. Gergen and J. Kaye, "Beyond Narrative in the Negotiation of Therapeutic Meaning," in *Inquiries in Social Construction,* ed. S. McNamee and K. J. Gergen (London: Sage, 1992), 166–85.
11. R. Harre and G. Gillett, *The Discursive Mind* (London: Sage, 1994).
12. M. Cole, "Cognitive Development and Formal Schooling: The Evidence from Cross-Cultural Research," in *Vygotsky and Education,* ed. L. C. Moll (Cambridge: Cambridge University Press, 1990), 167–88.
13. I. Illich and B. Sanders, *A.B.C.: The Alphabetization of the Popular Mind* (New York: Vintage, 1989); N. Postman, *Technopoly* (New York: Vintage, 1992).
14. S. Gablik, *The Reenchantment of Art* (New York: Thames and Hudson, 1991).
15. G. Bateson, *Mind and Nature: A Necessary Unity* (New York: Bantam, 1979).
16. A. L. Becker, *Beyond Translation: Essays toward a Modern Philology* (Ann Arbor: University of Michigan Press, 1995); Jose Ortega y Gasset, *What People Say: Toward a New Linguistics,* trans. W. R. Trask (New York: W. W. Norton, 1957).

Community, Spirituality, and Cross-Cultural Cooperation:*
A Joint Pluralistic Shabbat Experience for North American and Israeli Youth

Elan Ezrachi

Introduction

This is a case study of two groups of Jewish teens who spent a Shabbat retreat together. One group was from the United States and the other from Israel. The two groups were part of a fellowship program sponsored by an American Jewish foundation. The joint Shabbat, which took place in the United States, marked the concluding phase of a period of several months during which the two groups interacted.

This case study explores the dynamics of celebrating and practicing Shabbat in a pluralistic environment. In coming together, the groups represent a wide range of Jewish religious and secular approaches as well as many of the differences between Jews in Israel and the Diaspora.[1] The study of the Shabbat experience is an opportunity to examine the possibility of creating a shared meaningful spiritual community for people of different cultures. In this case, Judaism serves both as a unifying force and as an issue of contention between Israelis and Diaspora Jews. The Shabbat experience also exposes the diversity of Jewish interpretations that exists today across denominational lines.[2] The study

Elan Ezrachi was executive director of the Charles Bronfman *Mifgashim* Centre in Jerusalem. He was a doctoral student of Professor Joseph Lukinsky at the Jewish Theological Seminary of America.

*The author wishes to thank Tuly Flint for his involvement in the data collection and analysis of the findings described in this paper.

was conducted by way of on-site observations and a survey question-naire that was sent to the participants.

Background

The Shabbat program took place in the course of a visit of the Israeli teens to the United States. The Israelis, twenty in number, traveled to the U.S. for a seminar on the American Jewish experience. The tour focused on several themes: Jewish immigration to America; the structure of the Jewish community (the Jewish Federation, JCC, schools, and so on); visits to the Jewish communities of Boston and New York; the spiritual life of American Jews; and various models of "social action." Prior to the joint Shabbat program, the Israelis had spent Shabbat in homes on the Upper West Side of Manhattan, an area known for its rich and diverse Jewish life. In the course of the home hospitality, the Israelis were exposed to a variety of American Jewish religious alternatives.

On the eleventh day of the tour, twenty-one North American counterparts joined the Israelis. The two groups had met for the first time in Israel five months earlier, when the Americans had come for a summer tour of Israel. In Israel, they had spent a full week together in a *mifgash* (Hebrew for "encounter") program.[3] The structured *mifgash* began on Sunday and ended on Friday. At that point, the Israelis took the Americans home for Shabbat. There was no scheduled program for the Shabbat in Israel, and the guests went along with their hosts. The Shabbat in the Israeli homes was a mixture of rest, relaxation, visiting sites in the Israelis' communities, and nighttime entertainment. The Orthodox Israeli participants hosted the Orthodox North Americans, where Shabbat was kept in a way that suited their needs.[4]

After the *mifgash* in the summer, the two groups maintained contact through individual correspondence and telephone conversations based on their friendships. The organizers also attempted to keep the connection going in anticipation of the upcoming December reunion.

The Americans were invited to join the Israelis on their tour of America in the form of a four-day retreat. Twenty Americans and one Canadian registered for the reunion out of the twenty-four who were invited. The high participation rate was an indicator of the success of the joint fellowship program and of the motivation to continue the relationships. Generally, it seemed as though both groups were looking forward to their second *mifgash*.

The Mifgash

Some of the Americans arrived in Washington, D.C., as early as Wednesday evening. The retreat took place outside of Washington. On Thursday morning, the Israelis went to the Washington Holocaust Museum with some of the Americans. By the afternoon, all the Americans had arrived. The retreat began with greetings from the organizers, and the two groups held a discussion on the impressions that the Israelis had of America. The Israelis described their impressions of the American Jewish community, and the Americans were asked to respond. The rest of the evening was devoted to text study in small groups, followed by explanations about the rest of the program. Before the end of the day, the organizers announced that preparation for Shabbat would be delegated to six committees. Everyone was expected to join one committee that would be responsible for a specific aspect of Shabbat. On Friday, both groups traveled to the Jewish Community Center in downtown Washington and participated in a social-action project.[5]

The joint group returned to the retreat site on Friday around 2:00 P.M. Shabbat programming was scheduled to begin at 4:30. Because of the intensive scheduling, no preparations for Shabbat had been made. At that point, the organizers felt that there was some tension between the two groups. As a result, a special session was called, and each group met separately to discuss the problem.[6] The special session was over around 2:30, and the teens were rushed to the Shabbat planning committees. They were told that they had to finish the work by 3:45 so that people would have enough time to complete their personal preparations for Shabbat. The organizers had not prepared any program for Shabbat aside from arranging for candles, prayer books, blessing and song booklets. In other words, the organizers expected the teens to facilitate the Shabbat program themselves.

The Shabbat committees were arranged along the lines of the traditional Shabbat structure: kabbalat Shabbat (the opening service on Friday evening); Friday night dinner; *oneg* (social program after the meal);

Shabbat morning services; *se'udah shlishit* (the third meal in the late afternoon hours); and Havdalah (the closing ceremony of Shabbat). In most cases, the committees were made up of both Americans and Israelis. The organizers hardly needed to exercise any intervention for the division into committees.

The teens felt the pressure of Shabbat being so imminent. They quickly settled into their committees, and the entire retreat facility was filled with a buzz of discussions, material preparations, cutting and pasting of texts, and role assignments. Some committees had to resolve ideological issues, such as: the style in which Shabbat would be celebrated (Orthodox, Conservative, or Reform); the role of women; and combined services as opposed to separation according to denomination. By 3:45, the committees had ended their planning process and everyone went to their rooms to wash and change for Shabbat.

The Participants

As mentioned earlier, the retreat was a reunion for the two groups, twenty-one North Americans and twenty Israelis. All participants were juniors or seniors in high school. The organizers composed the two groups so that they would reflect the various religious and secular Jewish identities in Israel and in North America. Thus, in the Israeli group two participants were Orthodox, one Conservative, and one Reform. The rest of the Israelis considered themselves either traditional or secular.[7] Of the North Americans, three were Orthodox, and most of the rest were Conservative or Reform; only a minority had no particular affiliation.

Methodology

Two methods of research were employed in this study. I was among the organizers and happened to be Israeli. As such, this study is a reflective account of my work and impressions as an involved practitioner. The reflective data were collected through observations, interviews, staff meetings, and field notes.[8]

In addition to the reflective work, a questionnaire was sent to all participants two weeks after the Israelis returned to Israel. Twelve North Americans (60 percent) and sixteen Israelis (80 percent) returned the questionnaires. In the questionnaire there were two questions asking participants to define themselves and report on their specific role in the Shabbat program. The second group of questions addressed the planning process of the Shabbat activities. The third section was devoted to the evaluation of the Shabbat itself. The last set of questions asked the participants to express their views about the whole experience.

Findings from Observations and Questionnaires

Choice of Committee

The participants were free to choose a committee. Aside from minor interventions, the committees reflected a good balance of Israelis and Americans. Eighty percent of the Israelis and 75 percent of the Americans said that they went to the committee of their choice. When asked for the reason for choosing a particular committee, some voiced a firm interest in the committee's subject matter, while for others the participation in the particular committee was less significant. It appeared that the Shabbat committee method was more familiar to the Americans than to the Israelis. The Israelis, therefore, were made more anxious by what appeared to them as a vague structure. A few Israelis were unfamiliar with the purpose of some of the committees and were asking the organizers to clarify the procedure.

Two Israelis said that they had chosen a committee that would not expose their ignorance in the area of Jewish knowledge and skills: "The committee I chose does not require prior religious knowledge." "I was afraid to expose my lack of knowledge in the committees that dealt with prayer and ritual." Two Israelis chose their committee because they felt comfortable with that particular area. Eight of the Israelis reported that their choice was based on a desire to use the work in the committee to enrich their knowledge and experience and to deal with issues of tolerance and pluralism. "I chose the kabbalat Shabbat committee because I wanted to participate in the process of running an alternative [Reform] service and to understand the difference between the Reform and the Orthodox approach."[9]

For the Americans, who had had more experience in similar situations, the choice of committee seemed to be more instrumental, while for the Israelis it reflected an existential choice. The Americans had a clearer view of what the outcome of the Shabbat experience would be and also possessed a greater range of skills necessary for the task. Five Americans said that they went to the committee dealing with their favorite aspect of Shabbat, two felt that they had to represent their denominational affiliation, and two saw the experience of the committee as a vehicle to work with the Israelis.

The Planning Process

The organizers thought that the lack of preparation time could be advantageous to the process. Shabbat, being a holy time with a deadline that could not be moved, pushed the teens to work effectively and quickly.[10] The site was buzzing with activity.

In some committees, the work took on a practical direction, while in others there was a need for an ideological debate. At one point, I was approached by an Israeli girl who was sent by her committee to run a quick survey about the preferred format for the kabbalat Shabbat service. At stake was the issue of mixed seating, which is customary in Reform and Conservative services, as opposed to separate seating, as in the Orthodox settings. The Israeli girl, coming from a secular background, had little prior knowledge about this issue but was concerned that the solution should suit everyone. Some of the committees asked the staff to come in and help them resolve issues, while others managed by themselves.

The Israelis had an advantage in helping solve several logistical problems. Being more inclined to improvisation, the Israelis managed to find flowers to decorate the tables, arrange the spaces for the services, and find a solution for a place to light Shabbat candles despite the strict fire-safety rules at the facility.[11]

In the survey, participants were asked to recall who dominated the committees, i.e., Israelis or Americans, and whether the tone was set by people with stronger Jewish backgrounds. Some 66 percent of the Israelis felt that the work in the committees was balanced; 16 percent felt that it was dominated by the Americans; and 16 percent felt that Israelis set the tone. Among the Americans, 60 percent felt that the work was balanced, and 40 percent felt that the Americans set the tone. More important, 55 percent of the Americans said that the committees were dominated by those who chose to be there, based on their drive and ambition. Israelis gave more weight to prior knowledge as a basis for domination, thus expecting the Americans to have the upper hand.

Evaluating the Shabbat Experience

As the Shabbat officially began, there was a noticeable change in the atmosphere. The teens returned from their shared rooms, dressed up in accordance with the expected Shabbat dress code (as expected, Israelis were dressed more casually than their American counterparts).

The program began with a collective candle-lighting ceremony. Then the participants divided themselves into two groups: one with mixed seating to accommodate the Reform and Conservative participants; and the other with separate seating to accommodate the Orthodox style. The Orthodox group was very small, and in order to have the minimum quorum of ten males, there was a need for reinforcement. Most of the reinforcement came from the American males who were approached by the American Orthodox females.

The egalitarian kabbalat Shabbat service was conducted by an Israeli female who had some Reform background. The Israeli Reform style was unfamiliar to most of the participants, Americans and Israelis alike, and help was needed from the group to understand it. In the Orthodox service, which was conducted by one of the Orthodox staff members, there were also issues of style and format that had to be discussed as the service progressed. After the two services were over, the two groups joined each other, wishing one another a good Shabbat, hugging and kissing. The Israelis were less accustomed to this behavior but had no problems joining the revelry.

The dining room was set up by the committee in a three-part square, with white tablecloths and makeshift decorations. The seating was open, and there was full integration between the Americans and the Israelis. The meal began with the traditional blessings. As soon as everyone finished eating, spontaneous singing and dancing began. The committee in charge of the Friday night dinner did not interfere and had assumed that the singing and dancing would just happen. The Americans dominated the singing as well as the dancing. The collection of songs and dances was clearly from the American religious "camp style" tradition, with strong domination from the North American Orthodox females. At the beginning, the Israelis stayed out of the dance circle, but as soon as they were invited, they were all dancing. The Israelis did not try to organize a counter-dance initiative. However, the Israelis tried to lead the group in singing Israeli songs; several attempts were made, but the songs that they chose were either too quiet or unknown to the Americans. At some point, the Israelis simply gave up.[12]

Saturday morning was the highlight of the experience. The Shabbat morning service was carefully planned to include all the different religious styles. The room was set up with three seating areas: mixed, male only, and female only. An Israeli male of Iraqi-Yemenite background led the morning service. The tunes he used were unfamiliar to most of the participants from both sides, and they inserted different tunes as the service progressed. The centerpiece of the service was an alternative Torah reading.[13]

For each section of the reading, a mixed group of Americans and Israelis presented the text in a creative fashion, using drama, humor, role-playing, and rap. There was laughter and a comfortable atmosphere in the room, and people seemed to have a good time. Many Americans and Israelis thought that the Torah reading was the highlight of the Shabbat. The Torah service was successful because, while it was new for most of the participants, it was relatively free from formal religious restrictions. The rest of the Shabbat was spent with little programming, until the Havdalah service, which was conducted in a typical American Jewish camp style, with everyone standing in a circle and chanting together.

In the questionnaires, the participants were asked to evaluate their personal Shabbat experience based on the following categories: positive, meaningful, unifying, spiritual, Israeli-style, American-style, serious, or unique. Their answers indicate that the Shabbat experience was very positive for both groups. Still, there seems to be a noticeable difference between the Americans and the Israelis in their feelings about the experience. The Americans had experienced a familiar event, while the Israelis had much less experience or prior knowledge of such Shabbat experiences. This gap is supported by other questions that were raised in the survey. Most of the Israelis responded to the comment "The Shabbat as was celebrated was close to what I am used to" with the category "hardly," while most of the Americans responded to the same comment with the category "to a large extent." Both groups gave high marks when asked to comment on the extent to which the Shabbat was compatible with their ideologies.

Finally, the participants were asked, "What is the best group configuration to celebrate Shabbat?" Of the Israelis, 75 percent said that it should be a mixed group of Americans and Israelis; 80 percent of the

Americans said the same. Others made recommendations in reference to denominational divisions. None of the Americans or the Israelis suggested that the two groups should have been separated for the Shabbat according to nationality.

Discussion

The Shabbat experience was pleasant and the feedback was positive; however, several issues need to be considered. The first element is the recognition that the Shabbat was celebrated in a religious and American fashion. This means that, despite the parity that existed in the committees and the fact that both groups were equal in size, the Israelis felt that they were guests at an American Jewish scene. Nevertheless, they accepted this status and were willing to play by the rules of a game to which they were not accustomed.

In part, the American cultural domination was built in to the situation, since it took place on American turf. However, the Israelis were "inferior" on another level. The Shabbat, which was essentially a religious experience, excluded the secular Israelis. Israeli secular culture did not receive the place that it deserved in the menu of options.[14]

Secular Israelis felt like outsiders in two ways. First, secular Judaism did not receive recognition in the structure of the program, which was basically religious. Second, since secular Israeli culture did not equip the Israelis with cultural tools (texts, rituals, songs, and so on), they could not operate as equal players. It is recommended that secular Israelis who participate in similar religious experiences with Diaspora counterparts go through special training that will enhance their capability to express their secular position in similar situations. In short, the Israelis should be recognized for their effort to integrate despite the fact the Shabbat was not quite their style.

Perhaps the Shabbat was successful because the participants were motivated to have a good experience. Being in a prestigious fellowship program and having prior familiarity with one another ensured a high probability of success. Both groups felt mutual trust and were motivated to share a meaningful experience. In other circumstances, one would expect such an experience to be less harmonious.

Finally, we need to remember that the retreat was also a cross-cultural encounter. The two groups functioned in a relatively effective way, considering their differences. Still, there were always cultural gaps resulting from their differences that needed to be addressed.[15] In this regard, we should point out the differences that exist between Americans and Israelis in areas such as ceremonies, rituals, dress codes, aesthetics, music, gender, time management and scheduling, and matters of intimacy and distance.

Summary

Structured contact between Israeli and Diaspora Jews is a widespread phenomenon. However, in most cases the interaction tends to be social and recreational. In this study, we focused on the possibility of a joint spiritual experience. Shabbat is a focus of diversity in Israel and in the Diaspora. There are different practices of Shabbat that emerge from various ethnic, theological, and sociological approaches. The case study of the American and Israeli fellows is proof that these differences are not necessarily obstacles to a successful experience. Despite growing cultural gaps, there is a way to create a meaningful community in which the Jewish cultural heritage can serve as a unifying force.

Notes

1. Liebman and Cohen, *Two Worlds of Judaism: The Israeli and American Experiences* (New Haven: Yale University Press, 1990); S. Bochner, ed., *Cultures in Contact: Studies in Cross-Cultural Interaction,* (Oxford: Pergamon, 1982).
2. Z. Bekerman, "The Social Construction of Jewishness: An Anthropological Study of a Camp System" (Ph.D. diss., Jewish Theological Seminary, 1986).
3. L. Findling-Andy and A. Spector, *Mifgashim in the Israel Experience: Encounters of Diaspora Youth with Israeli Youth* (Jerusalem: Szold Institute, 1997); Bar-Shalom, *Encounters with the Other: An Ethnographic Study of Mifgashim Programs for Jewish Youth* (Jerusalem: Charles Bronfman *Mifgashim* Centre, 1998).
4. S. Deshen, "Israeli Judaism: Introduction to the Major Patterns," *International Journal of Middle Eastern Studies* 9 (1978): 141–69.
5. The program took place on Christmas Day. Hundreds of volunteers collected food, clothes, and toys and delivered them to needy people in D.C. The Israelis and the Americans participated in the distribution of the goods. Both groups were highly engaged in the program and were impressed by the special event.

6. The problem was felt more on the Israeli side. Many Israelis were complaining that the Americans were not interested in them, that they were focused on themselves, and that they were not interested in working toward the common goals of the retreat. The Americans recognized the problem and promised the organizers to change their ways. It seemed like a typical situation of intergroup conflict that could be resolved with proper intervention. See J. C. Turner and H. Giles, *Intergroup Behaviour* (Oxford: Blackwell, 1981).

7. Israelis usually define themselves using three categories: *Dati* (orthodox), *Masorti* (traditional), or *Hiloni* (secular). C. S. Liebman, *Religious and Secular: Conflict and Accommodation among Jews in Israel* (Jerusalem: Keter, 1990).

8. M. Hammersley and P. Atkinson, *Ethnography: Principles in Practices* (New York: Tavistock, 1983).

9. The Reform and the Conservative movements are very small in Israel, as opposed to the U.S. Israelis are therefore much less familiar with liberal religious approaches. See E. Tabory, "The Influence on Liberal Judaism on Israeli Religious Life," *Israel Studies 5* (spring 2000).

10. The policy of the program was that Shabbat is kept under strictly traditional standards in public places; thus, the work had to be done by the precise time of candle lighting, around sunset. The time pressure forced people to cooperate under what Sherif calls "superordinate goals"; M. Sherif, "Superordinate Goals in the Reduction of Intergroup Conflict: An Experimental Evaluation," in *The Social Psychology of Intergroup Relations*, ed. W. G. Austin and S. Worchel (Monterey, Calif.: Brooks/Cole, 1979).

11. On cultural differences between Americans and Israelis, see L. Shahar and D. Kurtz, *Border Crossings: American Interactions with Israelis* (Yarmouth, Me.: Intercultural Press, 1996).

12. See a discussion on the clash of two popular singing cultures in E. Ezrachi, "Encounters between American Jews and Israelis: Israelis in American Jewish Summer Camps" (Ph.D. diss., Jewish Theological Seminary, 1993).

13. There was no Torah scroll on site, and this allowed for a more flexible reading to take place.

14. When we talk about secular Israelis, we refer both to an ideological position as well as a culture that is reflected in the character of the sabra, the native Israeli. O. Almog, *The Sabra: A Profile* (in Hebrew) (Tel Aviv: Am Oved, 1997).

15. P. Pedersen, *A Handbook for Developing Multicultural Awareness*, 2nd ed. (Alexandria, Va.: ACA, 1994).

Training Teachers of Talmudic Literature in a Special Option of the Jewish History Department

Chaim Licht

Introduction

The Shenhar Committee in Israel presented its recommendations to the Ministry of Education and Culture in 1993,[1] declaring that the literature of the Oral Law was, for all practical purposes, not taught in state schools. The Committee recommended: "The schools should be required to teach Jewish studies, following an obligatory curriculum, at all age levels. . . . In schools where any compulsory subject within Jewish studies, such as the Oral Law, has been restricted or eliminated, care should be taken to see that the missing subject becomes part of the school curriculum."[2] The Committee detailed the reasons for the restrictions, which Marc Rosenstein has discussed extensively in "The New Jew."[3] The basis lies in the general Zionist perception of refashioning the cultural and intellectual values of the Jewish people to draw not only on Jewish heritage, but on general humanistic theories and moral codes. The Oral Law and its interpretation require commitment to a belief in revelation, in God, and in a divinely revealed law, all of which were barriers where the Zionist approach was concerned,[4] as long as Orthodox Judaism maintained that the Oral Law had to be taken by contemporary Jews as the normative basis for their way of life. As long as Israeli society in general, which does not define itself as religious, does not regard the Oral Law as a treasury of human and Jewish cre-

Chaim Licht is senior lecturer in Jewish thought in the Jewish history department of Haifa University. He was a doctoral student of Professor Joseph Lukinsky at the Jewish Theological Seminary of America.

ativity offering an option for Jewish cultural existence in a changing world, and as long as Israeli society in general does not find its own critical, innovative link to Jewish history, though freed from halakhic authority, there is but little chance of introducing the literature of the Oral Law into schools in the general state education system.

Such changes in the worldview of Israeli society do not seem imminent, so the education system must tread warily to assure gradual change and avoid counterproductive ideological confrontations.[5] The Shenhar Committee sees the possibility of implementing its recommendations only if priority is given to training suitable teachers of Jewish studies[6] at teachers' colleges or universities. The teacher of the future will specialize in an academic field that requires significant knowledge of the entire range of Jewish studies as well as the humanities in general.[7] The teacher is to have an open mind toward varied opinions and outlooks, a positive attitude toward democracy, human rights, and developments in the natural sciences, and should also be aware of changing times and historical circumstances. Such a teacher sees a knowledge of Jewish history and culture as essential in building the identity and intellectual world of the young Israeli; she or he regards Judaism as a pluralistic, evolving national culture that attempts to preserve personal, social, and national values from Jewish heritage. Such a culture can grow out of modern, not only ancient, Jewish experience as it combines Jewish and universal values.

That being so, with Shulamit Waller, my colleague in teaching talmudic literature, I proposed to Menahem Mor, head of the Jewish history department at Haifa University, that we compile a curriculum in response to the Committee's teacher-training recommendations. Professor Mor took up the challenge, and with his help and guidance the proposed study option received the necessary official approval.

To teachers holding B.A. degrees in the humanities and teaching licenses in the state schools at all elementary and secondary levels, we offered an M.A. in Jewish history and talmudic literature supervised by the Center for the Teaching of Talmudic Literature, with the opportunity to broaden their licenses to include those subjects. There were to be twelve class hours per week for two years, in structured courses at the same venue: a day and a half during the first year, and a day a week during the second year. Following a basic course in reading the Oral Law, a third of the time was devoted to the Second Temple period, the Mishnah, and the Talmud; a third to the literature of the Oral Law; and a third to related subjects.

These courses included enrichment in Jewish thought of medieval and of modern times, examining its roots in and references to the Bible and the Oral Law, and the didactics of this material. The curriculum was oriented toward practicing teachers of the humanities interested in enriching their knowledge of the Oral Law and prepared to take on additional training. Their curiosity and interest would give us strength to take them through the difficulties of acquiring knowledge in this new field. Since there are so few teachers of talmudic literature in the national education system, they alone could not possibly cope with the new curriculum.

Studying talmudic literature along with the history of the same period promotes a critical attitude, forging a link with world culture and with the historical events that so strongly influenced the world of the Talmud. Studying medieval Jewish thought brings with it a knowledge of the wide variety of later commentary on the Oral Law that attempted to bridge the gap between ancient forces and such worldviews—then new—as philosophy and the kabbalah.

Enrichment studies on the literature of modern times exposes its strong roots in ancient literary sources, despite the gap that appears to exist between the two eras. Thus, the learner has the opportunity to see how the study of Jewish culture over the generations enables it to renew itself, as modern-era authors make extensive use of language and literary creations of older times—even while disagreeing with many of the messages. The didactics course stresses the presentation of the material, with appropriate examples from the Oral Law that attempt to achieve the purposes that the Shenhar Committee set forth.

As a teacher in the course, I can report that the course at Haifa University is now in its sixth year, with fifty to sixty students in each class, three of whom have graduated and now hold M.A. degrees. The most talented are continuing as doctoral students. Most graduates are now seeking their own ways to combine the literature of the Oral Law with other subjects that they teach. While the Shenhar report stated that "hours for Jewish studies removed from the curriculum during the period of cutbacks should be restored,"[8] this has not been done. Hence, regrettably, there are no clear changes in the status of teaching the Oral Law in the state schools or any sign that in the near future the leadership of the Ministry of Education will make that necessary change. We shall continue training teachers using our curriculum as long as there is a demand for it, in the great hope that essential changes will eventually occur.

Basic Assumptions in Training Students to Teach Talmudic Literature

Our students are teachers with ten to twenty years' seniority, so it is unnecessary and even undesirable to show them how to teach a class. All already have methods for teaching their own subjects, and reinforcements or changes in the way that they do so lie in the province of school supervisors or specific in-service training programs. As they are from twenty-eight to fifty years of age, each has an integrated worldview. Every effort should be made to avoid making classes in talmudic literature an occasion for preaching. Rather, it should be presented as culture with which one engages in dialogue and criticism. The pluralistic approach is a tool by which to attain a deeper and richer culture, choosing among the options.

For most participants, the course has been their main encounter with talmudic literature. They studied as many as twenty pages of Talmud in the course, and they learned, among other things, to distinguish between the genres of aggadah, midrash, philosophical sayings, legal halakhic statements, and legal issues. At the same time, they are not sure of their own ability to study such a variety of texts independently, and if they cannot do that, there is little likelihood that they will actually teach the subject. Our classes have to give them the tools and methods for independent Talmud study.[9]

Intellectual Difficulties in Studying the Oral Law

Different Languages

The Oral Law uses both the Hebrew of the Bible and of the Sages, both of which were spoken in Jewish society in general and by the Sages in particular. While Israeli students know Hebrew, they encounter difficulties in understanding these two variants. The Talmud uses Galilean and Babylonian Aramaic, too, which had a great influence on Hebrew. Whether for active use or passive understanding, for today's students, Aramaic is an impractical tongue and as such, an unnecessary, irritating burden.

Because the Oral Law is just that, it expresses itself with the utmost brevity, sometimes merely hinting. The hints and short forms are based on cultural concepts that were abundantly clear to the authors and to students of earlier times. Contemporary students, by contrast, must learn a set of facts and use their imagination, filling in knowledge gaps with the help of dictionaries and traditional as well as critical commentators.

Moreover, this oral literature was committed to writing without punctuation to mark either the end or the internal divisions of sentences. There are no paragraphs or other signs that one subject ends and another one begins. Those accustomed to punctuation and paragraphing must get accustomed to the change, recalling that punctuation and paragraphing are in themselves a form of commentary that need not necessarily be accepted. Perusing a text without paragraphs or punctuation draws the reader into the dilemmas of interpretation.

Different Genres

Talmudic literature is composed of different literary genres. There is the tannaitic literature of the halakhah and the midrash. The aggadic literature includes statements, stories, proverbs, and other forms. The genre of negotiating a halakhic issue is found in both the Jerusalem and Babylonian Talmuds. Each genre has its own patterns through which it may be studied and understood independently, so genres must be separated and the patterns of each studied from the content. Since they are found one beside the other and sometimes one inside the other, context is significant. Understanding a text in context is different from interpreting it from within itself. These are complex skills, and learners must acquire them to attain confidence that they have indeed understood what they have studied.

A Different Reality

The subjects, affairs, and examples that this literature discusses seem quite irrelevant for contemporary students. How and why should they concern themselves with an ox goring a cow, forgotten asses and camels, or slaves, concubines, and bondmen? For these concerns of bygone days to be relevant, they have to be considered as part of a historical reality that requires study in order to see the culture and value principles that determined the relationship to reality at that time. Students have to work through the details of that different reality to cultural principles before they can relate to the course material.

The Logic of the Talmud

Strictly speaking, there is but one universal logic, and so it is in the exact natural sciences. Every individual, whatever his or her nationality or religion, uses it in studying and practicing science. Talmudic logic, however, is different. It is based not only on rules of logic but on parallels to cultural assumptions from its tradition, as well as on value-oriented approaches in the social, legal, and judicial spheres. The learner has to separate logical from value approaches and understand the tendencies behind the way that they are combined, so that he or she can take a critical attitude to one approach or the other.

Midrashim on the Scriptures

Present-day learners find the way that the Sages of the Mishnah and the Talmud expounded Scripture alien and unsatisfactory. This is not the way that the Bible was explained to them when they studied it. In most cases, the midrash goes far afield from the original text and does not relate to chapter, verse, or book as a whole. The midrashic explanation seems tendentious and forced. It is even more difficult to accept the religious principle that the midrash is the only way to interpret Scripture.

Learners must understand that their criticism is justified, that the midrashic method is not the way that the Bible is interpreted today, and it is certainly not binding on the reader. On the other hand, students must understand the function of midrashic explanations in reinforcing the Sages' views on that basic book of Jewish culture, the Bible. Students today can be critical, accepting what they can as commentary, and opposing what they cannot, while accepting it as a cultural trend.[10]

How the Sages Interpreted

In interpreting the Torah, their purpose was to achieve unity between the Bible, the tradition, and the generations of the Sages, with unity between logic and parallels over the generations. Such commentary is unacceptable to contemporary students, who are taught to look for differences, to separate the approaches and opinions of various persons, and to be alert to changes where the cultural sphere encounters tradition.

An interpretation that unites is of necessity tendentious, aiming to present one law, a single path marked out for a single people everywhere and at all times, not various laws for various groups. This interpretation is ideological, and as such appears unrealistic to modern learners who base themselves on the human spirit, environmental and sociological influences, key events, and encounters between various cultural worlds. Like those of many texts, the interpretations of the Oral Law appear forced and unacceptable. On the one hand, students are required to learn the unifying explanations as presented in the sources. On the other, they are invited to criticize and point out flaws, using the sources themselves to point out interpretations that indicate development and change over different periods of time. The encounter between the two types of commentary makes it possible to see the cultural point of view that makes change possible.

Judicial Matters

Much of the Oral Law deals with the law, halakhah, and legal issues, and today's students do not see themselves as lawyers. If that is what they wanted to be, they would have enrolled in law school. They understand the logical need for a law student to study Jewish law, since it applies in many spheres in Israel today, particularly in marriage and divorce. But why should humanities students have to concern themselves with law?

But going deeply into the legal issues of the Talmud, one sees that these are not merely legal matters, but rather an education to personal and community morality in a society that combines morality, law, and a judicial system. Students have to recognize the need to establish halakhic legal frameworks to protect a society that strives to be moral, just, and value-oriented. They must educate themselves to recognize that man is responsible for his acts and that ignorance of the law does not free him from that responsibility. Close scrutiny of the value approaches in social morality, law, and the judiciary enables students to recognize them as either acceptable or unacceptable to themselves as individuals.

Such observation will make it possible to develop a critical value-oriented approach, noting the way that approaches based on different values affect halakhic judgments. Students will be able to distinguish between a purely legal discussion and a moral one that affects judicial attitudes. Students must approach legal issues in various ways: the legal approach, alone or combined with a values approach; and criticism of text content for legal, logical, or value reasons.[11]

Talmudic Literature as an Academic Discipline

It is an educative, humanistic subject that creates a cultural framework from which one may extract the content and methods for renewed creativity as its values are applied to a new reality. Having thus defined talmudic literature, we now define the term "humanism." It means that man should seek to know himself within his environment, defining goals as an individual and as part of a particular society, aware of his moral responsibility as a factor with an influence on his surroundings. Humanism takes a universal position, but that position is applied according to the nature of particular persons and groups. Thus, the humanism of a Jew is Jewish, just as the humanism of others will correspond to particular national and religious backgrounds. Thus, one may speak of Jewish, French, English, Christian, or Muslim humanism.

The knowledge in the Oral Law consists of basic techniques and moral content. By basic techniques, we mean relating to a written text analytically and critically, giving students the tools—the terms and concepts—that will enable them to do this with skill, analyzing various aspects of language, style, genre, symbols, figurative language, and set language patterns.

As for moral content, our message is that the more one studies this literature, the more values will emerge in the personal, social, national, religious, and universal domains. The techniques are the basic tools of the adult in the modern Western world, which is flooded with information. Ordered categories are readily comprehensible, so that organizing content and values according to concepts and principles makes it easier to learn and understand a worldview. Talmudic literature is structured in a way that makes it easy to use in search of responses to personal, social, and cultural needs even in the course of theoretical study, a useful activity in itself. The independent teacher will find a multifaceted cultural heritage to pass on to future generations.[12]

We planned the didactics course with a knowledge of our students' difficulties in studying talmudic literature, as well as its knowledge structures. Students have to be given convenient tools[13] to overcome problematic technical aspects (language, punctuation, signs, and gaps in their knowledge of terminology) with minimum exertion. Texts were chosen for their stress on moral values, for their cultural relevance to our own times, and the presence of a transparent conflict between political conditions and the legal and moral aspects of the case. We also considered whether the issue related to the authority of the individual, of society, or of the Sages in determining judicial norms. Sources selected contained a sufficient variety of genres to make possible a study of basic patterns for understanding the content and its significance. Moreover, texts had to be short, with a clearly visible beginning, development, and end.

The traditional forms of commentary were used for studying the sources, and later critical commentary, with emphasis on differences between the two. These principles make it possible to impart to the students the ability to study talmudic literature as willing, interested, and independent learners so that they will truly want to teach it in their schools. In conclusion, I present an example of how the method works.

The Issue (Ketubot 103a)

1. THE TWO HUSBANDS CANNOT PLEAD, and so on.
2. A certain man once leased his mill to another for [the consideration of the latter's services in] grinding [his corn].
3. Eventually, he became rich and bought another mill and an ass.
4. Thereupon he said to the other, "Until now, I have had my grinding done at your place
5. but now pay me rent."
6. "I shall," the other replied, "only grind for you."
7. Rabina [in considering the case] intended to rule that it involved the very principle that was laid down in our Mishnah:
8. THE TWO HUSBANDS CANNOT PLEAD, "WE WILL MAINTAIN HER JOINTLY."
9. BUT ONE MUST MAINTAIN HER AND THE OTHER ALLOWS HER THE COST OF HER MAINTENANCE.
10. R. Awira, however, said to him, "Are [the two cases] alike?"
11. There [the woman] has only one stomach, not two;
12. but here [the lessee] might well tell the owner, "Grind [in your own mill] and sell; grind [in mine] and keep."
13. This, however, has been said only in a case where [the lessee] has no [other orders for] grinding at his mill,
14. but if he has [sufficient orders for] grinding at his mill, he may
15. in such circumstances be compelled [not to act] in the manner of Sodom.

Stages of Preparation for Independent Study

A. Reading, punctuating, and translating the text above into the Hebrew that the student speaks. Translating and punctuating lead to a preliminary understanding. (While the English translation is punctuated, the original Aramaic is not.)

B. Numbering the lines to enable other students to follow particular textual points.

C. 1. Separating tannaitic from amoraic passages.
   2. Separating attributed from unattributed passages.
   3. Separating a statement of opinion from support of an opinion.
   4. Separating supports based on logic from supports relying on earlier sources.
   5. Separating supports derived from the Bible, the tannaim, and the amoraim.

D. Stating the time, position, and place of activity of the Sages mentioned, helping to place the issue in the time and the academy from which it originated.[14]

E. Presenting methodological terms and linguistic expressions that make it possible to follow the flow and pattern of the issue as presented by the editor, for the convenience of the student, since these repeat themselves in other issues.

F. Recognizing value, legal, culture, and moral concepts. This helps the student discuss them in general and in relation to this particular issue.

G. Checking the performance of tasks A–F with one to three students, which allows for reexamination, corrections, and additions.[15]

How the Method Operates

Line-by-Line Literal Aramaic-Hebrew Translation

Line 1 quotes a Mishnah passage from an anonymous source, stating a position.[16] Lines 2–6 are an unattributed story from the amoraic period, containing a legal problem. Lines 6b–11a are a discussion between two amoraim, mentioned by name, on deciding this case. In the position of the first amora, Rabina (lines 6b–8), the language indicates logical thinking, and lines 7–8 refer to the anonymous Mishnah. In lines 9–11a,

R. Awira states a position with a justification based on logic. Lines 11b–14 are an anonymous amoraic passage that establish a position and give it a logical and moral justification.

The Sages cited by name are Rabina and R. Awira. Rabina was a great Babylonian amora of the sixth generation (375–425 C.E.), head of the yeshiva at Matta Mahsia. R. Awira was a Babylonian amora of the fifth–sixth generation (350–425 C.E.) and a friend of Rabina: both studied with Rava at Mahuza. Hence, one may conclude that most of the issue stems from the sixth Babylonian amoraic generation, in the Matta Mahsia yeshiva, near Sura. The final anonymous passage is later, possibly Savurai.

A certain man:	a linguistic expression indicating the beginning of a story
Intended to:	a linguistic form introducing a logical consideration
In our Mishnah:	a methodological expression that introduces a tannaitic source a tannaitic source from the six divisions of the Mishnah that Rabi edited the tannaitic source discussed here
Said to him:	a linguistic form indicating a face-to-face argument between the persons mentioned
Are alike?	a linguistic form rejecting a previously mentioned similarity
There:	indicates a source brought in for the sake of comparison
Here:	an expression referring to the case under discussion
Has been said only:	an expression that limits the previous interpretation to special instances

Thus the development of the issue:

A. Stating the case

B. Opinions of Rabina and R. Awira

   B1: Rabina's opinion based on a Mishnaic precedent

   B2: R. Awira's opinion rejecting the precedent and explaining the rejection

C. The anonymous Talmud limits the previous decision: justification is legal and moral. A and B are an issue from the Matta Mahsia yeshiva in the sixth amoraic generation. C continues the issue, seemingly at a later date, in an unidentifiable place. The issue was certainly edited after the time of the C source.

The specific value concept in the issue is not to act "in the manner of Sodom." It means that when one party benefits and the other does not lose, the court imposes the entire financial loss on the latter, even though formally and judicially it is right that the other man, who benefits, should pay. A person or a court that does act accordingly is behaving like the people of Sodom.[17] This value term will be examined later as a general principle and as one relevant to the issue under discussion.

Analyzing and Synthesizing: In-Depth Study

As the preliminary study showed, the issue is made up of interlinked units, like most talmudic issues, a knowledge structure typical of the Oral Law, with its systematically organized categories that are intellectually accessible as linked technical, content, and legal-moral units. The analytical-separating process makes it possible to relate to the written text analytically and critically and to see clearly how the material is organized. Hence I find it essential to study each link separately, and then combine them to show the issue as a single entity.

Our issue has four principle parts. Part A is the story (lines 2–6a). B1 is the discussion between Rabina and R. Awira (lines 6b–11a). B2 Rabina cites the Mishnah as a precedent for a possible decision (lines 7–8). Part C restricts the conclusion using an anonymous Talmud (lines 11b–14).

Each part is subdivided. In the story are two divisions (lines 2–3a; 3b–6a), as in the discussion between Rabina and R. Awira (Rabina's opinion in lines 6b–8 and R. Awira's in 9–11a), in the Mishnaic precedent (line 7, "the very principle"—line 8, "WE WILL MAINTAIN HER JOINTLY"). Restricting the conclusion has three divisions: 11b–12a, "only one stomach, not two; but here [the lessee] might well tell the owner"; 12b–13a, "Grind [in your own mill] and sell; grind [in mine] and keep"; 13b–15, where [the lessee] has no [other orders] . . . if he has [sufficient orders] . . . he may be compelled."

Part A: The Story

As in most units of the Oral Law, this story is written with extreme brevity, making it difficult for the contemporary student to understand.

The first task is to winnow out and understand the details, and the next task is to close the gaps and obtain a complete, comprehensible story. In so doing, a distinction must be made between gaps that can be filled through proven information in the textual language and those gaps where imagination is required and filling them is possible but not essential or contradictory to the written text.

In the first division of the story, we read of a man who leased millstones for grinding to his friend. Given the terminology, we are entitled to expand the story to include what we know from talmudic sources on lessor-lessee relationships,[18] which allows us to add some details: the lessor and the lessee made an agreement, oral or written, in which they specified its duration and the fee the lessor would receive from the lessee. Since the story does not contain specific details, this is a standard agreement for that period.

As appears from the second division of the story (line 5), the agreement stated how the lessee would pay the lessor—by grinding his corn free of charge. The story, however, contains no details as to how long this was to continue or when the grinding would be done, so that any additions of this sort are the result of imagination. The story says nothing of problems between lessor and lessee during the term of the agreement. The argument arose in the second division of the story because of a change in the lessor's position. He became rich, buying additional millstones and a donkey, as a result of which he tells the lessee, I will grind my corn with the new millstones and you are to pay me rent in money for the millstones I leased to you. The lessee refuses and tells the lessor, I will pay you rent by grinding your corn. We may expand the story as written by closing some gaps: the lessor claims that he is continuing to respect their agreement, which obliges the lessee to pay him rent. He agreed to accept rent by having the lessee grind his corn as long as this profited him. Since it no longer did, in view of his changed position, he is entitled to demand rent in money. The lessee, by contrast, claims that their agreement specified payment by grinding the lessor's corn and that the demand to change the manner of payment violates their agreement. Their argument is whether the lessor's demand is based on their agreement, as he claims, or deviates from it, as the lessee claims.[19]

Part B2: The Mishnah Cited by Rabina as a Precedent (Lines 7–8)

At once, it is seen to be part of a longer Mishnah. Rabina quotes "Two shall not say" and "provide for her," but we do not know who the two are and who she is. Our first stage is thus to find the entire Mishnah, an essential step regarding most quotations used as precedents, since the reference was a sort of code to jog the memory of the Sages, who would know it by heart; the modern student must turn to reference works.[20]

Having found the Mishnah, we study it by the analysis-synthesis method. To analyze it, we must interpret words and concepts that, if not understood, may lead to basic errors in using the method. A legal Mishnah is analyzed on the basis of the normative judgments that are always present. Having broken it down into its basic links, a pattern of an event, a solution, or a justification must be sought in each one. This is the full pattern, which is not commonly found. In most parts, an event appears without justification for the normative statement. One nonetheless notes that there is no justification so as to see at once that it is missing, as the amoraim always did, since giving or changing a justification determines a norm.[21] In the beginning, one must show the internal pattern in every part of the Mishnah in the language of the Mishnah, which clarifies what is actually written and what must be expanded to close gaps, as explained earlier.[22] Its internal structure revealed, the event has to be turned into a legal dilemma, shown from the viewpoints of the two parties. The briefer the written account, the more any expansion will be the work of imagination, a danger to be kept in mind, as it lays the base for a different normative judgment. The different "possibilities" for an event that has been judged normatively characterizes the talmudic issue. Possibilities should be kept close to the Mishnah text, so as to distinguish between those closer and those more remote. The latter indicate nonacceptance of the literal text, for legal or moral reasons.[23]

An Appreciation

This article is written in honor of my esteemed teacher Professor Joseph Lukinsky. Since the 1970s, when I had the privilege of studying under him and writing my doctorate for the Jewish Theological Seminary under his guidance, he has been a source of inspiration in teaching and educational planning. For more than twenty years, Professor Lukinsky has taken a special interest in my work in training teachers of talmudic literature in the state schools of Israel, and I discussed the articles and books that I wrote with him so that I could profit by his invaluable advice. I consider it a pleasure and a privilege to write this essay in an anniversary volume in his honor. May we have the opportunity of learning from him for many years to come.

For her expert editing of the English version, my thanks to Betty Sigler Rozen.

Notes

1. Aliza Shenhar, *Am ve'olam*, report of the Committee to Examine Jewish Studies in State Schools, Ministry of Education, Culture, and Sport, 1994.

2. Ibid., 16.

3. Marc Rosenstein, "The New Jew: The Place of Jewish Tradition in General Zionist Education in Palestine from Its Beginning until the Establishment of the State" (in Hebrew) (Ph.D. diss., Hebrew University, 1985), 1–2.

4. Avi Lavsky reviewed the subject extensively in "Integrating Subjects in the Jewish Studies Curriculum in State Secondary Education: A Case Study " (Ph.D. diss., Jewish Theological Seminary, 1994).

5. Scientific, critical study of the Oral Law at the universities has strongly influenced modern Orthodox society but has had only a marginal effect on Israeli society in general because it attracts so few non-Orthodox students.

6. Shenhar, 24–28.

7. Ibid., 25.

8. Ibid., 16.

9. The student is directed to use a method of independent study from "Modelim v'astrategiot behora'ah," developed by L. Kramer-Hiyyun, Ministry of Education and Culture, Teacher Training Dept., Curriculum Institute (Jerusalem, 1985), containing a Hebrew and English bibliography linked to each model.

10. For this approach to Bible midrash, see S. Libermann, *Yevanim veyevanut b'Eretz Israel* (Jerusalem: Bialik, 1962), 185–212; Y. Frankel, *Darchei ha'aggadah vehamidrash* (Tel Aviv: Massada, 1991), 45–88.

11. On coping with various difficulties, see *Hora'at hatorah shebe'alpeh,* ed. J. Heinrich (Jerusalem: Hebrew University School of Education and Ministry of Education and Culture, 1960). Particularly relevant is Y. Katz's article on the problem of studying Talmud in the schools, 36–53. Regrettably, little that is new has appeared.

12. For significance of knowledge structures, see M. Silbermann, *Mivnei hada'at shel hamikzo'ot vegishah ahdutit betickhnun limudim* (Jerusalem: Ministry of Education and Culture, 1989), containing articles by outstanding scholars in the field.

13. Adin Steinsaltz's book is a recent work that serves this purpose. More recently, Bar Ilan University issued the CD-ROM *Havruta lelimud,* which serves these purposes.

14. Work to be done using the CD or one of the following: A. Heimann, *Toldot hatanaim veha'amoraim* (Jerusalem: Boys Town, 1964); M. Margaliot, *Encyclopedia lehahamei hatalmud vehagaonim,* Y. Eisenberg's revised ed. (Tel Aviv: Yavneh, 1995).

15. Such exercises in independent study are done four weekly hours throughout the year in the course on the reading of talmudic texts.

16. It also states that the discussion in the previous passages is finished, and a new

one is beginning, as accepted in the Vilna printed edition. But this was not the practice in Babylonian Talmud (BT) manuscripts: it is not present in Munich MS 95, while in Vatican MS 113 it is. In the text-reading course, students learn how to go back to manuscripts and to recognize their importance, comparing these with the more readily available printed versions and to appreciate the significance of variants in understanding a text. In our course, however, I suggest avoiding such comparisons, as they are of little use to schoolteachers.

17. Rashi's explanation. The expression is found only in BT: *Eruvin* 49a; *Bava Batra* 12b, 59a, a value established by Babylonian amoraim, apparently in Nahardea and Pompadita, and unknown in Eretz Israel sources. In *Eruvin* 49a, it is attributed to Rav Judah in the name of Rav Samuel (second- and first-generation amoraim); in *Bava Batra* 12b, to Rava and Rav Joseph (third-generation); elsewhere, it is unattributed. Its applications in the above sources is beyond the present discussion, as is the association of Sodom residents with negative qualities.

18. While I prefer to focus on this one issue, the broader subject is presented in the laws of the four guardians in the Bible and the Oral Law, since the lessee of an object becomes its guardian for the entire period of the lease.

19. Group discussions would help internalize the story in full, with its legal problem, but we use them only in the analysis-synthesis stage.

20. Our students acquired skill in finding sources through reference works and a CD-ROM. They learned the difference between finding a source in manuscripts or in accepted printed versions, and between one found in scientific by contrast with a rabbinic reference work, and between an amoraic as against an original context. E.g., a Mishnah from one of the six divisions, and the same one as quoted in BT or the Jerusalem Talmud (JT).

21. See Y. Frankel, "Mekomah shel hahalakhah besipurei ha'aggadah," in *A Collection of Talmudic Research Studies,* ed. Y. Zussmann and D. Rosenthal (Jerusalem: Magnes, 1990), 205–7.

22. Using the written text, cultural terms and concepts, and rational assumptions.

23. This is especially relevant to talmudic negotiations, though found in the negotiating situation in tannaitic literature, too.

Teachers' Images
of Their Teaching Potency:
The Case of Bible Teachers

Asher Shkedi

Most of the literature that deals with teaching and teacher training relates to knowledge and beliefs in synonymous terms.[1] According to Richardson,[2] teachers' beliefs are a system of guiding principles about the phenomena with which they are dealing. One might say that the teacher's beliefs reflect the way in which she or he understands or grasps the teaching phenomenon and its components.

One feature of a belief system is that it does not require validation from others or from the research literature and does not even need internal consistency. A person's belief system can include different ideas that are not necessarily coordinated and may, in fact, contradict one another. Beliefs are, at their core, relatively unchanging, and when they do change, it is usually the result of a conversion or shift of gestalt, and not of new arguments that may have appeared.[3] Teachers' beliefs are also characterized by their situational nature, which means that in different situational contexts, different beliefs find expression.[4]

Although the connection between the teacher's beliefs and actions has not been sufficiently researched, research assumptions indicate that teachers' beliefs influence their teaching activity. One may say, at the very least, that the teacher's beliefs function as an internal filtering system through which pedagogical decisions are made.[5] If the teacher, for instance, believes that the student is a passive being whose role is to absorb knowledge, this will effectuate a particular teaching method, in

Asher Shkedi is a senior lecturer in the Melton Centre for Jewish Education and the School of Education at the Hebrew University of Jerusalem. He was a doctoral student of Professor Joseph Lukinsky at the Jewish Theological Seminary of America.

contrast to those methods arising from a belief that the learner is an active being who builds knowledge in internal thought processes.[6]

Teaching is basically a process of educating through content-based disciplines. The way that teachers know and understand the subject matter distinguishes them from the subject-matter specialists. This teachers' knowledge is known as "pedagogical-content knowledge."[7] Pedagogical-content knowledge is that dimension of subject-matter knowledge that is related to teaching. It includes the most useful representations, the most powerful analogies, illustrations, and demonstrations, and various ways of presenting and formulating the materials to make them most comprehensible to others. Despite the centrality of contents in the teacher's mind, teachers' ideas about content are not as purely content-based disciplines but rather as an amalgam of various elements of knowledge that at times reflect different points of view. Pedagogical-content knowledge includes references to the following components of teachers' knowledge: disciplinary content knowledge, knowledge of the learners, knowledge of curricula, knowledge of context, teachers' perceptions of self, and conceptions of their role.[8]

On the assumption that the components of teacher knowledge are interrelated, one cannot understand the teachers' conception of their teaching potency without relating to the other components of their pedagogical knowledge. Several studies of Bible teachers and their pedagogical-content knowledge[9] have found that these teachers view the biblical text according to their personal and pedagogical outlook on the particular text. These teachers' responses also reflect the demands of the school, of the educational system, and of society, all of which see the Bible as an invaluable component of education. Teachers' views of the educational potential of the Bible are influenced by all components of the educational process. Studies indicate that teachers' commitments and connections to the world of the text and their commitment to their students are both connected to their conceptions of their role. Teachers perceived their role as one of mediating between the Bible and the students.

The centrality of students in teachers' conceptions of their teaching potency is so salient that students perhaps constitute the most important personal factor in the teachers' professional world.[10] Sarason[11] points out that teachers are motivated by their own sense of duty and by others' expectations that they will lead their students to an acceptable level of achievement, and that they are troubled in the event that they do not have the proper conditions or sufficient time to achieve this level. Studies show that the positive feedback that teachers receive from their daily contact with students gives them a sense of satisfaction from their work and the appropriate reward for their efforts.[12]

Studies of pedagogical-content knowledge point out the narrative character[13] of teacher knowledge. "Images" are central in teachers' narratives.[14] The image can be viewed as a horizontal axis that links teachers' thought and action[15] and is a concentrated expression of complex knowledge. "Images serve to guide the teacher's thinking and to organize knowledge in the relevant area."[16] Images are expressed in teachers' actions, in the explanations that they give for their actions, and in the interpretations that they give of processes that take place in their classes. Images act as a type of glue that connects personal and professional experience, formally acquired knowledge and knowledge gained from experience. Teachers simultaneously carry different and sometimes inconsistent images about various aspects of teaching. While some images might relate to episodic matters, others may be more generalized.[17] Every teacher holds images consistent with his or her personality, knowledge, experience, and specific encounters with students. Nevertheless, patterns can be found among these different images of different teachers evidencing clear clusters of like "images."

Teachers operate within complex situations containing contradictions, tensions, and dilemmas.[18] The teachers' images would appear to serve as a theoretical and practical solution that each teacher finds for himself or herself in order to function within these complex teaching situations. These images provide teachers with a personal way of functioning creatively among the different obligations and commitments: to students—as a class and individually, to the subject matter, to society, and to personal ideology and ability. The different areas of emphasis and the differential significance that each teacher gives to components of the teaching framework will lead teachers to form their particular pedagogic beliefs and construct their own personal images about their teaching potency.

Our study of Bible teachers' beliefs about their teaching potency attempted to identify patterns of images expressing teachers' conceptions of their students and of their own teaching roles. When we analyzed the hundreds of pages of interviews and observations from our study of Bible teachers, we noted that, aside from attitudes, explanations, and beliefs, a "story line" could be discerned: a horizontal axis, a connecting motif that gave a certain meaning to the overall picture.

Study Population and Method

This study was based on a total of 60 informants—36 Israeli teachers and 24 teachers from abroad, the latter being participants in a one-year academic program in Israel. The study was conducted by interviewing 50 Bible teachers and further observations and stimulated-recall interviews with another 10 Bible teachers. The Israelis taught in local Israeli schools, and the foreign teachers taught in Jewish schools outside of Israel. Seventeen informants were elementary school teachers (7 from Israel, 10 from abroad), and 43 were junior high and high school teachers (29 from Israel, 14 from abroad). Although we cannot claim that this study was representative universally, the wide scope of teachers' backgrounds is likely to give voice to a wide spectrum of opinions and outlooks of teachers of Bible and perhaps of other culturally valued texts. In the course of conducting the study, it was noticed that in relation to this research question, there were no significant differences between the Israeli and non-Israeli teachers. Their commonalties were more significant than their differences. We therefore treated them as one group.

The data collected from the sixty teachers were analyzed according to categorization techniques.[19] At this stage, we focused on three main categories, each of which included several subordinate categories. The three main categories were: teachers' beliefs about student attitudes and interests; teachers' beliefs about student intellectual difficulties; and teachers' beliefs about their own teaching roles. At this stage of analysis, we noted that patterns could be discerned. These patterns were reflected in the connections among the categories mentioned above. We found four (listed below) main patterns of teachers' beliefs about their teaching potency. These patterns of beliefs, the teachers' images, were gleaned from the place that the teachers gave to each of their beliefs about student attitudes, student difficulties, and their own teaching role.

Findings: Teachers' Images of Their Teaching Potency

The research findings indicate that teachers' conceptions of their roles and their perceptions of students are connected to each other and influence their conception of their teaching potency. Some believed that teachers are limited in their teaching potency and thwarted by barriers such as cognitive difficulties or students' attitudes. Others believed that teachers do not feel limited in their teaching potency and that student learning is based first and foremost on good teaching. We also found one teacher who believed that she was entirely without any teaching potency. The differences among the teachers as expressed in the different weight that they give to their students' attitudes, to their students' difficulties, and to their own teaching role.

The Image of Teaching Potency as Regarding Students as "Clay in the Teacher's Hands"

Shosh, age forty-five, has over twenty years' teaching experience. She received her initial training in teaching in the field of special education, but over the years she began to focus on teaching Bible. Shosh has participated in academic courses in the field of Bible, and is currently completing her studies for a bachelor's degree.

> The first question students ask me is: "Are you a Bible teacher?" Because it always seems to them that I should look austere—skirt, brown bag. . . . I don't look religious, and that's exactly what I say—the Bible is mine, I don't need a costume in order to love it. . . . I see Bible as a reflection of life. . . . It is ours. . . . Within this "ours," I feel that it belongs to me.

The lessons take place in ninth grade, near the end of the school year. In the class are thirty-six students seated at desks for two, arranged in five rows. The lesson is dedicated to a historical introduction to the Book of Jeremiah. Although the subject matter is historical background data, Shosh is neither lecturing nor dictating to the children. Rather, the lesson is conducted in the form of dialogue between Shosh and the students as she tries to extract the information from them:

Shosh: What is the most important thing that Jeremiah did?

Student: Religious reform.

Shosh: Religious reform—great! How was this expressed?

Student: Concentrated ritual.

Shosh: Wonderful! What is "concentrated ritual"? [*writes on board*]

Some students cooperate with Shosh, some listen, others are busy with other things, but order and quiet are maintained. Here and there someone yawns. Occasionally, Shosh turns the students' attention to ideas that deviate somewhat from the historical events, here a joke, there an actual fact, focusing on maintaining the tension of the lesson:

> A teacher who educates is always an actor. . . . I always make an effort to combine the reality of today, so that the Bible does not seem to them to be an old, outdated book. . . . When preparing this class, I had strong doubts about how to make the lesson attractive, how to present it imaginatively. . . . If only I could have done what I wanted, I wouldn't have taught Jeremiah. I would have continued with the stories of Samuel, like the *Dallas* dynasty.

The next lesson is held a few days later. After a number of introductory words and tie-ins to the last lesson, Shosh begins by reading the first verses of chapter 1 of Jeremiah. "I do the reading myself so that it will be more distinct and attractive. . . . If the text is clear, they can read independently, whoever wants to. Some get lost."

Shosh mentions two types of difficulties in the course of the work: those in comprehending the text; and those that stem from negative messages from home. It appears, however, that these difficulties are overcome in light of Shosh's feeling of success and her belief that the students like studying Bible:

> I can show off and say that maybe they like me, too . . . but I feel that for the most part, they truly like the subject; they don't see it as just another subject. . . . I draw things out of them that are already there within them. . . . They bring quotations from the Bible—that comes from within them. Bible really flows from them.

What is the secret of success, according to Shosh? "What is a good teacher? Someone who loves the subject and the students. . . . I like to include a lot of drama in the lesson, so that the subject appeals to them. . . . They see how much this book belongs to everyone."

Explanatory notes. This teachers' image of their teaching potency as regarding students as malleable, like clay in the teacher's hands, was identified in the conception of twenty-three teachers (out of sixty) from the study population. The teachers who belonged to this group were characterized by the greater emphasis that they laid on their teaching role and the lesser emphasis that they placed on students' difficulties and attitudes. Typical of this group is a dominant reference to the teacher's role as a central performer in the teaching-learning process and less reference to students' interests or their difficulties as factors in the teaching-learning process. "Just as with all subjects in teaching, so it is with texts. . . . If the lesson and the teacher are interesting, they study. . . . Students do not want to study at all—that's the starting point. . . . It is the teacher's role to interest and appeal" (Pnina).

Certain teachers describe how, little by little, they attracted their students' attention and moved them to become interested in the topic. "When I first started, they really did not discover the depth and beauty in the Bible, and I think that somehow in these lessons I brought them closer to the beauty and charm. . . . In the world of texts, there is something nice, if you really know how to teach it properly" (Shimon).

These images highlight the weight that teachers give to their own teaching. It is in this respect that students are as "clay in the teacher's hands," susceptible to influence, attraction, and interest. Accordingly, students study not because the subject interests them, but because the teacher succeeds in moving them toward studying.

The feeling among teachers that the study process is dependent on them leads a large number of them to blame themselves for any failures: "There are things that are up to me. . . . It depends on how I teach, and I need to find a way to arouse their interest. . . . If the students are bored, it is a sign that I have a problem" (Reesa).

Turning the students into "clay in the teacher's hands" is not easily or rapidly accomplished. The teachers describe how they invest time and effort in planning the lesson, trying to make it appealing, encouraging the students and changing the course of the lesson according to their responses.

> When I teach a text, it is hard for me . . . because I have to translate it for myself so as to teach it to the children. . . . A teacher cannot take anything for granted or make any assumptions regarding the children. One has to look at who the student is, from where, what he or she knows and does not know . . . to put myself in the children's situation and think how they would relate. (Lori)

The Image of Teaching Potency
as Maintaining Students' Understanding

Ruth, age forty-nine, is a teacher at a vocational school and has over twenty years' experience. The school equips students with technological skills along with general subject knowledge. One required subject at the school is Bible. The lessons in which the case was observed were in the tenth grade. The students, all of whom are boys described as disadvantaged, number only fourteen. The subject of the lessons is the confrontation between Elijah the Prophet and King Ahab. "I have a lesson plan that I have to cover. . . . If the text is both boring and difficult, I refrain from teaching it. The points of emphasis are determined by the number of difficult words, difficulties with the ideas in the texts—I teach difficult texts in smaller stages."

The lesson opens with a short review of the subject matter learned in previous lessons. Ruth asks short and directed questions of knowledge, and the students respond correctly. Throughout the lesson, there are continuous disturbances, most of which are a result of students' responses to what is being discussed in the lesson. Ruth begins by reading the chapter. Throughout the reading, there is quiet in the classroom. "I read the section being studied, and it is significant that the children are listening. It focuses their thinking. I read in the correct manner and believe that intonation, punctuation, and exactness in reading are very important. They give a different meaning to the text."

After Ruth completes the reading, she asks the students to tell the story in their own words. One student summarizes the contents briefly, and a discussion ensues:

> Ruth: What is the accusation? "Bless God and the King"—that is the accusation. Look at these words. [*writes words on the board*]
>
> Student: To bless is in the positive sense.
>
> Ruth: Good, but that does not suit our story, because if Navot blessed, then what is the accusation here? [*Students offer all kinds of ideas.*]
>
> Ruth: The word "bless" in the Bible has two meanings: positive, as we all know, and negative.
>
> Student: To curse.
>
> Ruth: Right. . . . Navot cursed.

Ruth explains:

> It is not important to me that the children know every word,
> every meaning. It's important that they understand what is
> being read and that they understand the Bible in general bet-
> ter—to understand the story's message, and not to focus neces-
> sarily on the meaning of every word. . . . As long as the
> standard of the discussion is maintained and they aren't just
> saying things thrown out into the air, I'm pleased that the chil-
> dren make associations between current situations and things
> that we're studying.

After the entire chapter has been read and the children have a general
understanding of it, Ruth asks the students to take out their notebooks
and gives them a written assignment. Summarizing the chapter into a
few central issues appears to be a very important goal for Ruth—she
thinks that this is one of the most difficult points in the encounter between students and the Bible: "The students have a tough problem with
understanding the concept of time. . . . It is very difficult for them to
distinguish between the main idea and the secondary issues."

The lesson immediately following this one is also Bible and is dedicated to students' independent study. Most of the class is studying. Ruth
moves among the students, checking to see what stage of the assignment
each student has reached, and clearing up difficulties or words that are
not understood. Occasionally, there is a disturbance of sorts and a lack
of concentration, but Ruth quickly returns the situation to order. She
seems pleased with the results: "They know how to find their way
around the Bible; I worked a lot with them on that at the beginning of
the year, and now there are already results. . . . They are knowledgeable
about the Bible, and this is expressed particularly during independent
study in class."

Explanatory notes. Fifteen teachers from the study population were
characterized by their image of their teaching potency as maintaining
students' understanding. Typical of this group are the vivid references to
the students' cognitive difficulties in the teaching-learning process and
less reference to students' interest and to teachers' roles. They relate to
their teaching role mainly as the challenge of students' overcoming cognitive difficulties.

Certain teachers talk of the need to further their understanding of the children's learning process: "The more I study . . . the more I am conscious of and responsive to the problems of learning: how to read a text, how to present a text, and what problems students have with reading texts" (Shira).

More than anything, the teachers who emphasize maintaining students' understanding describe their didactic struggles with ways to overcome students' cognitive difficulties and their use of special methods: precise reading, practice, emphasis on main points of the text, and questions. Some teachers describe even more creative teaching activities, such as drama and games. These teachers frequently describe how they overcome cognitive difficulties of their students, how they adapt the text to the level and capacity of students, select suitable texts, and emphasize different components of each text. In these teachers' view, the key to success is the ability to assist students in overcoming the objective difficulties in the process of their encounter with the text.

The Image of Teaching Potency as Keeping Students Afloat

Amira, age forty-six, is a teacher with eighteen years' experience. She explained that it is no accident that she has chosen to teach Bible. Her love of Bible, she claims, stems from her background and upbringing and the traditional lifestyle that she maintains in her home: "I love Bible very much, I get excited. . . . I think that studying Bible transforms us into people with roots, . . . tied to the Land of Israel, to religion, to the earth upon which we live, to our past."

Amira teaches ninth grade twice a week in a public school in the center of the country. There are 36 students in the class—19 boys and 17 girls. The observed lessons take place during the last month of the school year, around the period of final exams. The subject of the lessons is the character of the prophet Jeremiah as reflected in his prophecies. "In my opinion, the most fascinating book is the Book of Jeremiah. I like prophecy very much, and I think that I know how to teach it. . . . You can understand my frustration when . . . I don't have time."

The class is organized in four long rows of desks; at each desk are two students. The lesson begins with a number of administrative announcements. Immediately after the organizational part, the class turns to reading the homework. The students are used to this routine and quickly respond to the teacher's requests. There is complete quiet in the classroom—it is obvious that Amira is successfully leading the class through its work and obtaining the desired behavior. For homework, Amira routinely gives students independent reading of the text accompanied by a detailed assignment page. Amira runs a discussion in class, based on the homework, the objective of which is to extract the desired answers from the students, only a limited number of whom actively participate. Her questions are short and limited, and she appears to have clear and definite answers to them:

> I try to press the students to do thorough work in the classroom, because that is the basis for analyzing texts. . . . I persist, and the students know that I am serious, very demanding, very consistent in my demands. . . . Bible is something that the students aren't excited about yet, so I feel like a frustrated policewoman.

Addressing contemporary issues is very important to Amira, and she believes that this brings students closer to the texts. She is convinced that the choice of teaching Jeremiah arises from the need to be relevant. Are the students also convinced as to the relevance of the text? Even Amira is not certain that this is the case. Amira is aware that the circle of interested students is quite small:

> Always when I start the first day of teaching Bible, the answer I get is: "There is no reason, it's just nonsense, it's past and pointless, and math is more important". . . .Also, the subjects are irrelevant to them in an emotional sense. . . . Why would a child be interested in the destruction of the Temple? . . . How can they identify with a prophet from whom they are removed by age and time?

As if to contradict the above, there is a sudden awakening of sorts in the class. A student raises his hand and asks permission to speak:

> Student: Could you characterize Jeremiah's image in light of all this?
>
> Amira: Would anyone like to answer him? [*Students talk among themselves.*]
>
> Student: When I must describe a figure in an exam, how do I go about it?

The classes are taking place at the end of the school year, just before final exams, and students are preoccupied with the question of how to characterize the figure of Jeremiah in an exam. There is no doubt that the school routine, through the rules and obligations it places on the students, helps in maintaining a learning framework in fields that students do not find interesting. Amira is aware of this and takes advantage of it for her own purposes. "I encourage them to study texts by heart, and for this they receive bonus points. They study for the grade, but in fact they gain familiarity and proficiency in the material." Does Amira feel that she is successful in reaching her goal?

> The children come with prejudice. For over half the students, anything that smells of religion is regarded as extremist, racist, and they are naturally "anti" texts associated with religion. . . . I am quite frustrated. . . . At this age, even if they are interested, they won't say so. I think that at this age, most of them do not like Bible. It depends a lot on the teacher: If the teacher is interesting and prepares interesting lessons and ties them to topical issues, certainly they have an attitude of respect.

Thus, for Amira, frustration and hope are interconnected.

Explanatory notes. This image of teaching potency as one of keeping the children afloat characterized twenty-one teachers from the study population. As mentioned, the majority of teachers in the study stated that students are uninterested in studying biblical texts. What distinguishes these twenty-one teachers is their emphasis on these students' attitudes and less reference to students' cognitive abilities and difficulties. While talking about their teaching roles, they focus mainly on the challenge of arousing their students' interest.

These teachers attempt to vary the lessons as much as possible. Many pointed out that they, too, try to emphasize the connection to the child's everyday world: "I listen to the criticism, and when I do, I ask that students elaborate as to why they feel that way, and what bothers them, and I am always ready to hear the reasons. Despite this, there is hostility and provocation" (Rivka).

Some try to take comfort in the fact that even if students will not take an interest, at least they will know and understand the text. However, most teachers do not see this as a possibility. "You always say, okay, at least they know. . . . What does 'know' really mean? So I'll give an exam and they'll write like parrots what they were supposed to study. . . . Maybe something stays with them, but I really doubt it" (Leah).

Nevertheless, despite their frustration, the teachers with this image of their teaching potency as keeping students afloat cannot be described as apathetic and do not show signs of giving up.

The Image of the Teacher as Impotent in the Face of Students

Marsha, age thirty-two, with eight years' experience, is a teacher in a Jewish supplementary school in the U.S. The students attend classes twice a week, after a long day of studying at a public day school. "It's irrelevant to their lives and not easy for them. . . . They don't care. They come to school because their parents want them to."

The students, the majority of whom come from homes where there is no observance of Jewish tradition, are sent by their parents to the school for social reasons and as an expression of Jewish belonging and not because of any intrinsic interest in the subject matter. Despite the fact that the parents send their children to the supplementary school, their level of involvement in the schooling process is almost nonexistent:

> Family involvement, . . . that is one of the greatest problems that I see. . . . Parents send their children . . . to school and say: "Make my kid Jewish." They have no idea that this is something that needs to be part of home, too. . . . Children need to see that it is important to parents. . . . It is very hard for them to study the material—they don't understand why it is important to study it. . . . Students have no background in Judaism or with biblical texts.

Marsha does not find great value in teaching culturally valued texts such as the Bible. The texts in themselves, she says, have limited educational impact. Most learning is a result of what children do, see, or hear at home. For her, schools are primarily arenas for teaching verbal skills and cognitive processes but must provide students with learning that is meaningful within the context of their daily lives. In contrast, Marsha has a dream of a different type of school altogether, a school where parents and children study together: "I would invite the parents and children to study together. I think that when children see their parents involved in conversation, it has influence on them, and there is a chance. . . . I think of when they get home and continue the discussion. . . . Then something is learned."

Explanatory notes. Out of the sixty teachers who participated in the study, only one voiced this belief. This teacher talks a lot about students' lack of interest in the subject as well as their intellectual difficulties. Typical of this image is the belief that whatever the teacher does, or however she or he teaches, there is no chance that the students will be brought toward meaningful achievement, even at the level of minimal expectations. It would appear almost impossible to function within an educational system with such a teaching image.

Marsha is not the only teacher in this study who taught in a supplementary school. As such, she is not the only one who faces difficulties characteristic of this type of schooling. Yet she is the only one who perceives herself as impotent in the face of her students. It would appear that this image is a result of the specific level of expectations that a teacher has of the teaching process. It is quite possible that in a different context, Marsha herself would perceive the same students in a different manner.

Conclusion

We have presented four main images of teachers' beliefs about their teaching potency within the context of teaching Bible: as regarding students as clay in the teacher's hands; as maintaining students' understanding; as keeping students afloat; and as impotent in the face of students. In accordance with constructivist-qualitative research presumptions, we do not claim that these patterns are true for all Bible teachers and in every context. However, this picture may be used to shed light on other cases of teaching Bible and other Jewish texts as well as on other areas of teaching.

What is the significance of the research findings for teacher education and curriculum development? This study claims that teachers' beliefs are formulated in an overall image that is derived from separate beliefs and, at the same time, that this image has an impact on these beliefs. These images influence the teachers' classroom activities and can strengthen or retard teaching improvement.[20] Many researchers point out that teachers claim that they were not adequately prepared for the real-life encounter with students and that the theories taught are seldom relevant to the daily life of the school.[21] Consideration of the concepts of teachers' images has demonstrated that the teacher-education process cannot be limited to acquiring elements of teachers' knowledge separately. Rather, all elements must meld and focus the learning from the teacher's perspective as part of the teacher's pedagogical knowledge. This perspective can bring student teachers and curriculum developers closer to the relevant reality of the field of teaching Bible and other Jewish texts.

Notes

1. M. F. Pajares, "Teachers' Beliefs and Educational Research: Cleaning Up a Messy Construct," *Review of Educational Research* 62, no. 3 (1992): 307–32; G. D. Fenstermacher, "The Knower and the Known: The Nature of Knowledge in Research on Teaching," in *Review of Research in Education,* ed. L. Darling-Hammond (Washington, D.C.: American Educational Research Association, 1994), 3–56; V. Richardson, "The Role of Attitudes and Beliefs in Learning to Teach," in *Handbook of Research on Teacher Education,* ed. John Sikula (New York: Macmillan, 1996), 102–19.
2. Richardson, "The Role of Attitudes and Beliefs in Learning to Teach."
3. J. Nespor, "The Role of Beliefs in the Practice of Teaching," *Journal of Curriculum Studies* 19, no. 4 (1987): 317–28.
4. Z. Fang, "A Review of Research on Teacher Beliefs and Practices," *Educational Research* 38, no. 1 (1996): 47–65.
5. Ibid.
6. G. Hillocks, *Ways of Thinking, Ways of Teaching* (New York: Teachers College Press, 1999).
7. L. S. Shulman, "Those Who Understand: Knowledge Growth in Teaching," *Educational Researcher* 15, no. 2 (1986): 4–14, and "Knowledge and Teaching: Foundations of the New Reform," *Harvard Educational Review* 57, no. 1 (1987): 1–22.
8. S. M. Wilson, L. S. Shulman, and A. E. Richert, " '150 Different Ways of Knowing': Representations of Knowledge in Teaching," in *Exploring Teachers' Thinking,* ed. J. Calderhead (London: Cassell Educational, 1987), 104–24; D. C. Smith and D. C. Neale, "The Construction of Subject Matter Knowledge in Primary Science Teaching," *Teaching and Teacher Education* 5, no. 1 (1989): 1–20; P. L. Grossman, *The Making of a Teacher: Teacher Knowledge and Teacher Education* (New York: Teachers College Press, 1990); Gudmundsdottir, "Values in Pedagogical Content Knowledge," *Journal of Teacher Education* 41, no. 3 (1990): 44–52.

9. A. Shkedi, "Teachers' Workshop Encounters with Jewish Moral Texts," *Journal of Moral Education* 22, no. 1 (1993): 19–30, and "The Tension between 'Ought' and 'Is': Teachers' Conceptions of the Encounter between Students and Culturally Valued Texts," *Educational Research* 39, no. 1 (1997): 65–76; A. Shkedi and G. Horenczyk, "The Role of Teacher Ideology in the Teaching of Culturally Valued Texts," *Teaching and Teacher Education* 11, no. 2 (1995): 107–17.

10. A. Lieberman and L. Miller, *Teachers, Their World, and Their Work: Implications for School Improvement* (Alexandria, Va.: Association for Supervision and Curriculum Development, 1984).

11. S. B. Sarason, *The Culture of the School and the Problem of Change* (Boston: Allyn and Bacon, 1982).

12. Sharon Feiman-Nemser and R. E. Floden, "The Culture of Teaching," in *Handbook of Research on Teaching*, ed. M. C. Witrock, 3d ed. (New York: MacMillan, 1986), 505–26; D. C. Lortie, *Schoolteacher* (Chicago: University of Chicago Press, 1975).

13. J. Bruner, "Narrative and Paradigmatic Modes of Thought," in *Learning and Teaching the Ways of Knowing*, ed. E. Eisner (Chicago: National Society for Study of Education, 1985), 79–115, and *The Culture of Education* (Cambridge: Harvard University Press, 1996).

14. F. M. Connelly and D. J. Clandinin, *Teachers as Curriculum Planners: Narratives of Experience* (New York: Teachers College Press, 1988).

15. S. Gudmundsdottir, "Story-Maker, Story-Teller: Narrative Structure in Curriculum," *Journal of Curriculum Studies* 23, no. 3 (1991): 207–18.

16. F. Elbaz, "The Teacher's 'Practical Knowledge' Report of Case Study," *Curriculum Inquiry* 11, no. 1 (1981): 61.

17. J. Calderhead and M. Robson, "Image of Teaching: Student Teachers' Early Conception of Classroom Practice," *Teaching and Teacher Education* 7, no. 1 (1991), 1–8.

18. A. Berlak and H. Berlak, *The Dilemma of Schooling: Teaching and Social Change* (London: Methuen, 1981); M. Lampert, "How Do Teachers Manage to Teach? Perspectives on Problem in Practice," *Harvard Educational Review* 55, no. 2 (1985): 178–94; Shkedi and Horenczyk, "The Role of Teacher Ideology in the Teaching of Culturally Valued Texts."

19. A. Strauss and J. Corbin, *Basics of Qualitative Research: Grounded Theory Procedures and Techniques* (London: Sage, 1990).

20. Hillocks, *Ways of Thinking, Ways of Teaching.*

21. Lortie, *Schoolteacher;* A. Shkedi, "Teacher Education: What We Can Learn from Experienced Teachers," *British Journal of In-Service Education* 22, no. 1 (1996): 81–97.

STUDIES IN JEWISH TEXTS

Postponing Spiritual Gratification:
Levinas's Perception of Religious Maturity as an Orienting Notion for Jewish Education

Jonathan Cohen

The writings of Emmanuel Levinas, one of the premier philosophers and Jewish thinkers of the twentieth century, have become increasingly well known outside of France, thanks to the efforts of scholars and English translators.[1] Levinas's continental orientation and his explicit and implicit references to Husserl and Heidegger and the phenomenologists of the French tradition do not always facilitate his accessibility to an English readership. Even his "occasional" pieces, devoted to patently Jewish subjects, are difficult to understand without some knowledge of his basic philosophical insights.

For readers of Hebrew, the situation is much the same. Although Israeli scholars of European extraction such as Ze'ev Levi and Ephraim Meir have written full-length works on Levinas's thought, and Annette Aronowicz, Michael Gillis, and Shmuel Wygoda have made important forays into the articulation of Levinas's philosophy for Jewish education, his writings remain virtually unknown among Jewish educators who do not specialize in philosophy.[2] In light of this situation, this essay should be regarded as a preliminary attempt to introduce aspects of Levinas's thought to the Jewish educational community.

To understand Levinas's unique perspective, let us first look briefly at his core philosophical insight and then examine his concept of religious "maturity," as opposed to "puerile" or "adolescent" orientations to religion and spirituality.[3] The crux of Levinas's philosophy touches on that realm where an intimation of absolute value, or a life of truth, becomes accessible to human beings.[4] Within the framework of most

Jonathan Cohen is senior lecturer in philosophy of education and philosophy of Jewish education at the Melton Centre for Jewish Education and the School of Education, the Hebrew University of Jerusalem.

European philosophy since the Greeks, claims Levinas, the search for truth takes place in the realm of cognition, wherein human beings strive to obtain genuine knowledge of the nature of the other beings they encounter in their experience, of themselves, or at the highest level of abstraction, of the nature and origin of Being itself. In more traditional philosophy, this involves a process of conceptualization and definition, whereby the knowing subject attempts to grasp the object of knowledge by defining its essential characteristics. Such a process yielded Aristotle's famous definition of a human being as "thinking animal," or Spinoza's definition of reality as consisting of one substance manifesting itself in two modes: thought (or consciousness); and extension (physical being).

Contemporary philosophers, however, such as Heidegger, with whom Levinas had occasion to study, claim that it is no longer either possible or true to reality to conceptualize man or the world in terms of univocal, overarching, and essentialist definitions like these. Whatever we understand of our surroundings or ourselves, they claim, comes not from the neutral conceptual inspection of objects by subjects, but by dint of our involvement with and implication in our world. The perspective we have on any matter of concern to us is determined by our "angle" (in more than one sense), and we would thus be wrong to suppose that it is final or definitive. For some, this situation implies an inescapable relativism that precludes claims to an experience of truth of any kind. Others regard such a finite understanding, colored by context and involvement, as the very way in which the world manifests and illuminates itself to us, enabling us to open ourselves to the world. Any contextual and "biased" knowledge that we may have reflects our legitimate, finite interaction with Being, which reveals itself and gives itself over to us precisely in this fragmented manner.

While Levinas did not de-legitimize the cognitive orientation summarized above in its proper sphere, he believed that European civilization had undergone its deepest crisis because of the unrestricted hegemony of this posture.

In contradistinction to this orientation, Levinas proposed ethics as that dimension wherein an intimation of the absolute may be glimpsed. He dared to make this proposal on the basis of what he regarded as a universal pre-philosophical experience, accessible to everyone—the sense of responsibility for another human being, particularly when there seems to be no choice in the matter. Levinas devised a unique vocabulary of experiential terms as part of an attempt to convey the structure of this archetypal situation. There are times, he says, when we sense that we cannot but react to the vulnerability of the other as reflected in the "nakedness" of a "face,"[5] and we feel persecuted by the haunting appearance of the need that we see in it, as though held hostage by its gaze. We are driven to come to the aid of the other even before we make an autonomous choice to commit ourselves. In such a situation, we substitute for others, taking on their sufferings and responsibilities as our own, even when they have brought about their sufferings through their own lack of responsibility.[6] "Shouldn't others be responsible for us as well?" Levinas has been asked. "Yes," he answers, "but that is the *Other's* affair. I must look to my own responsibility."[7]

While such situations are often perceived to be outwardly imposed, Levinas insists that the worthy human being must maintain a posture of readiness to respond to the Other, leading to a constant state of "insomnia."[8] There is no possibility of attaining to that state of rest imagined by philosophers, wherein perplexity is ended and the subject assumes an object into its consciousness. For Levinas, the most primordial human perception is ethical, not cognitive. The Other's otherness is always before me, and it is my task to assuage his wounds, not to absorb him into my world picture.

But there is another matter central to Levinas's philosophy that we must consider before examining his conception of religious maturity. While individuals may find themselves responsible to others even before they have constituted a sense of selfhood and identity that would allow for an autonomous decision, they are faced with the question of the relative status of others in the world who are likewise responsible. How are conflicts between respective responsibilities and needs to be adjudicated? It is at this point that law and justice become necessary, and politics emerges as the indispensable public arena wherein priorities between needs and duties are determined.[9] In fact, for Levinas, it is the practical need for justice and the administration of social life that initiate theoretical inquiries into society and the natural environment; these inquiries then give rise to the gestures of cognitive abstraction, definition, and quantification that are the very element of European philosophy and science. It is in this domain that they acquire legitimacy. Nonetheless, Levinas never ceases to stress that the more abstract and second-order dimensions of justice, law, political philosophy, and science must take their bearings from a primordial orientation geared to the disinterested service of the Other.

As we have mentioned, Levinas's claim that ethics be regarded as "first philosophy," the posture in and through which we originally per-

ceive what confronts us, and not only the mode by which we subsequently act upon it, is articulated and defended within the categories of
Western philosophy.[10] The pre-philosophical experience of responsibility
is described in non-confessional terms on the assumption that it is accessible to the perception of every rational human being, without appeal to
a discrete religious dimension or a given historical, revelatory tradition.
To hear and obey an external command emanating from the needfulness
of another, even before the obligation has been formulated and freely
taken on by an integrated self, is, at least potentially, a universal human
experience. It is in the nature of such an experience that it confronts one
as a non-negotiable command. This dimension of absoluteness in the
experience of responsibility leads Levinas to the insight that it is at the
locus of ethical obligation that the transcendent leaves its trace.[11] While
laboring to maintain the secular independence of ethical experience, the
absolute heteronomous normativity of the ethical moment leads Levinas
to assert that in the claim of the "other" can be found the "latent birth"
of a mature religion.[12]

The theme of maturity and immaturity runs like a thread through
Levinas's more direct discourses on religion. Expressions such as
"puerile," "infantile," and "adolescent" are sometimes used to describe
religious orientations that Levinas wishes to negate, whereas the adjectives "mature" and "adult" characterize those he would wish to endorse. Bearing in mind this developmental distinction as we examine
Levinas's religious or Jewish writings, it would appear that this criterion
is being applied to a wide range of religious phenomena. Although Levinas is not to be suspected of reducing religiosity to psychology, he
seems to imply, as the following examples will illustrate, that mature religiosity is largely dependent on the overall maturation of personality. It
is this feature of his thought that is so suggestive for religious education,
as we shall see.

Without making claims about what the discipline of psychology rel-
egates to childhood or adolescence, it is not difficult to notice that Levinas characterizes certain religious aberrations as rooted in personality
traits, whether individual or collective, that are often associated with either childhood or adolescence. For example, young children often need
consolation in the face of pain or failure. Without such consolation
from a parent or some significant other, the child will not be able to face
future challenges and inevitable disappointments. There is an expectation of positive feedback for positive feelings or intentions, and when
such feedback does not come, there is a sense of betrayal and a need for

consolatory affection to restore trust in the world and its workings. This, so Levinas would seem to intimate, is what lies behind the attitude of many believers to their God. Levinas calls this "the consolation of divine presence to be found in infantile religious feeling."[13] Mature religiosity, on the other hand, involves the realization that God does not intervene in the workings of history and does not even reveal His loving presence to the believer in the face of disaster in order to reassure him, as it were, that He is still somehow in control. It is precisely in the situation of the absence of God that mature religiosity can manifest itself. In Levinas's words: "The adult God is revealed through the void of the child's heaven."[14] The religious adult knows that only an ethical response to surrounding evil testifies to the trace of transcendence in the world. Such an attitude, however—Levinas is at pains to emphasize—in no way precludes the existence of a dimension of personalism or intimacy in the mature relationship to God. Says Levinas, also quoting the famous note allegedly found in the Warsaw Ghetto by Yossel ben Yossel of Tarnopol, "The intimacy of the strong God is won through a terrible ordeal. By belonging to the suffering Jewish people, the distant God becomes my God: 'Now I know that you are really my God, for you could not be the God of those whose *actions* represent the most horrible expression of a militant absence of God.' "[15]

The same feeling, however, could be distorted to mean that Jews are somehow intrinsically ethical so that God is reflected only in *their* actions. This can lead to a collective narcissism and misplaced pride in the supposed ethical attainments of the Jewish people.[16] This kind of exclusivism is often found among children who need to feel that "their group," or family, is somehow better than the rest. Religious maturity, on the other hand, consists in both the individual and the group seeing itself as "chosen" in a very different sense. For Levinas, "chosenness" involves irreplaceability in responsibility.[17] In the ethical situation, it is not as if an integral personality autonomously decides to assume responsibility, something for which it could be justly commended afterward. One is yanked so fast into a situation by the muffled cry or vulnerable gaze of the Other that there is no time to put together a self-identical ego that can claim the right to be considered "special." The very existence of a continuous self is displaced and disturbed by the gesture of being for-the-other. My uniqueness is disclosed only by virtue of the fact that *only I* can respond in this way at this time. A sense of being chosen, then, means a constant readiness for responsibility, a sense of "always being late"[18] for the moment in which my irreplaceable aid might be needed. The Jewish people has somehow taken upon itself to be the emblem, or historical symbol, of this ethical readiness. Belonging to the Jewish people means belonging to a group that has somehow carried this awareness of always "being on call" both in its literature and in its destiny. It is the figure of the typical gesture of humanity, whereby one is charged to take the suffering of the other upon oneself, to carry it in the other's place, to substitute for him.

Perhaps the essence of immaturity in Levinas's conception is the giving over of responsibility to others rather than taking it on oneself. In religious terms, this means the expectation of a God who "dishes out prizes, inflicts punishment, and pardons sins."[19] In addition, the childish religious sensibility wants its God this way or no God at all. If God should disappoint, then one will have nothing to do with Him. Atheism, to Levinas's understanding, is really an expression of the feeling that if I cannot have God the way I want Him, then I do not want Him at all. Adulthood, in this connection, would mean going beyond this "my way or nothing" attitude, with its expectation of a God who gives significance to events. Events of significance or moments of transcendence that point to the possibility of an absolute must be generated by human ethical activity.

Another well-known characteristic often imputed to childhood is naïveté. This has to do not so much with wanting the world to behave in a certain way, as with the inability to acknowledge that the world does indeed deviate in its behavior from our expectations. Naïveté can derive from lack of experience, namely, not having been sufficiently exposed to human imperfection and resistance to change, or from denial—refusal to see imperfections even when they stare one in the face. It is within the framework of this view of immaturity that Levinas confronts the issue of universalism and particularism. Those who would deny the continuing relevance of Jewish particularity in favor of a kind of humanist universalism are acting as if a certain homogeneity of humankind has already been attained.[20] We are reminded, some forty years after Levinas made these remarks, of those who continually advise us of the trend toward globalization and interdependence, while ignoring repeated outbursts of vicious tribalism all over the world. The continuing heterogeneity of humanity is denied, and those who insist on reminding us of it are condemned as retrogrades. Now a mature, non-idealizing religiosity is certainly not to be gained by a further regression to ethnic chauvinism. For Levinas, universal solicitation of the Other and universal justice must be placed before the Jewish consciousness always as the ultimate telos of the tradition. Yet a non-naïve religiosity will also be aware that in a reality characterized by finitude and incompleteness, the Absolute will always be carried in and through certain particular loci. In ethics, what is needed is not a theory of the universal ethical ideal but a phenomenology of ethical directionality as experienced by concrete human beings in all their uniqueness. As far as the relationship of the Jew to the rest of humankind is concerned, it must be remembered that the Jewish tradition, in contradistinction to the so-called humanist-universalist European tradition, carries a unique vision of justice. Western justice derives from a philosophical tradition characterized by a movement toward totalization, equalization, homogenization, and the reduction of the Other to the Same. This inevitably leads to some kind of violence or violation of the Other. In the Jewish vision of justice, the otherness of the Other is strictly maintained as a condition for the charge to dislocate oneself from one's natural interest in one's own being and stand ready to take on the Other's unique burden. Any more general attention to justice in society merely reflects the necessity to prioritize human need and response to that need. No naïve wishful thinking about the homogeneity of humanism or humanity can obscure this distinction between the classic Western and classic Jewish orientations to justice.[21]

Having decided to value Jewish particularity, the question arises as to what might be considered a desirable approach to its cultivation. Children are known for the difficulty they have in the postponement of pleasurable gratification. "Spoiled" children are characterized by their need for quick and easy stimulation and their inability to summon the concentration and perseverance necessary to master intricate tasks. Such difficulty in the postponement of gratification often figures, from Levinas's perspective, in the immature approach of many Jews who need to cultivate their religion amid "serene," "pleasant," and "undisturbed" surroundings that afford them a sense of belonging and experiences of "spiritual friendship." This, in lieu of the struggle to realize the "difficult freedom" enjoined by Judaism, namely, the opportunity to respond to vulnerability in the most unserene, unpleasant circumstances wherein it is most often found. Fashionable versions of Judaism as propounded by charismatic speakers are superficially adopted in place of individual and collective effort to master the "difficult wisdom" of Judaism as embodied in recalcitrant Hebrew and Aramaic texts. For Levinas, religious maturity means appropriating the implications of the charge to be responsible for the Other as a total way of life, both by study of the texts wherein the precedents for the realization of this orientation are recorded, and the effort to apply these precedents to ever-changing conditions.[22] In a number of articles written when the State of Israel was young, Levinas praises those *olim, halutzim,* and other Israelis who dedicate their entire lives to building up a society founded on principles of justice, applying (not always consciously) principles embedded in the Jewish legal tradition to the details of everyday life.[23]

If we were to summarize the tendencies to "childish religiosity" recounted above, we might say that they are all self-serving and self-promoting in some sense. Yet certain expressions of religious immaturity as articulated by Levinas proceed from a gesture of excessive self-deprecation—a feeling of smallness and insignificance that explains, for Levinas, the Pauline sensibility that "I cannot do that which I must do."[24] In contradistinction to this consciousness of inadequacy, Levinas maintains that "we can do what we must do." Human beings are essentially adequate to their moral responsibilities. It is not necessary that there be a figure that takes on our moral failures and substitutes for us. The opposite is true: we are to be ready to substitute for others, even to take responsibility for their lack of responsibility.[25] We must ask ourselves: What part have I had in not working to change the conditions that have begotten others' lack of responsibility? Instead of declaring their intrinsic weakness in the face of ethical challenges, and then turning to a helper figure, mature persons proceed on the assumption that they are strong enough to carry their moral burdens.

Another form of self-negation regarded by Levinas as childlike and immature occurs with the abdication of integral personality so as to become absorbed in the "womb" of a larger, more all-encompassing reality. Levinas sees in the hankering for a religious ecstasy (ek-stasis) that involves an "exit from one's state" and absorption into the holy, an infantile yearning for envelopment and protection from the difficulties of day-to-day moral decision making.[26] Again, for Levinas, it is within this very matrix of attention to ethical detail that witness to the Absolute is born.

While there are other religious phenomena that Levinas attributes to a childlike disposition, we turn now to those that he views as more typical of an adolescent attitude. Adolescence sometimes brings with it a tendency to insolence and rebelliousness. In order to establish a clearer sense of individuality and independence vis-à-vis parents and the adult generation, adolescents often spurn the advice of more experienced adults as old-fashioned and irrelevant, preferring to strike out on their own, regardless of the accumulated wisdom of the generations. Perhaps it is this kind of adolescent immaturity that Levinas sees as informing certain critical modes of text interpretation. In confronting this orientation, Levinas writes: "These ancient texts, both biblical and rabbinic, not only attract the learned curiosity of philologists who, in looking into them, *are already adopting a superior position*. . . . One must retain a keen ear: everything has perhaps been thought—before the Middle Ages covered the whole of Europe—by thinkers who were little concerned with *developments*."[27] Contemporary interpreters of canonical texts assume that they have outgrown certain old-fashioned notions to be found in the ancient texts. They also believe that they can understand, better than the authors of the texts themselves, by what stages and strata the tradition developed in order to attain to the insights approximating those of the interpreters. The mature attitude, on the other hand, so Levinas seems to imply, should be one of modesty. It may be that "everything has perhaps been thought" by masters who, long before modern humanism and scientific philology had a chance to take hold in Europe, addressed certain spiritual issues with unparalleled penetration. Levinas is not authorizing blind submission to ancient texts. Elsewhere, he writes that the "pious murmur of assent"[28] that our forefathers would emit before even opening a holy book is not available to us as moderns. Much of what we find in the old books cannot be appropriated in its original form, or in the form already digested by earlier interpreters. It is more mature, however, to assume a posture of modesty, allowing for the possibility that a renewed effort at interpretation will disclose insights latent in the text, rather than the presumption that we have superseded whatever the text might have to offer us.[29]

Along with their flaunted irreverence, we often find adolescents uncritically extolling the virtues of "spontaneity" and "naturalness." Levinas calls this "trust in the apparent innocence of our natural movements."[30] Freedom is seen as "the natural sense of arbitrary will."[31] A mature religious sensibility, however, should retain a modicum of mistrust toward uninhibited self-expression. Such a sensibility would favor some measure of formality, as well as a certain distance afforded by ritualization. This would have the effect of restraining the penchant for immediacy that often drives the mystical yearning for union with the sacred, and an unmediated encounter with the divine presence. We are reminded here of the remarks of R. Joseph Soloveitchik in his *Halakhic Mind*, that mature religiosity does not remain content with interiority, but demands objectification of its subjective insights in the spatio-temporal world through the medium of law.[32] We are also reminded of the comments of Yeshayahu Liebowitz in his famous article "Chinuch lemitzvot," that it is precisely the discipline of the law that liberates freedom of choice by preventing subjugation to one's natural drives.[33]

Law is also the medium for communal observance of religious tradition. For Levinas, community and tradition are important not only for the wisdom that they carry, but also as agents of maturation. This is to be understood not in the sense of socialization, but rather in the sense of the overcoming of narcissism and excessive individualism, tendencies that also often accompany adolescence. Just as Levinas is concerned that an excessive need to "belong" might lead to conformism, thereby dulling one's awareness of the uniqueness of one's most personal, irreplaceable responsibilities, so is he concerned that excessive self-absorption can lead to a self-serving attitude toward religion. The individual, turning inward, cultivates a yearning for private religious experience—a personal tête-à-tête with God, as Levinas puts it.[34] To counteract this, one is called upon to pursue a mediated spirituality, carried by an eternal people, an ancient language and a history-long commitment to the ethical condition of humanity. It is the communal-historical tradition that best models the orientation of devotion to the Other. Arduous devotion to the study of the details of the law coupled with an attempt to implement it in the full context of a total society is the best training for self-transcendence in the idiosyncratic, unrepeatable situations of one's personal life as well. Still, one must be on guard not to submerge oneself in community and tradition to the point where one's personal conscience, for Levinas the lens by way of which we have an intimation of the divine (he calls ethics a "Divine optics"),[35] is de-activated.

Having touched on the adolescent's need to belong, and the degree to which the peer group might actually tyrannize the young person, all in the name of "independence" and "spontaneity," we are led to the kindred distinction between what some psychologists today might call "outer-directed" and "inner-directed" personalities. Many people, says Levinas, derive their religious motivation from the "theatricality" of an external revelation. The divinity of the revealed text must be "dramatically" confirmed by a grand event, as well as be legitimated by the recurrent practice of the community. One's religious motivation becomes contingent on such external support.[36] The "immature" religionist has difficulty summoning the inner resources to provide an individual, personal justification for adherence to religious tradition. Someone who has reached religious maturity, on the other hand, derives his or her trust in the sacred text from an internally sensed correspondence between a truth-orientation that has been staked out personally, and the orientation seen as emanating from the text. For this inner-directed type, the text rings true in that it embodies a vision of life that in the considered view of the reader is that which is most needed, to borrow a phrase from Leo Strauss. The inner truthfulness of the message of the text as a whole takes precedence, as far as religious motivation is concerned, over issues of the empirical-historical veracity of the text's account of revelation.

One of the propensities perhaps most associated with adolescence, and mentioned specifically by Levinas as such, is a sense of alienation and ennui that often leads to a hankering for excitement and enthusiasm. This, for Levinas, is yet another drive that lies at the root of the yearning for the appearance of the sacred.[37] An attraction to the bizarre, the mysterious, or the luminous takes over. With oblique reference to philosophers and scholars of religion as distinguished as Kierkegaard and Otto, Levinas has no qualms in pointing out the dangers of "fear and trembling" before the sacred, or awe before the "numinous."[38] For Levinas, such yearnings for the thematization of religion as a discrete sphere of human experience leading to contradictory feelings of repulsion and fascination in the face of the "holy," emanate from an alienation from day-to-day reality, the real site of the possibility of transcendence. Perhaps paradoxically, a mature approach to religion would involve, for Levinas, the de-thematization of religion itself. Rather than fleeing reality in search of mystery, purity, or illumination, one would do better, in Levinas's view, to dirty one's hands and give succor to the Other in the morass of social reality where he or she is to be found.

There are further spheres in which Levinas's distinction between immature and mature religiosity finds expression. In concluding this preliminary enumeration of these dispositions, brief mention should be made here not only of the affective domain (wherein people feel adequate, inadequate, consoled, alienated, or whatever), but also of the cognitive domain. For Levinas, the kind of religiosity that is channeled through unceasing ethical awareness and activity is predicated on the development of a certain capacity for abstract thought. The immature mind cannot conceive of the divine except by way of some form of concretization or personalization. There is a need to have Him somehow "out in front" of one as a presence.[39] The developed mind, however, need not have reference to a presence to gain a sense of standing under the charge of the Absolute. God does not appear to one in a way analogous to the appearance of persons or objects to the senses, as He is assumed to do, say, in the thought of Yehuda Halevi. Neither, however, is His abstraction to be understood in the Maimonidean sense of that incorporeal being who exists essentially, and on whom the being of all entities contingently depends. The purity of God is revealed in and through human ethical turning. When one human being signals another: "I am here for you," whether or not there is as yet any opportunity to say or do something specific, testimony has been given to the possibility of the triumph of the good. It is through such a directionality, rather than through any presence or being, whether concrete or abstract, that the trace of the transcendent as ground and guarantor of the good may be intimated. The hiddenness or invisibility of God is not to be understood in the sense that God is the most abstract concept thinkable. Whatever trace we have of Him is hidden in the events of turning, whereby human beings, before they can even collect their own continuous presence or being, are displaced in the direction of substituting for and taking on the burden of the Other. To see His turning to us in the very event of our turning to others involves a kind of thinking that does not need to posit either an empirical or a conceptual referent as the basis for a real relationship. This unusual kind of capacity for abstraction would seem to entail a highly developed intellect indeed.

We turn now to a consideration of some overall implications for religious education, as well as certain serious educational problems that may be seen to derive from Levinas's notion of religious maturity. Needless to say, much more reflection on Levinas's orientation is in order, far beyond what the framework of this preliminary essay will allow.

First of all, it would seem that in Levinas's conception, there must be "therapy" before there can be "ultimacy." On the one hand, as we have already mentioned, religion is not to be reduced to psychology. The ends of religious education cannot be said to have been realized when the learner is no longer selfish, self-involved, impetuous, alienated, or other-directed. Nor is religion to be regarded as a mere means to the cultivation of a healthy personality. No matter how healthy the learners might end up being, if they have not sensed the absolute normativity of the call that comes from the vulnerability of the face of the Other, then the religious dimension, à la Levinas, has not been entered. On the other hand, it emerges from Levinas's writings that a healthy personality is a precondition for the manifestation of authentic religiosity. Personality aberrations will result in religious aberrations. Excessive individualism can lead to a retreat to private religious experience, away from the locus of genuine religiosity, namely, ethical involvement with the Other. On the other hand, an excessive need for acceptance by the group can beget an insensitivity to individual conscience, that organ that reads what it is that the irreplaceable and unique "I" must do for the Other in certain very particular circumstances. However much Jewish knowledge that students may amass in the course of their Jewish education, neglect of personality development may likely cause them to miss the whole point of being a Jew. If being a Jew means belonging to that people that models the posture of continuously "being on call" to come to the aid of the Other, and one's inhibited personality development makes it constitutionally impossible even to approximate this posture at certain times in life, then by Levinas's standards the whole point of Jewish education has been missed.

In our experience, educators introduced to Levinas for the first time often find his vision demanding in the extreme. In particular, they find it difficult to come to terms with his description of the ethical person as possessed of a sense of infinite responsibility and guilt. It seems to them that any healthy person would collapse under the weight of such guilt or else be so paralyzed as to be incapable of any ethical activity whatsoever. Reactions such as these make it necessary to clarify some of the implications of Levinas's ethics for the education of the ethical personality. Levinas, as philosopher, does not explicitly concern himself with the pathway from immaturity to maturity. He legitimately contents himself with delineating precisely what he believes immaturity and maturity to consist in. It is the task of the educational thinker to go beyond the often dichotomous formulations of the philosopher and consider the path by way of which the ends put forth by the philosopher might be led up to in the educational process. In so doing, it would appear that a further distinction must be made, between psychological guilt and existential guilt.

It is true that Levinas conceives of the ideal ethical posture as one of unlimited responsibility. The infinite is mediated precisely by this situation: no matter how much I do for the Other, my responsibility increases rather than decreases. Existentially, one is aware that one's guilt, or implication in the dereliction of the human world and responsibility to act to repair it, is limitless. This awareness, however, is not the same as the psychological guilt that derives from fear of disapproval, punishment, or the exposure of one's weaknesses (whether in the past, present, or future). The goal of existential awareness of guilt does not mean that young people must be led to feel guilty in the psychological sense. In fact, the very opposite would seem to be the case. Educators concerned with the growth of an ethical personality à la Levinas would have to give attention to the question of how young people are to be given the ego strength necessary to sense the responsibility and make the sacrifices demanded by maturity. Rather than replicate the adult situation for young people, it could very well be that educators will have to build up youngsters through approval, manageable (rather than seemingly limitless) tasks, and so on, until they have the sense of self that would allow for exposure to Levinasian ethical dislocation.

For example, early on in a young person's growth, we might need to reinforce ethical actions performed by saying or signaling "you did it," implying a completed ethical accomplishment, and an association of that accomplishment with the ego of the young person. This would seem to run counter to the Levinasian sense of things whereby ethics is always viewed as an infinite task. As that child grows up, however, the phrase "you are the only one who can do it" might become more central in the adult motivation of ethical behavior. This type of encouragement, given before ethical acts are performed, while perhaps appropriate at early ages as well, could very well become, with maturation, the only legitimate form of motivation authorized by the Levinasian approach.

Here, as elsewhere, the course of educational development leading up to maturity cannot be conceived simply as a miniature version of maturity. It often turns out that, within the framework of education, we are called upon to create situations with features that do not necessarily resemble our vision of maturity. In education for artistic excellence, for example, or for excellence in sports, we often subject youngsters to rigorous discipline so that someday they will acquire the buoyancy and spontaneity that make it look easy.

There is another sense in which the educator's awareness of gradual growth, the sense that the mere replication or miniaturization of adult standards is not viable as an educational strategy, could serve to modify the dichotomous structure of Levinas's distinctions between mature and immature religiosity. As will be remembered, Levinas believes that phenomenologically and ontologically, a posture of "dis-inter-esse," or *dis*-association with an *interest* in one's continued "*esse*," or being, must precede the legal and political adjudication of the relative place or rights of human beings in society. The spirit of ethical directionality toward the Other must infuse the process of the determination of justice as mediated by law. Yet, as R. S. Peters, working within the framework of a different kind of ethics, reminds us, young people are often constitutionally incapable of appropriating an independently conceived ethical orientation such as this before they have been led through the "courtyard of Habit and Tradition."[40] In terms of the Jewish tradition, this might mean induction into the method, content, and application of Jewish law well before exposure to its rationale or guiding spirit. Within the context of education, the order of appearance of ethical sensibility and the legal-political determination of ethical priorities might conceivably be reversed. First, the student would come to know the medium wherein decisions as to which Other is to be served first are made, and only later become acquainted with the full experiential and philosophical depth of the "Other-orientation" that animates it. Levinas's philosophy may be said to have a deductive structure, *from* the experience of the "face" and of being "for-the-Other" *to* the details of the implementation of this orientation in the face of conflict, while education, in keeping with Levinas's philosophy, may well have to appropriate an inductive structure: *from* deliberation on conflict and prioritization *to* a penetrating understanding of the posture of disinterested service.

The above comments do not exhaust either the educational issues or problems that suggest themselves to anyone who might be interested in reconceptualizing Jewish education along the lines of Levinas's view of religious maturity. For example, educators, even if guided by a Levinasian conception, would necessarily have to be more tolerant of those traits characterized by Levinas as immature than Levinas himself often appears to be. Rather than leave the Levinasian dichotomy in place, some conception of *shelo lishma* ("not for its own sake") and *lishma* ("for its own sake") would have to be evolved. Someone motivated by a theatrical view of revelation might well be moved to acquire a good deal of expertise in the nuts and bolts of talmudic deliberation, which for Levinas is the most quintessential particularistic locus of the "Other-orientation" and the struggle for justice. A young person in search of the presence of God, initially intuited immaturely as the mysterious or the holy, may be a better candidate for religious maturation in Levinas's sense than someone to whom the dimension of the transcendent is a matter of indifference. By Levinas's own testimony, an intense awareness of the disappointment of atheism with the providential God, however dangerous from the point of view of conventional religious instruction, would seem to be a prerequisite for the location of the trace of transcendence in human ethical activity within a disenchanted world.

Continued educational reflection on the implications of Levinas's insights would involve the articulation of other such mediate positions on the path to maturity.

Apart from considerations regarding the cultivation of the mature religious personality of the kind treated above, a number of additional questions would have to be addressed. For example: Are Levinas's standards for religious excellence so high as to lead to the restriction of "Levinasian" education to a moral and intellectual elite, even if this result were not intended by Levinas himself? How are individual differences to be taken into consideration? What of those whose ability to give to the Other has been compromised for whatever reason? Or another issue: Can religious institutions actually sustain the de-thematization of religion as a tenet of educational policy?

It is our hope that Jewish educational researchers might find Levinas's views challenging enough to warrant undertaking this kind of exploratory thinking. More comprehensively, we would be gratified if the preliminary consideration of the implications of one orientation, that of Emanuel Levinas, might encourage educationalists to turn to the writings of other modern Jewish thinkers as a resource for the enrichment of discourse on the ends of Jewish education.

Notes

1. Alphonso Lingis has translated *Totality and Infinity* (Pittsburgh: Duquesne University Press, 1969), *Existence and Existents* (The Hague: Martinus Nijhoff, 1978), and *Otherwise than Being* (The Hague: Martinus Nijhoff, 1981) and has compiled and translated *Collected Philosophical Papers* (Dordrecht: Martinus Nijhoff, 1987). Adriaan Peperzak has, with Simon Critchley and Robert Bernasconi, edited a collection called *Basic Philosophical Writings* (Bloomington: Indiana University Press, 1996) as well as provided an introduction to Levinas's philosophy, called *To the Other* (West Lafayette, Ind.: Purdue University Press, 1992) and a new study called *Beyond: The Philosophy of Emmanuel Levinas* (Evanston, Ill.: Northwestern University Press, 1997). Richard Cohen has translated and introduced *Ethics and Infinity: Conversations with Philippe Nemo* (Pittsburgh: Duquesne University Press, 1985) and *Time and the Other* (Pittsburgh: Duquesne University Press, 1987). Annette Aronowicz has translated *Nine Talmudic Readings by Emmanuel Levinas* (Bloomington: Indiana University Press, 1990) and has provided an excellent introduction with penetrating remarks on Levinas's hermeneutic approach. Sean Hand has translated *Difficult Freedom* (London: Althone, 1990), a collection of Levinas's writings

on topical Jewish themes, and has compiled *The Levinas Reader* (Oxford: Blackwell, 1989), containing representative Western as well as Jewish writings. For comparisons of Levinas and Rosenzweig, see Richard Cohen, *Elevations: The Height of the Good in Rosenzweig and Levinas* (Chicago: University of Chicago Press, 1994); and Robert Gibbs, *Correlations in Rosenzweig and Levinas* (Princeton: Princeton University Press, 1992). Susan Handelman has placed Levinas, with his Rosenzweigian background, in a series with Walter Benjamin and Gershom Scholem in her *Fragments of Redemption* (Bloomington: Indiana University Press, 1991). Warren Ze'ev Harvey has analyzed Levinas's thought as a paradigm in the context of the historiography of medieval and modern Jewish thought in *Paradigms in Jewish Philosophy*, ed. Raphael Jospe (Madison, N.J.: Fairleigh Dickinson University Press, 1997), 27–36; and Ze'ev Levi has written on teaching Levinas within the framework of modern Jewish thought in that same collection, 243–56. These are only some examples taken from the burgeoning literature on Levinas being published in English of late.

2. Annette Aronowicz has offered insights in this regard within the framework of a project undertaken at the Jerusalem Fellows in recent years. Michael Gillis, another former Jerusalem Fellow, has recently completed a doctoral dissertation for Monash University in Melbourne, Australia, a chapter of which is devoted to Levinas's hermeneutic approach to talmudic texts and its implications for Jewish education. Shmuel Wygoda, yet another Fellows alumnus, is currently writing a dissertation at the Hebrew University in Jerusalem on aspects of Levinas's implied philosophy of education.

3. See "A Religion for Adults," in *Difficult Freedom*, trans. Hand (henceforth, *DF*), 11–23, and also 143, 155.

4. For essays by Levinas particularly relevant to the summary that follows, see "Is Ontology Fundamental?" "Transcendence and Height," and "Essence and Disinterestedness," in *Basic Philosophical Writings*, ed. Peperzak et al., (henceforth, *BPW*), 1–10, 11–31, and 109–27, respectively.

5. For Levinas's phenomenology of the demand issuing from the "face" of the other, see "Philosophy and the Idea of Infinity," in *Collected Philosophical Papers*, trans. Lingis, esp. 54–56. See also "Ethics and Spirit," in *DF*, esp. 7–8.

6. For terms such as "persecution," "hostage," and "substitution," see the essay "Substitution," appearing in *The Levinas Reader*, ed. Hand (henceforth, *LR*), 88–125, and, in a different translation, in *BPW*, 79–95.

7. See R. Cohen, trans., *Ethics and Infinity*, 95–101.

8. For a characterization of insomnia, see Levinas's "God and Philosophy," in *LR*, 166–89 (esp. 169–70), and, in a different translation, in *BPW*, 129–48 (esp. 132–33).

9. For the role of justice, politics, and economics in Levinas's system, see "The Ego and the Totality," in *Collected Philosophical Papers*, trans. Lingis, 25–40, particularly his discussion of the "third man" and the "third party." See also *Ethics and Infinity*, 99–100.

10. For a discussion of the origin and meaning of the phrase "ethics as first philosophy," see Adriaan Peperzak's compilation of the same name, *Ethics as First Philosophy* (New York: Routledge, 1995), in particular Peperzak's own remarks in his preface, xi.

11. For the notion of "trace," see sec. "The Trace" in Levinas's "Meaning and Sense," in *BPW*, 59–63.

12. See "God and Philosophy," in *LR*, 181, and in *BPW*, 143.

13. See "Loving the Torah More than God," in *DF*, 142–45.

14. Ibid., 143.

15. Ibid., 144.

16. See "Religion and Tolerance," in *DF*, 172–74.

17. See "Israel and Universalism," in *DF*, 175–177.

18. See "God and Philosophy," in *LR*, 180, and in *BPW*, 143.

19. See "Loving the Torah More than God," in *DF*, 143.

20. See "Place and Utopia," in *DF*, 99–103, esp. 100. See also "Israel and Universalism," in *DF*, esp. 176–77.

21. For a characterization of the difference between the European and Jewish traditions regarding visions of justice and peace, see "Peace and Proximity," in *BPW*, 162–69.

22. In "Means of Identification," in *DF*, 52, Levinas writes: "It is not enough to take stock of what 'the rest of us Jews are,' and what we feel these days. We should run the risk of taking a compromised, alienated, forgotten, ill-adapted or even dead Judaism to be the essence of Judaism. . . . [T]he other path is steep but the only one to take: it brings us back to the source, the forgotten, ancient, difficult books, and plunges us into strict and laborious study." In "Reflections on Jewish Education," in *DF*, 268, Levinas writes: "Pure piety is no longer enough. We can still pull off a pedagogy of exaltation . . . but pure feelings which . . . pass for ideas have no future. Nothing is really vital, we have to say, unless it bears the mark of the intellect. No cheap acquiescence." For Levinas's attitude to "spiritual friendship," see "A Religion for Adults," in *DF*, 20, as well as Levinas's "Martin Buber and the Theory of Knowledge," in *The Philosophy of Martin Buber*, ed. Maurice Friedman (London: Cambridge University Press, 1967), 133–50.

23. See, in particular, "The State of Israel and the Religion of Israel," in *DF*, 216–20, and in *LR*, 259–63. See also "Space Is Not One-Dimensional," in *DF*, 259–64.

24. See "Judaism," in *DF*, 26.

25. See *Ethics and Infinity*, 98–100.

26. See "A Religion for Adults," in *DF*, 14–16, where Levinas emphasizes the need for separation from "elevation" to the "numinous." Levinas's suspicion of the magnetism of the "Sacred" can also be sensed in "The Diary of Leon Brunschwig," in *DF*, 43–45, and in "Place and Utopia," in *DF*, 102.

27. Foreword to *DF*, xiii (italics mine). On the "insolence" that assumes to have resolved all the questions of earlier civilizations, see "The Virtues of Patience," in *DF*, 154–55.
28. From *Nine Talmudic Readings*, 8.
29. For a more nuanced account of Levinas's hermeneutic approach, see Annette Aronowicz's introduction to *Nine Talmudic Readings*, ix–xxxix.
30. From "Antihumanism and Education," in *DF*, 283.
31. Ibid., 285.
32. See J. B. Soloveitchik, *The Halakhic Mind* (New York: Free Press, 1986), esp. pts. 2–3.
33. Appears in Yeshayahu Liebowitz, *Yahadut, am yehudi umedinat yisrael* (Jerusalem: Schocken, 1975), 57–67.
34. From "Education and Prayer," in *DF*, 270.
35. See "A Religion for Adults," in *DF*, 17, and Peperzak's preface to *Ethics as First Philosophy*, xi.
36. See "The Spinoza Case," in *DF*, 107.
37. See again "The Virtues of Patience," in *DF*, 154–55.
38. See again "Loving the Torah More than God," in *DF*, 144–45. See also "How Is Judaism Possible?" in *DF*, esp. 248, where Levinas speaks disparagingly of "savoring metaphysical anxiety and the presence of the Sacred in social quietude."
39. See "God and Philosophy," in *LR*, 184, and in *BPW*, 147.
40. See R. S. Peters, "Reason and Habit: The Paradox of Moral Education," in I. Scheffler, *Reason and Teaching* (London: RKP, 1972).

From Desert to Diaspora:
The Sages and the Holy Land

Marc Hirshman

The Nile, the Desert, Canaan, and the Diaspora in the Bible

Three geographical landscapes—the Nile, the desert, and Canaan—have shaped the Jewish people throughout their early history. The impact of these landscapes on rabbinic thought of the first four centuries of the common era will occupy our attention. After tracing their biblical contours, we will focus on the Sages' perceptions of the promise and dangers that each landscape held for the Jewish people. These Sages, *hachamim* in Hebrew, or *sophoi* in Greek, lived mainly in the Land of Israel, though the venerable and much-respected Babylonian community surged and assumed a dominant, if not predominant, position in rabbinic Judaism from the third century C.E. The relationship of these two great centers of rabbinic Judaism, Israel and Babylonia, has been the subject of numerous historical and ideological studies over the past century, of which I should like to note but two.

Simon Rawidowicz's great work, *Babylon and Jerusalem*,[1] published in 1957, months after the author's death, must be singled out as the most powerful exposition of the ideological conflict between these two centers.[2] Consonant with his historical-ideological survey, Rawidowicz went on to vigorously advocate a continued symbiosis of the two centers of his day, America and Israel. His paradigm was an ellipse of two foci rather than a circle with a single center. Isaiah Gafni recently published a fine volume, an even-handed treatment of the relationship

---

Marc Hirshman teaches at the Hebrew University of Jerusalem, where he is director of the Melton Centre for Jewish Education.

of Israel and the diaspora in antiquity, called *Land, Center and Diaspora*.[3] I will focus on one aspect of the question of the different centers and try to understand how biblical and rabbinic Judaism construed the relationship between geography and holiness.

It is remarkable that the term "Holy Land," *admat kodesh*, is extremely rare in the Bible. Its first and most famous appearance is at the burning bush, where Moses is instructed to take off his shoes, "for the place on which you stand is holy ground" (Exod. 3:6, NJPS). The holiness of the ground derives from God's presence at this remote site outside of Midian, a site that one modern scholar called "no-man's land,"[4] echoing a rabbinic tradition that we will soon take up. When Joshua meets the chief of staff of God's army on the outskirts of Jericho, he is also instructed to remove his shoes, for the place on which he stood was holy (the word *adama* does not appear in this citation). Both these instances clearly indicate that the holiness of the place derived exclusively from the immediate presence of God or God's emissary.[5] We encounter the sweeping usage of holy land or ground in Second Temple times. This is in the context of Zechariah's vision of the return to Judaea and specifically to Jerusalem: "The Lord will once again claim Judah as his own possession in the holy land, and make Jerusalem the city of his choice" (Zech. 2:16, NEB).[6] From these three passages, we can adduce that a particular geographical location assumes holiness only when the divine presence rests there. We have not yet seen the words "Holy Land," meaning the entire Land of Israel, as an intrinsically holy site.

But we would be mistaken if we were to conclude that the absence of the embracing term "Holy Land" in the Bible means that this notion is not recognized there.[7] Moshe Greenberg wrote an illuminating essay, "The Link between the People and the Land in the Bible,"[8] wherein he states that the Bible's view may be summarized in four principles: 1) The Land of Israel is God's gift to the people; 2) The land is God's land, with attendant legal implications (e.g., the sabbatical year, *shmita*); 3) The purpose of living on the land is to be a nation of priests and a holy people; 4) The people will be expelled from the land if they do not fulfill their mission. The Land of Israel, though never called by that name in the Torah, is God's special place and does not tolerate defilement. Like the Temple itself, so the land wherein God resides abhors defilement. One quotation of many will drive this point home: "You shall not defile the land in which you live, in which I myself abide, for I the Lord abide among the Israelite people" (Num. 36:34, NJPS).

Indeed, one can view the Book of Exodus as the saga of God's dwelling places. At the beginning of the book, God appears in a bush in the desert. Later, God rests on Sinai, and finally, God takes up residence in the tabernacle, dwelling among the people. Two prophets retain very different memories of this sojourn in the desert. Ezekiel, prophesying in Babylonia after the destruction of the First Temple, envisaged a renewed covenant that necessitated another purging of the people in the desert before their reentry into Israel. How different Ezekiel's vision of the desert is from Jeremiah's idyllic recollection of the romance between Israel and God in the desert: "I remember your youthful devotion, your bridal love, when you followed me through the desert, the unsown land" (2:2).

In a similar, but anthropocentric, view, one can sketch the Jews' intended movement in Exodus from the lush Nile area, through the arid desert, to "a land of hills and valleys, it drinks water according to the rains of heaven" (Deut. 11:11). It is a movement from relative independence or indifference to nature, to ultimate dependence on the supernatural in the wilderness, and finally to a recognition of dependence on God's nature.[9]

According to Ezekiel and the Psalmist, the seeds of diaspora were sown in the desert, when the Jews rejected the Holy Land. Ezekiel says, "Yet I did solemnly swear to them in the wilderness to scatter them among the nations and disperse them through the lands" (Ezek. 20:23). Psalm 106, which has some Second Temple language,[10] states: "They rejected the desirable land and put no faith in His promise. They grumbled in their tents and disobeyed the Lord. So He raised His hand in oath to make them fall in the wilderness and to disperse their offspring among the nations" (Ps. 106:24–26). In this view, diaspora was a result of the Jews' rejection of the land prior to their entering it.

I have briefly sketched some of the contours of "God's land" in the Bible—the no-man's land, the desert, where the Jews, on the one hand, prepared for entry into their land; and, on the other hand, where they sowed the seeds of the diaspora. What happens to the holiness derived from God's presence, be it at Sinai or in the Land of Israel, when God chooses to depart? Is God's holiness restricted to one particular place, or is it portable? Can the Jews enjoy a holy place outside the Land of Israel?[11] The Sages, at least some of them, addressed these formidable questions and developed their own unique responses.

Preambles and Priorities: The Tannaitic Midrash and the Holy Land

It is fascinating that the early tannaitic midrashim, of the first three centuries C.E., on the Books of Exodus–Deuteronomy all open with reflections either on the nature of prophecy or on God's dwelling among the people of Israel. Each one of these rabbinic investigations of Scripture speaks directly to our topic. Let us begin with what is arguably the earliest of the midrashim, the Sifra on Leviticus. The first verse of Leviticus reads: "The Lord called to Moses and spoke to him from the tent of meeting, saying. . . ." This verse prompts a discussion of the nature of the call to Moses and of the voice that Moses ostensibly heard. A parallel is drawn between the call to Moses at the bush and the call in the tabernacle. Prophecy here is mobile, and its contours are the same whether it is in a bush, in the desert, or in the holy tabernacle. Even more explicit is R. Yose the Galilean: "In three places, the Torah was spoken—in Egypt, at Sinai, and in the Tent of Meeting."[12] God's revelation was not only in the desert but also took place in the heart of what was considered by the Bible to be a debauched and tainted society, Egypt.

This approach is modified somewhat in the tannaitic midrash on Exodus, called the "Mekhilta." Its opening chapter deals with Exod. 12:1, which prefaces the laws of Passover with the following verse: "And the Lord said to Moses and Aaron in the land of Egypt." The Rabbis comment: "In the land of Egypt—outside the city. . . . And why indeed did God not speak with him within the city? Because it was full of abominations and idols" (Lauterbach ed., 3–4). Rather than returning to the direct interpretation of the verses in Exodus, the Mekhilta develops, at great length, the theme of the locus of prophecy, and states emphatically: "Before the Land of Israel had been especially chosen, all lands were suitable [kosher] for divine revelation [dibrot]; after the Land of Israel had been chosen, all other lands were eliminated" (Lauterbach ed., 4).

After developing this theme of succession in other areas, the Mekhilta returns to the theme of prophecy and claims that God deigned to speak to prophets, such as Ezekiel, outside the Land of Israel only by virtue of the merit of the ancestors, and then only by a body of water, which is considered ritually pure. This view is shored up by the Mekhilta's treatment of the prophet Jonah, which deserves to be cited in full:

You can learn from the following that the Shekhinah (God's presence) does not reveal itself outside of the Land of Israel. It is said: "But Jonah rose up to flee unto Tarshish from the presence of the Lord" (Jon. 1:3). Could he have thought of fleeing from the presence of God? Has it not been said: "Whither shall I go from thy spirit? Or whither shall I flee from thy presence? If I ascend up into heaven, Thou art there" (Ps. 139:7ff.). . . . But Jonah thought: I will go outside of the Land (of Israel), where the Shekhinah does not reveal itself. . . . They give a parable for this: A priest had a slave who said: "I will run away to the cemetery whither my master cannot follow me." (Lauterbach ed., 7–8; parenthetical expansions are my own)

The parable epitomizes the rabbinic view that only the Land of Israel, after it was chosen, was considered pure. The land outside of Israel was impure, and God's word could be revealed only at a pure site, as by a body of water. The capacity to receive God's word was the *sine qua non* of holiness. This capacity was eventually restricted to the Land of Israel, according to our passage on the Mekhilta. In what seemed to be a digression about successions, the Mekhilta developed its view of the chosen. God had chosen the Temple as a dwelling place, Aaron as the priest, David to be the king, and the Land of Israel to become the exclusive place of prophecy. As the medieval poet Judah Halevi put it, *evchar lenafshi lehishtapekh bemakom asher ruach elohim shefukha al bechirayikh*, "I would choose for my soul to pour itself out within the place where the spirit of God was outpoured upon your chosen."[13]

The opening section of the tannaitic comments on the Book of Numbers, called the *Sifre*, will give us a new perspective on the location of the holy. The verses in Num. 5:1–4 deal with the commandment to send the impure away from the desert camp of Israel: "Remove male and female alike; put them outside the camp so that they do not defile their camp in whose midst I dwell" (5:3). We will quote the comments on the last half of the verse:

"So that they do not defile their camp." From here, they say that there are three camps: the camp of Israel, the camp of the Levites, and the camp of God's presence [Shekhinah]. From the entrance of Jerusalem to the Temple mount is the camp of Israel. From the entrance of the Temple mount to the Temple court is the camp of the Levites. From the entrance of the Temple court and within is the camp of God's presence.

For the Rabbis, the encampment in the desert around God's ark became the paradigm for charting the location of the holy. They superimposed the holiness map of the desert encampment on the map of the Land of Israel.[14] God's first residence among the people in the desert was paradigmatic. Even more interesting is the next comment in the Sifre on the verse "in whose midst I dwell": "Beloved are Israel, for even though they are impure, God's presence [Shekhinah] resides among them."

The Sages' view set forth here is that God's holiness has accommodated itself to Israel's impurity out of love. This is a startling innovation. The essence of holiness is that it abhors impurity. Yet God's love for Israel is so overwhelming and God's holiness so inviolate that God can dwell in the midst of Israel's impurity.

To summarize this section: we have seen that the holiness of the desert was reconstructed in the Land of Israel, but only in the Land of Israel. According to this view, all other locations are no longer fit for God's revelation, although, of course, God fills the entire world. Outside of Israel is considered impure. And while generally God's presence abhors impurity, only out of a special love for Israel does God continue to dwell among them, even if they themselves are impure. This leads us to our next topic: Can the Land of Israel, according to rabbinic thought, lose its special holy status, entirely or even temporarily?

The Resilience of the Holy

So far, we have discussed Israel, the Holy Land, as the home of prophecy. For most of the Rabbis, however, prophecy had ceased soon after the destruction of the First Temple in 586 B.C.E. This was certainly not the position held by all Jews in Second Temple times, and there were some rabbis who believed in the availability of prophecy even after the destruction of the Second Temple.[15] According to the regnant rabbinic view that prophecy had ceased long ago, did an aspect of holiness remain that is unique to the Land of Israel?

The answer appears, quite appropriately, in the first chapter of the first tractate of the order of the Mishnah, which treats the laws of purity. We have seen above that, according to the Torah, the Land of Israel abhorred impurity. It is consistent, then, that the Rabbis, after spelling out the sources of impurity in the first chapter of the Mishnah of *Kelim,* moved to define the aspects of holiness of the Land of Israel. The Mishnah in *Kelim,* "Vessels," reads:

> There are ten "holinesses":
> The Land of Israel is holier than all other lands. What is her holiness? That we bring from her the *omer,* the first fruits and the two loaves.
> The cities surrounded by a wall (in Israel) are holier than her, for lepers are sent out of these cities. . . .
> Within the walls of Jerusalem is holier than them—for we eat there the lesser sacrifices and the second tithe.

The Mishnah continues with its ascending order of holiness, delineating the various areas of the Temple and their restricted access. The Mishnah culminates with the following two sites in the Temple:

> The Temple palace [*heichal*] is holier than it, for no one enters without having washed his feet and hands.

> The holy of holies is holier than them, for no one enters it except the high priest on the day of atonement during his ministrations [*avodah*].

Most of the list defines holiness by way of restrictions on access. But the very first category, the holiness of the Land of Israel, was defined not by individual purity, but by the fact that only from the Land of Israel did one bring three agricultural offerings to God's temple. This seems to be a clear indication, within the rubric set up by Greenberg, that the Rabbis considered the Land of Israel to be God's land. Therefore, its first fruits, the *omer* of barley, the two loaves of wheat, and the first fruits of the other five species with which the land was blessed, were brought to God's temple in Jerusalem. Only the produce of the Land of Israel was to be brought as first fruits to God, because it was God's land. This is the holiness of the Land of Israel. Does this holiness remain after the destruction of God's dwelling in Jerusalem—the Temple? The striking answer to this is found in the Mishnah *Eduyot* and reads:

> Said Rabbi Joshua: I have heard (that is, I have a tradition) that
> we sacrifice even though there is no temple, and eat the holiest
> sacrifices even though there are no curtains, and the lesser sacri-
> fices and the second tithe even though there is no wall—since
> the primary holiness made it holy for its time and made it holy
> for the future also. (8:6)

This was to be a hotly debated issue from early rabbinic times until the
medieval codifiers of Jewish law. Was R. Joshua's position restricted to
the holiness of the Temple, or was it true of the holiness of the entire
land? As we have seen, the holiness of the land was integrally related to
that of the Temple. It was R. Joshua's tradition that the destruction of
the Temple did not compromise the essential holiness of the Temple
mount. The destruction was indeed a sign of God's disfavor with the
people but was not to be taken as if God's presence was removed entirely. Once holy, always holy.

A Unique Diaspora: Babylonia

We turn to the great diaspora community of Babylonia[16] and consider
how the Babylonian rabbinic tradition understood its relationship to
the holiness of the Land of Israel. The issue is presented most
poignantly in a *sugya* of the Talmud that discusses the rights of a husband or wife whose spouse has decided to make aliyah. We begin with
the Mishnah and the Tosefta and proceed to the Babylonian response.
The Mishnah reads: "All are taken up to the Land of Israel, but none
are taken down from the land. All are taken up to Jerusalem, but none
are taken down. The same holds for men and women" (*Ketubot*
13:11). This fairly literal translation of the Mishnah will serve us well
in the long run. This Mishnah, which is located at the end of the tractate that deals with the *ketubah*, the marriage agreement, states in a
matter-of-fact way that all are to be taken to Israel, and within Israel to
Jerusalem, and no one is to be taken away. The Mishnah's language indicates a comprehensive law, beginning with the word *kol* ("all"), but
is vague about who exactly is intended. It compensates by tacking on
at the end the clause that "both men and women" enjoy the same status. The intensity of this legislation well reflects its editor's Israel bias.

But what happens if the spouse refuses to make aliyah? How far are the Israel-based rabbis willing to go to enforce this ruling? The Tosefta formulates this same law in a different way:

> He wants to come to Israel, but she does not want to; we/they compel her to come. She wants to, but he does not want to; we (do not—ms. Erfurt) compel him to come. He wants to leave the Land of Israel, but she does not want to; we do not compel her to leave. She wants to, but he does not; we compel her not to leave. (Tosefta *Ketubot* 12:5)

Again, each partner in the marriage has to follow the lead of the spouse who wants to be in Israel, and the Tosefta spells out that the court presumably coerces the reluctant spouse to comply. This tone of coercion was not used in the Mishnah, and one may wonder whether its omission is indicative of a more moderate stance. Most interesting are the final two cases in the Tosefta—if he alone wants to leave Israel, the family unit may be broken in order to allow her to stay in Israel; she is not compelled to leave. But if she alone wants to leave, she is compelled to stay. In the Tosefta's version, then, residence in Israel takes precedence over family unity, when she alone wants to remain, but the family unity is preserved when she wants to leave. The Tosefta sacrificed the strong egalitarian stance of the Mishnah by allowing the husband to leave Israel, albeit alone, and depriving the wife of that same right. On the other hand, we hear the astounding conclusion that, in the Tosefta's view, residence in the Land of Israel supersedes family unity. This is certainly an exceptional stance. It is also noteworthy that the Tosefta uses the verb "come" to the Land of Israel rather than "go up," which we saw in the Mishnah.

As noted, these sources originated in the Land of Israel. Their strong Israel bias is manifest. How did Babylonian Jewry react? For this, we turn to the *sugya* in the Babylonian Talmud (BT) that discusses this Mishnah. As is its custom, the Babylonian Talmud quotes relevant material from the Israel sources. In our case, the law we have seen in the Mishnah and Tosefta is repeated, though with a new twist. In the Tosefta, it sufficed to say that we compel the partner to comply. In the BT's version of this source, the sanctions or means of coercion are spelled out. If the partner refuses, even after "coercion," then the stipulated penalties are applied. In our case, the woman is deprived of the benefits in her *ketubah,* or, if the husband is recalcitrant, he has to pay out the marriage contract. This seems to be only a fleshing-out of the Mishnah-Tosefta rule. But in fact, this source has added a new and remarkable twist to the law of the Mishnah-Tosefta. For the first time, we see that there is an alternative to the unilateral enforcement of aliyah. There are economic sanctions, but there is also a limit to the extent of the coercive measures.[17]

The second tannaitic—that is, the oldest strata of Israel sources, quoted by the BT here—is a long paean to life in Israel as opposed to life in the diaspora. It is preferable to live in a pagan town in Israel rather than in a thriving Jewish community in the diaspora. Living abroad is as if one worships idols. This very strong language shows, it would seem, to what lengths the Israel sources were willing to go to make their point. According to them, living in the Land of Israel takes precedence over both family unity and community. Better to be in Israel among pagans than in the diaspora among Jews; better to be single in Israel than married in the diaspora. These positions sound anomalous to what are usually taken to be normative Jewish values: family and community. What, then, was the response of the Babylonians?

I will omit subtle interventions of the Babylonians in Israel texts, an example of which we saw in the law of coercion and paying out the *ketubah*. At the bottom of BT *Ketubot* 110b, we read:

> R. Zera was evading Rav Yehuda because he desired to go up to the Land of Israel, since Rav Yehuda said: All who go up from Babylonia to the Land of Israel transgress a positive commandment, as it is said (Jer. 27:22): "They shall be brought to Babylon, and there shall they be until the day that I remember them, saith the Lord."

Rav Yehuda, the founder and head of the great academy in Pumbeditha, who flourished in the mid-third century, read Jeremiah's prophecy concerning the aftermath of the first destruction of the Temple as a mandate also for the second destruction. It was God's will that the people remain in exile in Babylonia until God redeems them. This was, in halakhic terms (albeit ironically), a "positive" commandment. Babylonia was the designated asylum for the Jewish people until they would be restored to their homeland. Rav Yehuda has added Babylonia to the desert, the Holy Land, and diaspora. Babylonia was seen as a home away from home. Indeed, an early midrash, attributed to Rabban Yohanan ben Zakkai, gives a moving portrayal (Tosefta *Bava Kamma*

7:3): "Why was Israel exiled to Babylonia, rather than to all the other lands? A parable, to what is this comparable? To a woman who has disgraced herself [*kilkela*] to her husband. Whither does he send her? To her father's house."

Babylonia was perceived to be the home of Abraham. The Jews had been unfaithful in their covenant with God, their only spouse, and therefore they were sent back to their parents' home (whether permanently or temporarily is unclear here).[18] Rabban Yohanan was the leading figure in the restoration of Judaism in the Land of Israel after the Second Temple was destroyed. There is a message of consolation here: even in anger and disappointment, God punishes with mercy and understanding. But Rav Yehuda, one of the leading Babylonian rabbis, went far beyond mere consolation. Babylonia is not simply a runner-up, a consolation prize for world Jewry, as we will soon see.

The next two statements, attributed to Rav Yehuda or his teacher Shmuel in our *sugya* in BT *Ketubot* 111a, teach the following lessons:

> Rav Yehuda said in the name of Shmuel: As it is forbidden to leave the Land of Israel for Babylon, so it is forbidden to leave Babylon for other countries. . . . Rav Yehuda said: Whoever lives in Babylonia it is as if he lived in the Land of Israel, for it is said (Zech. 2:11): Ho Zion, escape, thou that dwellest with the daughter of Babylon.

In Rav Yehuda's view, Babylonia enjoyed all the rights and immunities of the Land of Israel. The two centers are to be in a permanent stasis: neither are Babylonian Jews to go to Israel, nor are Israel Jews to come to Babylonia. This astonishing stance surely has its roots in the unique position of Babylonian Jewry, who rightly saw themselves as descendants of the elite Jewish society that had been deported to Babylonia by Nebuchadnezzar in 597–596 B.C.E., and had founded their community. The Babylonian Jews continued to see themselves as the blue bloods of world Jewry. But we have only heard the Babylonian Jewish voice in our passage so far. The Babylonian Talmud, as is the entire corpus of rabbinic literature, is meticulous in presenting different views and voices in the treatment of almost every cardinal issue in Jewish thought and practice. Let us turn now to the voice of Israel rabbis, woven into our *sugya*.

It is R. Elazar in our *sugya* who is the vocal proponent of the primacy of the Land of Israel. It will not come as a surprise that this R. Elazar was himself a native Babylonian Jew, who had, like R. Zera, "made aliyah" in the latter half of the third century. One can read this page of the Talmud as a ping-pong match between the Israel views of R. Elazar and the Babylonian views of Rav Yehuda and later generations of Babylonian rabbis. Here is the first of R. Elazar's startling statements about the virtues of living in the Land of Israel: "Whoever lives in the Land of Israel rests without sin, as it says [Isa. 33:24], and the inhabitant shall not say, 'I am sick'; the people that dwell therein shall be forgiven their iniquity." This verse in Isaiah is understood to convey a wholesale dispensation for anyone who has sinned, as a result of residence in the Land of Israel. This is a desperate attempt to invest the Holy Land with a characteristic that flies in the face of one of the defining themes of the Land of Israel in the Torah. Leviticus taught clearly that the land will not tolerate sinners and will expel them. R. Elazar has turned the tables and claims that the land is expiative and living therein atones for sin. We have come back to the theme that we saw in the earlier Israel sources—residence in the Land of Israel as the overarching value. If, in the earlier sources, Israel took priority over both family and community, R. Elazar's stance is even more radical. The Jewish sinner is a saint if he lives in the Land of Israel. This is even one step beyond the source we saw above—which considered those who live in the diaspora to be godless or idolaters.

We can speculate as to what the theoretical basis of R. Elazar's view was. Our best attempt is to see it as an extension of the view that the daily offerings of the Temple atoned for all sin. That source reads: "Never did a person lodge in Jerusalem with sin in hand. For the *tamid* sacrifice of the morning atoned for sins of the evening, and the *tamid* sacrifice of the evening atoned for sins of the day." H. and Z. Safrai have already noted the trend in post–Second Temple times to transfer characteristics that were specific to the Temple and assign them to the entire Land of Israel.[19] They adduce R. Elazar's view here (elsewhere assigned to the earlier sage R. Meir)—that life in the Land of Israel is expiatory and alleviates sin—as a good example of that trend.

Let me bring two more strong statements by R. Elazar in this *sugya* and conclude with the Babylonian Talmud's ultimate response to his stance. The Talmud goes on to tell the story of Ulla, a Sage who carried traditions back and forth between Israel and Babylonia. The Talmud reports:

Ulla used to go up to the Land of Israel. His soul came to rest [he passed away] in Babylonia. They came and told R. Elazar.

He said, "You, Ulla, die on defiled ground." They told him that his casket was coming, and [R. Elazar] said, "It is not the same when one is received by the land while living as one who is received after death."

The final and ultimate pronouncement brandished by R. Elazar in his effort to fortify the position of Israel is: "The dead outside the Land of Israel will not live," presumably at the final resurrection. This is eventually softened by the BT and reformulated to say that those buried abroad will suffer travail at the resurrection while the dead of the Land of Israel will not suffer. Two more Israel rabbis close out the extravagant praise of the land in its son's eyes: R. Yirmiyah b. Abba in the name of R. Yohanan says: "All who walk four cubits in the Land of Israel are assured a place in the world to come." Probably the most audacious of all is R. Abbahu, a late-third-century rabbi who lived in Caesarea: "Even the Canaanite maidservant who lives in the Land of Israel is assured a place in the world to come." This is R. Abbahu's understanding of Isa. 42:5, that God who gives life to the nation, on the Land of Israel.

Gafni, in his study mentioned above, showed that most of the rabbinic literature that extravagantly praises the Land of Israel postdates the devastation of the land in the Bar Kochba revolt. Gafni argues reasonably that as the political situation of the land reached its nadir, the Rabbis began to become more pronounced and aggressive in their formulations of what I would call the almost mystic qualities of the land.[20] Alongside the political considerations, which reverberate throughout the sources, it is important to consider the theological implications of the Bar Kochba disaster. It is clear that up until the destruction of the Temple, the Temple's presence at the heart of the land was a major source of religious authority, side by side with a parallel claim made for religious hegemony based on excellence in Torah study. After the Temple's destruction, efforts were made to carry on, buttressed by a firm activist belief that the Temple would soon be rebuilt. Not sixty years later, Jerusalem was liberated by the Jews of the Bar Kochba revolt, and they enjoyed a renewed, if ephemeral, independence. In the aftermath of the Bar Kochba revolt, the Temple mount was plowed over, and a pagan temple, Aelia Capitolina, was constructed in its place. It became necessary to emphasize the holiness of the land in spite of the fact that the center of the land, the Temple mount, had been defiled. It is for this reason that historians note the surge in statements in praise of the Land of

Israel. The Rabbis had to convince their people that a body could remain holy while deprived of its most essential organ.

How, then, did the BT resolve this enormous effort of Israel rabbinic thought to emphasize the sanctity of the land in Jewish life? Two final passages from our *sugya* give the answer. The first, an anonymous continuation of the debate between R. Zera and his teacher, speaks of six oaths between Israel and God, which are derived from a midrash on the Song of Songs. The first three of the six oaths were: that Israel not make aliyah *en bloc* (*kehoma*); that Israel not rebel against the nations; and that the nations not oppress Israel too much (!). The other three revolved around the mystery of the final redemption. In short, Babylonian Jewry thought, after the second destruction, that it was a time for quiescent passivity. The Jews might even see their sojourn in the diaspora as a mission to enlighten other peoples, but at the least they themselves were to remain quiet and fixed to their place. It is not surprising that the extended treatment of the Land of Israel here in the tractate of *Ketubot* ends, on the one hand, with tales of individual rabbis and their love of Israel but, on the other hand, the final word and certainly the most telling, is a vision of the Land of Israel in messianic times. The final statement is that of Rav Hiyya bar Ashi, who quotes Rav, the third-century founder of the Babylonian yeshiva of Sura, a yeshiva that was to dominate Jewish life for the next eight centuries. Rav said, "In the future, all the barren trees of Israel will bear fruit." Israel, in this view, will enjoy a spectacular renaissance in the messianic future, but for now Babylonia is our home.

The Sages of the Land of Israel struggled to assert the land's primacy, even after the trauma of Aelia Capitolina. From biblical times, the seeds of the struggle between a land-centered religion to a Torah-centered portable religion are in evidence. The two ancient rabbinic centers, Israel and Babylonia, continued the debate, each fiercely advocating its own unique calling. Given in the desert, the Torah seemed to defy efforts to be pinned down to one geographical location.

Notes

1. Simon Rawidowicz, *Bavel verushalayim* (Waltham, Mass.: Ararat, 1957).
2. A lapidary translation of S. Rawidowicz's thesis on the relationship of the two centers appeared under the editorship of his son, B. Ravid: S. Rawidowicz, *Israel: The Ever-Dying People* (Rutherford, N.J.: Fairleigh Dickinson University Press, 1986; repr., *State of Israel, Diaspora and Jewish Continuity*, Waltham, Mass.: Brandeis University Press, 1998).

3. Isaiah M. Gafni, *Land, Center and Diaspora: Jewish Constructs in Late Antiquity* (Sheffield, England: Sheffield Academic Press, 1997).

4. Jon D. Levenson, *Sinai and Zion: An Entry into the Jewish Bible* (Minneapolis: Winston, 1985), 19.

5. See U. Simon, "Holy Place and Holy Land," in *The Hebrew Calendar,* publications of the President's Residence (in Hebrew) (Jerusalem, 1997). He emphasizes the fact that it is entirely the divine prerogative to invest a site with holiness.

6. Interestingly, the LXX here has simply *ten hagian,* "the holy" with the word "land" missing.

7. Robert Wilken's presentation of the material in the first chapters of his fine book *The Land Called Holy* (New Haven: Yale University Press, 1992) suffers by identifying the concept with the term. He locates the beginnings of the term in Ezekiel's theology, while Moshe Greenberg's treatment leads us to see its inception in Leviticus.

8. The essay appears in a collection of Greenberg's essays, *On the Bible and on Judaism,* ed. A. Shapira (in Hebrew) (Tel Aviv: Am Oved, 1984), 110–24.

9. I follow here an insight of Eliezer Schweid.

10. A. Hurvitz, *Bein lashon lelashon* (Jerusalem: Mossad Bialik, 1972), 173.

11. A fascinating tradition from Second Temple times is recorded in the Book of Jubilees (8:19), which relates that the Garden of Eden and Mount Sinai in the desert were also part of the land given to Shem, the ancestor of the Jewish people.

12. Sifra *Nedava,* ed. Finkelstein, chap. 2, p. 15.

13. *Selected Poems of Judah Halevi,* ed. H. Brody (Philadelphia: Jewish Publication Society, 1924; 1974), 4.

14. The paradigm of the desert encampment and the "holiness" of Jerusalem has received excellent and insightful treatment by D. Henschke, "The Sanctity of Jerusalem: The Sages and Sectarian Halakhah," *Tarbiz* 66 (1997): 5–28. Sectarian law, in the Qumran writings and in the Book of Jubilees 32:14, saw the desert encampment as the paradigm and denied any intrinsic holiness to Jerusalem save that which emanated from the Temple; the rabbinic stance, which itself goes back to Second Temple times (8 n. 15, which refers to S. Safrai, *Aliyah laregel bimei habayit hasheni*), invested Jerusalem with intrinsic holiness in the Deuteronomic tradition of the place that God had chosen. It seems to me, though, that our source is a rabbinic source based on the desert paradigm. Henschke's claim that *beit habehira* in the few places in the manuscripts where it actually appears (many mss. read *beit habira,* and not *habehira;* see n. 34) means the place that God chose, Jerusalem, is intriguing, but I find it unconvincing.

15. The classic source on this is Tosefta *Sotah* 13:3. On the possibility of continued prophecy, see B. *Bava Batra* 12a–b. E. E. Urbach's important article "When Did Prophecy Cease?" *Tarbiz* (1946): 1–11 (repr. in E. E. Urbach, *The World of the Sages* [Jerusalem: Magnes, 1988], 9–20) collects evidence for other Jewish views that maintained the continuing availability of prophecy. More recently, see C.

Milikowsky, "The End of Prophecy and the End of the Bible in the Eyes of Seder Olam, Rabbinic Literature, and the Surrounding Literature," *Sidra* 10 (1994): 83–94, who quotes also F. Greenspahn's article "Why Prophecy Ceased," *JBL* 108 (1989): 37–49.

16. See M. Beer's excellent depiction of the unique status and self-image of Babylonian Jewry from their first exile in 590 B.C.E. until their final aliyah some 2,500 years later, "Al sod kiyuma shel golah ahat," *Hauma* 5 (1957): 561–70.

17. My colleague S. Lewis pointed this out to me when we studied this *sugya*.

18. See Gafni's discussion of a later version of this source, in Song of Songs Rabbah 8:10, where it is clear that the wife is sent away temporarily and not permanently. In our early source, *meshalecha* probably also means only "sent away" rather than divorced, even though that same root serves the Bible as a verb of divorce (Deut. 24:2).

19. H. Safrai and Z. Safrai, "The Sanctity of Eretz Israel and Jerusalem," in *Jews and Judaism in the Second Temple, Mishnah, and Talmud Period: Studies in Honor of Shmuel Safrai*, ed. I. Gafni, A. Oppenheimer, and M. Stern (Jerusalem: Yad Izhak ben Zvi, 1993), 357.

20. Gafni, *Land, Center and Diaspora*, chap. 3 n. 2.

Differences between Chapter Divisions and the Parashiyyot:
The Case of Va'era (Exodus 6:2)

David Marcus

Throughout his teaching career, Joe Lukinsky has exhibited a special interest in the external form of the Masoretic text of the Hebrew Bible. In his classes and public lectures, he has often pointed out the exegetical ramifications inherent in the cantillation notes and in the *aliyyot* divisions. Inspired by Joe's interest in this area, this study in his honor will examine another type of Hebrew text division, that of the division of the text into chapters. We will examine how these chapter divisions compare with the *parashiyyot*, the weekly synagogue lectional readings. We will pay specific attention to those *parashiyyot* whose beginnings do not coincide with the beginnings of chapters. We will demonstrate that the different textual division leads to a different exegesis of the text because not only is the beginning of the *parashah* clearly separated from what is related in the earlier part of the chapter, but the material described in the first few verses of the *parashah* is highlighted by virtue of its prominent position in the *parashah*. To illustrate this point, we shall devote the second part of this paper to a case study of one particular *parashah* that does not correspond with a chapter head, namely *parashat Va'era*, which commences at Exod. 6:2.

The origin of chapter divisions is traditionally associated with Stephen Langton, archbishop of Canterbury (1150–1218). Langton was a member of the influential Paris school of theologians, which revised the Vulgate text in the thirteenth century.[1] Langton's divisions were based on the text of the Vulgate, and it was these Vulgate chapter divisions that were eventually applied to Hebrew manuscripts. In 1330, Solomon ben Ishmael used the chapter divisions with a Hebrew manuscript to facilitate references for polemical debates, and almost two hun-

---

David Marcus is professor of Bible at the Jewish Theological Seminary of America.

dred years later (1514–17) the editors of the Complutensian Polyglot adopted the chapter divisions to harmonize their Hebrew text with the Greek and Latin versions in parallel columns. Coincidentally, in the same year (1517) the editor of the first rabbinic Bible, Felix Pratensis, included the chapter divisions in his edition but also retained the *pisqa'ot,* the traditional Masoretic sectional divisions.[2] This arrangement was continued by Jacob ben Chayim in his celebrated edition of the second rabbinic Bible in 1524–25[3] and is now the standard procedure in all modern printed editions.[4]

At first in Hebrew texts, the chapter enumerations were in Roman numerals, but Pratensis, in his edition of 1517, introduced Hebrew letter numbers for the chapters. The practice of placing chapter numbers in Hebrew editions won such widespread acceptance that the enumeration of these chapters was placed alongside the other Masoretic notes at the ends of books in the Masorah Finalis.[5] In modern printed editions, different systems of enumeration for the chapters can be found. The editions of *Miqra'ot Gedolot,* Letteris, Snaith, and most Israeli Bibles use Hebrew letters. On the other hand, the critical editions of *Biblia Hebraica* (BH[3], BHS, and the new BHQ) use Arabic numerals, and some editions (e.g., HUP and Koren 1992) use both Hebrew letters and Arabic numerals.[6]

As mentioned earlier, the origin of the chapter divisions is credited to Stephen Langton. But he did not actually invent the chapter divisions. Before Langton, there were other types of divisions in existence, but his system is the one that gained prominence and became the standard.[7] Echoes of these other chapter-division traditions can still be seen by comparing the chapter divisions in modern printed editions of the Vulgate with the chapter divisions in modern printed editions of the Hebrew Bible that were originally taken over from the Vulgate.

Here are some examples: the Vulgate begins chapter 32 of Genesis with the words *Iacob quoque abiit itinere,* "Jacob also went on his journey," a division that is reflected in English translations such as the KJV (1611) and the NRSV (1989) as "Jacob went on his way." However, most Hebrew printed editions begin the chapter with the phrase *vayashkeim lavan baboker,* "Laban arose early in the morning."[8] The Vulgate commences chapter 13 of Numbers with the verse *profectus est de Aseroth,* "and the people marched from Haseroth," but modern Hebrew printed editions begin the chapter with *vayedabeir YHWH el moshe leimor,* "the Lord spoke to Moses saying,"[9] a division that is followed in this case by the KJV and the NRSV. Variation in chapter enumeration may even be seen among modern printed Hebrew editions themselves. For example, some printed editions (*Miqra'ot Gedolot* and Koren) begin chapter 26 of Numbers with *vayehi acharei hamageifa*, but in other editions (BHS and Snaith) this verse is verse 19 of the preceding chapter, and the chapter starts with *vayomer YHWH el moshe*. Again, in some editions (*Miqra'ot Gedolot* and Koren), chapter 31 of Jeremiah begins with *ko amar YHWH*, but in others (BHS, HUP, and Snaith) the chapter begins with *ba'eit hahi*.[10]

The original impetus of the chapter divisions seems to have been to divide the text into units of sense and into divisions of reasonable length. As far as sense is concerned, early biblical manuscripts often included headings at the beginning of a section containing a synopsis or summary of the contents of that section. These summaries were numbered and known as *tituli*, "superscriptions."[11] Thus, the introductory section to the Benedictine edition of the Vulgate[12] gives a comprehensive listing of Latin editions that divide the Book of Genesis into divisions under various headings. Each division is accompanied by a heading of a line or a few lines, depending on the size of the division. This tradition of providing a synopsis at the beginnings of chapters is still found in modern translations, as can be seen in the Douay-Rheims English translation of the Vulgate or in the NRSV translation of the Hebrew.

When one examines the current placement of chapter headings in the Pentateuch, two major contextual features stand out. The first is that the chapters often signal time breaks, many times introduced by the ubiquitous *vayehi*, "and it came to pass."[13] The second feature is that almost half the chapters in the Books of Exodus, Leviticus, and Numbers begin with the formulaic expression introducing the divine word *vayomer/vayedabeir YHWH el moshe*, "The Lord said/spoke to Moses." In Exodus, the phrase opens every chapter from chapters 6 to 13,[14] and in Leviticus it is used as a chapter heading on no fewer than nineteen of its twenty-seven chapters. In fact, the phrase occurs in fifteen successive chapters, from 11 to 25.[15] There can be little doubt that this phrase served as a literary marker and is probably further evidence of the original public reading of these chapters.[16]

As far as the length is concerned, it is possible to estimate the average length of a chapter in the Pentateuch by dividing the number of chapters (187) into the number of verses (5,845), yielding an average length of about 31 verses. In this respect, the chapters most tellingly resemble the Masoretic *sedarim*, the Palestinian sectional divisions used for the triennial cycle, the average length of which is either 37, 35, or 33 verses, depending upon which tradition one uses. In the normative *Miqra'ot Gedolot* tradition, which knows 164 *sedarim,* there are approximately 37 verses per *seder;* in the Leningrad Codex cycle, which has 167 *sedarim,* there are 35; and in the *Soferim* cycle, which has 175 *sedarim,* there are 33.[17] Because of this closeness in length with the *sedarim* and because of the fact that the beginnings of approximately 40 percent of chapters actually coincide with the beginning of *sedarim,*[18] it has been suggested that the original Vulgate chapter divisions were heavily influenced by these Palestinian triennial *seder* divisions.[19] But if the chapter divisions show a relationship in length with the *sedarim,* they display an even closer relationship with the older Masoretic paragraphing sectional divisions of *petuchot* and *setumot,* divisions that are found in the earliest Hebrew manuscripts.[20]

Of the 187 chapters in the Pentateuch, 150—or 80 percent—correspond with either a *petuchah* or *setumah* sectional break.[21] Because of this closeness between the chapters and the Masoretic divisions, it can be observed that when the chapter divisions ignore the Masoretic divisions, particularly those in close proximity to the beginning of a chapter, this must be the result of a different exegesis or a different understanding of the text.[22] For example, the present chapter division at the beginning of chapter 6 of Genesis has ignored the *setumah* sectional division that occurs before the immediately preceding verse at 5:32. The different division preserves two ways of interpreting the text. One way is that reflected by the chapter division that separates the genealogies listed in chapter 5 from the story of the intermarriage of the divine men and the mortal women that commences chapter 6. The other way is represented by the Masoretic division that separates Noah's genealogy from the other genealogies in chapter 5 and joins it to the intermarriage story in chapter 6.[23]

Another case can be seen at the beginning of chapter 22 of Exodus, where the chapter division again ignores a *setumah* sectional division at the end of the preceding chapter (21:37). Once again, the two divisions reflect different interpretations of the text. The chapter division has the effect of dividing up the laws of theft, whereas the Masoretic division keeps the laws together and preserves the regular Hebrew syntax pattern found in the rest of the laws of a primary protasis with *ki* followed by secondary protases with *im*.[24]

There are many other examples of discrepancies between chapter headings and Masoretic divisions,[25] but in this paper, we would like to focus on one particular cluster of discrepancies—namely, those involving Masoretic sections that contain *parashiyyot*,[26] the weekly synagogue lectional readings according to the annual cycle.

The beginnings of *parashiyyot* have always lent themselves to homiletical interpretation. For by placing certain material at the beginning of a *parashah*, the tradition not only gave it prominence but enabled the very name of the *parashah* to be derived from the first principal word in this section. Further emphasis to this segment is given by the fact that it is this beginning portion that is read four times in the normal course of the liturgical week,[27] and it is this opening portion that is more than likely to be the subject of weekly sermons. Thus, when a *parashah* does not correspond with the beginning of a chapter, a further opportunity for exegesis arises because the different divisions represent different understandings of the text. The chapter divisions represent alternate methods of exegesis. In these cases, it is apparent that, for its part, the tradition wished not only to highlight the material described in the first few verses of the *parashah* but also to separate the beginning of the *parashah* from what is related in the preceding text. Here are some examples from all five books of the Pentateuch.

In chapter 25 of Genesis, *parashat Toledot* begins with verse 19, which highlights the story of Isaac. It is thus detached from the account of the death of Abraham and the genealogy of Ishmael listed in the earlier part of the chapter. In chapter 13 of Exodus, *parashat Beshallach* starts with verse 17 and spotlights the actual Exodus narrative. It is thus separated from the earlier part of the chapter, which deals with the consecration of the firstborn and rituals for the Passover festival. In chapter 26 of Leviticus, *parashat Bechukkotai* starts in verse 3 to underscore the expected blessings for observance of the covenant and to separate the *parashah* from the warnings and admonitions mentioned in the first two verses of chapter 26. In chapter 4 of Numbers, *parashat Naso* starts with verse 21, thus honoring the Gershonite Levites while separating them from the Kohathite Levites, whose duties are described earlier in the chapter. In chapter 21 of Deuteronomy, *parashat Ki tetse* starts with verse 10, which outlines rules for a marriage with a war captive, as opposed to the rest of the chapter, which deals with a case of unexplained homicide.[28]

Each of the twenty-two (out of fifty-four) *parashiyyot* that do not correspond with chapter beginnings could be analyzed for its own interpretative possibilities, but here, as a case study, we shall explore the possibilities for just one *parashah*, *parashat Va'era* (Exod. 6:2).

Parashat Va'era starts at the second verse in chapter 6 of Exodus. Since the *parashah* commences with a *setumah*, this chapter represents another example of a chapter beginning not corresponding with a Masoretic sectional division. The chapter division is no doubt influenced by the occurrence of the phrase "The Lord said to Moses" in verse 1, which, as we have already observed, serves as a literary marker for chapter headings. For its part, the Masoretic division has the effect of highlighting new material in the opening of the *parashah* and separating itself from material mentioned earlier in the text. In this case, the earlier material consists only of one verse (v. 1). In this verse, God answers Moses' complaints of the preceding verses (5:22–23). Moses had confronted God with two grievances: one concerning the people and the other concerning Moses himself.[29] In the first, Moses asked why God had added to the people's misfortunes: "Why did you bring harm to this people?"; and in the second, Moses questioned why he was commissioned for his task: "Why did you send me?" (5:22). Moses then elaborates on these grievances in chiastic or reverse order. He first mentions that God has made things worse for the Israelites: "Ever since I came to Pharaoh to speak in your name, he has dealt worse with this people"; then he remonstrates on behalf of the people: "And still you have not delivered your people" (5:23). To both complaints, God responds in the order in which Moses originally framed them. God first addresses Moses himself: "You shall soon see what I will do to Pharaoh."[30] Next, He addresses the plight of the people: "[Pharaoh] shall let [the people] go because of a greater might; indeed, because of a greater might he will drive [the people] from his land."

This verse is followed by a *setumah* sectional division, and the new *parashah* Va'era begins in verse 2 to emphasize the reaffirmation of the covenant promise made to the patriarchs. In making this verse the beginning of the *parashah*, the Rabbis accomplished two things. First, they allowed for Moses' grievances to God to be answered by an encouraging response to end the previous *parashah*, Shemot.[31] This is fully in accord with the tradition of not concluding texts on a despondent or negative note, and in accord with the ends of other *parashiyyot* where a verse or verses of a positive or more upbeat note were added to make for a better conclusion.[32] Second, they enabled the new *parashah* to highlight not God's answers to Moses' grievances, but God's reaffirmation of the *berit*, "covenant" between God and the patriarchs. As the first major word of the *parashah* indicates (*va'era*, "I appeared"; lit., "I let myself be seen"), this *berit* was made in direct revelation to the patriarchs, all three of whom are mentioned individually by name. The *berit* to the patriarchs was twofold: much progeny and inheritance of the land of Canaan.[33] The former promise has come to fruition, since the Israelites are now a numerous nation in Egypt. The second promise, soon to be fulfilled, will lead to the salvation of the Israelites in Egypt. God declares that He has indeed heard the cry of the Israelites and is mindful of the *berit* made to the patriarchs. Because of this *berit*, God will deliver the Israelites from bondage, enter into a covenantal relationship with them, and will bring them to the land that He covenanted to give to the patriarchs.

The Masoretic division commends itself for two other reasons. The first is because it has long been recognized that verse 1 of this chapter is awkwardly placed and that verses 2–8 form a literary unit on their own. This literary unit is one that displays extraordinary rhetorical art.[34] It is framed by the words *ani YHWH* in verses 2 and 8 as a kind of literary inclusio, or envelope. The unit contains significant repetitions chiastically arranged (such as the names of all three of the patriarchs, the phrases *hamotzi etchem/vehotzeiti etchem*, "I will bring/who brings you out," and *sivlot mitzrayim*, "the labors of the Egyptians"), all serving to emphasize the primary theme of God's remembering the *berit* that He made with Israel's ancestors. In recognition of this literary unit, almost every modern biblical translation and commentary follows the Masoretic practice of dividing up the text so that verse 2 begins this new literary unit. In translations, this is indicated by beginning a new paragraph or indenting the text, and in commentaries by a new chapter or section.[35] As to the placement of verse 1, sometimes it is placed together with the last verse of chapter 5 (the Masoretic division)[36] or else, by means of spacing, it is made to stand by itself, joined either to the preceding or the following (JPS; NRSV).

Another advantage of the Masoretic division is that it avoids two problems that are produced by the current chapter division. First, it avoids the repetition of God speaking to Moses in successive verses without Moses replying. The first verse of chapter 6 begins with God speaking: "The Lord said to Moses"; it is followed in verse 2 by a second introductory phrase of God speaking to Moses: "God spoke to Moses." To offset this problem, it has been suggested that this duplication is merely a stylistic device,[37] or that the second phrase should be translated "God also spoke" for verse 2 (NRSV). But there is no "also" in the text, and it is much more probable, in accordance with the Masoretic tradition, that we are dealing with unconnected units of texts.

Second, the Masoretic division avoids the problem of God speaking within the space of two verses with two different names. The first verse mentions that *Elohim* spoke to Moses, whereas the second verse uses the divine name YHWH. The use of different divine nomenclature would be strange if verses 1 and 2 were part of the same passage according to the present chapter arrangement, but not so strange if verses 1 and 2 belonged to different sections (the Masoretic arrangement).[38] It is ironic, in this respect, that the Masoretic sectional division fits in neatly with the results of modern biblical scholarship, which also makes a major break at this point in the text. The prevailing opinion in critical scholarship today is that the section commencing with verse 2 belongs to the pentateuchal source identified as the Priestly (P) writer. Indeed, this very passage is one of the key pieces of evidence separating P from other pentateuchal sources such as J (the Yahwist writer).[39] Unlike the writer J, which uses the divine name YHWH throughout Genesis and in the beginning of Exodus, P only uses YHWH from this passage on. Before this passage, P uses *Elohim* or another divine name, such as *El Shadai* as expressly indicated in verse 3.[40] Hence, verse 1, which uses the divine designation YHWH, must be assigned to a different source from verse 2, which uses *Elohim*. If verses 1 and 2 are placed together, as under the current chapter division, then from a critical point of view, it could be argued that the two verses come from different sources, and it needs to be explained why the two have been placed side by side. Such a problem, of course, does not arise in the Masoretic division.

To sum up the results of our analysis of this test case: *parashat Va'era* is an example of a Masoretic sectional division that does not correspond with the beginning of a chapter. In this case, an analysis of the text shows that the Masoretic division is to be preferred over the chapter division. First, the Masoretic division allows Moses' grievances to be answered by God in the previous *parashah Shemot* and thus enables that *parashah* to end on a note of hope and encouragement. Second, it allows the new *parashah* (*Va'era*) to highlight God's reaffirmation of the *berit* between God and the patriarchs. Third, the Masoretic division respects the distinctiveness of the literary unit that starts at verse 2 and continues to verse 8. Finally, the Masoretic division avoids two problems that are produced by the current chapter division. It avoids the problem of the repetition of God's speaking in two successive verses without Moses replying, and it avoids the problem of God's speaking with two different names.

Notes

1. D. Barthélemy, "Les Traditions anciennes de division du texte biblique de la Torah," in *Selon les Septante,* ed. G. Dorival and O. Munnich (Paris: Cerf, 1995), 34.

2. C. D. Ginsburg, *Introduction to the Massoretico-Critical Edition of the Hebrew Bible* (repr., New York: Ktav, 1966), 25–26.

3. Ben Chayim's source for these chapter divisions was the Concordance (*Meir Nativ*) published by R. Isaac Natan in Venice in 1523; see now J. S. Penkower, "The Chapter Divisions in the 1525 Rabbinic Bible," *VT* 48 (1998): 361.

4. Nevertheless, only a few modern printed editions (e.g., Koren and Adi) actually distinguish the different *pisqa'ot* in their typographical layout. Thus, in both the Koren and Adi editions, spaces are left in the text on the same line for a *setumah*, "closed" division; and a *petuchah*, "open" division, is always marked by the text beginning a new line. However, most modern printed editions (even the critical editions of *Biblia Hebraica*) just mark these *pisqa'ot* by their first Hebrew letters, *pei* or *samakh*, and do not always begin a new line for *petuchot* divisions.

5. Joseph ben Abraham Athias in his edition of 1659–61 was the first to enumerate the chapters in this fashion, and later editors incorporated Athias's Masoretic notes into their editions as though they were regular Masoretic notes (Ginsburg, *Introduction*, 27–29).

6. Only the edition of Snaith uses Roman numerals alongside Hebrew letters.

7. See B. Smalley, *The Study of the Bible in the Middle Ages* (Oxford: Blackwell, 1952), 221–24; and R. Loewe, "The Medieval History of the Latin Vulgate," in *The West: From the Fathers to the Reformation,* ed. G. W. H. Lampe, the *Cambridge History of the Bible* (Cambridge: Cambridge University Press, 1969), 2:147.

8. A few Hebrew printed editions (e.g., some Koren eds.), the Septuagint (Göttingen), and some Peshitta traditions (Urmiah and Lee) follow the Vulgate division, but other Septuagint traditions (Rahlfs) and the Leiden Peshitta follow the normative Hebrew division.

9. Some Septuagint traditions (Wevers) follow the Vulgate division, but others (Rahlfs) and the Peshitta follow the Hebrew division. Other examples of differences in divisions may be found at the beginnings of Exodus 22; and Deuteronomy 13, 23, and 29.

10. A comprehensive study of the differences in chapter divisions between the various rabbinic Bibles and modern printed editions (esp. *Biblia Hebraica*) has been undertaken recently by Penkower, "The Chapter Divisions," 350–74.

11. Smalley, *The Study of the Bible in the Middle Ages,* 221.

12. *Biblia Sacra Iuxta Latinam Vulgatam Versionem* (Rome: Typis Polyglottis Vaticanis, 1926), 73–133.

13. For example, in Genesis, chaps. 6, 11, 14, 15, 17, 22, 23, 26, 27, 38, 40, 41, and 48.

14. And again five more times, in chaps. 25, 31, 33, 34, and 40.

15. The other occurrences are in chaps. 4, 6, 8, and 27. In the Book of Numbers, the phrase occurs at the beginning of seventeen of the thirty-six chaps. (1, 2, 4–6, 8–10, 13, 15, 17, 19, 26, 28, 31, 34, and 35).

16. C. Perrot, "Petuhot et setumot: Étude sur les alinéas du Pentateuque," *RB* 76 (1969): 83.

17. B. Z. Wacholder, "Prolegomenon," in J. Mann, *The Bible as Read and Preached in the Old Synagogue* (repr., New York: Ktav, 1971), xxvii–xxviii; C. Perrot, "The Reading of the Bible in the Ancient Synagogue," in *Mikra*, ed. M. J. Mulder (Assen, Netherlands: Van Gorcum, 1988), 140.

18. From the charts in Wacholder, "Prolegomenon," li–lxvii, one can see that there are seventy-six chaps. out of 187 that start at *sedarim* breaks.

19. Barthélemy, "Les Traditions anciennes," 51.

20. Perrot, "Petuhot et setumot," 52–53; J. M. Oesch, *Petucha und Setuma*, Orbis Biblicus et Orientalis 27 (Freiburg: Universitätsverlag, 1979), 165–314; Y. Maori, "The Tradition of Pisqaôt in Ancient Hebrew MSS: The Isaiah Texts and Commentaries from Qumran," *Tarbiz* 10 (1982): 1–50 (in Hebrew).

21. The breakdown of the other 20 percent of chapters that do not correspond with a Masoretic divisional break is: in Genesis, chaps. 3, 6–9, 13, 19, 28–33, 42–47 (most of the Joseph story), and 50; in Exodus, chaps. 4–6, 8, 16, 22, 32, 36, and 39; in Leviticus, chaps. 10 and 26; in Numbers, chaps. 14, 22–24 (the traditional book of Balaam), and 30; in Deuteronomy, chaps. 2, 3, 6, and 11–13.

22. E. Tov, *Textual Criticism of the Hebrew Bible* (Minneapolis: Fortress, 1992), 52.

23. This chapter division is followed by some Septuagint traditions (Rahlfs), the Vulgate, and the Peshitta. However, the Göttingen Septuagint follows the Masoretic tradition, and chap. 6 begins with "Noah was five hundred years old."

24. See 21:1–6, 7–12, 18–19, etc. It is most interesting that in this particular instance, the standard Vulgate editions and some Septuagint and Peshitta traditions follow the Masoretic division, whereas modern printed Hebrew texts and other Septuagint traditions (Rahlfs) have preserved the chapter divisions. Since the chapter divisions were originally taken over from Vulgate manuscripts (see above), this would represent another example of a variant Vulgate tradition.

25. See Genesis 31 (31:3), 32 (32:4); Exodus 6 (6:2), 16 (15:27), 32 (31:18), 39 (39:2); Leviticus 26 (26:3); Numbers 22 (22:2), 30 (30:2); Deuteronomy 2 (2:2), 6 (6:4), 13 (13:2).

26. The beginnings of all *parashiyyot* except one, *Vayechi* (Gen. 47:28), correspond with a Masoretic sectional division. *Vayechi* is not marked either as a paragraph or as a *seder*. It has been suggested that this *parashah* was a late development to the annual cycle and represents a deliberate change to avoid beginning a *seder* at

48:1, a verse that mentions Jacob's sickness; instead, the new *parashah* begins with "life" (Wacholder, "Prolegomenon," xxviii–xxix).

27. At the afternoon reading on the preceding *Shabbat;* on the preceding Monday and Thursday morning services; and on the Sabbath morning service itself.

28. The other seventeen *parashiyyot* that do not correspond with chapter beginnings are: in Genesis, *Noach* 6:9, *Vayetse* 28:10, *Vayishlach* 32:4, *Vayigash* 44:18, *Vayechi* 47:28; in Exodus, *Va'era* 6:2, *Tezaveh* 27:20, *Ki Tissa* 30:11, *Pekudei* 38:21; in Numbers, *Balak* 22:2, *Pinchas* 25:10, *Mattot* 30:2; in Deuteronomy, *Va'et-chanan* 3:23, *Ekev* 7:12, *Re'eh* 11:26, *Shofetim* 16:18, *Nitsavim* 29:9.

29. N. Leibowitz, *New Studies in Shemot (Exodus)* (Jerusalem: Eliner Library, 1995), 114–15.

30. Literally, our text reads, *ata tir'e,* "now you will see." Note that the Samaritan version reads the second-person pronoun *ata,* "you," for *'ata,* "now," suggesting a translation "as for you, you will see."

31. This point was noticed by *Beer Yitzhak,* one of Rashi's supercommentators (= Yitzhak Horowitz of Yaroslav, nineteenth century): "Communities did not wish to conclude the preceding *parashah* on a note of complaint and grievance, so they added the verse 'the Lord said' [6:1] to conclude with a promise of encouragement," *Sefer Beer Yitzhak, Bereshit-Shemot,* ed. J. Copperman (Jerusalem: Kiryah Ne'emanah, 1967), 1:145.

32. See the ends of *Bereshit* (Gen. 6:8), *Vayetse* (Gen. 32:2–3), and *Vayigash* (Gen. 47:27).

33. To Abraham, Gen. 12:2–3, 7; 13:16; 15:5; 17:5; 18:18; 22:17; to Isaac, 26:4, 24; to Jacob, 28:14; 35:11.

34. P. Auffret, "The Literary Structure of Exodus 6.2–8," *JSOT* 27 (1983): 46–54; J. Magonet, "The Rhetoric of God: Exodus 6.2–8," *JSOT* 27 (1983): 56–67.

35. See, for example, M. Noth, *Exodus,* OTL (Philadelphia: Westminster, 1962), 56; B. S. Childs, *The Book of Exodus,* OTL (Philadelphia: Westminster, 1974), 108; J. I. Durham, *Exodus,* WBC 3 (Waco, Tex.: Word, 1987), 71; W. H. C. Propp, *Exodus 1–18,* AB 2 (New York: Doubleday, 1999), 261.

36. Childs, *Exodus,* 92; Durham, *Exodus,* 67; E. Fox, *The Five Books of Moses,* Schocken Bible 1 (Dallas: Word, 1995), 285; Propp, *Exodus,* 244.

37. According to M. Shiloach ("*Wayyomer . . . Wayyomer,*" in *Studies of the Israel Bible Research Society in Memory of Dr. Y. P. Korngreen,* ed. A. Weiser and B. Z. Luria [in Hebrew] [Tel Aviv: Niv, 1964], 255), the two verbs of speech in close succession represent a rhetorical feature in biblical Hebrew whereby the second verb comes after an implied pause in the narrative. Here, the implied pause would come after God's answer to Moses' grievance.

38. It should also be observed that the divine name YHWH, used in v. 1, is the same one that is used in the preceding verses of chap. 5.

39. The designation "J" came from German scholars trying to represent the first letter of YHWH. Since there is no *Y* in German, German scholars used the letter *J*.

Biblical scholarship written in English perpetuates this designation of "J" as the Yahwist writer. For a good nontechnical account of the history of this area of biblical scholarship, see R. E. Friedman, *Who Wrote the Bible?* (New York: Harper and Row), 1989.

40. The covenantal nature of the divine name *El Shadai* has recently been elucidated by W. R. Garr, "The Grammar and Interpretation of Exodus 6:3," *JBL* 111 (1992): 385–408.

Beyond Hospitality:
Abraham at the Terebinths of Mamre

Lifsa Schachter

> The Lord appeared to [Abraham] by the terebinths of
> Mamre; he was sitting at the entrance of the tent as the
> day grew hot. Looking up, he saw three men standing
> near him. As soon as he saw them, he ran from the en-
> trance of the tent to greet them, and, bowing to the
> ground, he said, "My lords, if it please you, do not go
> on past your servant. Let a little water be brought;
> bathe your feet and recline under the tree. And let me
> fetch a morsel of bread that you may refresh yourselves;
> then go on, seeing that you have come your servant's
> way." They replied, "Do as you have said."
> Abraham hastened into the tent to Sarah and said,
> "Quick, three seahs of choice flour! Knead and make
> cakes!" Then Abraham ran to the herd, took a calf, ten-
> der and choice, and gave it to a servant boy, who has-
> tened to prepare it. He took curds and milk and the calf
> that had been prepared and set these before them, and
> he waited on them under the tree as they ate.
>
> *Gen. 18:1–8[1]*

As a reader coming across this section of narrative in the midst of the
majestic and momentous stories of the Abraham epic, I have often re-
acted with surprise. What is this story doing here? Why in the midst of

Lifsa Schachter is director of the Center for Jewish Education at the Cleveland College of
Jewish Studies. She was a doctoral student of Professor Joseph Lukinsky at the Jewish
Theological Seminary of America.

tales of vast migrations and encounters with mighty kings, why in the midst of the story of the origins of the Jewish people and the establishment of the eternal covenant between God and the Jewish people, do we have this seemingly simple domestic story, filled with relatively trivial details?

This question has been asked by many readers throughout time. Focusing on the detailed description of the way that Abraham hastened, hurried, and ran about, and the personal attention he lavished upon his guests, traditional Bible commentators have suggested that this story exemplifies the virtue of hospitality, especially to strangers, and highlights the importance of personal and direct involvement in hospitable activities. As we shall see, this interpretation is ancient, continues throughout Jewish history, and is frequently cited as an instance of the maxim *ma'asei avot—siman levanim*. As Abraham was engaged in acts of hospitality—even while indisposed as a consequence of his recent circumcision—so are we, his descendants, to emulate his example by also engaging in acts of hospitality, even when it is not convenient for us. The interpretive tradition is unanimous that this story has been included in the Bible to teach this lesson. In this paper, I review the history of the traditional interpretation—that this text is primarily intended to provide a model of hospitality. Then, despite the strength of this tradition, I suggest an alternative reading, leading to a different behavioral mandate for us, the *banim*, Abraham's descendants.

The Interpretive Record

That this is a story about hospitality is found in the earliest interpretations of the Bible available to us. Ancient texts, both rabbinic and non-rabbinic, focus on the courtesy with which Abraham greeted the strangers (whom he did not know to be divine), the energy he brought to the task, the generosity with which he treated his guests, and the extreme personal attention he bestowed upon them.

> [Abraham's action shows that] **hospitality to wayfarers** is greater than receiving the divine presence. (*Shabbat* 127a)

> That [Abraham] had a multitude of servants is clear . . . [yet] he himself becomes an attendant, a servant [to the visiting angels]

in order to show his hospitality. (Philo, Questions and Answers in Gen. 4:10)

Abraham . . . used to go out and look all around, and when he would find travelers he would invite them into his house. (Abot d'R. Natan A, 7)

The day whereon God visited [Abraham] was exceedingly hot, for He had bored a hole in hell so that its heat might reach as far as the earth, and no wayfarer venture abroad on the highways, and Abraham be left undisturbed in his pain. But the absence of strangers caused Abraham great vexation, and he sent his servant Eliezer forth to keep a lookout for travelers. When the servant returned from his fruitless search, Abraham himself, in spite of his illness and the searching heat, prepared to go forth on the highway and see whether he would not succeed. (*Bava Metzia* 86:b)

In this last midrash, Abraham's commitment to hospitality is portrayed as so great that he did not merely wait for guests, but actively sought them out. He did not ignore this mitzvah even when he could have done so because of indisposition.

James Kugel asserts that, in many cases, the power of the traditional rabbinic tradition is so strong that "gradually, as the centuries passed, these traditional understandings came to be *the* meaning."[2] The history of interpretations surrounding this episode is a case in point. Medieval commentators all affirm the idea of hospitality as *the* interpretation of Abraham's behavior. For example, Rashi (1040–1105) explains that Abraham sat at the entrance of the tent in order "that he might see whether anyone passed by, and invite him into the house." Similarly, Radak (1160–1235), commenting on the story, says that "loving-kindness [*gemilat hesed*] is to take guests into one's home and to honor them by filling their needs, such as washing their feet and providing food, drink, and rest."

This interpretation persists down to our own times in both liberal and traditional commentaries. Nahum Sarna titles these eight verses "Hospitality to Strangers." More specifically, he comments: "Abraham's openhearted, liberal hospitality to the total strangers knows no bounds."[3] Similarly, the Stone Edition of the Torah calls this section "Hospitality" and comments: "His manner of service was through being kind to people."[4] This consistent interpretation of the episode finds its way into most of the curricula of Jewish elementary schools, where it has been translated into activities encouraging children and families to invite guests to their homes.

An Alternative Interpretation

Perhaps it is the banality of these applications that led me to struggle with the question: Why is this story at this point in the Torah narrative? While not arguing against the virtues of hospitality, my exploration led to an alternative reading of this story, one that places the story at the center of narratives about Abraham and the moral mandate given to him. This alternative interpretation emerges by reading the story "in the moment," suspending for the time the developments that are to follow.[5] Reading "in the moment" also requires examining the concrete realities embedded in the episode, allowing other possible meanings to emerge.

"In the moment," Abraham sees three men. Because they are strangers, they must be travelers passing by his tent. "In the moment," he does not know that they will turn out to be heavenly messengers—they are simply travelers journeying through the hot wilderness surrounding Mamre.

Focusing on the concrete realities facing small groups of wayfarers traveling through this wilderness during this period of civilization frames and generates the questions: What would have been the likely experience of these travelers had an Abraham not invited them into his tent? What would they encounter? Would they find shelter and food? Would they be safe?

These questions led to my reviewing what is known about travel in those times from other biblical references to travelers. This method follows the hermeneutic principle *hamikra mefaresh et atzmo* (one section of biblical text can help explain another text elsewhere in the Bible). A brief allusion to the dangers of travel can be found in the Song of Deborah, "In the days of Shamgar son of Anath, in the days of Jael, caravans ceased, and wayfarers went by roundabout paths" (Judg. 5:6). The dangers of travel are more explicitly portrayed in two other biblical narratives. The first is a story that follows closely on the Abraham narrative, the story of Sodom. The second also comes from the Book of Judges.

In the Sodom narrative, we read what happens when Lot invites to his home the two men who arrived at Sodom one evening. The travelers are prepared to spend the night in the village square, but Lot strongly urges them not to do so. Lot's motive is not made explicit, but subsequent events point to the danger that strangers face in Sodom. Lot's home does not provide them with adequate protection, for even before they lay down for the night, all the townspeople gather around the home and shout to Lot: "Where are the men who came to you tonight? Bring them out to us so that we may know them!" (Gen. 19:5). Lot's attempt to dissuade them provokes an angry retort: "This person came as a sojourner, and he sets himself up to judge! Now we'll do more harm to you than to them" (Gen. 19:9).

This short exchange gives clear evidence of the risk facing a small group of wayfarers. The anonymous traveler is fair game for violence, with homosexual rape a real possibility. Sanctuary in someone's home does not provide sufficient protection to the traveler. The host who offers protection also places himself and his household at risk—especially if the host himself is an alien.

It may be argued that Sodom, a city known for its wickedness, presents an exceptional and isolated incident. But while the story is presented to highlight the wickedness of Sodom, it does not present a unique description of travel within the Bible. The story of the concubine of Gibeah (Judges 19–21) echoes and expands on the motifs of the Sodom episode. In the course of this story, the fate of the traveler is depicted in more explicit and graphic detail, dramatizing the dangers of travel during biblical times—both to the traveler and to the one offering protection.

This excerpt from the Book of Judges is part of an extended story describing the lawlessness that prevailed before Israel came under the strong central leadership of a king. This travel narrative describes the perils that befell a group traveling through the Judaean wilderness. A man, his concubine, and his attendant were on their way from Bethlehem, which is in Judaea, to the hill country of Ephraim. The text preserves their conversation as night was fast approaching:

> The attendant said to his master, "Let us turn aside into this town of the Jebusites and spend the night in it." But his master said to him, "We will not turn aside to a town of aliens who are not of Israel. We will continue to Gibeah." (Judg. 19:11–12)

This exchange between the travelers as they traverse the countryside presents clearly the master's perception of the danger in spending the night in a town that was not an Israelite one. It is testimony to the concrete reality of unprotected journeys through alien and often hostile territory during this time period.

The goal of the master to reach an Israelite settlement proves to be misplaced. Even in an Israelite settlement, no one would invite them "indoors to spend the night" (v. 15). It wasn't until a man from their own region, the hill country of Ephraim, witnessed their plight that they received an invitation. The man from Ephraim was clearly aware of the danger to an Israelite traveler, even within an Israelite settlement. This is captured in his words to the travelers: "Do not on any account spend the night in the square" (v. 20).

The travelers agree to spend the night with their kinsman, and the story continues in a manner that parallels the story of Sodom in many ways. As in the Sodom story, this home is surrounded. Here, too, apparently contrary to the expectations of the host and guests, the home offers inadequate sanctuary to the travelers. Lacking the divine intervention of the Sodom story, there is violence to the guests and the householder, culminating in the death of the concubine. These acts lead to dire consequences for the Israelite tribes, not relevant to this discussion.

The point being made here is that these stories function as an internal biblical midrash on the story of Abraham and his guests, leading to reflection on the qualities and strength of Abraham's character. These stories describe what could happen to a traveler in isolated settlements outside the protection of the law. They show the powerlessness and marginal status of the resident alien. For a person to step forward to offer protection to the traveler required great courage and a highly developed sense of moral righteousness. In this world, Abraham's behavior toward the travelers far transcends simple hospitality. It is an example of moral courage.

The Story in Context

This interpretation of Abraham's behavior is reinforced by a second hermeneutic principle, *semichut parshiyot* (interpreting biblical narratives in light of adjacent ones).[6] Reading the story in its context, we find that it is framed by two verses. In the selection immediately preceding the narrative describing the visit, God establishes His covenant with

Abraham. The basis for this covenantal relationship is made explicit. The charge given to Abraham is: "Walk with me and be blameless [*tamim*], and I will grant my covenant between me and you (Gen. 17:1–2). Immediately following the departure of the travelers, God once again emphasizes His reason for singling Abraham out: "For I have embraced him so that he will charge his sons and his household after him to keep the way of the Lord to do righteousness and justice" (Gen. 18:19).

I suggest that these two verses serve as bookends to the story of Abraham's welcoming the travelers. They reinforce the deeper meaning of Abraham's behavior. Accordingly, this story is placed in the Torah at this point to provide an example of what it means to "walk with God and be blameless," to "keep the way of the Lord to do righteousness and justice." This understanding highlights additional dimensions of Abraham's character and helps us understand why he merited being chosen as father of the Jewish people.

Hachnasat orchim is the traditional Hebrew term used to describe Abraham's behavior. It is conventionally translated as "hospitality," consistent with the way the tradition interprets this episode. But the literal meaning of *hachnasat orchim*, "taking in travelers," points us more directly to the true meaning of Abraham's behavior. As we have seen, in Abraham's time, traveling was fraught with danger—and those who offered protection to travelers put themselves at risk as well. *Ma'asei avot*, according to this reading, refers to Abraham's great courage in extending his home and protection to wayfarers—to those members of society who lacked all power and protection. *Siman le'vanim*—the mandate to us, his descendants, is to find ways, appropriate to our own times and circumstances, to offer protection to the defenseless and to act with righteousness to those without power.

Notes

1. All translations of Tanakh are from the new JPS translation.
2. James L. Kugel, *The Bible as It Was* (Cambridge: Harvard University Press, 1997), xiv.
3. Nahum M. Sarna, *The JPS Torah Commentary: Genesis* (Philadelphia: Jewish Publication Society, 1989).
4. Nosson Scherman, ed., *The Torah: Haftaros and Five Megillos with a Commentary Anthologized from the Rabbinic Writings*—The Artscroll Series/Stone Edition (Brooklyn, N.Y.: Mesorah, 1993).

5. I want to acknowledge my indebtedness to Joseph Lukinsky for introducing me to this way of reading biblical texts.

6. The rabbinic tradition uses this principle to link the story of Abraham's guests with his experience of circumcision (Midrash *Rabbah*, Genesis 48). The episode also begins a new weekly parashah and introduces the announcement of the birth of Isaac. Perhaps the linkage to Abraham's circumcision, the use of the story to introduce the birth of Isaac, and the changed realities for travel after there was a nation state all work together to help explain the closing off of alternative perspectives on this story.

Publications of Joseph Sander Lukinsky

Readings in the Teaching of Hebrew (with Dr. Azriel Eisenberg). New York: Jewish Education Committee, 1960.

"Role Conflict in the Rabbinate." Address presented at conference on ethics and the rabbinate, Herbert Lehman Institute for Ethics of the Jewish Theological Seminary of America, New York, 1962. Mimeographed.

"The Term 'Structure' as It Functions in Recent Educational Theory." Unpublished doctoral qualifying paper, Harvard Graduate School of Education, 1968.

"Teaching Responsibility: A Case Study in Curriculum Development." Unpublished Ed.D. diss., Harvard Graduate School of Education, 1968 (University Microfilms, Ann Arbor, Mich.).

"Morality and the Teaching of Mathematics" (with Stephen I. Brown). Ethical Education (summer 1970).

"Structure in Educational Theory." Parts 1 and 2. Educational Philosophy and Theory 2 (November 1970): 15–31; Educational Philosophy and Theory 3 (April 1971): 29–36.

"Jewish Education and Jewish Identity." In The Study of Jewish Identity: Issues and Approaches, A Symposium, edited by Simon N. Herman. Jerusalem: Institute for Contemporary Jewry, Hebrew University, 1971.

"The Implications of Trends in the Jewish Family for Jewish Education." Response to papers presented at the Consultation on the Jewish Family and Jewish Identity of the American Jewish Committee, in Proceedings, 23–24 April 1972.

"The Education Program at the Jewish Theological Seminary of America: Basic Distinctive Assumptions." Jewish Education 43, no. 3 (fall 1974).

"Jewish Education" (original title: "Formative Evaluation and the Hidden Curriculum in Jewish Education"). Proceedings of the Rabbinical Assembly, 1975.

"Let's Not Give Up Yet: A Response to the Menorah Curriculum." Conservative Judaism 31, no. 2 (winter 1977).

"Integration within Jewish Studies." Jewish Education 46, no. 4 (winter 1978).

"Integration of Religious Studies and Mathematics in the Day School" (with Stephen I. Brown). Jewish Education 47, no. 3 (fall 1979).

"Integrating Jewish and General Studies in the Day School: Philosophy and Scope" (keynote address), "Response to Panelists," and "Additional Discussion." In Integrative Learning: The Search for Unity in Jewish Day School Programs, proceedings of an invitational working conference, Atlantic City, N.J., 15–17 May 1978, edited by Max Nadel. New York: American Association for Jewish Education, 1980.

"Two Cheers for Being Confused about Our Values." Religious Education 75, no. 6 (November–December 1980).

"The Evaluator as Change Agent" (with Burton Cohen). Jewish Education 49, no. 1 (spring 1981).

"Two Pioneers of Jewish Education." Melton Newsletter no. 12 (spring 1981).

"Fairy Tales, Myths, and Jewish Education." Melton Journal no. 13 (winter 1982).

"Making the Seder a Personal Experience" and "Last Night a Seder" (fiction). Melton Journal no. 15 (winter 1983).

"Sports and Jewish Education: A Personal and Curricular Note." In Studies in Jewish Education and Judaica in Honor of Louis Newman, edited by Alexander Shapiro and Burton Cohen. New York: Ktav,1984.

"Religious Settings as Educators" (with Burton Cohen). In Education in School and Non-School Settings. 84th Yearbook of the National Society for the Study of Education, 1985.

"Law in Education: A Reminiscence with Some Footnotes to Robert Cover's 'Nomos and Narrative.' " Yale Law Journal 96, no. 8 (July 1987).

"Jewish Education and Jewish Scholarship: Maybe the Lies We Tell Are Really True?" In The Seminary at 100, edited by Nina Cardin and David Silverman. New York: The Rabbinical Assembly and the Jewish Theological Seminary of America, 1987.

Review of Commandments and Concerns: Jewish Religious Education in Secular Society, by Michael Rosenak. Teachers College Record (summer 1989).

"A Response to Brian Tippen" (original title: "A Jewish Perspective"). In APPRE plenary symposium, "Interpreting the History of Religious Education in the Twentieth Century: Major Transitions" (conference celebrating eighty years of the academic study of religion and education, 3–5 November 1990). Religious Education 88, no. 4 (fall 1993).

"Scholarship and Curriculum: What Jewish Scholarship Means for Jewish Education." In The State of Jewish Studies, edited by Shaye Cohen and Edward Greenstein. New York: Jewish Theological Seminary, 1990.

"Abraham Joshua Heschel" and "Jewish Theological Concepts." In The Encyclopedia of Religious Education, edited by Iris V. Cully and Kendig Brubaker Cully. San Francisco: Harper & Row, 1990.

"Starting with Yourself: A Model for Understanding the Jewish Holidays and Teaching Them" (with Lifsa Schachter). In Curriculum, Community and Commitment, edited by Daniel Margolis and Elliot Schoenberg. Springfield, N.J.: Behrman House, 1992.

"Reflective Withdrawal through Journal Writing." In Jack Mezirow et al., Fostering Critical Reflection in Adulthood. San Francisco and Oxford: Jossey-Bass, 1990. Reprinted (abridged) in Intensive Journal Studies, no. 12 (spring 1993).

"Robert Cover: A Jewish Life" (with Robert Abramson). Conservative Judaism 45, no. 3 (spring 1993).

"Narratives and the Program in Religion and Education." Union Seminary Quarterly Review 47, nos. 3–4, 1993 (Essays on Religion and Education in Honor of William Bean Kennedy).

"About the Haredim in Israel: A Review-Essay." Review of Defenders of the Faith, by Samuel Heilman. Melton Journal no. 28 (autumn 1994).

"The Joseph Story as a Master Story." Conservative Judaism 48, no. 2 (winter 1996).

"Are Questions Necessary?" (with Lifsa Schachter). Jewish Education News 17, no. 1 (winter 1996).

Review of Teachers of My Youth: An American Jewish Experience, by Israel Scheffler. AJS Review 22, no. 2 (1997).

"Remembering Professor Bettelheim." Melton Gleanings 2, no. 1 (autumn 1997).

"Commitment to Hebrew: A Story." Melton Gleanings 3, no. 1 (autumn 1998).

"Celebrating a Grand Role Model: Louis Newman at 80." Melton Gleanings 3, no. 2 (winter 1999).

"Writing Heschel's Life as Autobiography." Jewish Education News 20, no. 3 (winter 1999–2000).

Review of Scripture Windows: Towards a Practice of Bibliodrama, by Peter Pitzele. International Journal of Action Methods: Psychodrama, Skill Training and Role Playing 51, no. 4 (winter 1999).

In Press: "Teaching Hazal and the Thought of Max Kadushin." Proceedings of the conference on teaching Hazal. Melton Centre of the Hebrew University, Jerusalem, May 1999, forthcoming.